"One Man *Crazy* ...!"

The Life and Death of Colin Clive Hollywood's Dr. Frankenstein

"One Man *Crazy* ...!"

The Life and Death of Colin Clive
Hollywood's Dr. Frankenstein

by Gregory William Mank

Midnight Marquee Press, Inc.
Baltimore, Maryland, USA

ISBN 13: 978-1-936168-81-1
Library of Congress Catalog Card Number 2018952710
Manufactured in the United States of America

First Printing by Midnight Marquee Press, Inc., November 2018

For Chris
1980-2018

Mom and I Miss You and Love You So Very Much

Table of Contents

Colin Clive, circa 1931

"One Man *Crazy* ...!"

Preface

Researching a biography is always a drama ... sometimes a melodrama.

In investigating the tragic life of Colin Clive, Hollywood's long, late-lamented Dr. Frankenstein, I've had many adventures, and misadventures. I've perilously hung out a third-floor window in London to get a good picture of Clive's former house across the street. I've slid directly down a steep Hollywood hill after snapping a from-above view of Clive's final home, tumbling over what I later learned were rattlesnake nests. I've blithely trespassed at theaters, studios, back lots, a mortuary, and a crematory. Most recently, I stood on the roof of the Hollywood Tower Hotel, where Clive posed 85 years ago with the HOLLYWOODLAND sign on Mount Lee as his backdrop.

Perhaps researching an actor who personified obsession brings out obsession in the researcher.

Over the decades, I've written about Clive in various books and articles, so I'm long acquainted with his genius and his angst. However, several years ago, when first considering a full-length, freshly investigated biography, I never expected the maelstrom of startling new discoveries.

Colin Clive's life was brief and harrowing, so one might expect his ghost to be vigilant about his secrets. Fancifully, I now and then imagined a scowling specter, wearing a long white surgical gown (as Clive had as Frankenstein), smoking a cigarette (as Clive did in so many candid photographs), his hair hanging in strands over his right eye (as Clive's frequently did in films and real-life), glaring at me viciously.

"See here, my good fellow," growled his whiskey voice. "I don't much like this *spying* of yours."

However, ghosts don't scare me—biographers defy them—and the chase persevered. If the specter was intent on escape, I was at least as determined to pursue, into whatever rabbit holes and deep darkness necessary. In time, I caught him ... or maybe he allowed me to catch him. If so, considering the various surprise discoveries, he was quite gracious about it all.

This book is entirely factual. For Clive's personal life, the sources include ancestry and census records, school archives, immigration papers, marriage and divorce records, probate files, private archives, death certificates, and pieces of Clive's own correspondence. The information on his films comes largely from the surviving production archives of various Hollywood studios. There are some recently discovered Clive interviews that reveal his charm and humor, as well as his familiar anxiety. Where I describe the weather on a particular day, I checked the newspapers for that date and city. Everything is precisely cited in chapter endnotes and in the acknowledgments at the end of the book. The interviews cited, in some cases, go back over 40 years, to my earliest days as a writer.

As for conjecture regarding Clive's personal reflections, as expressed in various places in the biography, I accept full responsibility, while noting that this "poetic license" stems from the actual events of the time, and includes, in places, Clive's own words.

Also ... the book refers to Clive in *Frankenstein* and *Bride of Frankenstein* as "Dr. Frankenstein." Yes, the Mary Shelley novel presents Frankenstein as a medical student, not a doctor, and the movies provide the same inference. However, since film history

widely regards Clive as "Dr. Frankenstein," and to avoid any lingering confusion between the Monster and his Maker (yes, it still exists), and because, in my opinion, Pop Culture granted Frankenstein an honorary doctorate long ago, Colin Clive, in these pages, will be Dr. Frankenstein

 This is a dark book. However, as the research probed deeper and a more complete portrait of its subject emerged, the story also became, at least for its author, a strangely moving and inspiring one. The book covers, fairly and I hope compassionately, the life and death of a tragically tormented man, who left a legacy of brilliant film performances, deserved a far kinder fate ... and who, for whatever mysterious reasons, has fascinated me for much of my life.

GWM
Delta, PA
2018

Prologue
Summer Idyll

Mad dogs and Englishmen,
Go out in the midday sun ...
Song by Noel Coward, 1931

1935

2320 Bowmont Drive is high in Coldwater Canyon, above Beverly Hills. It's a sprawling Mexican farmhouse, deserted previously by Katharine Hepburn, who believed a ghost haunted the hacienda.

It's now the home of Boris Karloff ... Hollywood's Frankenstein Monster.

His friends love to visit his mountain sanctuary. There's "Dear Boris" himself—sporting his top hat and skimpy elastic swim trunks, followed by his 400-pound pig "Violet." There are the roses, the gardens and, a special treat in a California summer, the pool.

In fact, Karloff, an ardent member of the Hollywood Cricket Club, has created a new sport—"Water Cricket." The batter stands on the diving board, the pitcher throws from the other end of the pool, and the fielders float about in inner tubes, water wings, or car tires. Today, a trio of Karloff's fellow British actors joins the other cricketers. Nigel Bruce, destined to play Dr. Watson to Basil Rathbone's Sherlock Holmes, abounds with "Elizabethan humor" and takes all his drinks "bottoms up." Alan Mowbray who, with Karloff, is a founder of the controversial Screen Actors Guild, is a noted raconteur of risqué jokes, calculated to shock the ladies.

There's a significance regarding the third actor/water cricketer. He's Colin Clive, who in the original 1931 *Frankenstein*, had "created" Karloff's Monster. It was Clive who, like a crazed 21st-century rock star 87 years ahead of his time, virtually sang the words, passionately, apocalyptically:

"It's alive, it's alive ... *IT'S ALIVE!*"

"Dear Boris" in his casual attire. (Courtesy of Sara Karloff)

Indeed, in *Bride of Frankenstein*, the sequel recently released in 1935, audaciously directed (as had been the original) by James Whale, Clive and Karloff had reprised their

Clive and Karloff, between scenes on *Bride of Frankenstein*. Note the tension in Colin's body language, compared to the serenity in Karloff's.

Monster Maker and Monster. Dr. Frankenstein created the Monster's Mate, portrayed amazingly, and rather alluringly, by Elsa Lanchester.

"She's alive! *ALIVE!*" Clive had exulted, again as if belting an anguished love song.

He's played other roles in Hollywood, notably the "doped with whiskey" Captain Stanhope in 1930's *Journey's End*, the part he'd triumphantly portrayed on the London stage and which had made him an overnight star. Clive's shattering Stanhope had heartbreakingly epitomized the horror of war, and critics had praised the performance as one of the most magnificent portrayals ever captured on film. He's gone on to deliver performances in romance and comedy, and has portrayed a demon lover, whose favorite sex toy is a riding whip.

For most movie fans, however, Colin Clive is Dr. Frankenstein Incarnate.

He's a strikingly intense actor. Mae Clarke his leading lady in *Frankenstein*, will say over 50 years later, "Colin had the face of Christ." James Whale, who directed *Journey's End* as well as the *Frankenstein* shockers, says he had "the voice of a pipe organ." Clive's cinema specialty: Hysteria. His film legacy will be odd, to say the least; a critic in 1983 will salute him as "cinema's greatest sado-masochist ... leaving behind a short but striking film portrait of fanatic determination, humiliation, and hate."

It's natural that Karloff would invite Clive to the party. Both men love sports and animals. Although Karloff's super horror stardom had eclipsed Clive after *Frankenstein*'s release, Clive enjoyed working with Boris, both in the original and the sequel.

"I nearly laughed myself to death during the making of *Bride of Frankenstein*," Clive had told a female reporter for *Picture Play* magazine. "Again and again, the director would have to call, 'Cut.' Every time I looked at Karloff ...!"

Clive's an adventurous man, who's always dreamed of being a hero. Except for a disastrous horse fall in cavalry training at the Royal Military Academy Sandhurst, he might have been a Bengal Lancer, galloping in a cavalry through the mountains of India. In late 1934, Clive had soloed as a pilot, flying a biplane in the Hollywood skies. He has a sly, self-mocking sense of humor, and laughs about his supposedly "mysterious" reputation.

"Don't call me mysterious," he recently told a reporter. "Just call me quiet."

Yet Colin Clive receives few invitations. Fraught, hyper-tense, he frightens people. They fear he'll suffer a "blow-up," a "breakdown," or both. George Brent, who'd co-starred with him in 1935's *The Right to Live*, privately refers to Clive as "a maniac who might cut your head off some night and plunk it in the icebox."

A "mad dog and Englishman," in the eyes of many in Hollywood.

He has various addictions. Cigarettes. Gambling. Sex. Whiskey. Especially Acting. His attraction to his craft is seemingly masochistic—he spent over nine years struggling for recognition in London, despite an almost crippling stage fright. His first wife was an actress; she tragically died a few months after Clive had opened in *Journey's End* in London, shortly before Clive's court date to divorce her. His second wife was a famed stage vamp of the Roaring '20s London stage; she's largely responsible for his stardom, and they're now estranged. His current lover is a red-haired, leggy, 20-year-old actress/showgirl; she's the winner of a Hollywood "Perfect Physical Specimen of Girlhood" contest, for which she posed in her lingerie, stockings, and high heels.

Despite Clive's history with the ladies, rumors persist that he's actually homosexual—possibly a result of his friendship with openly gay James Whale.

He suffers various torments. The stage fright that plagued him in his early nights as an actor still dogs him viciously. He frets that his leg injury, which has worsened over the years, will possibly repel his young lover. And he has a terrifying anxiety about a curse perhaps passed down from his family ... a condition in those days called lunacy.

"One man *crazy* ..!" Dr. Frankenstein says of himself in the 1931 film—a line of dialogue that, for Clive, hits perilously close to home.

The agonies are taking a toll. Clive's life is fast becoming a High Hollywood Gothic saga ... the tragedy of a man perilously pursuing a fame for which his lack of ego prophesies disaster. The real Monster that Hollywood's Dr. Frankenstein created, in his own eyes, is himself—cursed by his own fragility, hypersensitivity, and genius, haunted by demons tracing to his childhood, wracked by his addictions. In fact, one of his addictions rages out of control.

Colin Clive, the actor with the "Face of Christ," is now suffering a slow, agonizing, self-crucifixion by alcohol.

This day, however, in the sunshine, the chain-smoking Clive, sporting swim trunks, takes his place as batter on the diving board, playing with the same ferocity with which he acts. Cheering the men on are wives Dorothy Karloff, "Bunny" Bruce, and Lorayne Mowbray, as well as Colin's lover, Iris Lancaster. The "Water Cricket" game goes on for an epic six hours, and as twilight falls over Coldwater Canyon, there's concern. Clive frequently starts drinking at night. His real-life personality can morph startlingly; his ideal horror role might have been *Dr. Jekyll and Mr. Hyde*.

For all the warning signs, no one at today's party could know that in his final two films, Colin Clive, who so wants to be a hero who conquers his fears, will be virtually decaying before the audience's eyes ... and that in less than two years, he'll be dead.

Danny Boy will be played at his Hollywood funeral. What happened to his ashes is a mystery.

Part I

The Union Jack, Crucifixes, Virgin Martyrs, and Greasepaint

It appears I am destined for something; I will live.

Robert Clive, "Clive of India," 1725 -1774

Chapter One
Ancestry and Addiction

The Kolkata Zoo in West Bengal, India is one of the most famous in the world. In recent years, the bestiary has boasted an African lion, a white tiger, a king cobra, a crested serpent eagle, and an olive baboon.

The star attraction, however, of the Kolkata Zoo for approximately 140 years was "Adwaita," an Aldabra giant tortoise, whose name translated as "The One and Only." Adwaita had resided there since the 1870s, having once been part of the private zoo of Robert Clive, the legendary "Clive of India."

Over 250 years ago, Clive had spearheaded the supremacy of Great Britain over

much of South Asia. It was, he believed, England's God-given right to claim India, the mystical land of the Taj Mahal, elephants with howdahs, and funeral barges on the Ganges River. Statues of Clive still stand in Saint James' Park, London and in Shrewsbury, despite the fact that the man's imperialistic arrogance caused the Bengal famine of 1770, reducing that area of India's population by one-third. A controversial figure, politically and personally, Clive was a victim of depression, an alcoholic, and an opium addict. Historian William Dalrymple has labeled Robert Clive "an unstable sociopath."

When Clive died in 1774, agonized by gallstones, the story quickly circulated that the empire builder had committed suicide by stabbing himself in the throat with a penknife.

A portrait of Robert Clive, "Clive of India," by Nathaniel Dance.

Adwaita the tortoise finally died at Kolkata Zoo in March, 2006, at the estimated age of 250, having outlived his master by over 231 years. He'd also outlasted, by over 68 years, an actor who, publicity claimed, was a descendant of Robert Clive. In fact, in 1935 Hollywood released the biopic *Clive of India,* starring Ronald Colman in the glamorized title role (no addictions, no penknife in the throat) and featuring the real-life Clive descendant as Johnstone, a political enemy of Clive. The actor Colin Clive, born Colin

"Adwaita," Robert Clive's pet tortoise, who lived until 2006.

Glennie Clive Greig, spoke out bitterly about his lousy role.

"I would have liked an opportunity to portray that hard-drinking ancestor of mine. Instead I was given a small role that required less than four days' work—a role that any actor could have played."

In fact, recent evidence casts doubt on the actor's ancestry actually tracing to Robert Clive. In 1990, the Seventh Earl of Powis, the expert on the family line, responded to an inquiry from historian Scott Wilson:

> So far as I know, none of Clive's descendants are called Clive-Greig.
>   I feel almost certain that I would know it if there was a descendant of that name. So I fear that I must say with almost certainty that your Colin Clive was not a descendent of Clive of India ...

Colin Clive clearly believed he was Robert Clive's descendant, and he'd come to identify with the man's agonies, depression, and addiction.

Come the late 19th century, and Great Britain was very much the world power that Robert Clive had helped establish. The Greig family, into which future actor Colin Clive would be born, boasted generations of British military men who'd proudly served Victoria. To trace back a bit:

Tuesday, August 24, 1869: Piercy Henderson Greig was promoted to Captain in the British Infantry in Bombay. He and his wife Fanny were the parents of nine-month-old Piercy Greig, who'd been born in Mhow, Bengal, India, on December 13, 1868. The book later addresses his tragic fate.

Thursday, May 26, 1870: Captain Greig and Fanny became parents of a second son, Colin Philip Greig. He'd become a Captain in the British Army in 1902, and a colonel over a decade later.

Tuesday, October 24, 1871: A third son was born, John Glennie Greig. He'd also join the military and, from 1893 to 1921, would be one of India's and England's superstar cricketers, eventually scoring an amazing 7,348 runs. (He received the nickname "Jungly," which translates in India to "wild," because most Indians couldn't pronounce "John Glennie.") In his mid-60s, John would be ordained a Catholic priest.

Monday, October 26, 1874: A daughter was born, Mary Greig. She will disappear from public record after 1881, at which time the six-year-old child was a student at a boarding school in Sussex, England.

John Glennie "Jungly" Greig, Colin Clive's uncle and legendary cricketer.

Tuesday, July 18, 1876: A fourth son was born, Hugh Irwin Greig. He was destined for heroism in the First World War.

As for second son, Colin Philip Greig, by January, 1896 at age 25, and having cloaked himself in glory at the Royal Military Academy, Sandhurst, he began an appointment as a garrison adjutant in Sierra Leone, Africa. The area is one of long, grim history: a swampy tropical rainforest, once considered impenetrable, guarded by the tsetse fly. In 1896, the British marched in, establishing "the Sierra Leone Protectorate," tossing the native Krios people out of power and inflicting a crippling tax on the natives.

Result: The Hut Tax War of 1898. Outcome: The British were victorious, exiling the native chief and hanging 96 of his warriors.

On Wednesday November 9, 1989, two days before the Hut Tax War ended in Sierra Leone, Colin Philip Greig wed Caroline Margaret "Daisy" Lugard Clive at the British Vice-Consulate in St. Malo, Brittany. Colin was 28 years old; the marriage certificate listed him as "bachelor." Daisy was 17 years old; the marriage certificate listed her as "spinster" (the official term for an unmarried British woman of the era).

It was Daisy who provided the family its purported link to Clive of India.

Daisy Clive, the daughter of high society British parents, had been born October 29, 1881 in Madras, India, and was baptized in Karachi three weeks later. Her early years suggest that she made the acquaintance of the Greig family in India.

As for the wedding site ... St. Malo sits on the English Channel, a citadel, and a walled port city founded by the Gauls in the first century B.C. Its history boasts of being the base of the "Corsairs," 19th-century pirates. Its architecture includes St. Malo Cathedral, with lofty bell tower, dedicated to Saint Vincent of Saragossa, a martyr executed by the Roman Emperor Diocletian circa 304. As with many of the saints, his executioners, according to legend, were merciless—stretching Vincent on a rack, tearing off his skin with iron hooks, rubbing salt into his wounds and, finally, burning him alive on a red-hot gridiron.

After the wedding, the couple went to Barbados in the West Indies, residing at Greenridge Cottage, near the Marine Hotel. It would be just one of the diverse locales where they resided over the next dozen years.

Meanwhile, Great Britain became engaged in another war in Africa—this one a *Holy* war.

The Boers, Afrikaans-speaking settlers of Dutch ancestry who'd settled in South Africa, had claim to the gold in Transvaal ... gold that Britain felt a divine right to possess. The "Second Boer War," as it was officially known, began October 11, 1899, waging in Swaziland. The week of December 10 to December 17, 1899 became known as "Black Week," due to horrific disasters suffered by the British. The Battle of Magersfontein, for example, resulted in 120 British soldiers dead, 690 wounded, and this verse (by a Private Smith of the Black Watch):

> *Such was the day for our regiment*
> *Dread the revenge we will take*
> *Dearly we paid for their blunder*
> *A drawing-room General's mistake.*
> *Why weren't we told of the trenches?*
> *Why weren't we told of the wire?*

And so on. The verse has an anti-war ring to it, but England was decidedly jingoistic. The Second Boer War became a bloodbath, generals of both sides believing that God wanted them to claim the gold. By the time the war ended May 31, 1902, Great Britain would be decisively triumphant.

It's likely, but not definite, that Colin Philip Greig was in combat in the Boer War. At any rate, as 1900 arrived, his wife Daisy was safely settled in St. Malo, awaiting the birth of their first child. She was surely glad to be where she was, rather than in war-torn Africa. She was also no doubt relieved not to be in imperiled London, where on January 9, an epidemic of influenza attacked the city.

St. Malo, France. The birthplace of Colin Clive.

Saturday, January 20, 1900, 1:51 a.m.: Two days after the death of his paternal grandfather, and two days before the feast of the martyred Saint Vincent, a son was born to Colin and Daisy Greig. He arrived in a freshly new century, where the 80-year-old Queen Victoria still ruled Great Britain. It was a country that still held sacred the concepts of Holy War, Ascetic Theology, God and Country, Faith, Duty, and Destiny.

Colin and Daisy christened him Colin Glennie Clive Greig.

"You see, my country was engaged in the Boer War," he'd tell a reporter in 1935. "My mother went to France to get away from the turmoil at home, and I wanted to be with her when I was born, so I had to be born in France."

There were many turn-of-the-century English newborns and children who'd eventually pursue variations on the British Raj establishment. In Enfield in 1900, a 12-year-old named Billy Pratt, who'd played the Demon King in *Cinderella* several years before in a parish play, was dreaming of defying his family's distinction in the consular service and becoming an actor. He'd grow up to be Boris Karloff. Near Dudley Castle in the Midlands, a 10-year-old named Jimmy Whale fantasized escaping his life of near-poverty and becoming an artist. He'd grow up to direct *Frankenstein*.

Come 1902, Captain Colin Philip Greig was an Army Paymaster. He and wife Daisy were soon blessed with two more additions to the family:

Saturday, April 27, 1901: Cicely Margaret Greig was born 95 days after the death of Queen Victoria.

Friday, December 11, 1903: Noel Audrey Greig was born.

Captain Greig, meanwhile, had departed six months before Noel's birth for South Africa. Daisy and the children lived in St. Malo and Greig would be gone for nearly four years, finally returning home to his family in February of 1907. The family set up residence in London, but the reunion of Colin and Daisy was not a happy one.

September 19, 1907: Colin and Daisy Greig entered a deed of separation.

1908: Records show that Captain Greig was stationed in West India.

1910: ten-year-old Colin Glennie (usually called Glennie), nine-year-old Cicely, and seven-year-old Noel were boarding at the school of the Convent of the Cross College for Girls in Boscombe, Bournemouth. Situated on the old Portman estate, near the sea, and run by the Sisters of the Religious of the Cross, the school, despite its name, also educated boys. The Gothic chapel's stained-glass window behind the altar depicted Jesus Christ's crucifixion on Calvary.

The three children were growing up having seen little of their father and, now at the Convent of the Cross, seeing less and less of their mother. Roman Catholic dogma and iconography had replaced hearth and home. For Glennie, Cicely, and Noel, life, at least part of the time, must have been Gothically foreboding.

Glennie loved animals, especially horses. His early dream: becoming a Bengal Lancer, fighting on horseback for Queen and Country, adventuring along the dangerous frontiers of India. Film fans will remember *The Lives of a Bengal Lancer* (1935), in which Gary Cooper runs afoul of Douglass Dumbrille's despicable Mohammed Khan. It's Khan who utters the infamous line, "We have ways to make men talk," and tortures Cooper by placing bamboo shoots under his fingernails ... the slivers of bamboo then set afire. Rousingly imperialistic, *The Lives of a Bengal Lancer* was one of Adolf Hitler's favorite movies. He saw it three times.

"I like this film because it depicted a handful of Britons holding a continent in thrall," said Hitler. "That is how a superior race must behave and the film is compulsory viewing for the SS."

Revisionist politics aside, surely one can understand Glennie's attraction to becoming a Bengal Lancer. He had a thirst for adventure and escape. The excitement of serving in India, where both his parents were born, was surely inspiring.

Then came real-life drama—actually, melodrama.

Friday, July 14, 1911: Captain Colin Philip Greig, then 41-years-old, officially filed a petition for divorce from Daisy Greig, then 29-years-old, accusing her of engaging in a love affair with a sculptor named Cecil A. Johnson, then approximately 33-years-old. The petition listed the marriage's history, the three children, and eventually got down to cases, generally and specifically:

> *That the said Caroline Margaret Lugard Clive has frequently committed adultery with Cecil A. Johnson.*
>
> *That on or about the 10th and 11th days of June 1911 at No. 12 Markham Street Chelsea in the County of London, the said Caroline Margaret Lugard Clive committed adultery with the said Cecil A. Johnson.*
>
> *WHEREFORE your petitioner prays:*
> *That his said marriage be dissolved.*
>
> *That he may have the custody of the said three children Colin Glennie Clive Greig, Cicely Margaret Greig and Noel Audrey Greig, and such further and other relief in the premises that may be just.*

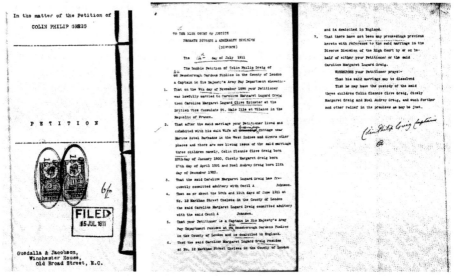

Divorce papers of Captain Colin Philip Greig and Caroline Margaret Lugard Clive, including Captain Greig's signature. (Courtesy of Scott Gallinghouse)

Captain Clive was living alone at 44 Bessborough Gardens, Westminster, S.W. Daisy resided at the aforementioned No. 12 Markham Street in Chelsea, presumably living with (or kept by) her sculptor lover. The three children, meanwhile, boarded at the Convent of the Cross.

Based on the presumption that there are, of course, two sides to every story ... perhaps Daisy, having wed at only 17, had suffered at the rigors of being an Army wife, especially with her husband away so much of the time. Then again, perhaps it had been worse when he was at home. Her life with Captain Greig, and his with her, had become intolerable.

At any rate, if Daisy deserved any sympathy in this matter, the Judge, Sir Henry Bargrave Deane, wasn't buying it. As Captain Greig requested, Judge Deane dissolved the marriage, awarding custody of the three children to the father. Even despite the adultery, it was a very unusual and severe decision for those days,

Monday, June 10, 1912: The final divorce decree took effect. Daisy and Cecil wed that summer, sailing on *The Corinthian* from London to Canada on September 14, arriving in Quebec September 28, crossing into the U.S.A. and settling in Schenectady, New York. In the wake of the scandal, Daisy's mother, Ellen, died in July of 1913; her father, Henry, succumbed in September of 1914; and her half-brother, Henry St. George Somerset Clive, died in May of 1914, although one imagines he would have been less traumatized by Daisy's perilous fall from grace than her parents.

Records indicate Cecil Johnson later acquired a new wife and, come 1940, was a widower, but the fate of Daisy is a mystery. In early 1915, a woman named Caroline M. Lugard married a man named Sam Morris in England. If this was "our" Daisy, it reveals that her marriage to Johnson had lasted less than three years, that she'd returned to England, and that, by her 34th year, she'd acquired three husbands.

Captain Greig would remarry in early 1920 to a woman named Jessie P. Hibbert. What eventually happened to Caroline Margaret "Daisy" Lugard Clive Greig Johnson Morris is a mystery. There's no record of Daisy being buried in the Clive family plot at the Municipal Cemetery in Richmond, Surrey, England.

Significant in this sad account is that Colin Glennie Greig's mother had virtually abandoned him when he was only 11-years-old.

Eight years after his parents' final divorce, Colin Glennie Clive Greig took the professional name of "Colin Clive." Did he do so because "Colin Clive" had a nicer ring to it than "Colin Greig?" Did he do it because of the distinction the name "Clive" had in British history? Or did he do so out of nostalgia and affection for his long-lost mother, despite her defection from his life?

Did he do it for all these reasons?

Chapter Two
The Athlete and the Horse Fall

By 1912 Colin Philip Greig and his three children lived in seaside Lytham, Lancashire, overlooking the River Ribble estuary. The name of their home: "The Hermitage." Perhaps Captain Greig needed a "hermitage" after his divorce scandal.

Tuesday, September 17, 1912: 12-year old Glennie entered Stonyhurst College, Lancashire, an all-male students Roman Catholic School, dating to 1593 and taught by Jesuits ("The Society of Jesus"). By 1912, its distinguished alumni included Charles Carroll of Carrolton, who signed the Declaration of Independence, Sir Arthur Conan Doyle, who created Sherlock Holmes, and Saint Thomas Garnet, S.J., one of the Forty Martyrs of England and Wales, who was executed at age 32.

The motto of Stonyhurst: "Quant Je Puis," meaning: "All that I can."

The beautiful grounds of Stonyhurst include the Sodality Chapel, which holds below its altar the relics of St. Gordianus, tortured and beheaded in 362 A.D. There are two observatories, one built in 1838 and one in 1866. The school became co-educational in 1999 and is the only surviving Jesuit preparatory school in England.

Glennie joined the "Upper Figures" class. The school records note he enrolled with a knowledge of French, and that during his first year, he was promoted to the "Lower Rudiments" class (Division 2). He ended the year in third place (out of 18); the following year, in "Upper Rudiments," he came in eighth (of 28 students). He spent the next two terms in "Grammar."

Coincidentally, Glennie had a classmate, about seven months older, also destined for fame as an actor. He was Charles Laughton. As such, Stonyhurst housed Hollywood's two future star blasphemers simultaneously: the title character of 1931's *Frankenstein*, who'll artificially create a Monster from stolen corpses, and mad Dr. Moreau of 1932's *Island of Lost Souls*, who'll surgically transform a panther into a woman.

Stonyhurst College, England. (Courtesy of David Knight, Stonyhurst archivist)

Saint Agnes, patron Saint of Stonyhurst's "Rudiments" Class.

Had the Jesuits at Stonyhurst only known!

Stonyhurst had a bevy of patron saints that watched over the young boys at each stage of their academic career.

For "Rudiments," where Glennie Greig had studied, it was Saint Agnes, virgin martyr, born in 291 A.D. She was so beautiful and so devoted to purity that, when she was only 13, the Romans spitefully dragged Agnes naked through the streets to a brothel. All men who tried to rape her were struck blind, and Rome promptly condemned her as a witch. Come her burning at the stake on January 21, 304 A.D., the fire wouldn't burn; a Roman officer, therefore, beheaded her. Portraits often show her holding a lamb, and she's the patron saint of, among others, virgins and rape victims. Her Feast day: January 21, the date of her martyrdom ... and the day after Glennie's birthday.

As for "Grammar," where Glennie progressed, the guardian was Saint Barbara, third-century virgin martyr, whose father, a rich Pagan widower named Dioscorus, had locked her away in a tower ... and wanted to marry her. Barbara refused his incestuous desire, and her piety worked miracles, making her impervious to her persecutor's horrific tortures. Like Agnes, she too was paraded naked through the streets, bleeding from wounds inflicted by hooks and rakes, and her own father beheaded her. God struck Dioscorus dead with a lightning bolt. Barbara is the patron saint of firemen and artillerymen. Her feast day: December 4.

Hence, the teenage boys of "Rudiments" and "Grammar" went to bed each night, praying to and watched over by two stripped, tortured, decapitated, female, virgin martyr saints.

While such baroque accounts had a lasting effect on Stonyhurst's Charles

Saint Barbara, patron saint of Stonyhurst's "Grammar" Class.

"One Man *Crazy* ...!"

THIRD PLAYROOM XI.

B. Whiteside.   F. Collins.   D. Cuffey.   B. Agostini.   L. Pearce.
J. Tayler.   A. Moorhead.   D. Feeney.   C. Greig.
J. Malone.   W. Jones.

Colin is seated on bench, far right.

Laughton, who according to his widow Elsa Lanchester dealt with cosmic guilt and fear to the night he died in 1962 (prayed over by a priest), it's not known if these macabre miracle tales had any impact on young Glennie Greig. What is clear, however, is that he soon became a Stonyhurst star athlete.

Sunday, December 15, 1912: Stonyhurst's "3rd Playroom" Football team battled Preston Catholic College, winning 12 to 4. *The Stonyhurst Magazine* (February, 1913), covering the game, recorded:

> *... from the last of a series of attacks on the right wing, Greig skillfully turned the ball goal-wards from a difficult position, and the goal-keeper could not get across the goal-mouth in time to save it.*

School records of 1913 also list Glennie coming in second as 3rd Division runner in both the 100 Yards Flat Race and the 880 Yards Flat Race, while placing third in the 440 Yards Flat Race. He also competed in the Long Jump, coming in third.

Thursday, March 13, 1913: Glennie played as a "Forward" in another match against Preston Catholic College. *The Stonyhurst Magazine* (April, 1913), reporting the early part of the game, wrote, " ... the ball traveled up and down the field till Greig, after a splendid run down the wing, brought off one of his most successful passes ... and Stonyhurst scored its first goal." The article also noted that Greig received an injury early in the second half, but "pluckily" kept playing. Stonyhurst won, two to one.

THE STONYHURST COLLEGE "UNDER-SIXTEEN" ELEVEN.
Who won the match played at Sedbergh on July 15, 1915, against the Sedbergh "Under-Sixteen" Eleven.

A. Moorhead.	W. Wadsworth.	R. Gibson.	G. Williams.
D. Cuffey.	E. Mahony.	F. Rockliff.	H. Broadbent.	H. Flower.
	J. Howitt.		C. Greig.	

Colin seated on ground, right.

Although Glennie didn't perform in school dramatics, he was a member of the Stonyhurst orchestra, playing the clarinet under the direction of Father Oswald Kellet, eventually earning a certificate for his talent. A second violinist was Charles Laughton.

Tuesday, August 4, 1914: England declared war on Germany. The boys of Stonyhurst surely prayed for victory and wondered how they'd eventually contribute to it.

Meanwhile, the film industry was maturing. In 1914, Charlie Chaplin introduced his character of "the Tramp" in *Kid Auto Races in Venice,* and Pearl White performed her own breathtaking stunts in *The Perils of Pauline.* The top stars in the U.S.A. were William S. Hart and Mary Pickford. "Gertie the Dinosaur" became the screen's first prominent cartoon character. All of these figures fascinated the boys, as did (in a different way) Theda Bara, the "vamp" of *A Fool There Was* (1915), especially after Fox Studios widely circulated the sexy, macabre photo of the dark-eyed Theda making love to a skeleton. March of 1915 saw the New York premiere of D.W. Griffith's *The Birth of a Nation,* as well as the gala opening of Universal City, California—which, 16 years later, would be the site of *Frankenstein.*

The Stonyhurst boys probably saw little of this 1915 entertainment; the Jesuits surely arranged no field trip to a cinema showing *A Fool There Was.* Yet they inevitably heard about it. Film was having a giant impact on popular culture—and was fascinating Colin Glennie Greig.

Incidentally ... 1915 also saw the release of two man-made monster movies: Germany's *Der Golem*, starring Paul Wegener as the 16th-century man of clay; and Ocean Films' *Life Without Soul*, based on *Frankenstein*, starring William W. Cowill and Percy Standing as, respectively, Monster-Maker and Monster.

April 5, Easter Monday, 1915: Glennie competed as a Second Division runner in "Sports Day." He won the Half Mile ("an exciting race with a good finish," wrote *The Stonyhurst Magazine*), coming in at two-minutes, 32 and one fifth seconds; came in second in both the 100 Yards and the 440 Yards; and came in third in the Long Jump. Glennie received the King's Cup for "Best All-Round Athlete in Second Division."

Another mystery follows: On April 10, 1915—only five days after his "Sports Day" triumph—Colin Glennie Greig left Stonyhurst. He'd stayed nearly three years. On its Internet site, Stonyhurst lists Colin Clive among its famous alumni.

The likely reason for Glennie's sudden departure from Stonyhurst was that an opening presented itself for the 15-year-old scholar/athlete/clarinetist at the D.J. Cowles School, an exclusive private academy that accepted a "limited number of pupils" in preparation for the Royal Military Academy Sandhurst. The D.J. Cowles School, originally based in France, had moved to the Manor House at Felixstowe, on the North Sea coast of Suffolk. It was the *alma mater* of Glennie's father, Colin Philip Greig, whom the D.J. Cowles School proudly exalted as the first student to have passed Sandhurst's final examinations in December.

Indeed, Sandhurst was a glorious tradition in the Greig family. Glennie's uncle, John Glennie Greig, had been the Royal Academy's star cricketer. His uncle, Hugh Greig, had been one of the Academy's "Gentlemen Cadets" in 1896. With the war raging in Europe, it seemed no better time for Glennie to perpetuate the family tradition at Sandhurst.

Then tragedy struck.

November 2, 1917: Major Hugh Irwin Greig, of the British Army's Royal Garrison Artillery, died in battle in Belgium. He was 41 years old. Major Greig was buried in plot 9, Row C of the Steenkerke Belgian Military Cemetery. In March of 1918, he was posthumously awarded the *Ordre de Leopold* (the Knight of the Order of Leopold) and the *Croix de Guerre* (the Cross of War).

The death of Glennie's Uncle Hugh likely bequeathed a new, even deeper, dynamic to the Greig military legacy. Come August of 1918, Colin Glennie Greig was at the Royal Military Academy Sandhurst.

Steenkerke Belgian Military Cemetery. Major Hugh Irwin Greig, Colin's uncle, killed in World War I, is buried here.

The Royal Military Academy Sandhurst. Colin is circled. (Courtesy of Dr. Anthony Morton, DPS, Curator, Sandhurst Collection, Royal Military Academy Sandhurst)

The few surviving records at Sandhurst on Colin Glennie Greig note that his paternal grandmother signed as his guardian, as his father was then in South Africa. Glennie, foreseeing the imminent end of the war with Germany, wrote that it was his wish, as it always had been, to join the "Indian Cavalry." The war ended November 11, 1918, and precisely how long Glennie was at Sandhurst isn't clear; the *Stonyhurst Magazine* notes in June of 1919 that he was "at Sandhurst."

Sadly, while in cavalry training, he suffered a spectacular accident: There was a horse fall and Glennie broke his knee.

Usually, Glennie would claim that one knee was broken. In a 1935 interview with Madeline Glass, however, he'd claim that *two* knees were broken, but considering he was charmingly flirting with Ms. Glass throughout the interview, it's possible he was exaggerating to impress her. At any rate, the accident forever shattered his dream of being a Bengal Lancer. For a young man who loved horses, it must have been heartbreaking. For the only male heir in a family of British military officers, it likely was devastating.

Colin Glennie Greig's military career was over.

The surprising attraction Glennie had for theater was certainly not in the blood, at least on his father's side. As such, he might have expected a thunderous denouncement when, as a heartbroken would-be soldier, he announced his hopes of becoming an adventurous would-be actor.

"My family did not object," he'd recall. "In fact, my father was extraordinarily decent about it and gave me every encouragement."

Duty, Identity, Heroism.

And, of course, Destiny.

It seemed to be a ringing bell, an alarm, almost a call to arms. There was a certain discord in it, perhaps, but that was to be expected, considering how very different it was from what he'd long dreamed of becoming.

Yes, perhaps it was meant to be. The horse fall at Sandhurst—maybe not the tragedy he'd once thought. Maybe he was destined to be an actor. Maybe that was why he'd developed this strange attraction to theater and the films, so off the street from anyone else in his family.

Not so shameful, really ... is it? Think of the actors who've been knighted. Sir Henry Irving, famed for his Shylock. Sir Herbert Beerbohm Tree, who'd founded the Royal Academy of Dramatic Art. Sir Johnston Forbes-Robertson, acclaimed as the greatest Hamlet of Victoria's age.

Yes, even Father approved. Acting was actually rather noble, in its own fashion. Entertaining the people. Taking their minds off their troubles. He'd witnessed the sadness in his own family ... so much sadness. If an actor in a play could succeed in relieving that sort of personal pain, or loneliness, even for a couple hours, he'd done something fine and worthy.

Actors gave people escape. They gave people dreams. It would be an honor to help people in this way ... yes, very much so.

There was only one problem. The very idea of standing on a stage before an audience absolutely terrified him.

Somehow, it unnerved him more than his lifelong dream of being a Bengal Lancer. He wasn't sure why. But it was something he had to over-come. After all, he came from a long line of heroes. It was what people were supposed to be in this world, be they the soldiers of his ancestry, or the female martyrs he'd prayed to at Stonyhurst, or all those who'd recently served and sacrificed in the Great War, such as his Uncle Hugh.

The motto of Stonyhurst ... " Quaint Je Puis" ... "All that I can." Yes, if he were an actor, he'd be all that he could be ... give it everything he had ... all that he'd have given to being a soldier. A hero on the stages of London, rather than the frontiers of India.

Heroes always conquered their fears ... didn't they?

Chapter Three
"Where Angels Fear to Tread," Bride
No. 1, and Death in a "Lunatic Asylum"

"Did you have any hard times at all, Mr. Clive?" Elisabethe Corathiel would ask in a 1931 interview for England's *Theatre World* magazine.

"Did I have any?" replied Colin. "At first I knew nothing else. I can honestly say that every penny I've ever had I've earned. I never had a sou from anyone. And knowing the precariousness of the profession, you can guess that the start wasn't all roses."

" ... 'where angels fear to tread'—you know the rest," Colin Clive, famed actor, would remember.

The London theater world of 1919 was a multi-ring-circus, enjoying "unprecedented prosperity" after the Great War. There was the West End, where the major productions played, including *Chin-Chin-Chow*, an "Oriental extravaganza" (starring British actors), based on Ali Baba. It had opened in 1916, playing to packed houses despite air raids and zeppelin bombings, and on the night of October 15, 1919, set a world's record as it played its 1,447th performance. Theaters were so desirable in the West End that they increased eight to 10 times in value. Meanwhile, there were the classical actors of the Old Vic, strutting and fretting in comedy and tragedy, "full of sound and fury." Conversely, there were the music halls, with their risqué, tights-busting chorus girls, provocatively adorned in top hats and corsets, acrobatically performing songs such as "The Man on the Flying Trapeze."

> *He'd smile from the air at the people below*
> *And one night he smiled on my love.*
> *She wink'd back at him and shouted "Bravo"*
> *As he hung from his nose up above*

It was a sensual time, zinged by a raucous post-war euphoria that spiked most of the world's theaters. In America, the Broadway sex farces were the craze: *Adam and Eva*; *Up in Mabel's Room; The Gold Diggers; Scandal*. Reformers attacked the theater, protesting, among other things, "Lingerie Displays and Scanty Skirts." In Germany, Weimar Berlin's bizarre erotica was becoming legendary.

It was also an epic era for the now-booming worldwide Film Industry. 1919 saw the release of D.W. Griffith's *Broken Blossoms*, Cecil B. DeMille's *Male and Female*, and Erich von Stroheim's *Blind Husbands*. In 1920, John Barrymore starred in *Dr. Jekyll and Mr. Hyde*, Mary Pickford in *Pollyanna*, and Douglas Fairbanks in *The Mark of Zorro*. Meanwhile in Germany, Conrad Veidt was scaring the crowds in *The Cabinet of Dr. Caligari*.

Actually, Colin Glennie Greig's apprehensions about becoming an actor were valid. For all its glamour, the theater could be a torturous existence, even for established luminaries. In early 1919, 60-year-old John B. Mason, one of America's greatest stage stars, suffered "a breakdown" while giving the premiere performance of the melodrama *The Woman in Room 13* at a tryout in Providence, Rhode Island. He died January 12 in a sanitarium in Connecticut. At the same time, 46-year-old Maude Adams, the greatest Peter Pan of her generation, was recovering from a nervous breakdown at a friend's home in Boston. She never appeared on stage again. On October 17, 1919, 48-year-old actor/manager Henry Brodribb Irving died in London. He was the son of the late and legendary British stage star Sir Henry Irving, the first knighted actor. One might presume that the young Irving, having grown up in the acting profession, would have been inured to its pressures—but he, too, died from a nervous breakdown.

"Where angels fear to tread ...," indeed.

Colin Glennie Greig had enrolled at London's Royal Academy of Dramatic Art. However, as he later said, " ... I do not want you to think that I say this in the least disparagement of this excellent academy when I remark that I consider the best training for an actor is experience. He should play every part he possibly can."

Did he have any true dramatic talent? Would he suffer as he feared, from stage fright? Could he adapt to the quirky challenges of an actor's life? Desperate to find out, Colin decided to test his mettle as soon as possible.

He was lucky. As a novice actor, Colin got to the West End immediately, if temporarily.

In 1919, the most prominent comic actor of the London stage was 61-year-old Charles Hawtrey, who would be knighted in 1922, the year before his death. Generosity to young actors, including Noel Coward, is how Hawtrey would be known. As Colin would relate:

Charles Hawtrey, who gave Colin his first theatrical job.

> *With the audacity of a beginner, I went to the Playhouse one night and sent in my card to Charles Hawtrey, who was then appearing there. He would have been quite justified in refusing to see me, for he had never heard of me in his life. But his goodness of heart is still famous, and to my great delight he not only saw me, but also offered me a part in his next play.*

Wednesday, November 12, 1919: At the age of 19, Colin, fresh from Sandhurst and his recalcitrant horse, made his London stage debut in the small role of Claude in *The Eclipse*, a musical farce directed by Hawtrey. The theater was the Garrick, on Charing Cross Road, and he was billed as Colin Greig.

"I believe I had one line to speak ...!" recalled Colin.

The Eclipse ran a respectable 93 performances and prophesized a comic career for Colin. He recalled:

> *Charles Hawtrey's kindness did not end there. He would often come behind and give me a few words of advice and encouragement. One day he said: "If you really want to learn your job, you will get out of London and go on tour. Play anything that comes along. Get experience."*
>
> *I took his advice, and for the next few years I travelled with different companies all over the country. It was then that I learnt what the hardships of the profession could be, although quite a lot of people considered themselves very lucky that the £3 a week minimum wage had recently been instituted. Before that, actors often earned as little as 30s. per week—without, of course, counting the slack times when no work of any kind was to be had.*

Colin, now taking the stage name of "Colin Clive," played the provinces, sometimes in classics, other times in farces, often in barns, firehalls, and other makeshift theaters in country villages. Young actors learned to recite a classic soliloquy and time comic delivery. They learned to fence, to dance, to apply makeup to make them appear younger, older, more attractive, or grotesque. They mastered controlling emotion and how to cry on cue.

It was a precarious existence, all the more so as the players found themselves co-habitating stages and boarding houses, often far from home.

Yes, the stage fright was merciless. He defied his fear. It's what heroes did.

Enter another inspiring figure in Colin's early theater life—the legendary Annie Horniman, whom George Bernard Shaw praised for "starting the modern theater movement." Notorious for smoking cigarettes in public (which women of that era were not supposed to do), and famous for having cycled over the Alps—twice—Annie had once been a member of the Hermetic Order of the Golden Dawn, which inspired Wicca. Amidst her jewelry: A dragon pendant, with ruby eyes and made from 300 opals.

Annie Horniman had established the Abbey Theatre in Dublin, and founded Britain's first repertory company, the Gaiety Theatre in Manchester, presenting both the Classics and works by fledgling playwrights. Colin later said, quite humbly:

> *I took part in the farewell season of Miss Horniman's at Manchester, though I came into it so late that I cannot claim to belong to that brilliant company of actors and actresses who were trained under her banner.*

Indeed, to a young man with a Catholic education and Sandhurst training, Annie Horniman must have seemed as if she'd arrived from another planet. At any rate, in 1921, Annie sold the Gaiety Theatre to a film company.

Annie Horniman was more than 39 years older than Colin Clive. When she died in August of 1937, she'd outlived him by six weeks.

Colin took to the provinces. He appeared in such plays as *The Love Divine* and *Paddy the Next Best Thing*. And he fell in love.

Monday, June 26, 1922: Colin wed Evelyn Taylor, an actress, at the Roman Catholic Church of English Martyrs in London. The newlyweds resided at 72 Lonsdale Road in

Barnes, on the River Thames, near the historic Hammersmith Bridge. They later moved to No. 5, Tregunton Road, in Kensington. There have been reports that the couple had met at the Royal Academy (possibly true), as well as stories that their marriage ended very quickly (definitely not true). For their first years together, they persevered, seeking theatrical fame and fortune.

Thursday, September 20, 1923: *Hassan: And How He Came to Make the Golden Journey to Samarkand*, a "poetic prose" extravaganza starring Malcolm Keen, opened in London. Evelyn was an "extra." The show was a big success, running 282 performances. For those eight months, Evelyn, not her husband, was appearing on the West End. For likely most of the time, she was the principal breadwinner.

As the story of Colin Clive evolves, the career of Evelyn Taylor isn't as critical as her unfortunate future. As will be reported, she was fated for a sordidly tragic death, becoming one of the taunting ghosts of her widower's short life.

The Roman Catholic Church of the Martyrs, where Colin Clive wed Evelyn Taylor in 1922.

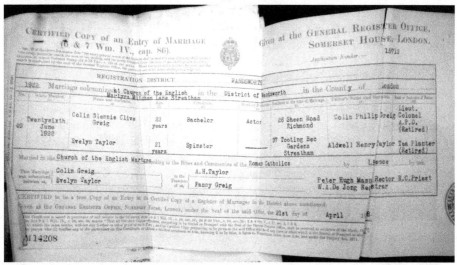

A marriage certificate of Colin Glennie Greig and Evelyn Taylor. This copy comes from their divorce file. (Courtesy of Neil Pettigrew)

St. Saviour's Hospital, England, also known as "The Public Lunatic Asylum, St. Saviour's, Jersey." Piercy Greig, Colin's uncle, died here in 1924.

First, the book must cover a different ghost, however. Only a few bare bones of evidence have turned up on this tragic topic, but it appears to have been a specter that haunted Colin, as well as his two sisters ... who'd become the end of their family line.

Sunday, February 10, 1924: Piercy Greig, Colin Clive's eldest uncle, died at the age of 55. The place of death: "St. Saviour's," located on King's Farm on the island of Jersey.

It was, basically and tragically, a Bedlam-by-the-Sea.

The 1911 British Channel Island Census had listed Piercy Greig as a patient at St. Saviour's. Under the heading of "Infirmity," his name appeared with others described as "Lunatics." The Census noted that his admittance date to the hospital as 1903, and as such, Piercy had been there for over 20 years at the time of his death.

The man signing the census listed the hospital as "The Public Lunatic Asylum, Jersey."

Mysteriously, little other data survives on Piercy Greig. He had worked in the British Civil Service prior to his incarceration. As for the Asylum ... in 1847, Whitehall had criticized the Channel Island States for their poor care of "islanders with learning disabilities and mental health issues." Most of the "afflicted" were kept at home, and many suffered horribly—regarded as animals, and kept in outhouses.

The General Hospital at the time accepted only a small number of these unfortunate souls, usually those who were paupers, as the hospital also served as a poor house. On Saturday, July 29, 1865, authorities laid the first stone for the asylum. The Crown leased the land for £84 per annum, and on July 11, 1868, The Jersey Lunatic Asylum had admitted its first 12 patients, transferred from the General Hospital.

Mental illness bore a ferocious stigma in the 1920s, vigilantly guarded by most families, especially those of social hierarchy. The mention of an asylum conjured sounds of

1911 British Census documentation of Piercy Greig's incarceration at The Public Lunatic Asylum, St. Saviour's, Jersey. Note Piercy's name, second from the bottom, line 39. Under Infirmity is the word Lunatics, which, as indicated by the line drawn, applied to everyone on this list. The last column shows that Piercy was admitted in 1903. (Courtesy of Scott Gallinghouse)

shrieks and screams in the night, and images of torturous strait-jackets and horrific shock treatments. It must have been a terrifying concern to the Greig family.

The frightening inference: There was "lunacy," severe enough to merit more than a decade of asylum incarceration, in the Greig family. Did any of the other members carry the curse?

Friday, May 16, 1924: Administration passed the effects of the tragic Piercy Greig— £416.16s.1d.—to his mother, Fanny. His legacy to his younger relatives, and a deeply frightful one, was the terrible fear of passing on insanity to a child. Neither of Colin's sisters, Cicely or Noel, would ever marry and lived with their father until his death. Colin would marry twice but have no children.

St. Saviour's Hospital recently closed. A blog spot titled *The Right of Reply* has posted various messages dated from 2011 to 2018 about alleged nightmarish events there: a girl patient who asked to be released to take a walk, received irresponsible permission, and was found six hours later drowned in the nearby Queen's Valley Reservoir; boy patients who were raped by male staff members in the basement; the basement housing patients who couldn't see, walk, or communicate; and patients doped with drugs. (This book doesn't claim those atrocities happened, just that they were reported.) A 2008 documentary film addressed in part St. Saviour's, the movie luridly titled *Sun, Sea & Satan*.

There's no current evidence of how fine or wretched a place St. Saviour's was nearly a century ago. One can only hope, that for the sake of Piercy Greig and his fellow patients, it wasn't wretched, as asylums too often during that era were a virtual chamber of horrors.

Was there mental illness on both his father's *and* mother's side of Colin Clive's family? While Daisy Greig's flagrant adultery would raise few eyebrows today, it had been startling behavior for a 1911 mother of three children in an era still consecrated to the memory of Queen Victoria. Had Daisy Clive Greig suffered, as had Piercy Greig, from "lunacy" to have behaved in so "unorthodox" a way?

Was Colin, too, prone to this illness?

In *Frankenstein*, Colin Clive will speak the word "crazy" six times, in regard to the role he so fervently plays. Each time, he says it with a bitter, almost vicious defensiveness.

No wonder.

Chapter Four
"God, What a Life This is!,"
The Dashing Young Villain,
and "Indian Love Call"

Saturday, September 13, 1924: A. R. Whatmore officially premiered the Hull Repertory Company, located in Kingston upon Hull in Yorkshire. The town sits on the River Hull, 25 miles inland from the North Sea. As historian Janet Sullivan Cross wrote of the company:

> *Designer Eric Hiller transformed a drab, barren hall, previously the local firehouse, into the Hull's main stage—and from there he conjured up a fog-shrouded Norwegian fjord for the British premiere of Bjornstjerne Bjornson's* Leonarda, *an English drawing room for C.K. Munro's* At Mrs. Beam's, *a country garden for A.A. Milne's* The Lucky One, *a run-down estate house for Ibsen's* John Gabriel Borkman ...

Whatmore ran 10-week seasons, hiring seasoned actors to work with the local beginners. A member of the troupe was Roland Culver, who'd been a fighter pilot in World War I and would appear prominently in such films as *Dead of Night* (1945), *To Each His Own* (1946), and *The Legend of Hell House* (1973). Culver and Colin co-starred at Hull in the play *Peter and Paul*. Attending a performance: the famed Annie Horniman, adorned in red and gold brocade, who came onstage afterwards to praise the actors.

Culver's memory of the Hull Repertory Company: "a bundle of temperaments, explosive as an arsenal."

A sampling of Colin's reviews during his first Hull sojourn reveal he acted a "terror-stricken brother," a "father," and "a vigorous brother," and he played leads in plays by A.A. Milne and C.K. Munro. Always polite, grateful, and gentlemanly, Colin later said, "Of very great value ... was the experience I gained under Mr. Whatmore."

A few months later, Evelyn Taylor landed a new West End gig. *A Kiss for Cinderella*, J.M. Barrie's version of the Cinderella tale, opened on Saturday, December 20, 1924, at London's Haymarket Theatre. Evelyn appeared as one of eight "Court Ladies." The show ran 63 performances, closing Valentine's Day, 1925.

Colin, meanwhile, had returned to the provinces, touring as the star of *The Way of an Eagle*. Notable is this February 25, 1925 review, from the *Gloucester Citizen*: " ... Mr. Colin Clive ... at times rough as Petruchio, at others devoted a lover as Romeo, and anon moody as Hamlet ... "

He would, in fact, have been a potentially terrific gloomy Dane. Unfortunately, based on the evidence, he never had the chance to prove it.

Colin came back to Hull for the fall 1925 season—this time with his wife. The *Hull Daily Mail* wrote that Evelyn Taylor, "... wife of Colin Clive, last year's popular member of the company, has a substantial claim on Hull's interest. Miss Taylor comes to Hull from Basil Dean's management."

Once again, Colin played impressively, and a fan wrote a letter to *The Hull Daily Mail*, published October 13, 1925: "... Mr. Clive is so versatile, yet so consistently good, that I find myself simply longing to see what character he will choose to delight us in next." The praise was important in sustaining his aspiration.

Although Colin had a passion for his chosen craft, he also had a certain contempt for it ... and, for whatever reasons, for himself. The idealism of his earliest nights in the theater was waning, surely nibbled away by his modest wages and the hellishly dogging stage fright. At times, he must have felt like a man who'd embraced a fetish as a way of making a living.

Still, he tried to deal with it, giving the theater all the devotion he'd have provided the military ... perhaps more so, considering his increasingly complex feelings about his chosen profession. In the memoir, *Fires of Spring*, writer Noel Barber recalled his nights as an actor with the Hull Repertory Company, specifically in the play *The Romantic Age*, by A.A. Milne. Colin had a prominent role, and Barber played, in his words, "a village idiot." As Barber wrote:

> *My big scene was with a quiet, very good-looking young man called Colin Clive. He had a deep, attractive, clipped voice. I liked him from the very start when he said, wearily:*
> *"God! What a life this is!"*

Colin applied Barber's makeup, the performance was a success, and Colin, Barber, and the company went out for bacon and eggs to await the reviews. As Barber continued:

> *Years later I saw Colin Clive again. By then, we had both gone our roads, he on the stage, I writing. He had behind him his magnificent triumph of* Journey's End—*he had in front of him Hollywood, a bitter disillusionment and a sudden, lonely death.*
> *He was earning two or three hundred a week then at least. But he still wore grey flannels, and he still said, wearily, "God! What a life this is!"*

Back in West London, the Q Theatre had opened near Kew Bridge on "Boxing Day," December 26, 1924. The building had previously served as a beer garden, swimming pool, roller rink, dance hall, and a cinema. The managers of the Q were Jack De Leon, a former lawyer turned playwright and director, and his wife Beatrice, who'd dreamed of becoming an actress, but made her mark as an enterprising impresario.

"No experience?" she'd ask a fledgling actor. "Well, you know we can't afford to pay you anything, but you've got to start somewhere."

At the "Q" Theatre, Colin Clive—no fledgling, but rather celebrating his sixth full year as a struggling actor—played in three consecutive plays: as Daniels in *Conflict* (November, 1925), as Sheridan Cleaver in *The House of Unrest* (December, 1925), and as both Hutchinson and Arthur in *The Long Lane* (January, 1926).

It was low pay, or more likely, no pay. A major break, however, was about to happen.

The Theatre Royal, Drury Lane, in London's Covent Garden, dates to 1663. After twice burning down, the current Theatre Royal arose in 1812. Edmund Kean had played

Shylock there. There have been operas and ballets. *The Whip*, presented in 1909, had featured an onstage train crash and 12 horses thunderously recreating the 2,000 Guineas Stakes, running on an on-stage treadmill. In 1922, a major renovation (the theater's last) created a four-tiered interior that seats a capacity audience of over 2,000.

Friday, March 20, 1925: *Rose-Marie*, the famed operetta, had opened at the Theatre Royal. The music was by Rudolf Friml and Herbert Stothart, the book and lyrics by Otto Harbach and Oscar Hammerstein II, and the show came complete with a chorus of 80. Set in the Canadian wilderness, it was the saga of Rose-Marie La Flamme, who loves miner Jim Kenyon—and who together sing the famous "Indian Love Call."

> *When I'm calling you,*
> *Oo-oo- oo-oo, oo-oo-oo-ooo,*
> *Will you answer too?*
> *Oo-oo,-oo-oo, oo-oo-oo-oo ... .*

In early 1926, 26-year-old Colin replaced Brian Gilmour as *Rose-Marie*'s Edward Hawley, the wealthy, caddish "other man"—Colin referred to him as "the villain." Hawley pursues the heroine, Rose-Marie, who even sang a song about Hawley, "I Love Him," although she never actually *does* love the swine. Apparently, Colin warbled a few lines in this song as well.

Hawley was a plum role, a scoundrel who, besides lusting after Rose-Marie, has a fling with a "half-breed" named Wanda. The wanton Wanda, whose big musical moment is the "Totem-Tom-Tom" dance, fatally stabs fellow villain Black Eagle after he discovers Hawley and Wanda canoodling. Suspicion of the murder falls on our hero, Jim. However, come the big Act II wedding finale, as a very reluctant Rose-Marie is about to marry Hawley, the wildly jealous Wanda crashes the nuptials, confesses to the murder of Black Eagle, and declares her mad love for Hawley. Rose-Marie jilts Hawley at the altar and runs off to the Kootenay Pass, where she and Jim climac-

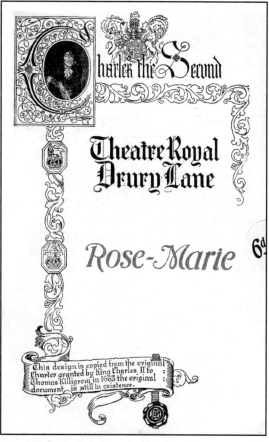

The Theatre Royal, Drury Lane program cover for *Rose-Marie*. Colin joined the show as a replacement in the role of Edward Hawley, the villain.

Theatre Royal · Drury Lane

Managing Director: ALFRED BUTT

Evenings at 8.15
Doors open at 7.45

Matinees :
Wednesday & Saturday at 2.30
Doors open at 2.0

—◦—

Rose Marie

A Musical Play

A Romance of the Canadian Rockies
in Two Acts

—◦—

THE CHARACTERS
in the order of their appearance

SERGEANT MALONE - -	MR. LEONARD MACKAY
LADY JANE ▮ - - -	MISS CLARICE HARDWICKE
BLACK EAGLE - - -	MR. PERCY PARSONS
EDWARD HAWLEY - -	MR. COLIN CLIVE
EMILE LA FLAMME - -	MR. MICHAEL COLE
WANDA - - - - -	MISS RUBY MORRISS
HARD-BOILED HERMAN -	MR. NELSON KEYS
JIM KENYON - - -	MR. DEREK OLDHAM
ROSE MARIE LA FLAMME -	MISS EDITH DAY
ETHEL BRANDER - -	MISS MARJORIE CHARD
A CARETAKER - - -	MR. GEORGE SPELVIN

T.11196

The cast list for *Rose-Marie*.

tically reprise "Indian Love Call." Hawley, presumably, never recovers from the social revelation that he and a homicidal squaw have been making the beast with two backs.

Rose-Marie ran a remarkable 851 performances, establishing Colin as a London stage player and providing plenty of exposure to West End audiences. It also prophesized the "other man" roles, which became one of his specialties in Hollywood. In time, a virtual beauty parade of actresses, including Katharine Alexander, Jean Arthur, Joan Bennett, Edna Best, Dolores del Rio, Josephine Hutchinson, and Diana Wynyard, would all find Colin in romantic triangles to be less-than-desirable, or sloppy seconds, or downright demonic. Based on how often producers would cast Colin in such roles, many audiences agreed.

When Jeanette MacDonald and Nelson Eddy starred in MGM's *Rose-Marie* (1936), Colin might have reprised his role as Hawley, but the character was written out of the script. So was the wicked Wanda.

Colin was now in a historic stage hit, earning a weekly salary, meeting London's luminaries. It was, by later indications, during the run of *Rose-Marie* that Colin and Evelyn Taylor separated. It had been a stormy union.

> *The dissonance was growing sharp ... the cacophony of conflicts roaring.*
> *So far away from the echoes of his early years. The hymns and rosaries of the Sisters at the Convent. The military marching bands. All crashing together now with the thunderous overture of* Rose-Marie.
> *The clashing iconography ... Christ Crucified, looming majestically in stained glass over the altar at Stonyhurst, where the beheaded martyrs Agnes and Barbara kept holy watch ... the Union Jack, flying over Sandhurst. Now sharing the stage in his mind with the British chorus girls, in black wigs, painted up as Indian squaws and cavorting in* Rose-Marie's "Totem-Tom-Tom" ...
> *The would-be Bengal Lancer ... an actor for seven years now. Almost a decade of toying with makeup, wigs and tights, fascinated in spite of himself by this strange, silly nonsense. A Bengal Lancer? Jesus!*

"One Man *Crazy* ...!"

Whatever made him think he'd be so heroic? The very sight and sound of those stiffs sitting out there in the audience terrified him, jolting him with stage fright, still biting and snapping at him even after seven years.

After the show, a whiskey often helped. But he knew he mustn't have more than one or two. And, despite the wretched stage fright, to take a drink before a performance was unthinkable. Drink was the kiss of death for an actor. Once word escaped, the actor was finished.

No, he'd carry on, as a soldier would. No crutches. No nets. Surely no bottles. The call came backstage ... the cue for his entrance was fast approaching ... Put out the cigarette ... Buck up ...

God, what a life this is!

Colin needed a person in his life to build his confidence, give him courage. He was about to meet a very significant London stage luminary, perfumed and exquisitely dressed, who would be eager to give him all that ... and more.

Chapter Five
The Corset Heiress Vamp,
"Life Upon the Wicked Stage,"
and A Divorce Petition

Jeanne de Casalis had a fascinating face.

Her eyes were large, her nose pointy; at times, she evoked a heroic angel in a stained-glass window. At other times, she seemed to appear as a witch in a fairy tale book—an alluring witch, but a startling one nonetheless.

The angelic aspect had served her well in Broadway's *The Tidings Brought to Mary*, the New York Theatre Guild's Christmas attraction of 1922. Performed as a medieval miracle play, it had starred Miss de Casalis as Violaine, one of two sisters in love with the same man. The earthy sister wins the man; the saintly Violaine becomes a leper. On Christmas Eve, the sister comes to Violaine with the corpse of her child—and, as the *New York Times* review wrote, "in contact with her leprous, saintly bosom, it lives again."

Miss de Casalis' bosom was less saintly in *Fata Morgana*, a 1924 London play in which the alluring witch quality dominated. Jeanne played a wildly capricious adulteress who breaks the heart of an innocent young man. Jeanne was so strikingly vile a vamp that this play ran at three different theatres, tallied 243 performances, and later had two London revivals—both times with Jeanne back in lascivious style.

Indeed, for British audiences of the mid-1920s, the brunette Mlle. de Casalis seductively personified the Mortal Sin of Adultery—and they adored her. She'd made her film debut in Gaumont-British's *Settled Out of Court* (1925), a divorce saga in which she played a slinky, faithless wife, co-starring with Fay Compton and Jack Buchanan.

An angel, a witch ... it depended on the makeup, the lighting, and of course, the role. However, for a 2018 viewer, the glamour diva portraits of Jeanne de Casalis—cruelly, perhaps, but quite accurately—evoke a Roaring '20s drag queen.

Yet she was, by all evidence, all-woman.

Jeanne de Casalis de Pury was born of French parents in Basutoland, South Africa, on May 22; the publicized year was 1897, although there's evidence she was actually four or five years older. Her father was proprietor of Charneaux, one of France's largest retailers of corsets, which makes it rather a mystery as to why the de Casalis family was in Basutoland. She later wrote that her earliest memory was of her birthplace:

> *... a far line of distant hills—very distant hills. Silence and the night descended over me. The clear, crystalline, rarefied night of the high veldt. In the stillness, I became conscious of the sound of footsteps ... footsteps on hard sunbaked soil. I was being carried. My face was pressed against a body ... its acrid smell filled my nostrils ... the acrid smell of a native body. I was being carried softly, stealthily in the cool night. Then, I slowly opened my eyes and SAW. It seems to me now that it was at that moment that I saw for the first time ever in my life. I saw the night. I looked into a deep, purple-black vault, and it was studded with gigantic stars ... the blazing, blinding, quivering stars of Africa—immense, near, terrible, almost touchable ...*

Jeanne de Casalis, the London theatre's star vamp and a theatrical force of nature. She'd become Colin Clive's lover and eventually his wife.

The memory (on which she didn't elucidate) gives an impression of her drama, talent, and eloquence. In her time, Jeanne would ambitiously make her mark not only as an actress, but also as a pianist, a playwright, a novelist, and even a comedienne. Come the mid-1920s, she was most celebrated, as the press often proclaimed her, as a "vamp."

Her stage name was pronounced with the accent on the first syllable; her nickname was "Cass." A widow, Jeanne was a sensualist who habitually celebrated good fortune by donning her sexiest lingerie. In most of her pictures from the 1920s, she appears to be wearing a wig and a heroic amount of makeup—what did she look like, one wonders, first thing in the morning? After she set her wiles on Colin Clive, he apparently soon

MISS JEANNE DE CASALIS IN HER MUCH‑DISCUSSED PYJAMAS.

LADY AYLESBROUGH AND HER VICTIM, ALLEN, THE CHAUFFEUR (MR. PAUL CAVANAGH).

"Potiphar's Wife," as its name implies, is a modern version of the old Biblical story, and deals with the infatuation of Lady Aylesbrough for Allen, her husband's chauffeur. He is wrongfully accused by her of attempted seduction, but in the end emerges with his innocence entirely vindicated. "Potiphar's Wife," which has had such a successful run at the Globe, was transferred to the Savoy on Monday last.

Scandalous! Jeanne de Casalis poses in her "shocking" pajamas in *Potiphar's Wife*, 1927. One suspects Jeanne's lingerie, that caused such an uproar in London, was adjusted a bit conservatively for this photograph. (Courtesy of Neil Pettigrew)

found out and, whatever he discovered, quickly and unconditionally surrendered to her considerable charms.

Jeanne de Casalis had enraptured him.

From all evidence, Jeanne and Colin first acted together in *Fire*, which opened at London's Everyman Theatre June 30, 1927. Jeanne starred as yet another adulteress, this one named Alice, and Colin was featured a poet, with the dashing name of St. John Sevening. *Fire* lasted only 11 performances, but for Jeanne, a spike in her celebrity—or infamy—was just around the corner.

Wednesday, August 17, 1927: *Potiphar's Wife* opened at London's Globe Theatre, starring Jeanne de Casalis as the Countess of Aylesbrough ... an adulteress. So seismic was the scandal unleashed by this play that the *New York Times*, "across the pond," reported:

**LONDON IS SHOCKED
BY "POTIPHAR'S WIFE"**
**Pajamas Worn in Play by Jeanne de
Casalis and Some Purple
Passages Stir Comment**

The article noted that most of the critics:

> ... *admit that some purple passages and Miss de Casalis' pajamas were more than they expected.*
>
> *"I thought up to last night, that I was unshockable," says Hubert Griffith* in The Evening Standard, *"but I found I wasn't."*
>
> *Miss de Casalis admits the pajamas were more scanty than is customary, but says the producer complained after the dress rehearsal that she was wearing too much and ordered her to remove the sleeves and part of the lining.*

On August 19, two days after the opening, Jeanne announced she'd wear "less risqué pajamas" for the rest of the run, but the publicity had its effect: *Potiphar's Wife* was a hit. It ran through September 10 at the Globe, then moved to the Savoy Theatre, playing through December 10, 1927.

Also in 1927, Jeanne played prominently in two Gaumont-British films. *The Glad Eye* is summarized on the Internet Movie Data Base thusly: "Men elude their wives by threatening to go on a dirigible. It crashes." *The Arcadians*, directed by Victor Saville, was a race track comedy, with Jeanne as a comic wife, played rather in a fluttery, Billie Burke style that she'd polish to great effect in later years.

While Jeanne was the rage of London's West End, her seven-or-eight-years-younger boy toy was back at the Hull Repertory Company for a third season. One of the plays—interesting, in light of his later Hollywood fame—was *The Witch*. It was a melodrama, based in Norway circa 1574, in which a town accuses a young beauty of witchcraft. The audience is righteously on her side, until the finale—when she lets loose a wild cackle, showing she's truly a disciple of Satan.

Come the close of the season, Colin returned to Jeanne. He was still largely an unknown; she was a true star of the London theater. Their bond was likely deep. Jeanne presumably believed in Colin's promise and was confident she could bestow some of her drive and assuredness on him. He was clearly in awe of her. She was a force of nature, theatrically, and the sexual attraction was apparently powerful.

In later years, after Jeanne's death and long after Colin's, the gossip suggested a "lavender" relationship, the couple allegedly homosexual, flagrantly using each other as "beards." The "flagrant" theory is highly dubious. After all, England was the home of King Henry VIII's Buggery Act of 1533, by which sodomy was punishable by death. Homosexuality was still illegal in England in 1927 (and remained so until 1967), the maximum sentence for sodomy life imprisonment, so "flagrant" behavior was ill-advised. (Of course, this seemingly failed to scare such theater folk as James Whale, who was openly gay but never flagrant.) It's entirely possible that Colin and Jeanne were fluidly adventurous and experimental in their sexuality—it was, after all, the Roaring '20s, and this was the London theater world. Nevertheless, an in-depth examination of both partner's later lives finds no such evidence.

Colin Clive would eventually find himself, during his lifetime and after it, playing in various legends. That he was a tormented homosexual was one of them.

Come the New Year of 1928, the lean, handsome ex-Sandhurst cadet with cool gray eyes, and the corset heiress who wore infamous pajamas, had youth and passion on their side. Colin, however, faced the humiliation of being overshadowed by a famous, glamorous lover.

Additionally, he and Evelyn Taylor, estranged, had never divorced.

Show Boat program.

Thursday, May 3, 1928: *Show Boat* opened, spectacularly, at the Theatre Royal, Drury Lane. Based on the Edna Ferber novel, with music by Jerome Kern and book and lyrics by Oscar Hammerstein II, it starred Sir Cedric Hardwicke as Cap'n Andy, Marie Burke as Julie, and featured Paul Robeson singing the unforgettable "Old Man River."

I gets weary, and so sick of tryin,'
I'm tired of livin,' but I'm feared of dyin' ...

Colin played the featured dramatic role of Steve, star actor of the *Cotton Blossom* riverboat and husband of actress Julie. When a villain exposes her as a mulatto, accusing her of miscegenation, Steve claims he too has black blood in him—and gallantly "proves" it by cutting his hand and Julie's, mingling the blood. He had little else to do in the show, but *Show Boat* was a gigantic hit in London, and Colin's long-running success in two famed musicals was impressive.

"Incidentally," he said, "in spite of acting in these two musical productions, I cannot sing or dance a step!"

Friday, May 4: The day after *Show Boat* triumphantly opened, Colin officially filed his Petition for Divorce from Evelyn Taylor. The document states:

> *That from about the first day of December 1927 down to the present date the said Evelyn Greig at 18c, Redcliffe Gardens, South Kensington aforesaid has lived and cohabitated and habitually committed adultery with Carl Harbord.*
> *YOUR PETITIONER THERFORE HUMBLY PRAYS that your Lordship will be pleased to decree that your Petitioner's said marriage may be dissolved and that your petitioner may have such further and other relief as to your Lordship may seem just.*

He signed the petition Colin G. Greig. The petition noted that Colin was living at 27 Upper Montague Street and included this message to Evelyn and Harbord, who were residing together at Redcliffe Gardens:

> *TAKE NOTCE that you are required within eight days after service hereof upon you inclusive of the day of such service to enter an appearance either in person or by your Solicitor at the Divorce Registry of the High Court of Justice at Somerset House Strand in the County of London should you think fit to do so and thereafter to make answer to the charges in this Petition and*

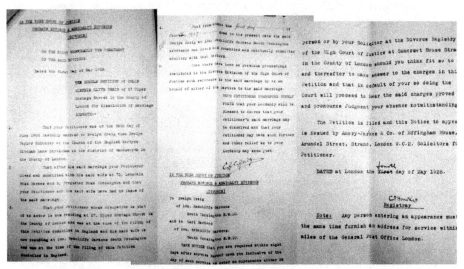

Colin's 1928 divorce petition to end his marriage to Evelyn Taylor. Note his signature as Colin G.C. Greig. (Courtesy of Neil Pettigrew)

that in default of your so doing the Court will proceed to hear the said charges proved and pronounce Judgment your absence notwithstanding.

As for Carl Harbord ... he was born John Kerslake Harbord in Devon on January 26, 1908. At the time of Evelyn Taylor's death, he was a featured film actor; in 1929, he'd appear in the first screen version of *The Informer*, as Francis McPhillip (the role played by Wallace Ford in RKO's 1935 version). Harbord would eventually come to Hollywood.

Apparently, Evelyn did not respond with a petition accusing Colin of dallying with Jeanne de Casalis. No action was immediately taken and come October, Colin would renew his petition of divorce.

Evelyn and Harbord continued their relationship.

It's significant that one of the songs in *Show Boat* was "Life Upon the Wicked Stage:"

> *I admit it's fun to smear my face with paint*
> *Causing everyone to think I'm what I ain't ...*
> *Life Upon the Wicked Stage ain't nothin' for a girl.*

Colin was coming to realize that, in his case, the Wicked Stage was nothin' for a guy, either. He chronically suffered stage fright, and while still feeling attraction to the theater, and a fascination with it, his love-hate involvement in it by now was virtually masochistic. One wonders if he'd have bailed out by now but for his relationship with Jeanne de Casalis.

Jeanne, meanwhile, starred in another film, *Zero* (1928). The plot concerned an author who fakes his own death so he can escape his wife and live with his mistress. Eventually, he returns to his wife. Guess who played the mistress?

> *The dissonance, the cacophony ... louder, more savage now.*
> *Yes, he was in* Show Boat, *a nice featured role, a weekly salary. Yet he was basically living at the tender mercies of his Ooh-La-la lover ... so much more famous than he was. Christ, her* Potiphar's Wife *pajamas were more famous than he was.*
>
> *An actor's ego's essential ... the link to survival. To go on stage every night, before an audience, without an ego, and instead with a repertory of torment and self-doubt, could be agonizing. Like a soldier, without a gun and helmet, or a sword and shield. But then, of course ... how the hell would he* know?
>
> *The ghosts had been visiting. His errant mother, who'd run away ... His lunatic uncle, who died in an asylum. Maybe he's inherited the licentiousness of his mother and the madness of his uncle to blame for where he was, and what he was doing ...*
>
> *All clanging together, roaring more loudly, more discordantly.*
>
> *Was he heading for Hell, as the Stonyhurst Jesuits would have surely warned him, for divorcing Evelyn, and "living in sin" with Mlle. de Casalis? Would the nightmare of inherited lunacy prove a reality?*
>
> *28 years old. His leg hurt worse, having never fully healed after that horse fall at Sandhurst. The Bengal Lancer-in-training turned jittery actor ...*

No, no whiskey. Won't hear of it. Still time to escape this bloody, God-what-a-life-this-is profession that threatens to destroy him, to still be a full man. After all, what were the odds of another break like Show Boat ... *Thousands to one?*

Actually, as Fate would have it, the theater was about to present Colin Clive a role that would, by a wickedly mocking irony, prophesize the tragedy he was soon to become. Almost sadistically, it would make him the sensation of the London theater.

Chapter Six
"The Bogey-Bogey" and "A Slice of Life— Horribly Abnormal Life ..."

Dudley Castle, Dudley, England.

Dudley is a city in the West Midlands of England. Dudley Castle, which sits appropriately on Castle Hill, dates at least to 1066. From a distance, it evokes the Gothic tower laboratory of *Frankenstein.*

In 2018, the castle is part of the Dudley Zoological Gardens, and there's a cinema at Castle Gate. Outside is a large memorial sculpture to a native of Dudley who, in 1889, was born into a life of near poverty. The memorial was erected in 2002, 45 years after its honoree drowned himself and four years after Hollywood released a biopic about him, *Gods and Monsters.* It has frames, as if in a reel of film, showing Boris Karloff's Frankenstein's Monster.

The honoree, however, isn't Karloff, but James Whale.

In 1928, "Jimmy" Whale, 39 years old, claiming to be 32, was a gay, wispy, red-haired, cheroot-smoking actor/director/scenic designer/stage manager, noted in London theatrical circles for dancing a wicked tango. He'd been a World War I POW in Holzminden, Germany, where he staged and acted in plays for his fellow prisoners. As the Los Angeles *Evening Express* would relate in 1930:

> *The camp held enough for both cast and audience. Every show was written by someone in the camp, the cast was chosen by debate, and if a sketch or play was successful, it had to be done every night for one week, because the dining room, with a normal capacity of 75, would not hold over 300, even with men standing on tables, etc.*
>
> *Two themes presented interest most frequently—satire of German officers, at which a few guards who slipped in to watch, would laugh uproariously, or satire of what well-meaning folks or institutions back in England sent through as gifts via the Red Cross.*
>
> *"It really was astounding," says Whale, "what extraordinary packages we received there from England. The good spirit behind them was apparent, but the contents of packages sometimes provided the biggest laughs we had."*

Whale didn't specify.

After the war, Whale drew cartoons for the *London Bystander*, and then entered the theater. Ernest Thesiger, whom Whale met in 1919 in a Manchester production of *The Merry Wives of Windsor*, would compare him to "a faun." Elsa Lanchester, who appeared in a 1926 revue that Whale stage managed called *Riverside Nights*, in which she wore a black top hat and a white ballerina tutu while singing risqué songs, described Whale as having "a face rather like a nice-looking monkey."

For anthropomorphic comparisons, the best, perhaps, was that Jimmy Whale was a fox.

"There was always a touch of the macabre, the sinister, the sadistic about Jimmy, you couldn't get away from it," said his friend, six-foot-five-inch co-player Alan Napier, best remembered as Alfred the Butler on TV's *Batman*. In 1928, Whale had given audiences a dose of those talents in the play *A Man with Red Hair*, based on Hugh Walpole's melodrama. Charles Laughton had played the title role of the whip-cracking, pain-obsessed Dr. Crispin, a maniac; Whale had played, as London's *Eve* magazine noted, "the maniac's bogey-bogey son," Herrick, a lunatic.

"A Man with Red Hair"

Hugh Walpole's novel makes a highly intellectual shocker at the Little Theatre

Comment on this intellectual thriller is impossible. If your nerves are strong and you have any liking for the art of acting do not fail to see the three most remarkable performances in London: those of Charles Laughton, James Whale, and J. H. Roberts. Mr. Laughton approaches the supernatural and makes one feel quite unwell.

Caricatures by
KETTELWELL

Herrick Crispin, the maniac's bogey-bogey son (James Whale)—a most remarkable performance with a marvellous exit

A sketch of James Whale as, according to the caption, "the bogey-bogey" in the 1928 stage melodrama, *A Man With Red Hair*. (Courtesy of Neil Pettigrew)

Whale went for a cadaverous corpse effect, wearing a dark suit with too-short sleeves. He'd pay a tribute to Herrick three years later when he helped stylize Boris Karloff's Monster in *Frankenstein*.

Unlike Colin Clive, James Whale had taken to London's theater world the way a ballerina takes to *Swan Lake*. "Come in pajamas," Whale once winked to heterosexual Alan Napier, inviting him to a gay party, "there'll be dancing." Curiously, the man who would direct *Frankenstein* had played *Frankenstein* in real life, both as creator and as his own fantasized creature. To advance, the once poor boy from the Midlands had fashioned a new "Jimmy," taking on the tones, mannerisms, and style of his upper-class gay lovers. It was, apparently, a fastidious process.

"Did you know," Alan Napier once asked me, "that gentlemen in England held their cigarettes and penises different than the working classes?"

Sunday night, December 9, 1928: The London Stage Society opened a two-performance run of a new play, *Journey's End*, at the Apollo Theatre.

The James Whale Memorial in his birthplace, Dudley. Note the pictures of the Frankenstein Monster in the frames of the sculpture.

James Whale was the director. The playwright was R.C. Sherriff, then working for The Sun Insurance Company, bicycling through villages as he settled claims. Sherriff had been wounded near Ypres during the Great War and had received the Military Cross. His play was a tragedy about a young, bitter, liquor-soaked Captain Dennis Stanhope, facing near-certain death in a World War I dugout in March of 1918. His men include middle-aged Lieutenant Osborne, a gentle, pipe-smoking schoolmaster who quotes from *Alice in Wonderland* and cares for the tormented Stanhope, and young Lieutenant Raleigh, the brother of Stanhope's girl-back-home. Raleigh had hero-worshipped Stanhope, but his arrival horrifies the Captain—who fears the boy will write home and tell "Madge" about the freakish alcoholic Stanhope has become.

There are no women in the play, and none of the three principals survives the saga. As such, it faced great trouble finding a producer. The London Stage Society eventually proceeded only after George Bernard Shaw, reading the play, gave his rather bizarre blessing:

"As a slice of life—horribly abnormal life—I should say let it be performed by all means."

Journey's End opened that December Sunday, with a star trio destined for varying degrees of greatness. Twenty-one-year-old Laurence Olivier, eventually praised as the supreme actor of his generation, was Stanhope.

Forty-three-year-old George Zucco, fated for Hollywood horror films, was Osborne. Zucco had served in the World War as a lieutenant and, in the trenches of France, nearly lost his right arm. He learned to camouflage the wound as he became a noted Shakespearean actor at Stratford-on-Avon and enjoyed success on the London stage. At the time of the try-out of *Journey's End*, Zucco had been rebuilding his career after a disastrous situation in Australia. As *Variety* reported (March 30, 1927):

Twenty-seven-year-old Maurice Evans, later an acclaimed Macbeth and, among many other things, Dr. Zaius in 1968's *Planet of the Apes*, was Raleigh. He'd already scored in London theater in the title roles of *Orestes* and *The Miracle of Saint Anthony*.

James Whale designed the set as well as directed. If the play won favor, there was a chance of a West End opening.

London drama critic (and war veteran) W.A. Darlington attended the Monday afternoon performance ("before a half-empty house," as he remembered), watching a play whose setting was the very sector of trenches in which he'd fought as a soldier. As Darlington later wrote in *Theatre Arts Monthly* (July, 1929), he struggled for self-control as Act I ended, afraid the audience would see "the shocking spectacle of a hard-boiled dramatic critic in tears."

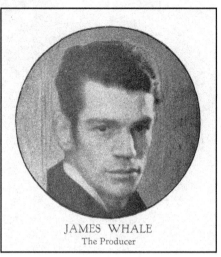

JAMES WHALE
The Producer

James Whale at the time of *Journey's End*.

> *I reached the end of the act safely, and my wife, turning to me, asked, "Was it like that?" I gave a couple of horrible gulps, and said, "Exactly like that." She nodded and said almost to herself, "I've never really known 'til now."*

However, Darlington cited a major flaw in the production. As fine as Olivier was as Stanhope, it was the second lead who was running off with the show:

> *... George Zucco, as Osborne, was perfect ... That I was not alone in thinking this was shown after the final curtain, when the deeply-moved audience called for Mr. Zucco and gave him an ovation, while being no more than politely enthusiastic over Mr. Olivier and Mr. Evans.*

The dream came true: producer Maurice Browne optioned *Journey's End*. The $12,500 necessary to mount the production came from Dorothy Elmhirst, a millionairess of America's Whitney family, wed to a Yorkshireman, the couple devoted to "benevolence, uplift, and constructive work." At this time, they were specifically intent on halting deforestation in Devonshire.

There was still, however, a major problem: with Zucco (the first of the star trio to die in the play) taking the top honors, the play was dramatically unbalanced. Zucco, despite his 1927 indiscretion in Australia, was basically a gentleman and certainly a superb actor—"He could have played God!" recalled his friend, screenwriter Charles Bennett. In a sense, as the wise, loving Osborne in *Journey's End*, Zucco was doing just that. After Osborne's

George Zucco as Lt. Osborne in _Journey's End_. Zucco signed this theatrical portrait to actress Stella Francis, who later became his wife. (Courtesy of the late Stella Zucco)

death, for Stanhope, the rest of the play is a virtual God-is-Dead despair.

Laurence Olivier had been very good—Alan Napier, who attended a performance, vividly remembered Olivier's portrayal the rest of his long life—but Zucco had been brilliant. Olivier himself provided the solution to this problem: He opted out of _Journey's End_ to star in a play version of _Beau Geste_—fated to flop.

Journey's End was to open in late January. A desperate search began for a new Stanhope.

It was Jeanne de Casalis, with her charm, aggressiveness, and London theater contacts, who reached Maurice Browne and arranged a _Journey's End_ audition for her lover. Colin had keen competition—notably from Colin Keith-Johnston, a splendid, handsome actor and a war hero both on the battlefield and in the air.

Were Keith-Johnston cast, _Journey's End_ would boast a director who'd survived a POW camp, a playwright who'd received the Military Cross, and two stars (Keith-Johnston and Zucco) who'd fought with distinction in the war. Colin Clive, too young to have been in combat, had been at Sandhurst on Armistice Day. Browne, Whale, and Sherriff had all but decided on Colin Keith-Johnston for Stanhope as Colin Clive reported for his 11th hour try-out.

While it's sheer speculation, one might imagine that Colin and Jeanne had hot words about his _Journey's End_ audition. He was probably deeply frightened by the prospect of actually starring in a West End drama. She perhaps pointed out that he'd been an actor for over nine years, and that he was potentially committing career suicide by forsaking this now-or-never opportunity.

The audition, at any rate, was very nearly a disaster.

Colin, terrified, nervously dragged on a cigarette. He misread the lines. He lost his place in the script. Yet, although he had no war experience to call upon, Colin tapped a pit of personal anguish that vividly came through in his jagged reading. Whale was fascinated. Maurice Evans, who'd watched both Keith-Johnston and Clive read for the role, crystallized what Whale instinctively felt:

"Keith-Johnston's got it _here_," said Evans, pointing to his head. "Clive's got it _here_"—and he pointed to his heart.

Colin won the role.

In his 1968 memoir, _No Leading Lady_, R.C. Sherriff described the painful rehearsals:

It was difficult for Clive to work his way into a word-perfect company. He alone was stumbling over his lines, drying up and being prompted. He was highly strung and temperamental, and one day after a bad rehearsal he went to Whale and offered to give up the part. Whale tried to reassure him, but everybody was worried. Stanhope, the Company Commander, was the rock upon which the whole play stood: if he failed, the play was doomed.

At the end of the first week of rehearsal, Clive began to show the strain. He seemed worn out and hopelessly despondent, but it was too late to make a change. I used to go and watch them at work, and one morning, after another bad rehearsal, Clive came over to me and apologized ...

Colin poured out his anguish to Sherriff—he'd tried to force his pace to catch up with the rest of the cast. "He had worked to all hours of the night on it," remembered Sheriff, "got worried, and slept badly, which made things worse at morning rehearsals."

R.C. Sherriff, despite his heroism in the war, was hardly a worldly man. He never married, and at the time of *Journey's End* (and for long afterward) lived with his mother. To help Colin, Sherriff made a suggestion that, almost 40 years later, the playwright still naively considered his "most useful contribution to the production" ... he advised Colin to rehearse after a shot of whiskey:

R. C. SHERRIFF
The Author

R.C. Sherriff, the author of *Journey's End*.

Stanhope, I told him, was an overwrought, nerve-shattered man through years of strain in the trenches. If Clive was feeling nerve-shattered and overwrought, then that was fine because it brought him more closely into sympathy with the character. But Stanhope had kept going, had driven himself on, with whisky. Did Clive drink it? Clive said he enjoyed a whisky at the right time, but never touched a drop of anything before rehearsals. It was fatal for an actor to get a name for drink. I suggested that, for the sake of his performance, he should stretch a point. Why not take a good stiff whisky at lunch, before the afternoon rehearsal—two, if need be—and see what happened?

What happened was that Colin went to a nearby public house, downed two whiskeys ("possibly three," wrote Sherriff), and came back to rehearsal, in the playwright's words, "like a man transformed."

He was no longer the anxious, diffident actor playing Stanhope: he was Stanhope, in every nerve of his body. He took command of the rehearsal as Stanhope had commanded the company.

Indeed, Colin did take command as Stanhope did—roaring drunk.

Colin autographed this portrait of himself as Captain Stanhope in the London stage's *Journey's End.*

"Whale was astonished and delighted," recalled Sherriff, claiming that Colin "didn't need the whiskey for subsequent rehearsals." Sherriff wrote these words over 30 years after Colin's death, and it's amazing in retrospect that he seemed oblivious to Colin's severe alcoholism that began and festered during the run of *Journey's End*.

It was a perverse "Method" acting, long before its time—and the sad addiction mirrored itself in one of Stanhope's lines as he remembers his love back home:

> *She doesn't know that if I went up those steps into the front line, without being doped with whiskey, I'd go mad with fright.*

Sunday, January 20, 1929: Colin Clive celebrated his 29th birthday. The next night, he'd open in *Journey's End*. His daredevil casting would make or break the careers of R.C. Sherriff, James Whale ... and himself.

Monday night, January 21: *Journey's End* premieres at London's Savoy Theatre.

The Savoy, having opened in 1881, was London's first public building entirely lit by electricity. It originally gained fame for hosting Gilbert and Sullivan operettas. This night's attraction is no operetta.

Act I: The curtain rises. It's March 18, 1918, in the trenches of Saint Quentin, Aisne. The first night audience sees the gloomy, candle-lit, catacombs-like dugout set, designed by James Whale. Two tunnels run into caverns, packing cases are used as chairs, and on the wall are drawings of ladies in "flimsy costumes" from *La Vie Parisienne*. Captain Hardy (David Horne), about to be relieved, is happily singing as the scene opens. George Zucco, balding, mustached, enters as Lt. Osborne. Hardy cruelly teases him about the battle to come and mocks Osborne's commander, Captain Stanhope.

"How *is* the dear young boy?" asks Hardy. "Drinking like a fish as usual?"

"You don't know him as I do," says Osborne. "I love that fellow. I'd go to hell with him."

Hardy departs. Soon Maurice Evans as 2nd Lt. Jimmy Raleigh arrives on-stage, a new addition to the company, thrilled to be joining Stanhope—whom he's hero-worshipped, and who's the beau of Raleigh's sister, Madge.

"You must remember he's commanded this company for a long time—through all sorts of rotten times," Osborne warns Raleigh about Stanhope. "It's a big strain on a man."

Now, Colin Clive makes his entrance as Captain Stanhope. Much of the preceding dialogue has concerned him, making the audience create its own images of the man. He must fulfill all these images. The captain is lividly angry at Hardy for the way he and his men left the trenches—"Dugouts smell like cess-pits; rusty bombs; damp rifle grenades; it's perfectly foul."

Mason, the cook (Alexander Field), offers him a bowl of soup.

"Damn the soup!" says Stanhope. "Bring some whiskey."

Osborne (whom Stanhope calls "Uncle") reluctantly informs Stanhope of the new officer. "Hullo, Stanhope!" exults Raleigh. Stanhope, shocked by his arrival, glares at him.

There's an awkward meal served by Mason. Stanhope basically drinks his supper. Second Lt. Trotter, plump, jolly, and played by Melville Cooper, takes Raleigh up into the moonlit trench. Colin's Stanhope, frightened, mortified that Raleigh has seen what three years of war has done to him, and increasingly drunk, shows Osborne the picture of Madge he carries in his uniform. The opening night audience hears Colin's heartrending delivery of the dialogue, sees his rising hysteria:

You know! You know he'll write and tell her I reek of whiskey all day ... He's not a damned little swine who'd deceive his sister. ... Hero-worship be damned! You know, Uncle, I'm an awful fool. I'm captain of this company. What's that bloody little prig of a boy matter? D'you see? He's a little prig. Wants to write home and tell Madge all about me. Well, he won't, d'you see, Uncle? ... Censorship! I censor all his letters ... Cross out all he says about me ... Then we all go west in the big attack—and he goes on thinking I'm a fine fellow forever—and ever—and ever ...

As always, Osborne calms the storm. He puts Stanhope to bed.

"Kiss me, Uncle!" jokes the drunken Stanhope, then falls asleep. Osborne winds his silver watch. The curtain falls on Act I.

Act II: The men discuss back-home memories to distract themselves from near-certain death. Trotter talks about his hollyhocks. Raleigh and Osborne share their love for playing rugby. Osborne recalls his days as a schoolmaster. The capture of a German soldier reveals the big attack is only two days away.

Meanwhile, the restless Stanhope confesses to Osborne that he got up in the middle of the night and was drunk when Raleigh had come down from duty.

Then he came in with Trotter—and looked at me. After coming in out of the night air, this place must have reeked of candle-grease, and rats—and whiskey. One thing a boy like that can't stand is a smell that isn't fresh. He looked at me as if I'd hit him between the eyes—as if I'd spat on him ...

Raleigh shows up with a letter to send to his sister. Stanhope demands the letter, taking it with a trembling hand, shrilly sending Raleigh to inspect rifles. He gives the letter to Osborne to read aloud:

... Dennis came in. He looked tired, but that's because he works so frightfully hard, and because of the responsibility. Then I went on duty in the front line, and a sergeant told me all about Dennis. He said that Dennis is the finest officer in the battalion, and the men simply love him ... I'm awfully proud to think he's my friend.

Lt. Hibbert, played by Robert Speaight, terrified of death, goes to Stanhope and announces he's leaving to seek medical aid for his neuralgia. Stanhope refuses to let him shirk his duty. Hibbert claims he'll die of pain if not allowed to go.

"Better die of the pain," says Stanhope, removing his pistol from its holster, "than be shot for deserting."

Hibbert attacks Stanhope with his walking stick. Stanhope smashes the stick across his knee and calms the weeping Hibbert, confessing he feels precisely the same fear.

I hate and loathe it all. Sometimes I feel I could just lie down on this bed and pretend I was paralyzed or something—and couldn't move—and just lie there till I died—or was dragged away.

Stanhope offers to go on duty with Hibbert in the trenches at four o'clock:

Maurice Evans as Raleigh and Colin as Stanhope in the play _Journey's End_.

Supposing the worst happened—supposing we were knocked right out. Think of all the chaps who've gone already. It can't be very lonely there—with all those fellows.

    Sometimes I think it's lonelier here.

The Life and Death of Colin Clive Hollywood's Dr. Frankenstein   **59**

Act III: A raid must take place. Osborne and Raleigh are among the men who will go. Beforehand, Osborne asks Stanhope, should he die, to send his watch and wedding band home to his wife. A countdown begins to the raid. Osborne and Raleigh talk of trivialities to keep focused; Osborne quotes from his favorite book, *Alice in Wonderland*.

> *"The time has come," the walrus said,*
> *"To talk of many things ... "*

They venture out into No Man's Land, where, indeed, Osborne is killed. Raleigh returns, and collapses onto the bed of Osborne.

"Must you sit on Osborne's bed?" bitterly asks Stanhope.

A macabre candlelight party takes place that night, after the death of Osborne, and shortly before the big attack. Stanhope, Trotter, and Hibbert get drunk, smoke cigars, and look at Hibbert's collection of risqué cards. Raleigh refuses to join the merriment. Stanhope demands to see him, and the two men have a showdown.

"Anything—*funny* about me?" demands the drunken Stanhope, his cigar clenched in his mouth, pathetically trembling. Raleigh asks how he can drink and behave this way after Osborne's death.

"To forget, you little fool—to forget!" howls Stanhope. "D'you understand? To forget! You think there's no limit to what a man can bear? ... Oh get out! For God's sake, *get out!*"

Stanhope falls beside Osborne's bed, sobbing bitterly. "His heart is breaking," notes the script. The scene blacks out.

The Germans launch the "Big Attack." The men go out to fight. Stanhope receives word a shell has hit Raleigh, breaking his spine. Stanhope orders Raleigh be brought back, and a soldier carries him into the dugout. The shells exploding, the guns rattling, the shadows closing, Stanhope tenderly cares for his mortally wounded friend.

"... I'm going to have you taken away," Stanhope says. "Down to the dressing station—then hospital—then home ..."

"Could we have a light?" asks Raleigh faintly. "It's—it's so frightfully dark and cold."

Stanhope gets two candles and two blankets. "Is that better, Jimmy?"

There's no reply.

Word comes Stanhope's needed in battle. He stands, runs his fingers over Raleigh's hair, and starts up the dugout steps, courageously facing his own journey's end. A shrieking shell explodes. The dugout is in near darkness. Only a single candle still burns, melting over a whiskey bottle. After a moment the flame goes out.

Curtain.

Colin's Stanhope has been a spellbinding performance—full of power, passion, and a strange, beautiful nobility. So overwhelming was the play that no one originally applauded after the final curtain. At last there was a solitary "Bravo," and the applause slowly began. It built considerably for Maurice Evans, tremendously for George Zucco ... and then thunderously for Colin.

Journey's End was a smash hit—and Colin Clive was an overnight star of the London stage.

The reception was incredible. Sherriff, wearing a tuxedo with a carnation, was pushed onstage by the actors, and made a speech. James Whale, also in tux with carnation, followed with a speech too. Then, remarkably, the audience, still standing, continued applauding, shouting the names of the individual actors. Sherriff wrote:

"One Man Crazy ...!"

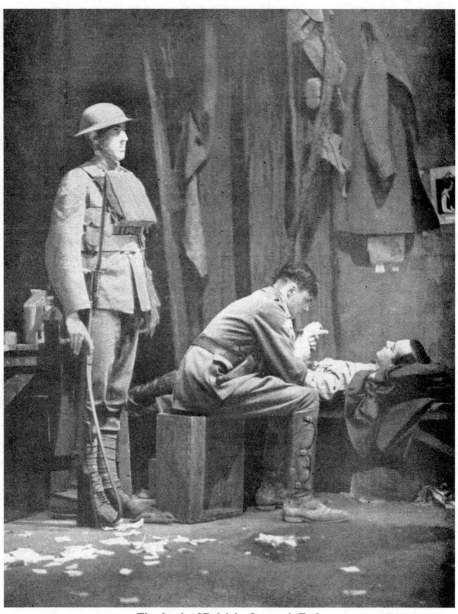

The death of Raleigh: *Journey's End.*

George Zucco, the most modest and retiring man who ever acted on a stage, was halfway up the stairs to his dressing-room when somebody ran after him and shouted, "Come back, George—they're calling for you!" and George went before the curtain to receive another round of cheers.

Colin Clive, as was natural, got the greatest ovation of them all, for nobody can resist the romantic appeal of the fairy story that lifts an obscure young actor to stardom in a night.

THE MEN OF JOURNEY'S END

MAURICE BROWNE
who presents the Play

R. C. SHERRIFF
The Author

JAMES WHALE
The Producer

CLIFFORD HAMILTON
General Manager

THOMAS WARNER
Stage Director

STANHOPE
COLIN CLIVE

OSBORNE
GEORGE ZUCCO

RALEIGH
MAURICE EVANS

TROTTER
MELVILLE COOPER

THE COLONEL
H. G. STOKER

A page from George Zucco's personal program for *Journey's End*, signed by Zucco and the cast. Colin signed his picture, but the signature is too faded to see clearly in this reproduction. (Courtesy of the late Stella Zucco)

Thus, along with R.C. Sherriff, it was a trinity of men, fated for Hollywood Horror films and real-life tragedy, who primarily made *Journey's End* a phenomenal hit. James Whale would direct a quartet of Universal horror classics and drown himself in his pool in 1957. George Zucco would play mad doctors, high priest to a Mummy, and so on, and die in 1960 after years of confinement in a sanitarium. Colin Clive would create the role of Henry Frankenstein on film and be dead in eight-and-a-half years.

"One Man *Crazy* ...!"

Indeed, the prophetic horror aspect had bled into *Journey's End's* aura of tragedy. For all of Stanhope's romantic quality, there was a haunting, frightening, almost freakish edge to Colin's performance; a living nightmare, created by war. As directed by Jimmy Whale, *Journey's End* was, in a sense, a grimly realistic horror play—*Dr. Jekyll and Mr. Hyde* in the trenches. Colin had made the nightmare come true.

Far more so, it was a story of supreme heroism. It was a not a super-hero's heroism, but that of a very real man who, facing despair, loneliness, and near-certain death, achieved the honor he so desperately wanted to attain, at a terrible price—and with the crutch of alcohol. Yet this crutch somehow made Stanhope all the more human, admirable, and heartbreaking.

The bond between Colin Clive, actor, and Captain Stanhope, character, was strangely and tragically intimate.

Before recorded performances, stage actors used to "carve in ice," as the saying went, meaning their work eventually melted away in the memories of the live audiences who applauded them. Over 89 years later, there are likely none still alive who were in the audience at the Savoy that first night. However, years ago, Sally Stark, a devoted Clive fan, visited a London bookshop, where the aged proprietor sold her a souvenir album from *Journey's End,* published later during the run. He'd seen opening night, and vividly remembered Colin Clive, whose raging, heartrending intensity as Stanhope still caused the proprietor to shudder. He told Ms. Stark about Clive's lightning-in-a-bottle performance, and said he'd have made "a terrifying Othello."

He added that, considering Clive's unforgettable intensity, he'd have felt worried for any actress playing Desdemona, as Clive's insanely jealous Moor murdered her in their bed.

On the second night of the play, R.C. Sherriff visited Colin in his dressing room before the performance:

> *No young actor for years had received such unanimous critical acclaim for his first big part in a West End play. His dressing room had been besieged by enthusiastic friends when the first night had ended, and when he had gone out of the stage door he had been mobbed by admirers with autograph books. For years he had plodded along with small repertory companies and thankless tours in the provinces, his name hardly known, and I wondered whether the wine of success had gone to his head.*
>
> *I expected to find admirers in his dressing room that evening, but he was alone. He was dressed for his part except for his tunic and was sitting before his dressing-table mirror in shirt sleeves. There was nothing about him to suggest a sudden spectacular leap to fame, only a humility and gratitude that an unaccountable twist of fate should have thrown the chance his way.*
>
> *He got up and shook my hand and said, "I'm glad you came in. It's the first chance I've had to thank you." I was taken aback: I had come to thank him. I told him how much I owed to him, but he waved it aside. "With a part like this," he said, "Any actor would have done the same."*
>
> *I didn't argue the point. I only knew how lucky we had been.*

Chapter Seven
A Bed at Nurse Dora White's

"The success of *Journey's End* is a fact of theatrical history," recalled Robert Speaight (who played the cowardly Hibbert) in his 1970 memoir, *The Property Basket: Recollections of a Divided Life*, "... and it owed much to Colin Clive ... *Journey's End* was his moment—and ours."

The man who most prospered materially from *Journey's End* was its producer, Maurice Browne. As Speaight wrote, Browne "became, almost overnight, a man transformed," buying a suite of offices on Charles II Street ("sumptuously appointed," noted Speaight), and marketing *Journey's End's* worldwide rights. Browne did not, however, raise the salary of anyone in the cast.

For London theatergoers, "Colin Clive was *Journey's End*," yet he continued at his starting salary—£30 a week.

Jeanne de Casalis had delivered the London theater a new star. Her young lover had come through, more spectacularly than she had perhaps imagined; he was now a major name, and for the moment at least, as big a name as she. Maybe hoping she and Colin might reign together simultaneously over the West End theater scene, she revived her 1922 New York success, *The Tidings Brought to Mary*, in which, as noted, she'd played the leper with a "saintly bosom." The play opened March 20, 1929 at the Arts Theatre, but folded after only six performances.

The press pursued Colin, and he provided a funny anecdote about *Journey's End*:

> Women have been coming in large numbers to the Savoy. Their own great part in helping to win the war should have disposed of the legend that because this is a war-play, women for that reason would dislike it.
>
> Not all of them, however, even now, have lost the illusion that the war was rather a fine and picturesque adventure. The member of the audience I have in mind was very kindly in compliment about what we had to show her, but she had a criticism to make.
>
> "The dugout is so very dirty and dingy," she said. "Why can't you set the scene in a nice clean tent? It would be so much prettier to watch!"

Did the overnight success affect him? How could it not?

Early in the run of *Journey's End*, Stella Francis, a blonde London actress who'd just returned from a 20-month world stage tour, including South Africa, Australia and New Zealand, attended the play. She was in awe of George Zucco's "beautiful performance," and Stella and George would marry in 1930.

As for Colin ... "I didn't know him well," said Stella, laughing, over 60 years later, "but I knew him well enough!" A specific critique of Stella's was that Colin, in the flush of his *Journey's End* success, believed that "he was God's gift to women." Undoubtedly, he now had reason and opportunity to think so.

Jeanne was concerned—and jealous.

One night, George Zucco hosted a party, where the guests included Stella Francis, Jeanne de Casalis ... and Tallulah Bankhead. The legendary Tallulah was at her liquor and

A March, 1929 advertisement with Colin Clive and, among others, Jeanne de Casalis. Considering the role Colin was playing in *Journey's End*, his endorsement here is rather funny!

cocaine peak, and the party would present the spectacle of an epic catfight. Many years later, Stella Zucco, in her 90s, vividly remembered:

> Well, Tallulah and Jeanne got into a fight over Colin Clive—and I mean a fight (pantomiming fist-fighting)! They had to be separated! George did partly, and several of the guests helped him. I imagine Tallulah and Jeanne were fighting over who got to go home with Clive that night.

The Life and Death of Colin Clive Hollywood's Dr. Frankenstein

I don't recall who won. I couldn't have cared less! (Laughing) *Fancy two women fighting over Colin Clive!* Why?

Colin Clive fan: Tallulah Bankhead.

In truth, Jeanne had more to worry about than female jealousy. Colin, terrified by his own success, was still facing the audience the same way Stanhope faced his own annihilation—"doped with whiskey." The eight performances-a-week regime demanded a rigid discipline, but the alcohol was becoming a requisite of that discipline.

Playing the alcoholic, near-hysteric Stanhope, he was becoming an alcoholic, near-hysteric actor.

And now, as he walked a tightrope of success, there came a tragedy that cast a new demon in his private repertoire ... and almost knocked him off the high-wire.

Tuesday, April 9, 1929: Evelyn Taylor Greig, Colin's estranged wife, died at the home of Nurse Dora White at Colesville Terrace, Bayswater. She was 28 years old. Cause of death: "Septic poisoning consequent on having had an abortion."

Colin, still legally her husband, had to identify the body.

The tragedy had commenced April 1, 1929, when Evelyn, with an unwanted pregnancy, came to the home of Ms. White and gave her first payment in advance for care. The father of the child was Carl Harbord, who'd been named in Colin's 1928 divorce suit.

Evelyn's death, coming 78 days after the opening of *Journey's End*, threatened to damage seriously Colin's career. Abortion was a shocking action; indeed, the procedure wouldn't become legal in Great Britain until 1968. Even the peripheral connection of having been the long-separated spouse of the dead woman might have proven disastrous.

Saturday, April 13: Four days after Evelyn's death, the coroner, Mr. H.R. Oswald, interrogated Harbord about the tragedy in an inquest at Kensington Town Hall. Harbord informed the coroner that he was "unmarried" and had been living with Evelyn for three years. This would date approximately to 1926, when Colin had joined the company of *Rose-Marie*. Harbord testified that he knew Evelyn's estranged husband, was "friendly" with him, and that in March, Evelyn had talked with Harbord concerning her situation:

"One Man *Crazy* ...!"

Coroner: *Did she do anything in respect to her health?*
Harbord: *Yes, she had visited a chemist. I don't know what she got.*
Coroner: *Did Mrs. Greig tell you she was pregnant?*
Harbord: *No.*
Coroner: *You knew she was taking medicine?*
Harbord: *Yes, and I told her not to take it.*
Coroner: *Why?*
Harbord: *Because I thought things would be righted naturally.*

The inquest noted that Evelyn had gone to Nurse White's, where Harbord visited her every day. He said that she'd told him on Monday, April 8, that she'd sprained her wrist. He returned the next day:

> Coroner: *Did she complain about her arm?*
> Harbord: *No, sir. She did not because she was dying.*

The Coroner then interrogated Nurse Dora White, who claimed to be a certified midwife who'd been in practice since 1920. She said Evelyn had seemed fine when she came to her house, and "took her food well." She also testified that on April 9, Evelyn's elbow appeared to be bruised, so she and Harbord summoned a doctor about 11:00 a.m. The doctor arrived just before midday:

> Coroner: *What did he say when he saw her?*
> Nurse White: *He said that she was dead.*

The *London Times* covered the tragedy, including this information:

> *Colin Glennie Greig, of 27 Upper Montague Street, W., identified the body as that of his wife, who he said had not lived with him for three years at least. He had started proceedings for divorce.*

It's telling that the *Times* made no mention that "Colin Glennie Greig" was in fact the birth name of Colin Clive, the sensational star of *Journey's End*. Clearly, the play's management and/or the *Times* were protecting the actor and the play from what could have become a devastatingly ugly scandal. (Carl Harbord's birth name, John Kerslake Harbord, appeared as well, rather than his professional one.)

Assuming that Colin was asked to identify Evelyn's body the same day she died, he would have had to perform that night in *Journey's End* under what must have been an almost unimaginable stress.

In fact, the timing was especially explosive. Colin and Jeanne de Casalis had co-au-

Carl Harbord, Evelyn Taylor's lover.

DEATH OF A FILM ACTRESS.

AN OPEN VERDICT.

The Coroner's inquiry into the death of Mrs. Evelyn Greig, 24, a film actress, who died last Tuesday, was held on Saturday at the Kensington Town Hall. Last Thursday the case of Greig v. Greig and Harbord was struck out of the list in the Divorce Court on Mr. Justice Hill being informed of the woman's death.

Detective-inspector Horwell was present at the inquiry, and Mr. S. Coleman attended on behalf of Nurse White, at whose home Mrs. Greig stayed. Mr. Walkes watched the case on behalf of Messrs. Parkes and Co., representing someone interested in it.

The CORONER (Mr. H. R. Oswald) said that Mrs. Greig was suspected of having died from the effects of an abortion. The jury would have to determine, if this was the case, how this came about, and, who, if anyone, had any hand in the matter. If the evidence was insufficient to implicate anyone else, and it was proved that she did it herself without anyone's assistance and was of sound mind at the time, the verdict would be *Felo de se.*

Colin Glennie Greig, of 27, Upper Montague-street, W., identified the body as that of his wife, who, he said had not lived with him for three years at least. He had started proceedings for divorce.

Mr. John Kerslake Harbord, an actor, living at Redcliffe-gardens, South Kensington, told the Coroner that he was unmarried and had been living with Mrs. Greig for three years. During that time she had never had

London Times headline: "Death of a Film Actress." Note the article refers to Colin as "Colin Glennie Greig," not as "Colin Clive." (Courtesy of Sally Stark)

"One Man Crazy ...!"

thored a play, *Let's Leave It at That*, a comedy about a highly temperamental couple—he a singer, she an authoress. The play was set for a one-night showcase that Sunday, April 14, at the Prince of Wales Theatre. Colin and Jeanne were playing the star roles, and the play was rather a *Journey's End* affair. George Zucco had a part and was directing the play, and Melville Cooper was also in the cast. Colin and Jeanne hoped *Let's Leave It at That* would attract a producer and boost their celebrity.

As such, Colin had to give eight performances of *Journey's End* and rehearse and perform a play he'd co-authored with his lover ... all in the same week he'd identified his estranged wife's corpse.

Sir Bernard Spilsbury, the Home Office pathologist, said that he had made a *post-mortem* examination of Evelyn Taylor Greig's body, and that the cause of death was heart failure due to abortion, with septic poisoning and acute general peritonitis. There was no evidence of any instrumental interference. The Coroner, in summing up, said that Mrs. Greig must have known by March that she was pregnant, and must have obtained the drugs with the idea of bringing on a miscarriage. The jury agreed. The coroner also said the open verdict did not preclude the police from taking action, "if they found reason to do so."

There are curious nuances to the tragedy. Colin had just become a major star while Evelyn was languishing in obscurity. Her last London stage credit had been *The Pigeon*, a fantasy by John Galsworthy that had opened at the Everyman Theatre May 25, 1928 and lasted only 17 performances. Evelyn had played one of "Three Humble People." Brember Wills, later the maniacal "Saul" in James Whale's *The Old Dark House* (1932), was in the cast.

Additionally, the case of "Greig v. Greig and Harbord" was set to come up in the Divorce Court of Mr. Justice Hill. Two days after Evelyn's death, the case was officially struck from the Court's list.

As for Carl Harbord ... he'd go on to play in such Hollywood films as *Sahara* (Columbia, 1943), starring Humphrey Bogart, and *Dressed to Kill* (Universal, 1946), the final Basil Rathbone/Nigel Bruce Sherlock Holmes film, in which Harbord's "Inspector Hopkins" was a none-too-satisfactory replacement for Dennis Hoey's Inspector Lestrade. Harbord's final documented credit: "The Lucky Cat" episode (May 7, 1955) of TV's *The Adventures of Superman*. He died in Los Angeles October 18, 1958 at the age of 50. His widow was prolific British character actress Isobel Elsom.

The late Michael Hoey, son of Dennis Hoey and a family acquaintance of Harbord, described him to researcher Scott Gallinghouse: Hoey called Harbord "a very nice, gentle man when sober, but horrifying when drunk."

As for Evelyn Taylor, the *London Times* had identified her as "a film actress," although no credits have emerged. No information has become available as to what disposition was made of her body.

Late in her long life, Stella Zucco surprised me by sending me one of George's few keepsakes from his career: his personal program from *Journey's End*. The program had pictures from the play and small portraits of everyone in the cast, and the players had signed the program by their portraits. After learning of the Evelyn Taylor Greig tragedy, I looked again at the program and checked the date.

It was for the matinee of Wednesday, April 17, 1929—eight days after Evelyn Greig's death, four days after the coroner's inquest, and three days after the performance of *Let's Leave It at That*.

Tuesday, April 23, 1929: Colin appeared in a special matinee performance of J.M. Barrie's *Shall We Join the Ladies?* at London's Palace Theatre. He was in all-star company: Gerald Du Maurier, Gladys Cooper, John Gielgud, Gwen Ffrangcon-Davies, Jean Forbes-Robertson, Heather Thatcher, Sybil Thorndike, and Lady Tree.

Monday, June 3: *Journey's End* moved to the Prince of Wales Theatre.

Monday, June 10: *Let's Leave It at That* opened at London's Queen's Theatre, in hopes of a run. As Colin was, of course, still in *Journey's End*, Michael Stern replaced him, while Jeanne reprised her role, as well as designed the scenery. George Zucco again directed. *Let's Leave It at That* lasted for only eight performances.

Saturday, June 22: "A Leading Vamp Engaged," headlined the *Dundee Courier*, noting that "Miss Jeanne de Casalis" was to marry Colin Clive. Significantly, despite his *Journey's End* fame, Jeanne snared the headline.

Saturday, June 29: Colin Clive, two-and-a-half months after Evelyn Taylor's death, wed Jeanne de Casalis at the register office in Ashford, Kent. The bride gave her name as Jeanne Bawden Wilson, widow, age 34. The groom gave his name as Colin Glennie Clive Greig, widower, age 29, son of Colin Philip Greig, retired colonel.

Jeanne was a strong, brilliant, self-confident woman. She surely believed she'd help Colin control the drinking that was threatening to go out of control. She'd help her dashing young husband conquer his pet devils.

The pet devils felt otherwise.

Journey's End played on, Colin living the role of Stanhope eight times a week.

The corpse in the bed at Nurse Dora White's was only the most recent ghost to haunt him. All the private demons had latched on, offstage and onstage, firing up Colin's raw-nerved Stanhope portrayal, fueled by alcohol. They gnawed away, through the summer, while Jimmy Whale, who'd directed a hit Broadway version of *Journey's End* (starring Colin Keith-Johnston as Stanhope), pursued high hopes of success in the movies.

Whale had gone west to Hollywood ... determined to direct the film version of *Journey's End*.

"One Man *Crazy* ...!"

Chapter Eight
"So Marvelously Sham"

Cheer up little girl
You're a long-time dead
And besides when you cry
Your nose gets red.

Sunday, June 16, 1929: James Whale, in Hollywood, had written to a London acquaintance he addressed as "Renee darling."

The slyly irreverent "Jimmy," who'd penned the letter on Paramount Studios stationery, claimed to have discovered the above poem in "a lovely Hollywood church of Los Angeles Spanish ... hanging up over a really smart altar." Among his news shared with Renee:

> *Whoopie, I must tell you, is the lovely new swear word & it means HELL.*
> *Yes, it is nice isn't it ... we find it lovely to use ...*

Now and then, Whale broke into verse:

> *When you meet 'em you like 'em*
> *When you like 'em you kiss 'em*
> *When you kiss 'em you love 'em*
> *When you love 'em you lose 'em*
> *Damn 'em!*

In Hollywood, Whale had learned about movies as "dialogue director" for Paramount's *The Love Doctor*. Clearly, he wanted to be in place as director when *Journey's End* became a film ... and Hollywood, with its hilltop castles and towering palms, was proving intoxicating. As Whale wrote to Renee:

> *WHY aren't you out here in this glorious place ... everything is so ludicrous*
> *and unreal ... The whole place is so marvelously SHAM that I now believe*
> *that Buckingham Palace is made of plaster of Paris, the King & Queen were*
> *never really married, the Prince of Wales is really Peter Pan & the secret of*
> *Journey's End is that it has never begun ...*

The HOLLYWOODLAND sign languished up on Mount Lee, vaguely Paganistic, looking from a distance like the giant skeleton of a dug-up dinosaur, lit up at night by 4,000 light bulbs. Nearby was "Wolf's Lair," a storybook castle, overlooking Lake Hollywood. Late at night, weird screams came from Wolf's Lair—the howls of a pet gibbon monkey, who lived in one of the turrets.

There'd be 707 film releases in 1929. Box office receipts would tally $720,000,000. The top stars were Lon "The Man of a Thousand Faces" Chaney and Clara "The 'It' Girl" Bow. Sound was revolutionizing the movies, and MGM produced its final silent, *The Kiss*, starring Greta Garbo.

James Whale, ready for fame and fortune in Hollywood.

The first Academy Awards Ceremony had taken place May 19, 1929 at the Blossom Room of the Hollywood Roosevelt Hotel. The award, designed by MGM art director Cedric Gibbons, definitely had its suggestive connotation: a naked man, stabbing a sword into a reel of film with five holes. (The holes, Gibbons claimed, represented the five branches of the Academy.) The gold-washed statuette stood 13.5 inches tall, weighed 6.75 pounds, and the back of its head was flat.

"One Man *Crazy* …!"

"... I saw it as a perfect symbol of the picture business," quipped Frances Marion, MGM screenwriter. "A powerful athletic body, clutching a gleaming sword, with half of his head—the part which held his brains—completely sliced off."

The very word "Hollywood" evoked a crazy sexuality, a sensual savagery. Thirty-year-old Joseph Moncure March had celebrated it with his 1928 banned-in-Boston epic poem, *The Wild Party*, whose heroine was an ill-fated Hollywood blonde voluptuary named Queenie:

> *What hips—*
> *What shoulders—*
> *What a back she had!*
> *And her legs were built to drive men mad.*
> *And she did ...*

Many a "Queenie" was dreaming of fame in Hollywood, including 18-year-old Jean Harlow, who had albino blonde hair and who applied ice cubes to her nipples before slinking on camera.

It was a city of bizarre fetishes and rituals—for example, on September 14, Joan Crawford had been the latest star to place her high heel prints in the fabled courtyard cement of Grauman's Chinese Theatre. And in reality, as a "Sin City," Los Angeles was definitely a horrific contender.

Police often found murder victims dumped in the Hollywood Hills only after coyotes had devoured much of the corpses. So many people had jumped off the 170'-tall Colorado Street Bridge in Pasadena that it was called "Suicide Bridge," and authorities were considering stringing nets under it to catch the jumpers. Then there was the "Witch-Woman," amok in Hol-

The HOLLYWOODLAND sign.

lywood, who in November had tempted a four-year-old boy with candy, taken him to a restroom in South Park, stripped him, and as the *Los Angeles Times* reported, "whipped him fiendishly with a sharp branch broken from a piece of shrubbery." The boy escaped and ran screaming from the park. There'd been a half-dozen similar "Witch-Woman" attacks on children previously that year.

All in all, Hollywood of 1929 was an awesomely creative and hideously vicious place, coldly unforgiving, where the gravest of Mortal sins was failure to deliver professionally. Many drank heavily, and some used drugs, but addicts received precious little sympathy. For example, in January, actress Alma Rubens, a drug addict, suffered "a public display of hysteria" on Hollywood Boulevard. Authorities shipped her off to Patton State Hospital in San Bernardino.

The hospital's official name a few years before: The Southern California State Asylum for the Insane and Inebriates.

HOWARD HUGHES
Thrilling
Multi-Million Dollar
Air Spectacle

Hell's
Angels

JEAN
HARLOW
Ben Lyon
James Hall

Hap
Hadley

James Whale did not get on well with Jean Harlow when he "ghost-directed" her scenes for Howard Hughes' *Hell's Angels*.

As Maurice Browne in London moved toward producing the film version of *Journey's End* in Hollywood, James Whale had acquired a wealth of film skill: Howard Hughes, who'd spent $2,000,000 producing and directing the epic *Hell's Angels*, signed Whale as "ghost director" of the film's new Sound sequences. Stealing the show from the biplanes and a zeppelin that exploded (in Technicolor), the aforementioned Jean Harlow vamped her star-making line: "Would you be shocked if I slipped into something more comfortable?"

Come the Halloween season of 1929, and it was hardly a love match: the synthetic English aristocrat who held his penis like a gentleman, vs. the blonde bombshell who iced her nipples. *So marvelously SHAM*, as Whale might have put it.

He mocked her attempts to act, and she would probably have mocked the way he held his penis, had she known; at any rate, work soon wrapped on *Hell's Angels*. Whale was happy to take his $7,000 bonus from Hughes, buy a Chrysler, and fully devote his time to a Platinum Blonde-free *Journey's End*. Maurice Browne dispatched George Pearson, a balding, mustached, professorial-looking pioneer producer in the British film industry, to join Whale and supervise the film, to be shot at Tiffany Studios.

All the while, Colin was in the play in London, wringing himself out as Stanhope. R.C. Sherriff later said, "Not only was he a very fine and very sincere actor, but he lived his part every night." Sherriff never got the double meaning of his own remark.

Colin *was* living the role of Stanhope, and it was ripping him to pieces.

There'd been skepticism that Hollywood would do right by *Journey's End*. Even *The Hollywood Spectator* had cynically editorialized:

> *... wait until Hollywood gets a crack at this stage masterpiece! Wait till we touch it up with a theme song and some comedy relief! No woman in it, eh? Well, we'll soon fix that. We'll pep it up with a bunch of hot love scenes ... the final fade-out must be of the hero and heroine indulging in a long and passionate exchange of lipstick ...*

Determined to stick to the spirit of Sherriff's play, Whale engaged, perhaps surprisingly, *The Wild Party's* Joseph Moncure March. The poet had written the dialogue for the sound remake of *Hell's Angels*, including presumably Jean Harlow's "Would you be shocked ...?" line. Whale had been comfortable working with him and wanted him to work on the film script already prepared by Gareth Gundrey. March greeted the *Journey's End* boys with a practical joke.

"I suggested that we really ought to have a lot of young-love interest, two or three pretty girls, including a wild flapper," said March. "Imagine how they took that, those English stage managers and actors!"

Auditions began for the various roles. Whale, however, eventually realized that only one man was truly worthy of playing Stanhope on the screen.

"I had to send for Colin Clive," he later said, "because we could find nobody in Hollywood who could play the part. I think I tested no fewer than 250 people."

Maurice Browne agreed to grant Colin Clive a leave of absence from the play, but at cutthroat terms. The actor would sail to New York City, take a train to California, complete his role, train back to New York, and sail home again to England ... all in just under eight weeks. In 1929, this was almost unheard-of; a days' late arrival or inclement weather could crack the clockwork. Still, Browne was adamant.

Colin learned he'd be going to Hollywood to star in *Journey's End*.

Tuesday, November 19: Cyril Gardiner would play Stanhope during Colin's leave-of-absence. Colin's *au revoir* performance in *Journey's End* was a special one—presented before the King and Queen, and the Duke and Duchess of York. He packed the "Sam Brown belt" that R.C. Sherriff had worn in the war and had given Colin to wear in the play, and which had been with him for over 300 performances.

The next day, Colin left Southampton on the White Star liner, *Homeric*, sailing for New York City.

> *So ... I'll star in a movie, eh? Well, all my ghosts and pet devils should star in it too. After all, aren't they part of my Stanhope performance? Christ, for months now, they could have all lined up on stage at the curtain call and taken a bow with me.*
>
> *Yes ... do come along. Sail across the Atlantic with me, ride the rails across America with me. Be there to watch and laugh and jeer as I play Captain Stanhope ... a cracked, funhouse mirror reflection of myself.*
>
> *Oh, it'll be such fun! A bloody, goddamned joyride to Hollywood!*

Part II
The Shooting of *Journey's End* ...
and the Aftershock

To me, his face was a tragic mask ...

David Manners, remembering Colin Clive, his co-star in the film *Journey's End*

"One Man *Crazy* ...!"

Chapter Nine
Jekyll and Hyde

The sea voyage was frightening.

The *Homeric* hit wicked weather, strong Atlantic gales day and night, rocking Colin and such fellow passengers as Metropolitan Opera singer Mario Chamlee, cartoonist Bud Fisher, artist Countess M.B. Pecorini, and orchestra leader Ben Bernie.

"New York's skyline looked like an *Arabian Nights* entertainment to me," said Colin. The ship finally docked Thanksgiving, November 28, 24 hours late, in New York City. The weather had already compromised Maurice Browne's rigid schedule—Colin had only 25 minutes to make his train—and escorts frantically hurried Colin to Grand Central Station. A reporter, tagging along, filed this report to the Detroit *Free Press*:

> *While being rushed, bag and baggage, from the docks to the train for the west, Clive exclaimed: "I say—but you Americans are speedy. What? It's tremendously invigorating. I like it, you know. I like all this bustle." And then he asked, as the taxi crossed Broadway:*
>
> *"What street is this? Oh, see the women! Aren't they smart? Just like our British girls. American and British girls are becoming very much the same in style, vivaciousness and beauty. I can hardly tell them apart. So, this is Broadway. Well, well—and what street is this?"*
>
> *"Fifth Avenue," he was told.*
>
> *"This isn't right," he exclaimed. "I should be permitted to see your New York. You're rushing me a bit too fast. Your speed is astounding. Only a short time ago I stood on the steamship's deck admiring your skyline and the Statue of Liberty. Next, you give me a lightning-like glance at Broadway, Fifth Avenue, your public library, and now?"*
>
> *"Grand Central," yelled the driver of the car. Clive was hurried through the gates, boarding that train two minutes before it started. When he reached his compartment, he asked:*
>
> *"Where do I sleep?" Told that a berth would be dropped down for him, he put both hands to his head, sat down in thought and as the humor of it all burst on him, roared:*
>
> *"This is jolly well astounding. Just like* Alice in Wonderland, *you know. I sit in a room without a bed, but it will appear from the ceiling. I expect to be serenaded by the Walrus and the Carpenter. However—oh, good-bye. See you when I return."*

When Colin finally settled for lunch, he ordered a bottle of Bass. The waiter reminded him he was in a country of Prohibition.

The U.S.A. of the fall of 1929 was the land of Herbert Hoover, Al Capone, Aimee Semple McPherson, Babe Ruth, and Charles Lindbergh ... all in the wake of October's Stock Market Crash. Colin would see little of American life as he rode the train across the country ...

... until we came to the prairie. I felt we might be traveling through any country, but I was thrilled out West to find that cowboys, dressed as they are in the films, rush about madly on horses.

At last, Colin arrived in Hollywood. *Journey's End's* supervisor George Pearson was awaiting him as, of course, was the film's director, Jimmy Whale. Colin found a room reserved for him at the Roosevelt Hotel, had a meal at the Brown Derby, and saw the HOLLYWOODLAND sign. As he wrote of his arrival:

> *Everything was done with machine-like precision. This is what amazed me. I had been told that the methods in production in Hollywood were rather loose. But they were not in this particular production. I met Mr. Whale, the director, who is an old friend. He gave me a copy of the scenario, and I was told to spend the evening in studying it and report at the studio the following day, which I did ...*

Tiffany Studios, 4516 Sunset Boulevard, was located in east Hollywood. Across the street, 4473 Sunset Drive had been the site of the Babylon set of D.W. Griffith's *Intolerance* (1916). "Babylon" had fallen in 1919, having been declared a fire hazard by the Los Angeles Fire Department.

Colin signed his contract—having been earning £30 per week in the play of *Journey's End*, he'd receive £500 (or $2,500) per week for the film. He remembered:

> *There were rehearsals. All were agreed on every detail of the film play. Every set was arranged ...*

Colin met his co-stars and the members of the *Journey's End* Company, all of whom had been rehearsing with a stand-in while awaiting Colin's arrival. For Osborne, Whale had selected Ian Maclaren. The 54-year-old British-born actor was an incisive choice: he played "the Christus" every Easter time in the Passion Play in Los Angeles, presented in the Pilgrimage Theatre in the Hollywood Hills. As such, Maclaren was an almost mystical presence in the film colony, and as Osborne, would have the same God-like essence George Zucco possessed in the London *Journey's End*.

Indeed, while the gray-haired Maclaren would seem God-like, Colin, with his ascetic features, would appear as if he were His only begotten Son.

As for Raleigh, Whale had discovered 29-year-old, Nova-Scotia-born David Manners, who would become a legend as the romantic male ingénue running afoul of Bela Lugosi as *Dracula*, Boris Karloff as *The Mummy*, and Karloff *and* Lugosi in *The Black Cat*. He'd grown up in the Canadian wilderness and in England (where he'd picked up a British accent) and had acted on Broadway and with the Theatre Guild.

In 1976, Manners, in his Pacific Palisades home, gave me one of his rare interviews, and recalled his casting in *Journey's End*:

> *I had actually decided to leave the stage and had letters of introduction to the owner of a sugar plantation in Hawaii. En route, I stopped over in Los Angeles and looked up some friends from New York. They were having a party, I attended, and Jimmy Whale was there. All through the party, he kept staring at me, and listening to me (my English accent was far more pronounced than*

"One Man *Crazy* ... !"

The Tiffany-Stahl Studio, Hollywood, site of the filming of *Journey's End*.

it is now); I was really quite embarrassed. Finally, he pointed at me and said, "You! Have you ever been on the stage?" I replied that I had, and he snapped, "Good! I want you to come to the studio tomorrow and make a test!"

Well, I just looked on the whole thing as an adventure. But I never got to Hawaii—and I might add that I've never been there in my life!

The Life and Death of Colin Clive Hollywood's Dr. Frankenstein

The cameraman would be Benjamin Kline, whose resume would include everything from The Three Stooges' *Disorder in the Court* (1936), to Edgar G. Ulmer's *noir* classic *Detour* (1945), to 29 episodes of TV's *Thriller*, including two of its most frightening hours: "The Incredible Dr. Markesan" (starring *Thriller's* host, Boris Karloff), and "A Wig for Miss Devore" (both 1962). Colin said:

> *As part of the Merlin-like atmosphere surrounding the talking film, the arrangements were affected so that the scenes in which Stanhope appeared were played first. Now, here I was before the movies for the first time, in my life—acting. The sensation was an extraordinary one. As Stanhope on the stage in London I had sensed audience reactions and was able to gauge my lines accordingly. As Stanhope on the screen I faced only those terrific studio lights.*

Colin also met two major challenges. He failed his voice RCA recording test, but it was the machinery's fault, not his, and adjustments fixed the problem. There were also the ligatures of Prohibition, but with so many speakeasies and bootleggers in Los Angeles, Colin easily found the whiskey that he so desperately craved.

Frazzled by his 5,400-plus-mile trip, scared about his film, and homesick for London, Colin Clive, perilously drunk, began work on the film of *Journey's End*.

> *Colin's entry on that set, as Stanhope, seemed in some miraculous way to turn make-believe into sudden stark reality.*
> George Pearson

The words of *Journey's End's* supervisor George Pearson related, of course, to the brilliance of the star. They also evoked the tragedy on the set ... truly a "stark reality."

The company, anticipating an actor playing Stanhope, met a frightening incarnation of Stanhope. Colin was a chain-smoking nervous wreck, terrified by the camera, wracked by fear about his Hollywood debut, horrified by the real-life nightmare that his drinking would go out of control. For his co-players, Colin's Stanhope had a perverse twist, with a sideshow freakishness—an addict, playing an addict.

Especially affected was David Manners, whose hypersensitivity would cause him to flee Hollywood for good in 1936. Colin's Jekyll/Hyde nature would haunt Manners all his life:

> *To me, his face was a tragic mask. I know he was a tortured man. There seemed to be a split in his personality ... one side that was soft, kind and gentle; the other, a man who took to alcohol to hide from the world his true nature.*
>
> *Today, he would find help. Every one of us wanted to help then, but when he was on the bottle—which was most of the time—he put on the mask of a person who repelled help and jeered at his own softness.*
>
> *He was a fantastically sensitive actor, and as with many great actors, this sensitivity bred addiction to drugs and alcohol in order to cope with the very insensitive world around them.*

Indeed, what if Colin truly went on an alcohol binge? Fortunately, 10 months of playing Stanhope onstage had made him letter-perfect, but if "Hyde" escaped, under all this incredible pressure ... what happened next?

As noted, addiction in Hollywood, be it alcohol or drugs, was hardly unheard-of ... and rarely forgiven. Even John Barrymore, at his movie star peak in 1929 and proclaimed by Warner Bros. as "The World's Greatest Living Actor," was dreadfully fearful that his own alcoholism would eventually cause him to be locked up in an asylum. If Colin Clive had an alcoholic breakdown in Hollywood, he might never complete the shooting of *Journey's End*, possibly not return to London as scheduled to resume his role in the play, and maybe even find himself incarcerated in a sanitarium in California. The nightmarish scenario must have caused Colin to remember the fate of his Uncle Piercy, who'd died five years before at the Lunatic Asylum on the island of Jersey.

Whale, naturally, kept a careful eye on Colin. Maurice Browne, in London, telegrammed his concerns, not so much for Colin's health, as for fear Colin might decide to "go Hollywood," sign for another movie, and not return to London's *Journey's End* as dictated in the original deal. Whale basically told Browne he didn't give a damn if Colin did or didn't (royalties promised Whale by Browne on *Journey's End* had not been forthcoming, and he and Browne weren't on cordial terms).

Every day and night, the pressure built intensely.

Director James Whale, supervisor George Pearson, and an executive welcome Colin Clive to Hollywood. Note Whale's knickers.

David Manners, who'd play Raleigh, stands with Colin Clive between scenes of *Journey's End.* Colin's sensitivity and Jekyll and Hyde nature would haunt Manners for the rest of his long life.

Colin, for all his demons, was a great professional, and he and Whale had the same strange bond they'd formed in London. In fact, on Saturday night of December 14, Whale and Colin appeared together on a radio variety show, broadcast over three California stations—KHJ, KFWB, and KNX—giving a talk about *Journey's End.* Fred Niblo, Will Irwin, and Jack Oakie were the emcees, and other guests included D.W. Griffith, Anita Page, Sally Blane, John Boles, and Inez Courtney.

"There was a blank feeling about it at first," said Colin about the filming. "But after a time, I liked it. The whole thing began to seem very realistic, just as though we were actually in a war." In fact, it *was* a war—a film company's war against a near-impossible deadline, and an actor's war against his own demons.

As with Stanhope, Colin Clive was determined to be a hero, and alcohol was his crutch.

It was Yuletide in Hollywood, as Colin and company acted on the Tiffany stage in their wartime passion play. George Pearson, having been dealing with *Journey's End's* daily and nightly challenges as its supervisor, remembered:

> *Christmas Day arrived ... Hollywood was one mad whirlpool of merry-making, banners and balloons, woolen snowmen, a Father Christmas at every corner, crowded saloons, constant health-drinking punctuated with carol-singing, strangers shaking hands with strangers and persistent calls of "Just one for the road!"*

"One Man *Crazy* ...!"

Colin and Ian Maclaren, who played Osborne. Here Osborne gives Stanhope his watch and wedding band to return to his wife in case he dies in a front line raid – which he does.

Pearson (who'd clearly witnessed a Yuletide Hollywood thumbing its nose at Prohibition) found himself dreaming of a "saner English Christmas" with his wife and children. Meanwhile, he'd been invited to a party at Victor McLaglen's. Colin was invited too, and when he arrived, it was clear, Pearson wrote, that Colin "had been a victim of the festivities."

Billy Bevan (as Trotter), Charles Gerrard (as Mason), and Anthony Bushell (as Hibbert) join Colin's Stanhope, reviewing "saucy" post cards. (Courtesy of Neil Pettigrew)

> *Whale suggested that a ride in an open car to the cold wind of the Pacific coast might restore him. We went, but it only sent Clive off into a deep sleep. In the darkness, we lost our Hollywood bearings, and couldn't locate McLaglen's home. A brilliantly lit building attracted us; we might get information there. We rang the bell. Clive slept on. A perfect butler opened the door. He politely asked us to wait; he would call his master. We were struck by the strange furniture of the large hall, for it seemed to consist only of huge tables of white marble piled with flowers of an intoxicating scent. An immaculately dressed gentleman of imposing appearance greeted us ... We were surprised by his smiling welcome. Yes, he knew where McLaglen lived. So that helped us. But when he said he was sorry for our sad mission, but that even death can be consoled by reverent obsequies, we realized we had struck a funeral parlor! How we got away, I don't know, but it was certainly the strangest Christmas Day experience I ever had.*

They escaped the funeral parlor, Clive still resembling the living (or not-so-living) dead:

> *We found our way to McLaglen, and deposited Clive, still somnolent; it was obvious that bed was the best place for him, so we drove him back to his hotel, and tucked him up on a couch, to dream maybe of dug-outs and millions of whisky bottles.*

Colin's harrowing Stanhope, heartbroken after the death of Osborne. (Courtesy of Neil Pettigrew)

Colin made it through the picture. The company presented the chain-smoking actor with a silver cigarette case. As scheduled, he was to leave New Year's Eve to start the trip back to London. Word of Colin's brilliant performance spread throughout Hollywood—the studio had tried to keep a lid on his personal difficulties—and agents hounded Colin to try to keep him in town.

Death scene: Colin's Stanhope tenderly cares for David Manners' dying Raleigh in the powerful climax of *Journey's End.*

The company of *Journey's End.* Colin is center with James Whale on his left. Ian Maclaren is at the picture's far left. (Courtesy of Neil Pettigrew)

"One Man *Crazy* ...!"

"They tried to steal his luggage," said James Whale. "They tried to make him lose the train. They tried to make him lose the boat. But Clive had to come back."

He headed east, having made an indelible impression on the men of *Journey's End*. He'd also impressed David Lewis, James Whale's lover, who'd later be executive producer of such films as Garbo's *Camille* (1937), Bette Davis' *Dark Victory* (1939), and Elizabeth Taylor's *Raintree County* (1957). In 1983, four years before his death, Lewis wrote to me:

> *I knew Colin Clive, dined with him several times. He was a very shy man and his misfortune was that he was an actor totally without ego. As you know, ego is essential to an artist.*
>
> *He was a beautiful actor with a wonderful speaking voice, and once he got going, he was one of the finest performers I have ever known. James Whale had the deepest respect and admiration for him and his work.*
>
> *Clive drank heavily, but he was the most gentlemanly of men.*

Lewis' words displayed a fondness and defense of Colin that both he and Whale must have loyally and admirably shared. Tragically, neither took any action to save him from what promised to be, in 1929, a long, lingering suicide by whiskey.

Chapter Ten
Accolades

Come the New Year of 1930, and James Whale continued work on *Journey's End*, shooting battleground exteriors at night on the old Pathé lot, which still held the castle of Jerusalem from DeMille's 1927 *The King of Kings*.

Playing the small role of Sergeant Cox in *Journey's End* was Australian Gil Perkins, who'd worked on the set at Tiffany Studios and vividly recalled the long, cold nights at Pathé. Later a legendary stunt man, who'd double Bela Lugosi as the Monster in *Frankenstein Meets the Wolf Man* (1943), Perkins admired Whale as a great director and "a nice guy. Very quiet—he'd explain to you what he wanted, not yell in front of everybody. He'd say, 'Come here, Gil ...'" As for *Journey's End's* star, Perkins said:

> *Colin Clive—a hell of an actor. He'd die young—from drinking. We had a lot of tremendous actors we'd lose that same way.*

Colin had a brief stay in New York City before setting sail for London. A reporter for the *New York Times* spoke with him in his room at the Warwick Hotel, where Colin claimed he still had a buzzing in his ears from the trains on the tracks. He said he found Americans "delightful," "charming," and "interesting," but launched into a tirade on, of all things, ice water.

> *Ice water was the bane of my visit. You are surrounded by ice water. Continually one has ice water poked at one from the drinking fountains, at the tables, in your homes. I sit down in a restaurant before a glass of ice water. I sip perhaps an eighth of an inch from its brimming surface before a lackey jumps up to my elbow and fills up the glass. Ice water, bah!*

He followed up with a rant about overheated rooms in America. All the windows were open in his hotel room on this cold, windy January night, and the reporter was clearly nervous as Colin "jumped up and leaned far out of the window, which was 17 stories above Sixth Avenue."

"This is what I like best," said Colin, indicating the view of small, lighted windows. "And there is another thing I must remember while here, and that is that tomato is not pronounced with a broad 'a.'"

He set sail on the *Berengaria* Saturday, January 4, 1930, arrived in Southampton Friday, January 10, and was back onstage in *Journey's End* Monday, January 13. He was likely relieved to have Hollywood behind him and to be back in London, and every reason to be proud. He'd heroically mastered an Olympian challenge, completing the film *Journey's End* and returning to the play without falling prey to, or at least being overcome by, his pet devils.

The play's one-year anniversary party took place at London's Kit Cat Club, in a private room decorated to resemble the *Journey's End* dugout set. Overhead were 18 maps with ribbons, showing cities and towns where *Journey's End* was playing this night all over the world. Hannen Swaffer, filing a report to *Variety*, wrote that "the proudest person there,

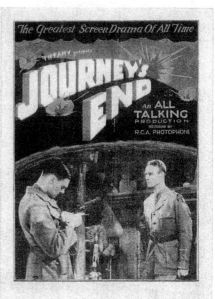

An advertisement for the world premiere of *Journey's End* at New York City's Gaiety Theatre, April 8, 1930. (Courtesy of Tracy Surrell)

I have no doubt," was the mother of R.C. Sherriff, and describing "old Mrs. Sherriff" as "a modest but beaming mother."

"Sherriff made a very poor speech," wrote Swaffer, "and so did Colin Clive, who like most actors, is apparently useless without words written for him to say."

Meanwhile, Whale had completed *Journey's End* in Hollywood, at a final cost of about $280,000. The film would preview in March, with release set for April.

February 2, 1930: Colin, still playing in *Journey's End*, starred as Michael Shannon in *Forty-Seven*, sponsored by the *Journey's End* company, which played this Sunday night and the following Monday afternoon. The play was based on the "Irish troubles," and the playwright was Sydney Loch, author of the book, *Ireland in Travail*. The *New York Times* reported the play had been "excellently staged" by George Zucco.

February also saw the release of *Knowing Men*, which featured Jeanne de Casalis and was the first British "Talkie" directed by a woman. The woman was no less than Elinor Glyn, the "racy" novelist who based the film on her book and shot it in an early two-color process called "Talkicolor." The result was a technical disaster, and the film was released in black-and-white.

Also in February, Jeanne had starred in the short film *Infatuation*, in which a young man falls in love with an aging actress ... and discovers she's his mother. Considering that Jeanne was at least seven years older than her husband Colin and, to be frank, by now looked even older in comparison, *Infatuation* was a strange choice for her.

Meanwhile, in Hollywood, *Journey's End* was ready for preview. Would the film, and Colin's performance, duplicate the play's success?

Publicity for *Journey's End* heralded it as *The Greatest Screen Drama of All Time*.

Monday, March 17: Dorothy Herzog of the Los Angeles *Evening Herald* wrote that she'd attended a standing room only preview of *Journey's End* in Glendale. She hailed the film as "magnificent," Colin as "superb," and especially praised the showdown scene between Stanhope and Raleigh.

"This grief-saturated scene of Clive's," wrote Herzog, "has few equals in the annals of the motion picture." Her review concluded by calling *Journey's End* "one of the few great achievements of this young century."

Friday, March 21: Anabel Lane of the *Film Mercury*, also seeing a preview, wrote:

> *Occasionally a piece of work is so perfect that even the mob recognizes its beauty and sincerity. Colin Clive's performance makes words a bit too inadequate for description. It seems inspired. Natural in every movement, not worried about poor camera angles, this actor made the role of Captain Stanhope the most vital and living performance it has been my joy to see.*

While both reviewers were women, perhaps responding to Colin's romanticism as well as his brilliance, his admirers weren't only female.

Tuesday, April 8: *Journey's End* had its New York City premiere at the Gaiety Theatre. Mordaunt Hall wrote in his *New York Times* review:

> *One almost forgets that what one sees are but photographs of the actor ... Mr. Clive's performance is magnificent.*

William Bolitho, writing for the *New York World*, was a noted author with a remarkable story of his own; he'd been buried alive in a mine explosion in the Somme in 1916, the only one of 16 men to survive, albeit with a broken neck. He eloquently described *Journey's End*'s powerful finale:

When Stanhope stumbles at last up the steps of the dugout to find what has had a rendezvous with him for three hellish years, there comes a gradual darkness. For whole minutes, measured by the heart, not the watch, the audiences watched all lights but one, the candle in the bully-tin, fade; and at last that went out, and unable to move or blink, forgetting that we were merely looking at an unlighted screen, we sat and peered in silence into primeval night, the end to which only high and true tragedy can lead us securely.

Bolitho continued:

I have actually come across a critic, a friendly one too, who did not understand that the drunkenness of Stanhope (how good the ravaged, handsome Colin Clive is in the role) is the measure of his superhuman courage. The mere

A program for the film *Journey's End*.

mention of "three years," his front-line service, did not convey quite enough explanation, apparently. Well, if you look at the boy Raleigh, and realize what had happened to him was merely the horrors of one day, you may get the three-yearer Stanhope in scale ...

Thursday, April 10: Journey's End had its gala Los Angeles premiere. It took place at the Mayan Theatre, which had opened in 1927, was designed as a Pre-Columbian temple, and boasted a lobby called "The Hall of Feathered Serpents." A number of the cast were there "in person," KMTR Radio broadcast from the lobby, and the attendees included Lt. Governor George Carnabon, District Attorney Buron Fitts, Carl Laemmle, Sr., and such stars as Gary Cooper, Nancy Carroll, William Powell, Jean Arthur, Richard Arlen, Mary Astor, Ruth Chatterton, and Pauline Starke. Monroe Lanthrop of the *Evening Express* praised the film as "overwhelming in its power to pierce the heart of the spectator," and wrote:

> ... Colin Clive, who came from London, plays the nerve-wracked Stanhope magnificently, mingling in his portrayal passion and tenderness, strength and weakness with an art so fine as to seem artless.

In April, the film opened in London, with James Whale in attendance; Colin, of course, was still in the play. Once again, the reception to the film, and especially Colin's Stanhope, was rapturous, as it would be all over the world.

Colin Clive, as directed by James Whale, had created one of the great lost souls in Hollywood history.

Colin apparently never saw *Journey's End.* He'd never willingly go to see any of his films, and if trapped into attending one, he'd look away from the screen at the wall or the floor. The idea of seeing himself as a 25 foot giant, flickering on a screen, terrified him.

Reality, in his eyes, was frightening enough.

Journey's End was a triumph ... but there quickly came an eclipse. On Monday night, April 21, 1930—only 11 days after *Journey's End's* opening at the Mayan Theatre—Universal's *All Quiet on the Western Front* had a gala premiere at the Carthay Circle in Los Angeles. It came precisely one week before the 22nd birthday of its producer, Carl Laemmle, Jr., whose father, Universal founder Carl Laemmle, Sr., had appointed as General Manager. "Junior" Laemmle had spearheaded *All Quiet* ... against vehement opposition by his father and Universal's bigwigs. Aware of the similarity to *Journey's End,* they'd nicknamed *All Quiet* ... "Junior's End."

The *All Quiet on the Western Front* premiere was a historic night in Hollywood, as testified to at the Embassy Club dinner after the premiere, attended by guests Douglas Fairbanks, Mary Pickford, Charlie Chaplin, Marlene Dietrich, D.W. Griffith, Cecil B. DeMille and many more. The film was an epic, swamping *Journey's End*, still critically and popularly praised, in its wake.

However, as fine as Lew Ayres' butterfly-petting Paul Bohmer is, he's never as starkly haunting as Colin Clive's Stanhope.

June 25, 2017 marked the 80th anniversary of Colin Clive's death. A few nights later, to commemorate, I watched, for the first time in several years, *Journey's End*.

The best-available DVD copy of the film is definitely watchable, but not very sharp. In several scenes, the actors on film look like ghosts, which fits this late weeknight viewing. Fireflies dart outside my window; a few hours earlier, an albino raccoon, which I'd never seen before, came loping across our yard. The whole day and night had seemed a bit off.

Colin makes his entrance in *Journey's End*, and it hits me again what a unique actor he was. His voice, as one on-line critic described it, "sounds a bit like Glynis Johns if she were to be possessed by Satan," as he vehemently rasps his first lines about cess-pits and rusty grenades. The young face is ascetic, and his Stanhope (pronounced by the men as "Stan-hupp") instantly takes a wicked possession of the film.

He's brilliant. His acting is realistic and doesn't date at all. The late film historian, William K. Everson, wrote many years ago that Colin's performance was "powerful, subtle, and very moving ... in its original appearance, his Stanhope must have been as arresting a piece of theater as Marlon Brando's Kowalski ... "

Whale directs with great intimacy and sensitivity. When Clive's Stanhope says his famous line—"She doesn't know if I went up those steps into the front line, without being doped with whiskey, I'd go mad with fright"—he says it directly to the camera, his eyes looking right at the viewer, a stark, personal confession. A moment later, as he becomes increasingly drunk, he suddenly bursts into laughter—a chilling sound.

In the showdown scene with the cowardly Hibbert, Colin's Stanhope says, "Supposing we were knocked right out. Think of all the topping fellows who've gone already. It can't be very lonely there, with all those fellows." The camera moves in closely as he says, "Sometimes I feel it's lonelier here." Again, I sense what Whale and Colin clearly wanted—it's as if Stanhope were confiding his despair to each individual member of the audience.

He has a young beauty and a sense of heroic, terrible tragedy, and when he breaks down crying near the end of the film, kneeling by the dead Osborne's bed—"his heart is breaking," noted the play script—his grief is so agonizing that it almost feels as if he's in the room with me.

The film plays on. The final shell hits. The dugout collapses. Black out.

THE END.

Fireflies dart by my window.

Chapter Eleven
Palpable and Not-So-Palpable Hits and *The Picturegoer* Interview

Tuesday, April 22 (Shakespeare's birthday eve), *Friday, April 25*, and *Monday, May 19, 1930*: Colin, still starring in *Journey's End*, played Laertes, aiming his poison-tipped rapier in special performances of an all-star *Hamlet* at London's Haymarket Theatre.

These charity matinees aided The Actors Benevolent Fund, The Actors Orphanage Fund, The Theatrical Ladies Guild, and The Denville Hall for Elderly Actors. The May 19 date was a Command Performance before the King and Queen. Henry Ainley played Hamlet, and the guest stars included Cedric Hardwicke as the First Grave Digger and Ernest Thesiger as Osric. Hardwicke later played Colin's "second son" Ludwig von Frankenstein in *The Ghost of Frankenstein* (1942), while Thesiger, of course, would entice Colin to create a Monster's Mate in *Bride of Frankenstein* (1935).

As for the Haymarket's *Hamlet* ... the overwhelming critical consensus was that Colin's Laertes died in more ways than one, and that Thesiger's camped-up Osric, mincing "A hit! A very palpable hit!" as Hamlet and Laertes duel, was a travesty. London critic/reporter Hannen Swaffer found both actors effeminate in their performances, and posted to *Variety* (May 9, 1930):

THE BROTHER WARNS HIS SISTER AGAINST HAMLET. LAERTES
(MR. COLIN CLIVE) AND OPHELIA (MISS GWEN FFRANGÇON-DAVIES).

Colin as Laertes in the Royal performance of *Hamlet* at London's Haymarket Theatre, April, 1930. Playing Ophelia is Gwen Ffrangcon-Davies.

> *Oh, Ernest Thesiger! Colin Clive's Laertes is generally talked about—so bad was it—while Ernest Thesiger, as Osric, made him look like a perfect lady. I do not think the Elizabethans were as purringly gentle as that.*

Swaffer went on to argue that Thesiger "should not do this sort of thing," and to eulogize, "the Shakespeareans are dying."

As these were special matinees, Colin was playing Laertes in the afternoon and Stanhope at night.

Tuesday, May 27: Hell's Angels had a spectacular premiere at Grauman's Chinese Theatre. Biplanes flew over Hollywood Boulevard, and Jean Harlow, at the microphone, thanked Howard Hughes—but didn't mention James Whale. The sexed-up war saga

"One Man *Crazy* ...!"

attracted giant box office and drove another nail into the coffin of Whale's film version of *Journey's End*, as far as the industry and public forgetting about it.

Saturday, June 7: Journey's End played its final, 593rd London performance. Colin gave a curtain speech.

Monday, June 30: Colin scored as Professor St. Nicholas Agi in Molnar's *The Swan* at London's St. James Theatre. His co-stars were Herbert Marshall, who'd lost a leg in World War I (and did perfectly well with a wooden leg) as "the Prince," and Edna Best, who was then married to Marshall, as "the Princess." (Best was the second of Marshall's five wives.) Colin was acclaimed as "so powerfully romantic" as "the Professor" that audiences were disappointed when the "Princess" resisted his allure to caress her "Prince."

Then came a new career milestone: Colin was to make his Broadway debut.

The play was titled *Overture*, an anti-Communist tragedy set in post-World War I Germany. Its author was the aforementioned William Bolitho (who'd reviewed *Journey's End* for the *New York World*) and who'd written the 1929 book *Twelve Against the Gods*. A crony of Noel Coward and Ernest Hemingway, Bolitho had died in France after an appendicitis attack on June 2, 1930, at the age of 39. As such, there was considerable interest in his posthumously produced play. Colin's role in *Overture*: Captain Karl Ritter, a saintly revolutionary, victimized by his own rebellion and climactically shot as a traitor. On October 17, 1930, Colin arrived in New York on the *Aquitania*, accompanied by his Great Dane, Remus. Among the other passengers: Chinese actress Anna May Wong.

As Colin rehearsed for *Overture*, the time came for Hollywood's official recognition of films released in 1930. At the Academy Awards Banquet on November 5, 1930, held in the Fiesta Room of the Ambassador Hotel in Los Angeles, *All Quiet on the Western Front* won for Best Picture; *Journey's End* wasn't nominated. Lewis Milestone received the Best Director award for *All Quiet* ...; James Whale wasn't nominated. George Arliss won the Best Actor prize for Warner Bros.' *Disraeli*; Colin Clive wasn't nominated.

Of course, the very concept of the Academy Awards was a union-busting maneuver by Louis B. Mayer and other Hollywood potentates, so there was almost no chance for little Tiffany Studios to place a contender among the major studios output. In less political arenas, *Journey's End* won recognition: On the *New York Times'* "Ten Best" list, it placed third, right behind *All Quiet* ... (Number One was Paramount's *With Byrd at the South Pole*). In *The Film Daily* poll, *Journey's End* placed Number Four (*All Quiet* ... was Number One, *Abraham Lincoln* Number Two, *Holiday* Number Three), and Whale placed eighth in the Director's poll. Incidentally, *Hell's Angels* placed ninth in *The Film Daily's* poll, which was another feather in James Whale's hat.

Photoplay magazine, in its May, 1930 issue, included Colin in its "Best Performances" list. Among the 14 other winners: Anthony Bushell for playing the cowardly Hibbert in *Journey's End*, and Lew Ayres for *All Quiet on the Western Front*.

By the way, Carl Laemmle, Jr., who'd courageously produced *All Quiet on the Western Front*, suffered a humiliation on Academy Awards night as his father, Universal founder Carl Laemmle, Sr., beamingly accepted the award.

"Next to the thrill of becoming a grandfather, this is the proudest moment of my life!" said Laemmle.

"Junior" Laemmle had his compensation. He was completing another project his father had tried to scuttle. The title: *Dracula*.

Colin at sea, with his dog, "Remus." (Thanks to Kerry Gammill)

Saturday, December 6: Overture had its opening night at New York's Longacre Theatre. Colin's Broadway bow was bizarrely timed. "7 Escaped Maniacs Are Hunted in City," headlined the front page December 5, 1930 *New York Times*. Six of the "maniacs" had escaped from the State Hospital for the Criminally Insane in Mattawan; the 7th had escaped two weeks before and had returned with two gunmen to free his friends. One of the escapees: Harry "The Butcher" Gordon, a real-life butcher who'd killed two other butchers. New York City was in a panic, but nevertheless, the curtain rose on *Overture*.

The play, and Colin, received mixed reviews. J. Brooks Atkinson of the *New York Times* praised Colin's performance for its "unassertive pride of character and adroitness of touch." However, John Mason Brown of the *New York Post* critiqued that Colin "made but little perceptible effort in mannerism, speech or appearance to differentiate the romantic German officer he is now playing from the cricketer [Stanhope of *Journey's End*] he once played. And the inevitable result was that *Overture* was robbed of much of the truth it might otherwise have held."

Colin got raves, professionally and personally, from his costar, Pat O'Brien, who played the Marxist heavy. In his memoir *The Wind at my Back*, the future Knute Rockne of the screen warmly remembered Colin as "what the trade calls 'a beautiful actor and a grand guy.'" O'Brien added humorously, "*How* can an Irishman say such things about an Englishman?"

Unfortunately, it was while Colin was in New York that his grandmother, Fanny Agnes Sharkey Greig, died in Southampton, England on December 23, 1930. She was 85-years-old. Colin's Broadway engagement prevented him from giving his grandmother a final good-bye.

Overture ran 41 performances. On January 16, 1931, Colin set sail on the *Aquitania*, returning home to England and to Jeanne, from whom he'd been away during the Christmas and New Year's holidays, both in 1929 and 1930.

Colin Clive's Broadway debut: *Overture*, December, 1930.

As for Jeanne, she'd enjoyed further theatrical success and was scoring a big hit on radio as "Mrs. Feather," a daffy, elegant lady who engages in comic, risqué telephone monologues. On April 20, 1931, Colin appeared with her on England's National Programme Radio in the episode, "Mrs. Feather's Fire."

On the stage, Colin played "The Apparition" in *The Romantic Young Lady* (Embassy Theatre, April, 1931) and Christopher Merryman in the satire *The Crime at Blossoms* (Playhouse Theatre, May, 1931). The latter saw Colin's Christopher and his wife Valerie (Joyce Bland) returning from a trip to find a

Colin Clive, with fellow passenger Anna May Wong.

double murder has occurred in their Elizabethan cottage in Sussex. As "Chris" is lazy and concerned only with his wife and garden, Valerie tries to relieve their debt by opening up their cottage as a murder scene bait for morbid tourists. In fact, Valerie even dresses up in "flowing crimson garments" six times a day to enthrall the visitors with a horrific recital about the double murder. Eventually her "ghastly exhibition" stirs Chris from "tolerant spectator to outraged husband," and the play to a hilarious finale.

"This is a play out of the ordinary rut," wrote *Theatre World*, "brilliantly acted by Colin Clive and Joyce Bland."

Colin had also starred in a new British film, Gainsborough's 1931 *The Stronger Sex*. His role: Warren Barrington, a nasty miner who weds his wife (Adrianne Allan) for her money, cheats on her, but redeems himself in a climactic mine cave-in by placing the one available gas mask on the man he knows his wife truly loves. His co-players included the "Bride" he'd later create in Hollywood, Elsa Lanchester.

Elsa, by the way, had married Charles Laughton in February of 1929. In the summer of 1931, Charles, Elsa, and Jeanne de Casalis starred in the London play, *Payment Deferred*. Charles played a murderer who poisons his nephew and buries the body in the backyard, Elsa portrayed Charles' daughter, and Jeanne acted Mme. Collins, a vamp.

The play won Jeanne special notice: "Gallant Actress Plays Her Part in Agony as Audience Applauds," headlined *The Ottawa Journal* (July 4, 1931). The story reported that Jeanne had broken her wrist in an accident that nearly overturned her car in the countryside; however, she insisted on going on in the play. "Her part demands great agility and the constant use of the hands for gesticulation," the article stated. "Miss de Casalis took off the sling with which she had been nursing the injured arm and acted the part with all her usual polish."

By now, Colin and Jeanne, when time allowed, enjoyed a 400-year-old cottage in County Kent, about 30 miles southeast of London. The River Medway runs through the center of Maidstone, Kent's "county town," and the beautiful area is known as "the Garden of England." Colin enjoyed motoring about the countryside, playing with his half-dozen blue-ribbon Sealyham terriers, and playing golf and tennis.

Elsa Lanchester remembered visiting Colin and Jeanne at their retreat in Kent, and sensing trouble in paradise:

> *Charles and I had stayed in the country with Colin Clive and his wife, Jeanne de Casalis, once or twice ... Theirs wasn't a very happy marriage. She was very precious, very affected ... He was very nice, an English gentleman.*

It was during the run of *A Crime at Blossoms* that Colin gave two interviews, which as David Manners of *Journey's End* might have said, revealed the "split in his nature."

Colin was gentlemanly and earnest in his interview with London's *Theatre World* titled: "How I Began." Several quotes from this interview have already appeared in the text, with Colin graciously paying tribute to Charles Hawtrey, Annie Horniman, and A.R. Whatmore. He concluded with this advice to "beginners" in the acting profession:

> *There is only one thing. They must work like Hell. They must concentrate on their job. Anyone will bear me out in this: Work is the only road to success.*

THE STRANGE CASE of COLIN CLIVE

BY his astonishing performance as Captain Stanhope in the talkie version of *Journey's End*, Colin Clive made a great name in filmdom, despite the fact that previous to this he had never even put foot inside a studio.

Journey's End enjoyed a world-wide release. Mr. Clive's mail bag was laden to bursting point with requests for signed photographs.

I sat back and waited with enthusiasm for his next picture.

Nothing happened for quite a considerable time. Then one day I read that the Gainsborough Company had signed him up to act in a talkie called *The Stronger Sex*.

At last, I thought, we shall be able to see some more of the man who made Stanhope a living personality.

The Stronger Sex was made in 1930. Colin Clive has done no more movies.

Determined to investigate the strange case of the film star who disappeared, I went along to the Playhouse Theatre recently, where Mr. Clive is acting

COLIN CLIVE and ADRIANNE ALLEN in " The Stronger Sex," and (below) COLIN CLIVE with ELSIE LANCHESTER in the same picture.

in a legitimate play, *The Crime at Blossoms*. I waited in his dressing-room for him. On a sideboard reposed a photo-frame. In the frame were two photographs, both of Jeanne de Casalis, the actor's wife.

The Clive-de-Casalis marriage has existed for quite a long time. In fact, no pukka film star would dare to flout convention by such outrageous marital endurance !

COLIN CLIVE in " Journey's End."

Colin Clive entered, looking very much younger than Captain Stanhope. He proceeded to crack a bottle of beer.

"Why haven't you done any more films since *Journey's End* and the *Stronger Sex* ?" I asked him.

"Because I am not in the least bit interested in motion pictures," he told me.

I pointed out that many filmgoers all over the world were inquiring about him. That after his portrayal of Stanhope he had fired the popular imagination. In short, that the public were wanting to see more of his work.

Then he told me the truth about himself. *Journey's End*, he said, was a fluke. Any fairly capable actor could have got away with the part of Stanhope. The cameraman was also responsible for a lot of his success.

When he finished the war film he made up his mind that nothing would induce him to act in another talkie.

An English company approached him with a big money offer to take part in a picture called *The Stronger Sex*. As he wanted money at that time, he took the job.

I asked him whether his distaste for films ...

The first page of "The Strange Case of Colin Clive," from England's *The Picturegoer*, June 27, 1931. In addition to Colin's rather bitter remarks about film stardom, the article promoted his British film *The Stronger Sex*. The actress center is Adrianne Allen. The actress below is Elsa Lanchester (captioned "Elsie Lanchester") who would later star with Colin in *Bride of Frankenstein*. (Courtesy of Sally Stark)

However, London's *The Picturegoer* also visited Colin in his dressing room between acts of *A Crime at Blossoms*. The reporter found two framed pictures of Jeanne de Casalis in the room, and Colin in a stormy temperament.

The interview, frankly, was a disaster.

"Why haven't you done more films since *Journey's End* and *The Stronger Sex*?" asked the reporter.

"Because I am not in the least bit interested in motion pictures," replied Colin.

Colin ranted so vehemently that one wonders if he'd had a nip, or several, before and during the performance. Among his remarks, as reported in the story:

> Journey's End, *he said, was a fluke. Any partly capable actor could have gotten away with the part of Stanhope. The cameraman was also responsible for a lot of his success ...*
>
> *Colin Clive would rather have two lines to speak on the stage than a star part in the biggest super film that ever came out of Hollywood ...*
>
> *When he went to Hollywood, he stayed at the Hotel Roosevelt ... He really isn't sure whether he did or not. Frankly, he wants to forget all about the film capital.*
>
> *He will kill in cold blood the very next person who asks him whether it was real whiskey he drank in* Journey's End *...*

On he went, claiming he'd only done *The Stronger Sex* because "he wanted money at that time," opining that "true dramatic art can only be successfully accomplished by living people before a living audience, with the footlights intervening." He vowed he'd only consider another Hollywood film if "the terms are so fat that it would be folly to refuse the offer."

He then said that, if he ever again ventured to Hollywood, he'd hurry back to the London stage as quickly as possible and "wash the taste of canned drama out of my mouth!"

The reporter found Colin "a little skeptical" that he had fans "craving" more of his film appearances:

> *True, I still get letters from all parts of the world, but my consistent absence from the screen will cause the public to forget all about me and pin their affections to some other player.*

Perhaps the interviewer sensed the "split" in Colin Clive that David Manners had witnessed. *The Picturegoer* slyly titled the feature *The Strange Case of Colin Clive*—similar to the title Robert Louis Stevenson had given his 1886 novella, *The Strange Case of Dr. Jekyll and Mr. Hyde.*

Meanwhile in the States:

Thursday, February 12, 1931: Universal Studios' *Dracula* had opened at New York's Roxy Theatre. "I am—Dracula," announced Bela Lugosi, standing on the staircase of his Transylvania castle, holding a candle, listening to the wolves howling ... "the children of the night."

Dracula epitomized a new, audacious genre that would become modern folklore. Come the haunted summer of 1931, James Whale and Colin Clive would join this unholy sect. And if Lugosi had baptized the Talking Horror Film with three words—"I am Dracula"—Colin would consecrate the genre with only two words:

"It's Alive!"

Part III
FRANKENSTEIN

Queer family, those Shelleys.
While the husband was writing about skylarks,
the wife was creating this tale of monsters!

Colin Clive, on the set of *Frankenstein*, 1931

Chapter Twelve
"Insane Passion"

The home of Boris Karloff, Hollywood, 1931. This is the view from the bedroom, showing the approximately 100 steps Karloff walked up each night after a day's work on *Frankenstein.* (Photo by author)

Sara Karloff, daughter of Boris Karloff, and Don Watkins, son of Marilyn "Little Maria" Harris, at Malibou Lake, 2016. (Courtesy of David Colton)

A fan of 1931's all-hallowed *Frankenstein* can make a Hollywood pilgrimage and see historic sites ... if he or she knows where to look.

There's the Spanish-style house, atop approximately 100 wooden steps in the Hollywood Hills, where Boris Karloff lived at the time of the filming of *Frankenstein.* After a long, hot day of suffering in Monster makeup and costume, Karloff made this torturous climb.

There's the villa, high in the hills of Los Feliz, where James Whale, *Frankenstein's* director, elegantly resided in 1931. "Villa Sophia," as it's known today, offers a spectacular view of Los Angeles, and is available for weddings and photo shoots.

Far west, in the Santa Monica mountains, there's Malibou Lake, where Whale staged *Frankenstein's* most shocking episode: Karloff's Monster drowning Marilyn

"Villa Sophia," the home of James Whale, 1931. (Photo by author)

Harris' "Little Maria." In 2016, 85 years after the shoot, Karloff's daughter, Sara, and the late Ms. Harris' son, Don, sat by the lake at this precise site, meeting for the first time.

"I don't float, so don't throw me in," laughed Sara to Don. "I don't want closure."

The back lot, Universal City, California.

Of course, Universal Studios, which produced *Frankenstein*, still exists in North Hollywood, both a studio and one of the largest theme parks in the world. Little survives there from 1931. The European Village, where *Frankenstein's* torch-bearing villagers paraded at night to pursue the Monster, burned down May 15, 1967 and, rebuilt, has burned down time and again. The "Black Tower," Universal's corporate headquarters, casts its shadow over the lot, with little awe for its 103-year history. In fact, in 2014, Universal demolished Stage 28, built for Lon Chaney's 1925 *The Phantom of the Opera*, to make way for a new park attraction.

There still exists Stage 12 ... the world's eighth largest soundstage, standing 49 feet tall, and measuring 199 feet long and 146 feet wide. Built in 1929 by Carl Laemmle, Jr. for his doomed musical, *Broadway*, it later held the castle stairway of *Dracula* (1931), and over the decades sets for such films as *Spartacus* (1960), *Thoroughly Modern Millie* (1967), *The Sting* (1973), *Earthquake* (1974), *Jurassic Park* (1993), and *Pirates of the Caribbean: Dead Man's Chest* (2006).

Once upon a time, Stage 12 housed one of the most famous sites in film history: the interior laboratory tower of *Frankenstein*.

Mary Shelley, in her prologue to *Frankenstein* wrote:

> *I have found it! What terrified me will terrify others; I need only describe the specter, which haunted my midnight pillow.*

Universal City, California of 1931 looks like a place where one might create a Monster.

Below the mountains of the San Fernando Valley, Universal has a fairy tale ambience, rather like *Dracula's* Borgo Pass village. Sets from silent films still loom on the back lot, such as the cathedral from the late Lon Chaney's *The Hunchback of Notre Dame*. By day, a shepherd, complete with a bell on a crook, leads his flock over the hills and past the lakes. By night, he guards the sheep against the coyotes that howl in the hills ... Universal's own "children of the night."

There'd been Universal's Best Picture Academy Award for *All Quiet on the Western Front* and *Dracula* is making a fortune, yet the studio's still eccentric. Five-feet-tall, 64-year-old Carl Laemmle, Sr., looking like a 20-years-older hobgoblin, marches about the lot, waving to the faithful like a Semitic Pope, welcoming his employees each week with a new front gate billboard, bearing such divine sentiments as "Be Kind to Others—signed, Carl Laemmle." Then there's 23-year-old "Junior" Laemmle, barely taller than his Dad, a playboy/hypochondriac, greeting starlets in his office while standing on a box concealed behind his desk.

Meanwhile, a strange irony is at play:

During what had become famous as "the Haunted Summer," Mary Shelley, Percy Shelley, and Lord Byron, staying at Villa Diodati above Lake Geneva in 1816, had challenged each other to create a ghost story. Modern astronomers, writing recently in *Sky and Telescope* magazine, have pinpointed it was between 2:00 a.m. and 3:00 a.m on Sunday, June 16, 1816 that Mary had her moonlight vision that led to *Frankenstein*:

> *... I saw the hideous phantasm of a man stretched out and then, on the working of some powerful machine, show signs of life, and stir with an uneasy, half vital motion. Frightful must it be; for supremely frightful would be the effect of any human endeavor to mock the stupendous mechanism of the Creator of the world ...*

Precisely 115 years later, on Tuesday, June 16, 1931, Robert Florey is directing a test for a film of *Frankenstein*, on a still-standing *Dracula* set, featuring Bela Lugosi as the Monster. Universal is dickering with MGM for Leslie Howard as Dr. Frankenstein, so a studio stock player essays the role in the test. Edward Van Sloan and Dwight Frye, Prof. Van Helsing and Renfield in *Dracula*, are in the test too as, respectively, wise Dr. Waldman and hunchbacked dwarf Fritz. In Florey's original *Frankenstein* script (with dialogue by Garrett Fort), the Monster is a mere ... well, monstrosity. Little wonder that Lugosi has protested the role, campaigning to play Dr. Frankenstein. Florey chooses to shoot the creation scene for the test, so all Lugosi has to do is open his eyes, hardly a showcase for his talent. The actor has reportedly applied his own makeup, evoking the Golem—and between test set-ups, a very *angry* Golem.

"I was a star in my country," rages Lugosi on the set, "and I will not be a scarecrow over here!" Edward Van Sloan's late-in-life memory of Lugosi's Monster: He looked "like something out of *Babes in Toyland*."

Also on June 16: James Whale, who'd joined Universal in March, begins seven straight nights of back lot shooting for *Waterloo Bridge*, based on the Robert E. Sherwood play. His heroine is one of Whale's "lost souls"—Myra, a streetwalker, beautifully played by Mae Clarke. During this week, Whale directs her suicide scene as Myra runs along Waterloo Bridge, into the path of a bomb dropped by a German zeppelin. Mae Clarke will

Carl Laemmle, Jr., Universal's "Crown Prince," about to produce *Frankenstein*.

remember Whale, perched high on a boom crane tower late on a cold night, wanting to see her from the zeppelin's point of view.

"It was *his* picture," Mae Clarke will recall reverently. "A James Whale Production!"

Junior Laemmle returns from New York City and sees a rough cut of Whale's *Waterloo Bridge* and Florey's *Frankenstein* test. The producer is so impressed by Whale's artistry (and so delighted he's shot the film under budget) that he green-lights a new, lavish opening scene for the film.

His response to Florey's *Frankenstein* test, in Junior's own words: "I laughed like a hyena!"

Robert Florey will strongly rebut this traditional testimony, mainly after most of the other principals involved are dead. However, one fact is crystal clear: Come Monday June 29, 1931, less than two weeks after Florey had completed his test, *The Hollywood Daily Citizen* announces that James Whale "will start working out plans for *Frankenstein*. Bela Lugosi, you know, will be starred in the production."

After James Whale enters the *Frankenstein* arena, the project takes on profound changes. In Whale's eyes, both Henry Frankenstein and his Monster are lost souls, even if the man-made Monster isn't supposed to have one. Both will inspire sympathy, and both will climactically die at the windmill on the mountain ... Frankenstein killed by his Monster, the Monster burned alive by the howling villagers. In 1952, film historian Gavin Lambert will meet Whale in London and later recall:

> *He talked about the fact that Lugosi was basically scary and scared audiences, and he said the Monster, in his view, although he could scare people, was also scared.*

Both Frankenstein and the Monster, Whale hopes, will profoundly haunt audiences. It will require incisive casting.

Bela Lugosi as *Dracula*, with Helen Chandler. The entire purpose of *Frankenstein*, originally, was to provide Lugosi a follow-up to *Dracula* with Lugosi as the Monster.

The last *Frankenstein* clipping that Bela Lugosi adds to his scrapbook is dated June 30—the day after the *Hollywood Daily Citizen* had reported Whale will direct the film. Whale apparently immediately expresses his ideas about casting, and that he doesn't want Lugosi as the Monster.

Thursday, July 2: The *Los Angeles Examiner* reports that Universal has switched Lugosi to *Murders in the Rue Morgue*. Robert Florey will direct the Poe film. It's apparently a consolation prize for having lost *Frankenstein.*

Friday, July 3: Whale begins two days of additional scenes for *Waterloo Bridge*, including a gala musical opening on a theater stage.

It's about this time that Whale quickly finds his Monster: Boris Karloff, a gaunt 43-year-old Englishman exiled by his British family over 20 years ago for his desire to be an actor. Karloff has a dark, satanic face, beautiful deep-brown eyes and, as Whale later expressed it, a "queer, penetrating personality." An on-the-rise character actor, Karloff is lunching in Universal's commissary while playing a gangster in *Graft*—snarling such lines as, "That dame's dynamite!" *Graft* wraps up July 12, so it's within two weeks of Whale's assignment to *Frankenstein* that he beckons Karloff to his table, tells him his face has "startling possibilities," and invites him to take a screen test.

"For what?" asks Karloff politely.

"For a damned awful Monster!" quips Whale.

"I'd be delighted!" says Karloff.

Karloff soon begins nightly experiments with Universal makeup chief Jack P. Pierce on the Monster makeup, with input by Whale. Meanwhile ...

Tuesday, July 14: Variety reports that Carl Laemmle, Sr. has left for New York, from where he'll sail to Europe and not to return until mid-September. This leaves Carl Laemmle, Jr. unfettered to call the shots. Meanwhile, as part of his 25th anniversary as Universal's founder, Laemmle, Sr. had engaged British poet and playwright John Drinkwater, noted for a play about Lincoln, to write his biography: *The Life and Adventures of Carl Laemmle*. Also on July 14, *Variety* notes:

> *Not to be outdone by his father, Carl Laemmle, Jr. is having his biography written. No title as yet.*

Junior is only 23-years-old, a bit young for a biography. At any rate, he relishes his power, and soon has the nickname of "Little Napoleon."

Thursday, July 16: *The Brooklyn Standard Union* publishes this significant story:

> *Junior Laemmle is going to give director James Whale the best cast available for Universal's new picture,* Frankenstein. *Bela Lugosi, who was originally slated for the picture, has been assigned a role in* Murders in the Rue Morgue *instead.*
>
> *However, negotiations have been completed with MGM, and Leslie Howard, one of MGM's contract players, will be borrowed for the leading role.*

Howard is a good choice; one of his recent stage successes was *Berkeley Square*, John L. Balderston's fantasy play that Howard had produced, directed, and starred in on Broadway, in 1929/1930. He was also the star of Warner Bros.' mystical *Outward Bound* (1930). Howard's dashing, gifted, and is co-starring with Norma Shearer, Clark Gable, and Lionel Barrymore in MGM's big summer hit, *A Free Soul*.

James Whale doesn't want him. He wants Colin Clive.

The director is totally upsetting Universal's *Frankenstein* apple cart. Howard's a major star. Additionally, the whole reason for Universal producing *Frankenstein* is to mount a *Dracula* follow-up for Lugosi. Junior wants to pamper his new prized director, but also craves box office names to sell *Frankenstein*. Colin Clive, despite *Journey's End*, is no Leslie Howard, by box office standards. And who the hell is this Karloff, anyway?

As destiny will have it, Junior is otherwise focused in July of 1931.

Leslie Howard, Universal's first choice for the title role in *Frankenstein*.

Besides seeking a biographer, he's personally producing *Strictly Dishonorable*, a risqué comedy starring his paramour of the moment, Sidney Fox. Ms. Fox is a four foot, 11 inch brunette, one of the few actresses in Hollywood who, in high heels, isn't taller than Junior (although about the same height).

John M. Stahl, whose clout at Universal exceeds even Whale's, is directing, under scrutiny from Junior to show Sidney to best advantage. Aware that she's hardly a great beauty, Stahl cautiously minimizes Sidney's close-ups. He also tries to conceal her slightly plump figure but isn't entirely successful.

"Don't eat starchy foods, Sidney," one reviewer will snipe after *Strictly Dishonorable*'s premiere.

Whale constantly pitches for Colin as *Frankenstein*. Junior, emotionally involved in *Strictly Dishonorable* and always a gambler, has to go either with big box office casting, or trust his new director's instinct.

Tuesday, July 28: The following news appears on page six of *Variety:*

> Clive For "Frankie"
>   *Universal cabled to London for Colin Clive to come over for* Franken-
> stein. *James Whale used him in* Journey's End *and wants him back. Francis
> Edward Faragoh is now writing the dialogue, succeeding John Russell, who
> succeeded Garrett Fort.*

Tuesday, August 4: "Clive Insisted Upon," headlines *Variety*, reporting that Colin will

James Whale. He had his own very distinctive ideas about *Frankenstein*'s casting.

return to Hollywood with a 10-week guarantee for *Frankenstein*. Noting that Colin comes at the "insistence of James Whale," *Variety* infers controversy: "Studio choice for the lead is Leslie Howard. Whale demanded Clive on the strength of what he did with him in *Journey's End*."

The wording sounds suggestive, probably intentionally. From this point on, Hollywood gossip will claim Whale and Colin are lovers. Some still believe it over 85 years later. The rumor will even impact some writers' analyses of *Frankenstein*—two homosexual men, as director and actor, creating their own man, and similar agenda-driven interpretations.

Impossible to disprove? Probably. Likely to have been the case? Definitely not.

Colin Clive has accepted a new Hollywood film, despite what he'd told *The Picturegoer* shortly before about never wanting to do another movie. He's agreed without seeing a script and clearly out of loyalty to James Whale, who's now triumphed in his choice for *Frankenstein*'s title role.

The fight over who'll play the Monster continues.

Saturday, August 8: Colin Clive sails from Southampton, heading to New York on the *Aquitania*.

Meanwhile, as Colin makes his way to Hollywood, James Whale attends an evening party at "Dias Dorados," the Laemmle estate in Benedict Canyon, to honor the widow of Notre Dame football coach Knute Rockne. On March 31, Rockne died in a plane crash in Kansas while en route to appear in Universal's *The Spirit of Notre Dame*, and the studio postponed production until this summer. The film stars Lew Ayres and features the college's famed "Four Horsemen" and others of its gridiron stars. At "Dias Dorados," an orchestra plays, a buffet is served, Chinese lanterns light the grounds, and the many celebrities include Lew Ayres, Mae Clarke, Walter Huston, Ginger Rogers, Paul Lukas, and Jean Harlow.

It's a safe bet that Whale doesn't ask Harlow for a dance.

Mae Clarke in *Waterloo Bridge*, Whale's premiere film for Universal. As the doomed prostitute Myra, Mae Clarke played one of Whale's "lost souls."

Colin Clive arrives in New York Friday afternoon, August 14. Awaiting him is a special delivery parcel from James Whale, with this letter:

> *I am sending you herewith copy of the script* Frankenstein.
> *It is a grand part and I think will fit you as well as Stanhope. I think the cast will be old Frederick Kerr as your father, Baron Frankenstein; John Boles as Victor, Bela Lugosi or Boris Karloff as the Monster, Dwight Frye as the Dwarf, Van Sloan as Dr. Waldman, and I am making a test of Mae Clarke as Elizabeth. Although it is largely an English cast, I do not want too much English accent about it, so in studying the part please keep this in mind. Of course, I do not want an American accent, but it is well to talk to as many Americans as you can to get that looseness, instead of what Americans think of as English tightness, in speech. Do not let this worry you, it is merely a note.*

There are several significant things in the paragraph. Note that Whale writes that it will be "Bela Lugosi or Boris Karloff as the Monster," with Lugosi mentioned first. Presumably, Junior Laemmle is still pushing for Lugosi—who, despite his later remarks that he'd rejected the role, really has no legal or financial footing to do so (and likely would have been blackballed by Universal if he had). Karloff's tests with Jack Pierce are apparently still continuing. Also, notice that Whale, aware of Colin's temperament, is clearly concerned that he not upset him, with his "Don't let this worry you" in regard to the accent.

> *I see Frankenstein as an intensely sane person, at times rather fanatical and in one or two scenes a little hysterical, and a little reminiscent of the breakdown in* Journey's End. *Similarly to Stanhope, Frankenstein's nerves are all to pieces. He is a very strong, extremely dominant personality, sometimes quite strange and queer, sometimes very soft, sympathetic and decidedly romantic. He hates causing anxiety to Elizabeth and his father, but his passionate zeal and his invention forced him to do so. He is pulled two ways—his love for Elizabeth and his almost insane passion for his experiments. In the first scene in his laboratory he becomes very conscious of the theatrical drama and goes a little insane about it. All the time one should feel that Frankenstein is normally extremely intelligent, a sane and loveable person, never unsympathetic, even to the Monster.*

The words reveal Whale's insight that will give *Frankenstein* its subversive brilliance. Robert Florey's original script had delineated Frankenstein as a bully who sadistically tortures his Monster. Whale's "sympathetic and decidedly romantic" Frankenstein, in his "almost insane passion," loves his creature. Come the climactic chase, as he leads the torch-bearing villagers in pursuit of the Monster, his melancholy bearing will be almost that of a mercy killing.

> *There are none of Dracula's maniacal cackles. I want the picture to be a very modern, materialistic treatment of this medieval story—something of 'Doctor Caligari,' something of Edgar Allan Poe, and of course a good deal of us. I know you will understand that none of this is to alarm you. It is just to make you feel certain about it, because I know you are absolutely right for it. I thought I would let you have the script so that you could think about it on the train. Some of the lines may be slightly altered, as this is an unfinished script, so do not get too set on the lines. We shall have about three days' rehearsals and tests before we actually shoot the picture.*

The "maniacal cackles" line seems another slam at Lugosi—who actually never cackles once in *Dracula*—yet Whale makes his point. His words that "none of this is to alarm you" is again testimony to his caution in handling Colin, as is his rather touching assurance, "I know you are absolutely right for it."

As for Whale's reference to reading the script "on the train"—Colin, rather than embarking by train, takes a plane to Hollywood, quite an adventure in those days. The *Los Angeles Record* reports on Wednesday, August 19:

> *Colin Clive, the actor who came all the way from London to play* Franken- stein, *made it here in eight days flat. His boat was a day and a half ahead of schedule because of some nice winds, and the same cause brought his airplane in eight hours ahead of time.*
>
> *If this keeps up he should finish* Frankenstein *in about a week.*

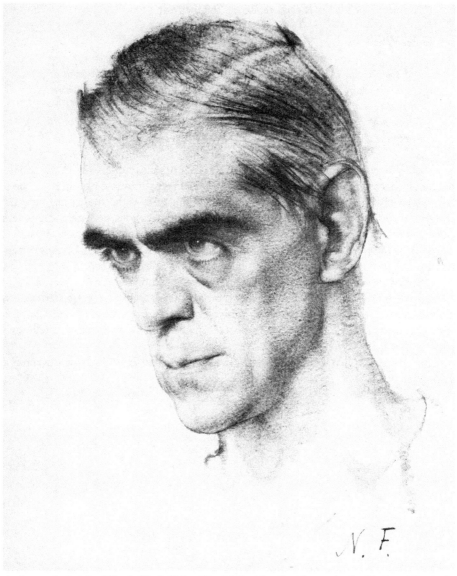

A charcoal sketch of Boris Karloff, by Nicolai Fechin, that hangs in the National Portrait Gallery, London. James Whale thought Karloff's face and "queer, penetrating personality" made him ideal as Frankenstein's Monster.

This visit, there will be no pressure such as the merciless schedule on *Journey's End*. Whale, aware of how perilously close Colin had come to an alcoholic breakdown on that shoot, will see to that.

Indeed, this time, things will be different. Colin will find himself working at a beautiful, almost pastoral lot, rather than the hotbox confines of Tiffany Studios. Universal, always peculiar, will offer its share of laughs, often at its own expense. Indeed, Colin arrives just in time for a new "crisis:" USC fullback Jim Musick, working in *The Spirit of Notre Dame*, has helped himself to two lunch boxes—and is promptly fired.

"Disgraced," headlines *Variety,* reporting the incident.

James Whale said:

> *I chose Colin Clive for* Frankenstein *because he had exactly the kind of tenacity to go through with anything, together with the kind of romantic quality that makes strong men leave civilization to shoot big game. There's also a level-headedness about Clive that keeps him in full control of himself even in his craziest moments in the picture.*

Colin's 10-week guarantee allows for several days of rehearsals, as well as time allotted for any necessary retakes. He has a director who'll pamper him, a leading lady who'll fall in love with him virtually at first sight, star-billing and, at the studio, his own star cottage. *Frankenstein* will be, with a few startlingly ugly exceptions, perhaps the happiest engagement of Colin Clive's film career.

During the week of rehearsals, almost on the eve of shooting, Universal finally selects its Monster. Junior Laemmle, at the 11th hour, approves Whale's choice.

"Karloff's eyes mirrored the suffering we needed," Junior will say.

There's more in Karloff's eyes than suffering—there's a striking, eerie star quality. Colin's Fallen Angel handsomeness and "shoot big game" presence, along with Karloff's stitched-together corpse look and "queer penetrating personality," will unleash the "insane passion" that James Whale desires.

Frankenstein will transcend being a mere follow-up to *Dracula.* It will become a phenomenon.

Chapter Thirteen
1931 Prometheus

Monday, August 24, 1931: *Frankenstein* begins shooting at Universal City, California. The previous day, the Los Angeles temperature had shot into the 90s, creating a mass rush to the beaches. Today is fair, cooler, and quite beautiful.

The approved final budget is $262,007; the schedule, 30 days. James Whale will shoot, wherever possible, in sequence, a rarity in Hollywood, and the first episode filmed is the cemetery scene opening. The mourners climb the soundstage graveyard hill, following a priest reverently carrying a cross, from which hangs a black banner bearing the image of a skull-and-crossbones.

The first principal we see: Dwight Frye, as Fritz, the hunchbacked dwarf, peeking over a spiked iron fence that surrounds a grave. His crazed eyes convey his character's mania. The 32-year-old Frye, the fly-gobbling Renfield in *Dracula*, had been an acclaimed Broadway actor, playing in comedies, dramas, and musicals ... with a manic intensity. Frye acts Fritz with similar "Method" approach, scuttling between scenes in ghoulish character. As such, he's a bit unappetizing during the 11:00 a.m. and 4:00 p.m. tea breaks, which Whale calls "elevensies" and "foursies."

Frye ducks behind the grave, clearing the screen for our Byronic hero ... Colin Clive as Henry Frankenstein. Dark eyes, an almost ghostly white face ... he looks every bit "the pale student of unhallowed arts" that Mary Shelley described seeing in her 1816 vision.

"Down ... down, you fool!" he says to Fritz.

Colin Clive, in a shot designed to make Henry Frankenstein appear to have devil horns.

The opening scene of *Frankenstein*. Dwight Frye, Colin Clive, and the Grim Reaper.

Whale, with cinematographer Arthur Edeson, adds another clever touch. As Colin looks over the fence, the iron spikes frame his face and seemingly rise from his temples, as if they're horns. The subtle but definite impression—Colin's Frankenstein is a devil.

The mourners depart. The grave robbers attack. Whale delights in the Gothic atmosphere, showing us a cemetery statue of Christ Crucified ... and one of a robed Grim Reaper. In a shot cleverly symbolic of Frankenstein's contempt for the sacredness of Death, Colin casually tosses a shovel-full of dirt into the Reaper's skeletal face.

"He's just resting," says Colin's Frankenstein, almost affectionately patting the exhumed coffin. "Waiting for a *new* life to come!"

Incidentally, also on August 24, another horror picture has started shooting: Paramount's *Dr. Jekyll and Mr. Hyde*, starring Fredric March and directed by Rouben Mamoulian.

Tuesday, August 25: The graveyard scene continues. Whale also films that day the episode where Frankenstein and Fritz cut down the hanged corpse. Frye wriggles across the gibbet beam with a knife in his mouth to cut the rope; Colin watches below, holding a lantern whose light gives his face a satanic glow.

With these two wildly intense actors, Whale's fully aware he's handling dynamite.

Wednesday, August 26: Elizabeth (Mae Clarke) and Victor (John Boles) visit Dr. Waldman (Edward Van Sloan), who warns them about Frankenstein's "mad dream." Mae Clarke is the "Queen" of Universal, due to the "buzz" after her performance for Whale in *Waterloo Bridge*, set to premiere in Los Angeles next week. She hopes it makes audiences forget James Cagney smacking her in the face with a grapefruit earlier in '31 in Warner Bros.' *The Public Enemy*—a notoriety she'll despise the rest of her long life.

Also on August 26th: The Laemmles, hoping lightning strikes in *Frankenstein* in more than one way, offer Boris Karloff, yet to start work on the film, a Universal contract based on his screen test.

> *The producer hereby employs and engages the artist to render his exclusive services as an actor in the portrayal of the role of "THE MONSTER" in the producer's photoplay now entitled "FRANKENSTEIN," and the actor hereby accepts such employment ...*

The studio takes no risk in the seven-year contract. If *Frankenstein* proves a hit, the Laemmles have a "New Lon Chaney"; if it's a debacle—and Karloff's Creature proves the most grotesque white elephant in Hollywood history—the studio can simply drop him at its first option. The contract starts at $500 per week and features the traditional morals clause, insisting that "the Monster":

> *... conduct himself with due regard to public conventions and morals, and that he will not do or commit any act or thing that will tend to degrade him in society, or bring him into public hatred, contempt, scorn, or ridicule, or that will tend to shock, insult or offend the community or ridicule public morals ...*

Thursday August 27: Edward Van Sloan as Dr. Waldman addresses a group of extras at "Goldstadt University" about the "Normal Brain" and the "Criminal Brain." As they leave, Frye's Fritz pries open a window with his tiny cane and hobbles into the darkened

Edward Van Sloan as Dr. Waldman lecturing on brains.

room. A gong startles him, he drops the normal brain on the floor ... and escapes with the criminal brain.

The past two days off provide Colin a mid-week mini-vacation—a luxury he'd never enjoyed during the filming of *Journey's End*. He's quick to discover that Hollywood offers all variety of sports and games. Later asked by the *New York Times* if he'd enjoyed *Frankenstein*'s shoot, Colin will reply:

> Oh crikey! I should say that I did. It was marvelous ... What pleased me most there was the frankness and cordiality of every one's welcome. I have a tremendous admiration for America.
>
> As a visitor to your country, and particularly an English visitor, I especially welcomed this readiness on the part of every one to make friends and to meet one more than half way. I had no trouble in getting golf and tennis games. As a matter of fact, the only trouble I had in regard to sports was to get the time to engage in them. I took up coffee drinking and I am only hoping that I will find some place in England where I can get coffee as it is made in the United States.

He works hard and plays hard, but this time, fortunately, he doesn't drink hard. The coffee helps keep him on the wagon.

Come late in the week, Colin is on Universal's Stage 12, feverishly acting on the tower laboratory set. Dwight Frye is with him, along with a bevy of unholy electrical gadgets provided by electrical special effects maestro, Kenneth Strickfaden.

In his white laboratory gown, the tall, willowy Colin seems both wizard and witch, an androgynous demon lover, magnificently capturing Frankenstein's "mad dream," his daring ... his agony. He also captures his romantic fervor; as played and directed, Colin's Frankenstein is more heroic than horrific.

> The storm will be magnificent. All the electrical secrets of Heaven! And this time we're ready. Eh, Fritz? Ready!

The special effects lightning and thunder abound. And now joining the show, half-naked under a sheet, his face covered, awaiting the Monster's unholy birth: Karloff.

This weekend, there's a full moon over Hollywood.

Monday, August 31: All the principals of *Frankenstein*—Clive, Karloff, Clarke, Boles, Van Sloan, and Frye—will be in the tower laboratory for a week. Next Monday is Labor Day, a holiday, so the company will work this coming Sunday. Colin Clive is at the top of his Grand Guignol game:

> That body is not dead. It has never lived. I created it! I made it with my own hands, from the bodies I took from graves, from the gallows, anywhere!

Mae Clarke, blonde, nervous, 21 years old, has met her leading man at the rehearsals. Colin, dramatically unleashed in Frankenstein's tower laboratory, totally awes her. The hair that falls over one eye, the restlessness as he smokes between scenes, his charm as he jokes with her, teases her ...

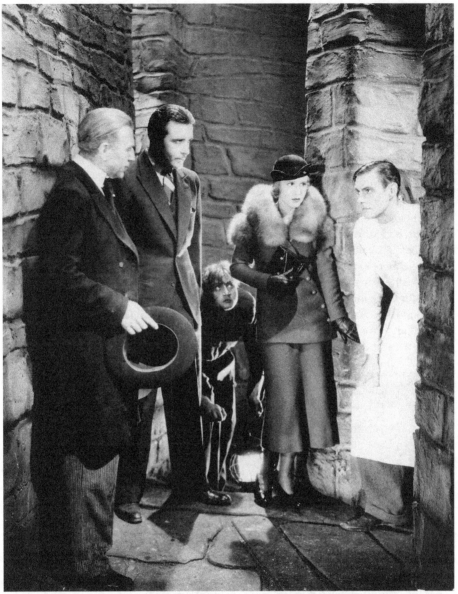

Edward Van Sloan, John Boles, Dwight Frye, Mae Clarke, and Colin Clive.

Colin Clive was the dearest, kindest man, who gave you importance. He was so wonderful, so clever. When he started acting in a scene, I wanted to stop and just watch. I'd think, "Here I am, playing scenes with this marvelous actor!"

Mr. Whale would say, "Colin's voice is like a pipe organ. I just pull out the stops, and he produces his music."

Colin was electric. I was mesmerized by him—so much that I hoped it didn't show! When he looked at me, I'd flush. I was afraid he could tell I was having these terrific thoughts about him!

Mae is fragile emotionally; within six months she'll suffer a breakdown and enter a sanitarium. To her, Colin Clive seems a Byronic fantasy hero in the flesh. The infatuation will last the rest of her life.

The laboratory tower episode climaxes, indelibly, with the creation of the Monster. Whale directs with brilliant theatricality.

"Quite a good scene, isn't it?" says Dr. Frankenstein, increasingly hysterical. "One Man *CRAZY* ... three very sane spectators!"

The storm peaks. The unholy miracle begins. "One great and special Fourth of July fireworks display—just for us!" Mae Clarke will recall. The Strickfaden gadgetry sparks and roars. Karloff goes on the star-making ride of his life, the operating table rising on chains, over 40 feet up to Stage 12's tower roof, the crew in the rafters shaking white-hot carbons to simulate lightning.

"I hoped no one up there had butterfingers!" Karloff will say 30 years later.

The table lowers, its chains rattling. The magic moment arrives. The newborn's stitched wrist quivers ... and moves.

"Look ... it's moving ... it's alive ..."

Then, more loudly, passionately, insanely, exultantly.

"It's alive, it's alive ... *IT'S ALIVE!*"

Colin Clive lunges, his body seemingly out of control, like a suddenly violent un-caged animal. Edward Van Sloan and John Boles rush to restrain him.

"Henry" says Boles, "in the name of God!"

"In the name of God!" cries Colin. "Now I know what it feels like to BE God!"

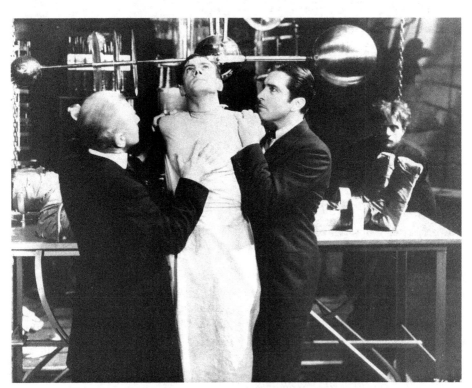

"It's alive!"

The "It's alive!" line is honored today as #49 among the American Film Institute's "100 Years ... 100 Movie Quotes." The "In the name of God ..." blasphemy, cut for the late 1930s reissue, will finally return in the Digital Age. Colin Clive's wild mix of crazed laughter and exultant triumph is brilliant, as is the dash of raw anguish; there's a fear, an anger, that God in His Heaven has allowed this blasphemy to happen.

After all, ... Isn't *He* watching? Shouldn't *He* have sent one of those lightning bolts that gave birth to the Monster down into the laboratory ... to strike Frankenstein dead for his audacity?

Yet, there's an extra spark. Perhaps the special magic of Colin's delivery is its tingling sense of sexual climax—the sensual euphoria that he's actually "turned-on" playing God. This is what the mimics inevitably try to imitate, but always miss. Only one actor ever really nailed it.

"Insane passion," indeed!

During this week leading to the Monster's birthday, there's a curious sideshow. Thursday, September 3, is the Los Angeles premiere of *Waterloo Bridge*, for which all of Universal, especially James Whale and Mae Clarke, have such high hopes.

Mae so admires her *Frankenstein* leading man—and has such a crush on him—that she invites Colin to be the Master of Ceremonies at the premiere tonight at the Orpheum Theatre.

There is, of course, a dangerous risk in this invitation.

For Colin, who still suffers anxiety and stage fright, the idea of a Hollywood "personal appearance" terrifies him. He's also quite frazzled, having been playing the past several days with such high-caliber intensity.

The invited guests list boasts Clark Gable, Douglas Fairbanks, Jr. and Joan Crawford (the couple married at the time), Lew Ayres, Helen Twelvetrees, Walter Huston, Marilyn Miller, Wheeler and Woolsey, Robert Montgomery, and Richard Dix. Junior Laemmle will be there too, as will Sidney Fox. KECA Radio will broadcast the premiere, with Ken Murray and Freeman Lang describing the arrival of the guests.

If, by chance, Colin has a "slip" during his M.C. appearance, he'll do so over the airwaves and before the eyes of a star-studded crowd. It would be disastrous. However, for Mae, who clearly adores him, and for "Jimmy," who recognizes the danger but trusts him, he agrees.

8:30 p.m.: The festivities begin. Mae Clarke will later describe the night as a "mini-premiere" ("only one searchlight," she said), but the crowd cheers the attending celebrities ... and the powerful film is a hit. Afterwards, Colin takes to the Orpheum stage, and presents the cast: Bette Davis (in one of her first film roles as the sister of Roy, the soldier who falls in love with Myra), Enid Bennett (Roy's mother), Frederick Kerr (Roy's father, and also playing Colin's father in *Frankenstein*), Doris Lloyd (Kitty, Myra's streetwalker crony), Kent Douglas (aka Douglass Montgomery, as Roy), and Mae Clarke (Myra), adorned "in a love-bird green lace dress, with velvet wrap to match, and an orchid corsage." Colin also introduces James Whale.

Colin Clive is, by all accounts, a dashing Master of Ceremonies, despite his nerves. Mae, more agog over him than ever, is glad her fiancé is there, lest she succumb to "my stormy waves of fancy for Colin."

James Whale and Colin, as seen from the rafters of Soundstage 12.

Colin's pulled it off ... and is due back on the *Frankenstein* set the next day.

> *Where should we be if nobody tried to find out what lies beyond? Have you never wanted to look beyond the clouds and the stars, or to know what causes the trees to bud? And what changes the darkness into light?*

"One Man *Crazy* ...!"

Incredibly, in *Frankenstein*, only a short time after revealing himself to be Hollywood's Maddest Doctor, Colin Clive's Henry Frankenstein also delivers as a virtual poet. The Monster Maker is at his leisure, sitting in the tower lab, smoking a cigar. Jimmy Whale, who favors cigars and frequently smokes one on the set, surely suggested the cheroot. As a former actor, Whale vicariously sees himself playing Frankenstein some days, the Monster on others. He also undoubtedly had asked for this marvelous "Where should we be ..." speech, that was missing in Florey's script and was, apparently, a late addition to the final script by Garrett Fort and Francis Edward Faragoh:

> *But if you talk like that, people call you crazy. Well, if I could discover just one of these things—what eternity is, for example—I wouldn't care if they did think I was crazy!*

Colin Clive speaks these words so fervently, so sensitively, that he performs one of the miracles of *Frankenstein*—he seduces a viewer to want to *be* Frankenstein.

Yet the most remarkable miracle of *Frankenstein* is about to make his official entrance.

Boris Karloff said:

> *The most heartrending aspect of the Creature's life, for us, was his ultimate desertion by his creator. It was as though man, in his blundering, searching attempts to improve himself, was to find himself deserted by his God.*

He enters, as brilliantly staged by Whale—backwards—turning slowly for those classic close-ups ... Karloff, as the Monster. The makeup by Jack P. Pierce is still a shocker—a sewn-and-stitched-together corpse, bolts in his neck, a wild creature, zapped to

The introduction of Karloff's Monster. Note the insane yet seductive eyes.

"Man looking at God!" – Karloff's Monster sees the sun.

life by lightning. Yet most amazing of all are Karloff's eyes. Hooded by the lizard eyelids made of mortician's wax, the eyes instantly convey insanity ... yet also *beauty*. Karloff had perhaps the most striking eyes of any actor in 1931 Hollywood, and his Monster's eyes seem almost feminine, as if we're seeing the eyes of Garbo—exhumed after being buried alive, and having gone stark crazy.

Once again, a macabre seduction seems at play as the Monster's eyes stare at the audience, pleading for acceptance ...

Henry Frankenstein gently tries to teach his Creature. The Monster reaches for the sun, shining through the open skylight. Mae Clarke, although not on call, is on the set this day—all the females want a peek at the Monster—and will remember:

> *I thought Karloff was magnificent. That scene with the skylight! When he looked up and up and up, and waved his hands at the light, it was a spiritual lesson: looking at God! It was like when we die, the Beatific vision, which makes people understand the words: "Eye has not seen, nor ears heard, the glories that God has prepared for those who love Him."*

Indeed, come the Monster, and *Frankenstein* takes on an increasingly bizarre religious tone—odd, perhaps, since Whale is agnostic and neither actor is religious, at least in a formal sense. The skylight scene almost suggests a medieval miracle play—the soulless Monster pleading to God for a soul, and—based on Karloff's evolving performance—God giving him one.

Frankenstein is joyful at his Creature's early mime—"See? He understands!" he exclaims to Waldman. Then comes the true horror: Fritz, tormenting the frightened Monster.

"Get away with that torch!" orders Frankenstein, protective of his newborn.

Yet the hunchbacked dwarf, thrilled to abuse a being more grotesque than he, defies him. We see Karloff's Monster in the tower dungeon, thrashing in chains, his high-pitched screams almost female, his fear and agony painful to see and hear. Frye's Fritz goes at him with his torch. The pitiful anguish in Karloff's face, and the sadistic glee in Frye's, are so intense that the censors will cut them from *Frankenstein's* re-release in the late 1930s.

Karloff, Colin, Frye, and Van Sloan: The fight to control the frightened, dangerous Monster.

Karloff relaxes as Jack Pierce and an assistant touch up his makeup.

"Oh, leave *it* alone, Fritz," Frankenstein says wearily, too frazzled to be forceful. "Leave *it* alone." His synthetic being, which he previously referred to as "he," is now an "it."

Now Fritz lashes the Monster with a whip. And when the Monster breaks his bonds, killing the dwarf—hanging him with his own whip—we side with the Monster. We see how this tragedy has ravaged Frankenstein, and we sense his depth of guilt at Waldman's offer to mercy-kill the Creature. But the Monster kills Waldman ... and escapes the tower laboratory.

Karloff's Monster is amok.

"Boris Karloff," Mae Clarke remembers a half-century later. "A pussy cat!"

"Dear Boris" is a joy, bravely professional in his torturous Monster makeup and costume, funny and charming as he relaxes between scenes, sprawling in a striped beach lounge chair, smoking a cigarette, sipping his tea or coffee, slyly smiling as he sings Cockney Music Hall ditties:

> *In Westminster, not long ago*
> *There lived a Rat Catcher's Daughter ...*
> *Doodle dee! ... doodle da!*

Whale addresses the actors by their role names; he calls Colin "Henry" and Boris "Frankenstein," which surely would have upset a purist scholar visiting the set. The Monster certainly attracts attention, and Universal fans the fire with stories, some published, some leaked:

"One Man *Crazy* ...!"

• There's the penny dreadful tale that a secretary on the Universal lot, coming around a corner, saw Karloff—and instantly fainted.

• There's the follow-up that Karloff must walk to and from the set with a veil over his face, escorted by Jack Pierce, by order of Carl Laemmle, Sr.

• A rumor spreads at Universal that Karloff, who must strip off his perspiration-soaked Monster costume every noon or risk pneumonia, has lunch daily in his own private bungalow stark naked. Imaginations boggle.

There's even a saga that Karloff, who's been married four times, allegedly has a reputation as "a swordsman." The rumor: Jimmy Whale cast Boris as the Monster due to tales about the actor's quite splendid natural endowment.

"Monster indeed!" Karloff might have laughed. It's perhaps luridly prophetic of Teri Garr's "schwanzstucker" line in Mel Brooks' 1974 *Young Frankenstein*.

Karloff makes his way, his face shrouded, Jack Pierce at his side.

Mollie Merrick, reporter, visits the *Frankenstein* stage. Colin Clive sits amiably with Ms. Merrick, talking of his choice of the role:

> *Naturally, I like everything that is different and this is a distinct variation from the part of Stanhope and from the sort of thing I attempted last winter in New York [Overture]. The theme of the story—a young scientist who creates a human being and imbues it with life—fits in with some of the most recent scientific experiments of the day. That he brings to life a monster who understands nothing but murder—a fiend whose compulsion is to kill—makes the weird story one of the most gripping and compelling things ever filmed.*

Of course, the approach to the Monster is calculated for sympathy, but Colin knows how to appeal to a 1931 female reporter. Mollie is all eyes as Karloff arrives on the set, and the actor charmingly captivates her:

> *In transit from his dressing room to the stage, Karloff wears a sort of cage over his head with thick veiling which conceals him from the studio staff as well as casual passers-by ...*
>
> *Karloff speaks the most perfect English one could wish for. His voice, a mellow exquisite baritone, will be heard to excellent advantage ...*

Obviously, Ms. Merrick has no idea Karloff only howls and screams as the Monster, but no matter. She's impressed properly, and concludes her report:

> *Colin Clive—half-British, half-French (sic)—has English reserve and modesty coupled with Gallic charm ... James Whale is considered one of the truly inspired directors of this locale ... No finer cast could possibly be assembled.*
>   *The trend of the times is toward the unearthly, the ghoulish, the weird, the fourth dimensional.* Frankenstein *achieves all of these things ...*

Whale is pleased that Mollie Merrick ends her report with a salute to Colin Clive and to him. However, he fears the inevitable: Karloff is taking *Frankenstein*. Whale's desire to make a film, as he expressed to Colin, with "a good deal of us," is in peril: Overshadowing them is an actor who'd agreed to fourth billing.

Jimmy Whale isn't very nice about it. Aware of Karloff's early struggles and survival jobs, he starts referring to him as "the truck driver."

Anxiety infiltrates *Frankenstein*. The film is falling behind schedule. Colin, who has no ego, is content to allow Karloff his success, but likely frets, characteristically, that he himself is not delivering to full effect. Karloff is having his own troubles. For all his humor and professionalism, the actor is finding playing the Monster to be harrowing, physically and emotionally; for all his sympathy for the Monster, he realizes how horrific he is. As the appalled critic for *The Sun* newspaper will write in November after *Frankenstein* opens in Baltimore:

> *... this fiend is the embodiment of everything evil in human experience ... It will hold the spectator spellbound ... and afterward come to him in nightmares ...*

"I dreamed *Frankenstein*," Karloff later confesses, admitting he suffered his own nightmares while playing this "fiend." Especially agonizing for him is the scene where the Monster drowns Little Maria in the mountain lake. It makes him ill to think about it. Perhaps, before Whale shoots the episode, he can reason with him ...

Colin, meanwhile, shows increasing anxiety. In his restless way, he wants to ask Mae Clarke for a date and asks Whale's advice. Whale nixes the idea, telling Colin, perhaps a bit stingingly, that Mae won't go out with married men.

Also, Mae Clarke, originally finding her leading man so romantic a figure, now senses something else ... an unusual melancholy. She'll recall over 50 years later:

> *He was the handsomest man I ever saw—and also the saddest. Colin's sadness was elusive; the sadness you see if you contemplate many of the master painters' and sculptors' conceptions of the face of Christ—the ultimate source, in my view, of all sadness.*

Strange words, and a strange irony—considering the actor was playing a man daring to be God.

Pauline Moore, a 17-year-old Universal starlet, is one of the bridesmaids in *Frankenstein*. She'll remember over 60 years later:

Boris Karloff was funny! He'd be standing around in his Monster suit, and he liked to walk up behind the girls, who were new on the set (like me), and—Boo—he'd hover till they turned and saw him and screamed! There was a nice friendly feeling on the Frankenstein *set.*

CARL LAEMMLE presents

"FRANKENSTEIN"
THE MAN WHO MADE A MONSTER

A UNIVERSAL PICTURE

Pauline Moore, amongst the bridesmaids, was saved by real-life hero Colin Clive during filming on the set of *Frankenstein*. Mae Clarke is shown here as the unconscious Elizabeth surrounded in the scene by many of the wedding guests and bridal party cast members.

There's a horrific near-disaster—a huge klieg light rips away and falls from a catwalk. Colin, seeing and hearing the light, grabs Pauline and yanks her to safety.

"If Colin hadn't pulled me into a doorway," Moore would recall, "we both would have been crushed!"

Colin Clive, hero of *Frankenstein*, becomes a real-life hero.

The fears, insecurities, and very nature of the film ... all these things sizzle like a witch's cauldron. Yet on the surface, high spirits prevail. The morning and afternoon tea, Whale's "elevensies" and "foursies," are always a sight to see, marked by English etiquette. "Everyone on the set had his own cup and saucer," remembered Mae Clarke. "No Dixie cups would do." On especially hot days, they relax outside, under an old eucalyptus tree. Colin, with "the face of Christ," smokes a cigarette. Boris, "the embodiment of everything evil," sings in his beach chair. "Jimmy" elegantly presides, as the shepherd and sheep walk above on the hillside.

A candid taken at Busch Gardens, Pasadena, Saturday, September 19, 1931. Colin's expression is almost frightening. (Courtesy of Sally Stark)

Saturday, September 19: The *Frankenstein* Company visits Pasadena's Busch Gardens for the brief episode where Henry Frankenstein and Elizabeth discuss their upcoming wedding. Colin and Mae Clarke, the latter in a bonnet and beautiful dress, sit on a platform in the garden, dogs at their feet. The film has been in production now for a full four weeks. Colin's becoming increasingly jittery.

"One Man *Crazy* ...!"

Between scenes, somebody snaps a picture.

The shot is almost frightening. Mae Clarke, who will always cherish the memory of Colin sending her a six-foot box of flowers one day during *Frankenstein* when she was indisposed, smiles sweetly, as an infatuated ingénue should. Colin's face, however, is a lightning bolt. He glares at the camera, his eyes angry, and his expression almost chillingly sad. If he has the Jekyll/Hyde nature David Manners remembered on *Journey's End*, this is Hyde.

Mae Clarke, although disturbed by the picture, saves it. Many years later, she shows it to an acquaintance, who asks about Colin Clive. Startled again by her co-star's expression, she gives the acquaintance the picture, saying sadly, "Keep this for me." The acquaintance later gives the picture to Clive fan Sally Stark ... who provides a copy for me.

At times a picture, for good or ill, is truly worth a thousand words.

Colin stays sober. Golf games. Tennis games. Horseback riding. Coffee.

There's pageantry, especially in the night scene of Colin Clive's Dr. Frankenstein, marching with the torch-bearing villagers through the back lot Tyrolean village, the bloodhounds barking, pursuing the Monster, Whale directing the spectacle with flair.

Yet there's also a sense of escalating tension, and a trace of sadism in the way Whale treats Karloff. Late in his life, Karloff will confide to a friend at a London theatrical club that Jimmy Whale behaved at times like "Queen of the Flippin' May" during *Frankenstein*, refusing to allow Karloff time off even to go to the toilet. Whale tells the Monster to go off in a corner and pee in a bucket. One guesses that, by rights of *Journey's End* and his top billing, Colin Clive continues bathroom privileges.

When the cast moves inside a soundstage, with artificial mountains and a night sky backdrop that looks, depending on your opinion, either wrinkled or Expressionistic ... or both—trouble escalates. Whale demands realism as Clive and Karloff fight as Frankenstein vs. Monster. At a recent theater showing of *Frankenstein*, the audience gasped when Colin, having dropped his torch, clearly falls on top of the flame—but continues the scene.

Monday, September 28: It's the final week of the shooting, and *Frankenstein* hits its Circus Maximus of offscreen angst.

It happens at Malibou Lake, far west in the Santa Monica Mountains ... the Drowning of Little Maria episode. Seven-year-old Marilyn Harris, in real life the haunted child of a sadistic mother—"Oh, she was a *witch!*" trembled Marilyn over 65 years later—arrives on location in a limousine, having driven the nearly 30 miles with Karloff in full Monster guise.

> *Boris Karloff was a very sweet, wonderful man, and I just loved him. Immediately ... I just loved him. I had no fear of him, whatsoever. We seemed to have a rapport together—and it was like magic ...*

Away from the child, Karloff pleads his case to Whale ... why can't the Monster and Little Maria just play with the flowers? Why must he drown her? The crew, aware of the debate, emotionally sides with Karloff.

"You see, it's all part of the *ritual*," replies Whale.

Karloff obeys—he has no choice. They throw flowers into the lake. Karloff's Monster laughs like a baby, giving a falsetto giggle. Then there are no more flowers. He reaches for Little Maria. The child splashes into the lake. Making it all the more horrible is the shriek of Marilyn's hysterically excited mother, screaming:

"Throw her in again! *Farther!*"

The flower game at Malibou Lake. Boris Karloff and Marilyn Harris.

A retake is necessary—on the first toss, Marilyn actually floats, like the flower. The death scene will require a change of costume and ultimately take two days to shoot. Whale offers Marilyn anything she wants to do the scene again. She asks for a dozen hard-boiled eggs. Whale will send her *two*-dozen.

The scene is bewitching cinema. There's no more horrible an atrocity than the killing of a child, yet Karloff's Monster—in his joy to have a playmate, his happy bewilderment, his spastic hysteria after he realizes what he's done—makes the Monster profoundly pitiable, despite the fact that he's drowned a little girl before our very eyes.

Nevertheless, Karloff never gets over it. "It was wanton brutality ...," Karloff, at age 80, will tell a reporter in 1968. "But Whale was the director and I was only an actor."

The truly wanton brutality was about to come.

The *Frankenstein* Company arrives back at the studio Tuesday, September 29. Whale announces he'll shoot tonight on the back lot—the scene where the Monster carries Frankenstein over his shoulder and up the hill to the windmill. Colin, who's had off the past two days, reports to Universal. Karloff is physically and emotionally wracked after two days on a hot location, and after having been in Pierce's makeup chair at 4:00 that morning. The "villagers" are there with their torches and bloodhounds. Karloff hoists Colin over his shoulder.

"Action!" cries Whale.

Karloff runs up the hill in his costume and heavy boots, barely outracing the bloodhounds and posse of villagers.

"Again!" shouts Whale.

And so, on Universal's back lot, under a waning moon, all of *Frankenstein*'s intensity explodes as Jimmy Whale tortures Boris Karloff. Anxiety, jealousy, revenge against Karloff

Michael Mark as Ludwig (Little Maria's father), Lionel Belmore as the Burgomaster, and Colin as Henry Frankenstein lead the villagers to kill the Monster.

for the insurrection at Malibou Lake ... it's an atrocity of ego and spite. Even the religious flourish that has become part of *Frankenstein* is evident: Boris Karloff is the Christus, carrying his cross up to a Universal Calvary; Colin Clive is his cross. Jimmy Whale, a sadistic Pilate, keeps this perverse Passion Play grinding all night long, taking the scene over and over, permanently damaging Karloff's back. The coyotes sounding their nightly howls in the hills add to the sadistic spectacle.

The sadism backfires. Although word of Whale's behavior doesn't leak outside Universal, it spreads like wildfire within the studio—raising Karloff from "Dear Boris" to "Saint Boris." In November of 1957, six months after Whale's suicide, Jack Pierce will appear on TV's *This Is Your Life* tribute to Karloff and tell this story. Pierce will mention Colin Clive, but significantly will not mention James Whale.

Karloff never forgets that horrible night. Little wonder that, in 1933, he'll become one of the most aggressive founders of the Screen Actors Guild.

Whale stays vicious. Clive and Karloff fight on the windmill balcony. The realism Whale demands throughout the Creator vs. Monster tussles ultimately causes Colin to dislocate an arm. The Monster hurls Frankenstein (a dummy) from the balcony ... we see his corpse riding on one of the windmill sails, then falling to the ground. The villagers set the windmill afire. Again, we hear the Monster's shrill, heartbreaking screams as the flames reach him.

The windmill burns on the mountain. Fade-out. THE END.

Classic climax: Colin's Frankenstein faces the Monster he created.

Saturday, October 3: There are only pick-up shots left to do. *Frankenstein* wraps up, five days over schedule. Colin, whose *Frankenstein* contract is still in effect, enjoys vacations at Lake Arrowhead and Palm Springs, while awaiting word from Whale if any retakes or revisions are necessary. There are none.

Tuesday, October 13: *Variety* writes that Colin can't decide "whether to return to home or remain here for pictures." The article claims that he has "offers from Paramount and Metro and an additional bid from Universal."

Monday, October 26: Colin had made his decision—he starts the long trip home this week. The moon is full again.

Thursday night, October 29: Whale previews *Frankenstein* in seaside Santa Barbara, 95 miles north of Los Angeles.

He would have liked Colin to have stayed, naturally, and see the film with an audience, but Colin had been as adamant as ever about not looking at himself on screen. The preview follows a screening of MGM's *New Adventures of Get-Rich-Quick Wallingford*, starring William Haines, Jimmy Durante, and Leila Hyams. *Frankenstein*'s opening credits show the cast list, with this teaser in fourth place:

The Monster ... ?

As such, despite being merely a "?," "the Monster" steals the cast list. The final credits will reveal the name, "Boris Karloff."

The *Frankenstein* preview is, as Harry Mines will report in the L.A. *Illustrated Daily News*, quite an event:

Frankenstein and his Monster, high on the windmill balcony, the villagers below. (Courtesy of John Antosiewicz)

Don't mention the name of James Whale to anyone in Santa Barbara. Else you will have a frantic, screaming mob on your hands.

Shades of Dracula, Edgar Allan Poe, and Honore de Balzac! Well, these boys have nothing on James Whale, when it comes to spreading horror. His production of Frankenstein *won for him a reputation in the northern city that is equal to none in motion pictures.*

During the preview, men and women in the audience, so it is said, looked like so many ostriches, in their attempts to hide their faces from the screen.

Those who weren't busily engaged in this occupation were being led from the theater, or else filling the air with lusty bellowing. Some were drawn to the screen by a weird fascination, others were frozen still, while one lady sitting in front of Mr. Whale was taken sick.

So now you see how terrifying this Frankenstein *thriller is.*

Oh, it was a night of nights in Santa Barbara!

The story quotes Whale: " ... I'll never, never forget that preview at Santa Barbara. It was worth making the picture just for that one showing. Such a reaction!"

As for Boris Karloff ... he prepares to celebrate Halloween with an all-new perspective, having put his heart and soul into portraying Frankenstein's Monster. He's fearful that *Frankenstein* has ruined his career (and his back) and has little or no faith in Universal extending his pot-of-gold contract.

Colin Clive – Frankenstein incarnate.

"One Man *Crazy* ...!"

"The Queen of the Flippin' May" didn't even invite him to the preview in Santa Barbara.

Top-billed Colin, meanwhile, boards the *Europa* in New York, to sail to Southampton. He chats with a reporter from the *New York Times*, who finds him sitting on a table in his cabin, happily "swinging his long legs to and fro," and homesick for England:

> *I think* Frankenstein *has an intense dramatic quality that continues throughout the play and culminates when I, in the title role, am killed by the Monster that I have created. This is a rather unusual ending for a talking picture, as the producers generally prefer that the play end happily with the hero and the heroine clasped in each other's arms.*

Actually, Colin had died in both *Journey's End* and *The Stronger Sex*. It is, perhaps, an unusual factor in his selecting his roles ... but don't most actors love death scenes?

Colin says he'd like to return to Hollywood for a new film, maybe as early as next spring; "I have not signed a contract to do one," he says, "but if I do so, I would like it to be under the direction of James Whale." He "jumped off the table and exclaimed excitedly" when asked about the sports he enjoyed in Hollywood.

On October 30, the *Europa* sets sail. Colin is relieved that he came through the new picture so relatively well. He has no idea of the phenomena about to follow.

> *Halloween night, 1931. On the* Europa, *out in the Atlantic.*
>
> *Yes, Hollywood had been fun, this time. Of course, Jimmy could be a nasty bit of goods—what he did to Boris that night on the back lot was absolutely beastly. Poor Mae ... he hopes she'll be all right. Something broken inside her, he thought—he sensed these things. Maybe she'd sensed the same thing in him ...*
>
> *Yes, all in all, a great role, a great director ... a great time. A great film? They all thought so, but what the hell happens when the churches and bluenoses see him digging up corpses, to make a Monster ... who drowns a little girl?*
>
> *Best be ready for anything. A triumph or a disaster. Only time will tell ...*

The original *Frankenstein* one-sheet, featuring Karloff in the test makeup.

"One Man *Crazy* ...!"

Chapter Fourteen
"Warning! The Monster is Loose!"

Tuesday, November 3, 1931: Colin Clive is at sea on the *Europa* as *The Hollywood Reporter* runs its review of *Frankenstein*, five days after the Santa Barbara preview. The headline: *Frankenstein 100% Shocker*. The trade paper has high praise for the film's two top attractions:

> *Colin Clive as the doctor and Boris Karloff as the Monster give tremendous performances ... They are magnificent.*

Yet the powers-that-be at Universal are jittery—has James Whale gone *too* far? The day this review appears, the studio shoots a revised Happy Ending—Frederick Kerr as old Baron Frankenstein, toasting his son's recovery from the windmill toss. The audience will see the figures of Henry Frankenstein and Elizabeth deep in a room; Colin's at sea, so a double (reported to have been Western actor Robert Livingston) represents him.

"Here's to a son to the house of Frankenstein!" says the Baron, raising his glass, as a bevy of maids smile coyly.

Also added: The pre-credits prologue, with Edward Van Sloan in tuxedo, giving the audience a "friendly warning" about *Frankenstein*:

"I think it will thrill you. It may shock you. It might even ... *horrify* you!"

The final cost of *Frankenstein*: $291,129.13.

Friday night, November 6: Universal premieres *Strictly Dishonorable*. Junior Laemmle, hoping it means major stardom for Sidney Fox, has been ill since late October, recently recovering at an undisclosed "desert retreat." Concerns about *Frankenstein* are adding to his hypochondria.

Friday, November 13: *Motion Picture Daily* reviews *Frankenstein*. " ... Karloff has truly created a Frankenstein Monster," writes Leo Meehan, noting, "Women come out trembling, men exhausted." The Friday the 13th review finally mentions in the last paragraph, "Colin Clive gives a splendid performance as the mentally perverted Frankenstein, who creates the Monster."

Universal sets a chain of late November east coast *Frankenstein* openings. The reception will determine who the real star is—Clive or Karloff.

Tuesday, November 17: Variety reports that Colin, now vacationing in Paris, has signed with British Paramount Studios to star in *The Light that Failed*, based on Rudyard Kipling's 1891 novel. The star role of Dick Heldar is a superb fit for Colin—an artist who paints a prostitute, making her the model for a portrait titled "Melancolia"—only to have the prostitute destroy the painting, and for Heldar to go blind. Alexander Korda, who'd soon direct Charles Laughton in his Oscar-winning performance in *The Private Life of Henry VIII*, is likely to direct. Additionally, Colin has an option for five more pictures with British Paramount.

The deal has basically assured Colin's major film stardom.

Friday, November 20: Frankenstein opens at the Rialto Theatre in Washington, D.C. Nelson B. Bell reviews the film in the *Washington Post*:

COLIN CLIVE   MAE CLARKE   BORIS KARLOFF

CARL LAEMMLE presents

"FRANKENSTEIN"

The Man Who Made A Monster!

with

COLIN CLIVE, MAE CLARKE, JOHN BOLES, BORIS KARLOFF

Dwight Frye, Edward van Sloan, Frederic Kerr

Directed by
JAMES WHALE

A Universal Picture

Produced by
CARL LAEMMLE, JR.

JOHN BOLES   DWIGHT FRYE   EDW. VAN SLOAN   FREDERIC KERR

Universal publicity for *Frankenstein*, showing the principals.

The most remarkable performance by far in Frankenstein *is that of the giant fiend himself by Boris Karloff... It is a skillful but unsavory bit of imaginative and grotesque portraiture that the delicately constituted will dream about through many haunted nights.*

The role of Frankenstein is played by Colin Clive, who conveys considerable conviction as the young scientist who sought to usurp the power

"One Man *Crazy* ...!"

The Alhambra Theatre, Milwaukee, presents *Frankenstein*, **November, 1931. (Courtesy of Dan Gunderman)**

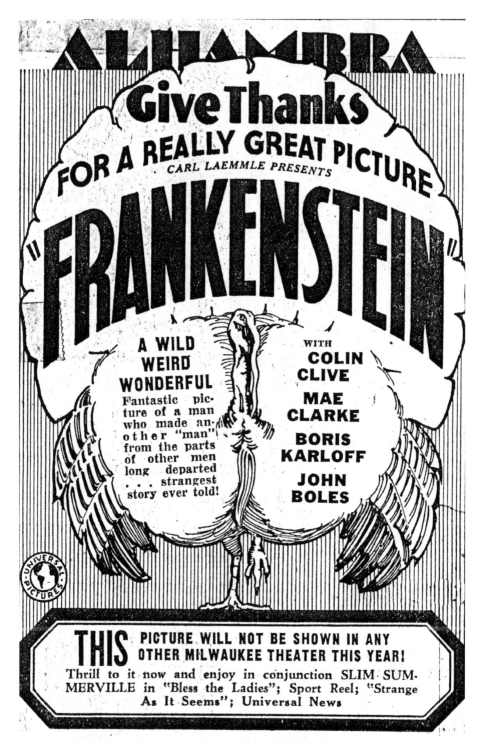

Alhambra Theatre, Milwaukee, Thanksgiving, 1931. (Courtesy of Dan Gunderman)

"One Man Crazy ...!"

of the Creator. His performance is high-strung, tense and as convincing as such a thing can be.

Wednesday, November 25: Frankenstein plays an 11:00 p.m. Thanksgiving eve performance at Keith's Theatre in Baltimore, officially opening the next day. *The Sun* critic Donald Kirkley who, as previously noted, hails Karloff's Monster as "the embodiment of everything evil in human experience," adds:

The Monster is perfectly played by Boris Karloff, and his makeup is a masterpiece. He snarls, screams, groans and growls most fearfully.

As for Colin Clive, Kirkley includes his name as part of "a consistently good cast."

Wednesday, December 2: Universal picks up its option on Karloff's contract.
Thursday, December 3: Frankenstein opens at Chicago's State-Lake theater. *The Chicago Tribune's* Mae Tinee (whose name is a play on "matinee") praises Whale's "astute direction" and writes:

Colin Clive—the Captain Stanhope of Journey's End—*is magnificent as the burning young scientist who knows no rest until he has concluded his experiment—and certainly none afterwards. As the Monster, Boris Karloff is a terrible, terrible THING!*

Friday, December 4: It's the feast day of Saint Barbara, Colin's heavenly guardian at Stonyhurst, and *Frankenstein* opens at the RKO-Mayfair Theatre in New York City. It will break the house record. *Variety* reports:

Looks like a Dracula *plus … Colin Clive … plays it with force but innocent of ranting. Boris Karloff enacts the Monster … with its indescribably terrifying face of demoniacal calm, a fascinating acting bit of mesmerism …*

Sunday, December 6: Colin, home in County Kent, has heard about *Frankenstein's* triumph. On this day, the date *The Film Daily Yearbook* will give as the official national release date of *Frankenstein,* he suffers a serious accident that evokes a ghost from his past: He tries to ride his horse over a high gate at Charing, Maidstone, and the horse falls, throwing him.

Back at Sandhurst, Colin had broken his knee in a horse fall; this time, he fractures a hip. Following an X-ray at a hospital, he's moved into his London home. On Thursday, December 10, the Boston *Herald* provides a grim account of the accident:

A curious irony of fate is that Colin Clive, who survived all the fake horrors of Frankenstein—*which is now piling up box office records all over the country, Boston included—should sustain so painful an injury, merely by falling off his horse, that he will be confined to bed for six weeks at least with a broken hip. It's hard luck. For Mr. Clive had recently signed a fat contract … and was planning to make a number of English films, which must now be held up indefinitely. It is to be hoped that the injury, which sounds pretty serious, will not cripple him permanently.*

Monday, December 14: The originally set starting date for *The Light that Failed* comes and goes without the film beginning shooting. With fear that Colin might be crippled for life, British Paramount cancels the film.

Back in the U.S.A., *Frankenstein* is a Yuletide sensation, Colin Clive's Frankenstein and Boris Karloff's Monster amok on U.S.A. movie screens. Strangely, as Christmas approaches, celebrating the Virgin birth of the Christ Child, filmgoers stand in long lines to behold the blasphemous creation of a Monster.

Colin and Jeanne meanwhile travel again to Paris, where they'll see in the New Year as he continues recuperating from his injured hip. He enjoys gambling, visiting the casinos of Cannes and Monte Carlo.

Friday, January 1, 1932: Frankenstein opens in Los Angeles at the Orpheum Theatre. The *Los Angeles Times* advertisement, presented as if penned by Henry Frankenstein himself, has a decidedly sexual flavor:

> *I Made a Living Monster ... Do YOU Dare to See It?*
> *... Half Man ... Half Fiend ... Knowing every Sensation But the Love of Woman!*

The lurid words went on, climaxing with:

> *It was a MONSTER! Sweating Death and Madness!*

Frankenstein will smash the Orpheum's house record. Louella Parsons in the *Los Angeles Examiner* writes:

> *So grotesque and horrible is the characterization of Boris Karloff in* Fran-kenstein *that all adults become little children, afraid of the dark ... James Whale has done an unusually deft job of direction ... Colin Clive ... leaves nothing to be desired as young Frankenstein, the scientist ...*

Of course, you can't please all the people all of the time. "Personally," writes Relman Morin, critic for the *Los Angeles Record,* "I think it is a shame that an artistic triumph like *Frankenstein* should be ruined by a set of olfactory nerves." He explains himself, describing the "Flower Game" between the Monster and Little Maria, specifically where the Monster smells a daisy:

> *And right there is where the horrible thing happens. He can't smell daisies, because he hasn't any olfactory nerves. They aren't made—they're born in you.*

As for Clive and Karloff, Morin finds them "unusually adequate for their roles."

The January, 1932 issue of *Photoplay* lists Karloff and Clive among "The Best Performances of the Month," and *Frankenstein* among the best films, writing:

> *It introduces a successor to the late Lon Chaney, who out-horrors anything Chaney ever gave us ...*
> *Boris Karloff plays the Monster. During the making of the picture he lost 21 pounds. You won't wonder when you see him. He's great, as is Colin Clive as Frankenstein. The direction and photography are magnificent ...*

January, 1932: Colin Clive, triumphant star of *Frankenstein*, at home in London, recovering from his horse fall in December of 1931. His wife Jeanne de Casalis poses with him.

Monday night, January 25: *Frankenstein* has its London premiere at the Tivoli Theatre. Outside is a giant electrical display of Karloff's Monster and Colin's Monster Maker. Colin, who's been recovering nicely from his horse fall, is at the premiere, along with royalty and celebrities. England's *To-day's Cinema* reports:

THE TIVOLI

Manager: W. P. FISHER

Phone: Temple Bar 5625

6D.

COLIN CLIVE

in

" FRANKENSTEIN "

Programme

The program for *Frankenstein*, Tivoli Theatre, London, 1932. (Courtesy of Tracy Surrell)

"One Man *Crazy* …!"

Colin Clive as Frankenstein, with the Monster's shadow.

While a big crowd clamored outside for admission, the doors had to be closed for this gala premiere, at which every seat was filled, and receipts in the box office were greater than any other night in months.

The same night, Boris Karloff makes a personal appearance at the Orpheum in Los Angeles, where *Frankenstein* is still packing the house. Like Colin, Karloff suffers stage fright, but has long ago decided he has "the fire in the belly" to be an actor and would never be happy as anything else.

P.D.926

Boris Karloff as the Monster, with Frankenstein's shadow.

As for Colin ... trapped into seeing the film in London, he doesn't look at the screen. The critics who *do* look are impressed properly:

> Empire News: *Think of all the horrors Lon Chaney gave you, double them, and you have some idea what to expect from* Frankenstein ... *It's strong stuff ... Karloff is nothing short of remarkable ... Clive is excellent.*

Impartial Film Report: *Boris Karloff walks away with the picture, but all the others do excellently.*

Perhaps never in the history of films has a featured player so spectacularly upstaged the star. Yet, as *Frankenstein* marches on—placing Number Seven on the *New York Times'* "Ten Best Films of 1931" list, rating a showing at the first Venice Film Festival, and reaping a staggering worldwide rental of $1,400,000—there's plenty of glory for Colin as well. He's the dynamic top-billed title player of a powerhouse film that makes show business history. He wins a generous share of lavish reviews, and the *Hull Daily Mail*—no doubt aware that Colin had spent three seasons in the city's repertory company—lavishly praises him.

"Colin Clive is one of the greatest film actors in the world," all-hails the reviewer.

Then there's the fan mail. Colin will enjoy telling the story about a package delivered to his home shortly after the release of *Frankenstein*. To his horror ... the package ticked! Fearing a bomb, he tossed it into his morning bath. An hour later he removed the wet packet, opened it and found "a curious contraption of wire, pipes, pulleys, miniature motors and an electric battery." A letter the next day explained the curiosity:

> *Dear Mr. Clive:*
> *Having just seen your picture* Frankenstein, *I want to have you look over my own invention, which is similar to the one you use in the picture. It can't make a living man, but if you put the current through the body of a dead mouse, it will restore life!*

For all the attention won by Karloff, and for all the crazed horror movie scientists to follow, Colin Clive, although he's too humble to realize it, predict it, or enjoy it, has become the all-time greatest mad doctor in the history of film.

Eighty-seven years later, *Frankenstein* still has its power and poetry, primarily due to the two actors who gave the film its macabre magic.

A haunted addict, his pet devils lurking but at bay during *Frankenstein,* brilliantly makes a hero out of a Maker of Monsters.

A sad-eyed exile, his performance a virtual sacrament, gives a soul to the soulless Frankenstein's Monster.

As directed by a self-created "gentleman lover" who'd played Frankenstein in his own life, Colin Clive and Boris Karloff provided *Frankenstein* its "insane passion." As such, the ghosts of Clive, Karloff, and James Whale have a timeless showcase.

"It's Alive!" is their rallying cry.

Part IV
Walking the High Wire
1932 to 1934

You see, I'm little more than a puppet really
as far as film work is concerned.
The director does all the brain work.
He is the man who makes *the picture.*

Colin Clive, *Picture Show*, May 28, 1932

Chapter Fifteen
A Whale That Got Away,
"Eyes Too Bright and Too Blue," and
Katharine Hepburn with Antennae

Colin Clive had created two of the movies' most powerfully haunting characters. Almost a decade's struggle for recognition had climaxed with a stardom he'd likely never imagined.

He was incredibly fortunate and he knew it. He was lucky to have had a wife who'd basically forced him into auditioning for *Journey's End*, and a director who'd bravely defied a studio to cast him as *Frankenstein*. Yet, however dynamic a part Jeanne de Casalis and James Whale had played in providing stardom for Colin Clive, they couldn't act the parts for him after the stagehands raised the curtain, or the cameraman started filming.

Colin would never quite come to terms with this fact—he'd continue almost desperately attributing his success to others. He was, however, fully aware of his great luck, something most actors never received. He'd be a fool to toss it all away in what he perceived as weakness and self-indulgence. For much of the next few years, he'd fight to keep control, and aspire to be what he'd started out being: the would-be-soldier as actor, a spit-and-polish professional.

He'd had the good fortune of his hip healing after the recent horse fall—an injury that was originally considered so serious as likely to cripple him. He and Jeanne enjoyed both their retreat in Kent and a handsome townhouse at 66

66 Gloucester Place, London. This was the in-the-city home of Colin Clive and Jeanne de Casalis in the early 1930s. (Photo by the author)

Gloucester Place in London. He'd had his share of blessings and would fight to make himself worthy of them.

Meanwhile, Jimmy Whale wanted him for a new film in Hollywood.

Imagine ... *The Old Dark House*, Universal, 1932, directed by James Whale, and starring Boris Karloff ... as well as Colin Clive and Jean Harlow!

It might have happened. On New Year's Day, 1932, the same day *Frankenstein* opened in Los Angeles, the Los Angeles *Evening Herald Express* reported that James Whale had sold Junior Laemmle on acquiring the rights to the J.B. Priestley novel. On February 16,

The Old Dark House, **Universal, 1932. Left to right, Raymond Massey, Lilian Bond, Gloria Stuart, Melvyn Douglas, Boris Karloff, Charles Laughton, and Eva Moore. James Whale originally wanted Colin Clive and Jean Harlow for the roles played by Douglas and Stuart.**

Mollie Merrick, who'd visited the *Frankenstein* set the previous summer, wrote in the New Orleans *Times-Picayune*:

> *Colin Clive will be coming back here shortly to make another horror story. James Whale will direct again and the picture will be called* The Old Dark House. *Clive, who played the role of Dr. Frankenstein in the film of that name, scored a tremendous hit. He does that with almost everything, for that matter. As Captain Stanhope in* Journey's End *he was a knockout.*

February 25, 1932: Jimmy Starr wrote in the *Evening Herald Express*: "James Whale is thinking about using Jean Harlow as the star of his next Universal production." It all made sense. Whale wanted Colin to play Roger Penderel, the cynical ex-soldier, who on a wild and stormy night, finds himself in the mountains of Wales, riding in a car with married couple Philip and Margaret Waverton, taking shelter in ... an old dark house. Colin would have been excellent delivering this Penderel self-assessment:

> *War generation, slightly soiled. A study in the bittersweet, the man with the twisted smile ... and this, Mr. Femm, is exceedingly good Gin!*

As the hero, he'd have battled the drunken, bearded, broken-nosed butler, Morgan—played by a top-billed Boris Karloff—as well as have climactically overcome the maniacal Saul (Brember Wills), a religious pyromaniac who tries to set the house afire. And he'd win the girl—red-haired Lilian Bond, who also arrives at the house that night as the companion of Sir William Porterhouse, played by Colin's Stonyhurst classmate, Charles Laughton.

As for Harlow ... Whale told Gloria Stuart (who played Margaret) that he wanted Gloria to appear as "a white flame" when Karloff's Morgan pursued her in hopes of raping her. Platinum Blonde Harlow would have suited Whale's pictorial concept ideally. Ms. Stuart (also a blonde) remembered too that the sexy dress she wore in *The Old Dark House* was "what we used to call a Jean Harlow dress—a pale, pink, bias-cut, satin velvet evening dress, with spaghetti straps." It's fun to imagine Harlow in the undressing-in-the boudoir episode, with Eva Moore, as old Miss Femm, ogling Harlow's body and saying her famous line, "That's fine stuff, but it'll rot!"

It would have been a fascinating reunion for Whale and Harlow after *Hell's Angels*, to say the least. Melvyn Douglas is fine as Penderel. Gloria Stuart is a very alluring Margaret, and her "Jean Harlow dress" so provocatively fits her derriere that it almost qualifies as a Production Code violation. Still, imagine ... a new Whale/Clive collaboration, with a rampaging Karloff and a strip-teasing Jean Harlow!

Instead, 1932 film audiences saw Colin in a disaster that convinced Paramount Studios to scrap making films in England.

Variety's September 20, 1932 review of *Lily Christine* wrote:

> *... Colin Clive is not without reputation on both continents as an actor ... but they've managed to keep his ability a dark secret in this instance.*

Corinne Griffith, star of *Lily Christine*.

A publicity picture of Corinne Griffith and Colin on the set of *Lily Christine*.

Colin was back in the movies. British Paramount still had its deal with him to star in *The Light that Failed*, and an option for five more films. It was too late now to revive the postponed *The Light that Failed*, so Paramount tossed Colin into a very different production.

The title: *Lily Christine*, based on a novel by Michael Arlen. Its purpose: to provide a comeback vehicle for Corinne Griffith, "The Orchid Lady" of silent films.

The movie (which is elusive to track down today and possibly lost) was shot at Paramount's base in Elstree and directed by Paul Stein. The basic story: Lily Christine (Griffith), her eyes "too bright, too blue," and who wears glasses, spends a platonic stormy night with Rupert Harvey, a novelist (Colin). Lily's caddish husband, Ivor, leaves her for an actress, a vain creature who insists that Lily admit to an affair with Rupert, to save the actress' reputation. It's a lie, but Rupert's wife, Muriel, believes it. Rupert asks Lily to reconcile with the unspeakable Ivor so that Rupert can save his marriage.

Lily, emotionally overwhelmed, removes her glasses while walking home ... and gets hit by a bus, or a truck. (Summaries of the film vary.) She dies. *The End*.

Lily Christine was Corrine Griffith's show all the way—it even provided a flash peek of the lady in "scanty attire." To guarantee her dominance, her husband, Walter Morosco, personally produced the picture. Colin's role gave him little opportunity. He's basically his leading lady's stooge, and it's amazing that, after the success of *Journey's End* and all the buzz about *Frankenstein,* that this was the best the British film producers had to offer him.

Thursday night, April 28: *Lily Christine* had its world premiere at London's Plaza Theatre. The Prince of Wales and Prince George were in attendance and proceeds aided the League of Mercy. The *London Times* reviewer wrote:

> *Miss Griffith very nearly succeeds in making Lily Christine a credible human being, and Colin Clive, realizing that Rupert is a simple and rather stupid man, praiseworthily refuses to try to make him anything else.*

In the U.S.A, *Variety* would catch up with *Lily Christine* in September of 1932, playing on a double-bill at the Playhouse Theatre in Mamaroneck, New York. The critic noted the film was so remarkably dull that the audience "grew very impatient with it," expressing "audible irritation."

Colin saw it as experience. He told England's *Picture Show*:

> *I used to hate film work, at first. But now I prefer screen work to acting on the stage. There is something about the Talkie business, which fascinates me. It is extraordinary how interesting this type of work has become.*
>
> *It took me 10 years to learn my job on the provincial stage—of course, I'm still learning now; but I'm afraid it will take me a lot longer to learn anything really worthwhile about films. The technical side is so interesting, and if ever I do master this part of making pictures, I would like to produce pictures and give up acting altogether.*

By "produce" pictures, Colin used the British term for direct. It's notable he hoped he might one day direct films, thereby still working in a craft that fascinated him, while avoiding the agony of stage fright and the feeling he was merely a "puppet" for the director.

Lily Christine was basically a debacle—so much so that Paramount Studios pulled the plug on its British studio. In its wake went Colin's contract for five more films. His

Corinne Griffith and Colin Clive in *Lily Christine*.

The Life and Death of Colin Clive Hollywood's Dr. Frankenstein

second major horse fall had caused severe consequences: it had cost him *The Light that Failed*, which might have been a triumph for him, and led to the flop of *Lily Christine*. It also had seriously injured him, and while the fall had damaged his hip rather than his leg, it impacted his previous injury. The shattered leg would steadily grow worse.

As for Corinne Griffith, *Lily Christine* was her cinema swan song. The late DeWitt Bodeen, screenwriter of *Cat People* (1942) and ace film historian, wrote in *Films in Review* in 1975:

> *Hollywood's real Woman of Mystery may well have been the orchidaceous Corinne Griffith.*
>
> *When in the mid-Sixties she was on the witness stand in a Los Angeles court of law, seeking annulment of her 33-day marriage to Danny Scholl, she threw a bombshell into the proceedings by maintaining that she was then only 52 years of age, that she had never made a silent film, and that the real Corinne Griffith had died in her mid-30s. She testified that she, her stand-in, a physical twin in beauty, had quietly replaced her as a talking feature star ...*
>
> *If this be true, Miss Griffith is living the real-life story for a suspense movie that would be dear to the heart of an Alfred Hitchcock.*

So ... did Colin actually co-star with Corinne Griffith's stand-in in *Lily Christine*? Probably not. The press would report that Corinne Griffith, silent screen star, died July 13, 1979, age 84, one of the richest (and possibly most deluded) women in the world.

Picture Show, England, May 28, 1932.

Meanwhile, things were proceeding well for Colin in the theater.

March 28: Colin starred at the London Palladium in *Elegant Edward*. *Variety* reported that Colin's salary was $1,100 per week, and that the show had "opened nicely."

Had he been more confident and aggressive, he might have attempted, in the wake of the giant successes of *Journey's End* and *Frankenstein*, a triumph in Shakespeare—Colin Clive as *Richard III*, perhaps. However, the critical trouncing he'd suffered as Laertes in the 1930 all-star *Hamlet* likely scared him away from any such ambition.

From July to September, 1932, Colin played at the Garrick Theatre in a John Galsworthy festival. Galsworthy was one of his favorite playwrights, and Colin portrayed Matt Denant in *The Escape*, Captain Ronald Dancey in *Loyalties*, and William Adder in *Justice*.

And inevitably—was there ever any doubt—he co-starred in a movie with Jeanne de Casalis. It was actually a short film, titled *A Matter of Good Taste*, released in October of 1932. *To-day's Cinema* hailed *A Matter of Good Taste* as "Ten minutes with Big Stars" and "800 Feet of Brilliant Photography and Lighting."

Charles Laughton, Colin's fellow alumnus from Stonyhurst, plays mad Dr. Moreau in Paramount's *Island of Lost Souls* (1932). Kathleen Burke plays the Panther Woman.

Late in the year, new offers came from Hollywood. One was for Universal's *The Kiss Before the Mirror*, to be directed by James Whale. The story: After a man murders his unfaithful wife, the man's lawyer begins to believe that his own wife is unfaithful. However, RKO Studios outbid Universal and, quite flatteringly, offered Colin the distinction of being the onscreen lover of a sensational new female star.

Friday, December 9: Colin set sail on the *Bremen*, once again without Jeanne.

As he made his way to America, the Horror genre, electrified by *Frankenstein*, was in full bloom. Whale's *The Old Dark House* had been a Halloween release. *The Mask of Fu Manchu*, starring Karloff on loan-out from Universal to MGM, had opened in New York December 2. *The Mummy*, for which Universal would bill its star on the posters simply as KARLOFF, a là MGM's GARBO, would open in Chicago December 23. On the same date and in the same city, Paramount's *Island of Lost Souls*, starring Charles Laughton as Dr. Moreau, would open.

Incidentally, in *Island of Lost Souls*, Laughton has a line of dialogue similar to Colin's famous words in *Frankenstein*: "Now I know what it feels like to BE God!" Laughton, regarding his animal-to-human creations, says, "Do you know what it means to feel like God?" However, unlike his Stonyhurst classmate, Laughton speaks the blasphemy with no hysteria, but rather a calm, cool self-assurance.

Two alumni of the same Jesuit school ... two different approaches to delivering blasphemous dialogue.

> *... a startling romance of forbidden love! The story of a world-famous avi-atrix who tried to quench the flames of desire with speed, thrills, danger ... and failed!*
> Publicity for RKO's *Christopher Strong*, 1933

RKO Studios, 780 Gower Street in Hollywood, had two big attractions in place for 1933 audiences: Katharine Hepburn and *King Kong*. Colin was about to work with the former.

Hepburn had scored big in her film debut, RKO's *A Bill of Divorcement* (1932), starring John Barrymore. RKO offered Colin the romantic lead opposite Hepburn in her first starring film, *Christopher Strong*, based on the Gilbert Frankau novel. Hepburn replaced original choice Ann Harding, while Colin, as with *Frankenstein*, once again claimed a title role initially set for Leslie Howard.

If there were a fly in the ointment, Colin would be playing a man old enough to be Hepburn's father, when in fact he was only seven years older than she.

The love tragedy is intriguing, largely due to its decidedly offbeat cast. Sir Christopher Strong (32-year-old Colin, with a mustache) is long and happily married to Lady Strong (48-year-old Billie Burke), and they have a grown blonde daughter, Monica (26-year-old Helen Chandler). The vibes are already bizarre: Henry Frankenstein, married to the future Glinda the Good Witch of *The Wizard of Oz*, with *Dracula's* "Mina" as their daughter!

Nose-diving into their life: Lady Cynthia Darrington (25-year-old Hepburn), a dazzling, Amelia Earhart-style aviatrix. She even flies a plane that's the same model as Ms. Earhart's—a Lockheed Vega. Sir Chris has been faithful for 22 years. Cynthia is a virgin ... temporarily. She is soon with child via her knighted lover, and—rather than destroy him and his family—goes up in her plane, breaks an altitude record, and crashes to her death.

It's an intriguing death scene: Cynthia appears to think twice, tries to save herself, but it's too late. Perhaps the producers, feeling she was also killing her unborn baby, decided to finesse the finale.

At the helm of this elegant high-flying soap opera: 35-year-old Dorothy Arzner, who was then Hollywood's only female director. There was no secret in Hollywood that

***Christopher Strong*, RKO, 1933.**

Arzner was a lesbian—her mannish grooming and attire rather shouted the fact. Women tended to suffer due to men in her films; in her previous movie, Paramount's audaciously titled *Merrily We Go to Hell* (1932), an heiress (Sylvia Sidney) dealt with a drunken lover (Fredric March).

Wednesday, December 21, 1932: Christopher Strong began shooting, under the title *The Great Desire*. Hepburn was (and remains) a sight to see and hear as Lady Cynthia—favoring beret and slacks, barking her dialogue like a happy canine, aggressively striding about the sets as if she owned RKO lock-stock-and-barrel. Colin complemented her perfectly, never playing the cad that Arzner's agenda perhaps preferred, making the title character sympathetic, even as he strays from his wife and leaves Cynthia "with child."

Colin adored Hepburn. They played together beautifully. One of their love scenes is a stunner—the two stars, drifting in a motorboat one night in a canal in Cannes, the ride leading to a passionate kiss. Colin said:

> *Katharine Hepburn is a grand girl. She is certainly different. There is nobody else quite like her in Hollywood—or anywhere else, for that matter … Katharine has got something bigger than beauty; she has got brains. And above all, she is an actress, to her fingertips. She is not just a face, but a great personality … She can talk. Few stars talk interestingly on any topic—except themselves, but Katharine Hepburn is the delightful exception … I have never known a star to be as painstaking as is Miss Hepburn.*

Katharine Hepburn in her remarkable "Moth" costume (with antennae!), dazzling Colin in
Christopher Strong.

Weather was stormy, inside and outside the RKO soundstage. One might have expected two ahead-of-their-time women, Hepburn and Arzner, to have worked smoothly together. Instead, they clashed explosively. Colin, trapped in the middle, was definitely on Hepburn's side. Nevertheless, in his gentlemanly way, he later tried to say nice things about Arzner. He claimed that working with a female director was a "novel experience," his choice of words a bit politically incorrect for modern sensibilities:

> *Miss Arzner is a clever technician, but it seemed a bit queer, at first, being told what to do by a woman!*
>
> *I got used to it after a while, though another thing that struck me as a bit strange, until I got over the shock, was that Dorothy Arzner never lost her temper. I suppose she leaves that privilege to the male directors. She is very reserved, very gentle, very clever, and she is an "ace" for camera angles.*

Colin was devoted to Hepburn. As the troubled production went on, Hepburn became ill, and on January 26, was rushed from the set to Good Samaritan Hospital. *The Hollywood Reporter* claimed she was suffering from appendicitis, while Charles Higham, in his biography *Kate*, cited influenza and "gynecological problems." Whatever her ailments, the always hyper-tense Colin worried terribly about her health.

Perhaps the most memorable vision from *Christopher Strong* is Colin's Sir Christopher beholding Kate's Lady Cynthia adorned for a costume party, wearing a silver form-fitting moth costume—complete with antennae! It was a magnificent camp creation, designed by Walter Plunkett. He actually made the moth costume from bits of metal, and it had to be taken off piece by piece—lest its removal literally skin Hepburn alive.

Colin, onscreen and off, was dazzled.

Indeed, based on all evidence, Colin had fallen in love, or at least infatuation, with his fascinating co-star. Hepburn took home movies on the set, and one of her favorite candid scenes was Colin, profanely battling to fasten a collar button.

Christopher Strong wrapped up February 3, 1933. The cost was $283,766—about $10,000 less than *Frankenstein*. "She Scores Another Blazing Sensation!" promised RKO as *Christopher Strong* premiered at New York's Radio City Music Hall (where it followed *King Kong*) on March 9, 1933. Mordaunt Hall of the *New York Times* was impressed:

> *Billie Burke gives an able portrait ... Mr. Clive is at his best ... Helen Chandler adds to her list of flawless portrayals ... As for Miss Hepburn, she delivers an excellent character study ...*

Hollywood Filmograph saw it all very differently:

> *It's one of those plays where every member of the cast suffers and is heroic. Katharine Hepburn is strong, talkative and suffering; Colin Clive is strong, silent and suffering; Billie Burke is weak, silent and suffering; Helen Chandler is flighty, playful and suffering; and the audience just suffers ...*

Indeed, modern film fans might be surprised at how polarizing a star Katharine Hepburn was in her early days. As *Hollywood Filmograph* ranted:

> *Katharine Hepburn, RKO's publicity-made star, is at times loud, at times uncouth, and at times—when she carelessly permits herself to be so—charming. Her hideous make-up—in one scene she was an absolute double for "Frankenstein"—makes her at times actually repellant. At times when her make-up is censored, she looks rather attractive.*
> *Colin Clive gives a fair, suppressed, old-fashioned stage performance ...*

It's all in the eye of the beholder. Seen today, *Christopher Strong* plays nicely, largely due to the ethereal quality of the two stars. It has a filmic antique quality, rather like an animated old first edition with an engraved cover. Both Hepburn and Colin make for engagingly illicit lovers; indeed, when Colin says to Hepburn, "I've been so lonely—so desperately lonely," he truly makes you believe it.

Christopher Strong wasn't strong at the box office, its worldwide rental a very modest $386,000. The loss: $35,000. Fortunately for RKO, *King Kong* came rampaging from the studio gates at the same time, saving the lot with an international rental of $1,856,000 and a profit of $626,945.

As to Helen Chandler, who played Monica ... it should be noted that she was at least as severe a victim of alcoholism as Colin was, and in 1933, perhaps more so. Her addiction killed off her career, a 1950 fire scarred her face, she spent years in a sanitarium in the California desert, and she relied during her final years on the Motion Picture Relief Fund. *Dracula's* leading lady died April 30, 1965, almost 28 years after *Frankenstein's* leading man had passed away.

Helen Chandler, Mina of *Dracula*, plays Colin's daughter in *Christopher Strong*. They shared a private demon in real life.

As for Dorothy Arzner ... her final feature film was Columbia's *First Comes Courage* (1943), starring Merle Oberon. In 1975, four years before Arzner's death, the Director Guild of America (of which Arzner had been the first female member) honored her, and Katharine Hepburn sent a telegram:

> *Isn't it wonderful that you've had such a great career, when you had no right to have a career at all?*

Hepburn probably meant it as a compliment, i.e., that as a woman, Arzner had faced incredible odds in Hollywood. Then again, considering how Arzner and Hepburn had battled during *Christopher Strong*, Hepburn might have intended the ambiguity.

All in all, the Hepburn and Clive *Christopher Strong* survives as a creaky yet admirable love tragedy. It's intriguing to watch the two young stars, each so full of promise, and to realize that one would continue for more than 70 years, while the other would be dead in little more than four years.

Yet for classic film lovers, *Christopher Strong* perhaps fascinates most in the Old Hollywood fantasy vision it conjures: Henry Frankenstein, making love to Katharine Hepburn, who's costumed as a silver moth with antennae.

Chapter Sixteen
Looking Forward,
The Hollywood Earthquake,
A Would-Be Invisible Man, and
A Different Haunted Summer

Marion Davies, as much of the 1933 world knew then and virtually every Golden Age movie fan knows now, was the mistress of William Randolph Hearst.

The publishing tycoon had set up Cosmopolitan Pictures at MGM, the home of "Leo the Lion" and "More Stars than the Heavens," to produce his lover's film vehicles. Next on her slate was *Peg O' My Heart*, the tale of a woman from a fishing village in Ireland who, to claim an inheritance, must live with her family of impoverished nobles in England. She falls in love with Sir Gerald "Jerry" Markham, a charming baronet.

Hearst and Marion wanted Leslie Howard for Sir Gerald. Howard, aware of this, boosted his asking price from $65,000 to $75,000. At that time, as Mollie Merrick reported, MGM "decided Colin Clive looked pretty good to them." Once again, as with *Frankenstein* and *Christopher Strong*, Colin was in line for a role originally envisioned for Leslie Howard. On the night of February 1, while *Christopher Strong* was in its final days of shooting, Colin reported to MGM to film a test for *Peg O' My Heart*.

Colin won the role of "Sir Jerry" ... very briefly.

Cosmopolitan Pictures was simultaneously producing a film titled *Service*, based on a British play by C.L. Anthony, about a Britisher laid off in the Depression after decades as a bookkeeper in a department store. It starred MGM's two venerable warhorses: Lionel Barrymore as the bookkeeper, and Lewis Stone as the store owner. The supporting cast featured Onslow Stevens as "Geoffrey," Stone's secretary, in love with Stone's daughter. The director was Metro stalwart Clarence Brown.

Apparently, the MGM powers decided Onslow Stevens would be more suitable as Sir Gerald than Colin. Stevens got the leading man role in *Peg O' My Heart*—and Colin got shifted (and one might say shafted) into assuming Stevens' role in *Service*.

Obviously, this didn't sit well with *La* Davies. On February 10, *The Hollywood Reporter* wrote:

> Marion Davies' desire to have Colin Clive play the leading role opposite her in Peg O' My Heart *has resulted in a second screen test being made of the English player. Miss Davies made the test with him and hopes to induce the MGM execs to switch the player into her production from the spot he has been signed for in* Service, *which Clarence Brown is about to place into production.*

MGM usually pampered Marion Davies, but not this time. Onslow Stevens stayed in *Peg O' My Heart*, and Colin remained in *Service*. Geoffrey was a milquetoast part, one that nobody would ever have imagined Colin playing, and that only happened due to the 11th hour casting switch. Stevens got second billing in *Peg O' My Heart*. Colin, in *Service*, retitled *Looking Forward*, named after a speech by newly elected Franklin D. Roosevelt, ended up with sixth billing.

Many Golden Age actors have their conspiracy theorist fans, and Clive's might argue that Hearst kept Colin out of *Peg O' My Heart* for fear Marion would fall prey to Colin's charms, or do the preying herself. However, as Hearst allowed Marion such leading men as Clark Gable, Gary Cooper, and Dick Powell, it's unlikely he'd scuttle Colin's casting. As for Colin, he was so embarrassed by his role in *Looking Forward* that, for once in his career, he fibbed, claiming he took it because the Los Angeles banks had closed due to the Depression. (Actually, the banks did close, but he was committed to MGM by that time.)

Looking Forward began shooting February 13. *Peg O'My Heart* started the same day. Meanwhile, Colin had commenced a far-from-home Hollywood romance with 19-year-old Helen Mack, whom 1933 filmgoers would enjoy as the ukulele-playing heroine of *Son of Kong*. When Helen learned Colin had, as *The Hollywood Reporter* noted, "a wife in Merrie England," she promptly dumped him.

He also had a reputed brief fling with Raquel Torres, the spicy Mexican starlet who's the recipient of one of Groucho Marx's famous lines in Paramount's *Duck Soup* (1933): "I could dance with you till the cows come home. Better still, I'll dance with the cows and *you* come home." Colin was achieving a bit of notoriety as a lady-killer. How much of this news was getting back to Jeanne de Casalis in London isn't known.

Looking Forward poster, 1933. Note that Colin's name doesn't appear.

Colin spoke respectfully about his *Looking Forward* co-stars:

> *I have never met an actor with less personal pride than Lionel Barrymore. He is an extraordinarily well-read and intelligent man. When he talks it is always about something worthwhile, though I think he likes sleeping almost better than anything else. I have seen Lionel Barrymore enjoying a sound sleep in his chair at the side of the set, yet the instant his cue comes up he is wide awake and ready for his shot!*
>
> *Lewis Stone is another very delightful man; in fact, he is one of the nicest men I have ever met. Reserved, cultured, charming and courteous to everybody, he certainly seems to know all there is to be known about picture*

Elizabeth Allan shows Colin her legs in *Looking Forward.*

acting, yet, with all his experience, he never questions his director or makes
suggestions of his own about how the scene should be played.
Lewis Stone always does what he is told, and how well he does it!

Colin was fortunate in Hollywood to work with a bevy of striking female co-stars, including *Looking Forward's* Elizabeth Allan, hailing from Skegness, England. By various accounts, the red-haired "Liz" Allan bedded her way to prominence, when her talent and attractiveness should have advanced her nicely. Her Hollywood lovers would range from Clark Gable to Marlene Dietrich; by the time of *Mark of the Vampire* in early 1935, she'd be the mistress of Metro's palooka of a general manager, Eddie Mannix. Bela Lugosi, watching out for his teenage friend Carroll Borland, who played his vampire daughter "Luna" in *Mark of the Vampire*, wouldn't allow Carroll to go near Liz between scenes, due to the star's "bad reputation."

During the shoot of *Looking Forward*, Colin spent weekends in the countryside with Liz and her husband, Bill O'Bryen, a London theatrical agent. Over the next couple of years, O'Bryen would make multiple round trips to and from Hollywood in hope of saving their marriage. At any rate, Colin and Elizabeth Allan worked nicely together in *Looking Forward*. Her "Caroline" is a daffy free spirit, and his "Geoffrey" is a bit of a charming prig. In a garden scene that plays almost as screwball comedy, Liz slightly lifts her dress, coyly showing the erstwhile Frankenstein her legs. Colin, taking it all in character, nevertheless looks ready to start screaming, "It's alive!"

Considering Elizabeth Allan's reputation-to-come, Colin's 1933 tribute to her after *Looking Forward* had a surely unintended innuendo: "It's a grand break for an English girl to win personal popularity in Hollywood, but Liz Allan seems everybody's favorite."

Friday, March 10, 1933: Looking Forward was still in production when, at 5:54 p.m., the historic Long Beach earthquake erupted. It left 115 to 120 people dead and caused $40,000,000 in property damage. Colin described the disaster:

> *I was sitting in my hotel room writing to Jeanne when suddenly the radio started to screech and the lights flickered. Then I heard a rumble, the house quivered, my books came tumbling down and great cracks appeared in the ceiling. I rushed downstairs and out into the street. There was tremendous*

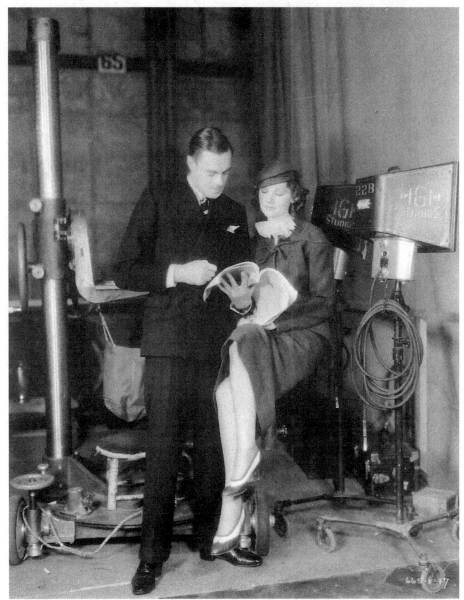

Colin and the soon-to-be-notorious "Liz" Allan, on the MGM set of *Looking Forward*.

excitement. People looked scared. Two girls fainted just in front of me. For a few moments there was panic. Then, though it seemed longer at the time, a few seconds later it was all over. There followed a series of small shocks but I wasn't taking any chances and I went back to my room and stood in the archway of the open door. That is the safest place I was told to stand when an earthquake is on.

Wednesday, March 15: *Looking Forward* wrapped. Cost: $288,726.93. Colin is convincing in it—indeed, everybody is, including Benita Hume as Stone's treacherous young wife, and Phillips Holmes as Stone's loyal son.

Thursday, March 23: A surprise notice in *The Hollywood Reporter*: "Fox yesterday dusted off *My Dear* and turned it over to Harry Lachman's direction. It is a musical and Colin Clive is being considered for the lead." What a pity *that* one never happened!

Also on March 23: *Peg O'My Heart* completed shooting. The next day it began 12 days of retakes.

Thursday, May 25: Looking Forward opened at Loew's State Theatre in Los Angeles. The Los Angeles *Record* praised the film as being "distinguished by its cast and excellent direction," concluding, "Colin Clive gives an excellent performance."

By this time, *Motion Picture Herald* offered a feature titled "What the Picture Did for Me," in which exhibitors chimed in on how films performed for them at the box office. A number of them would let loose at *Looking Forward*:

Walter H.E. Potamkin, Cedar Theatre, Philadelphia, PA:

> *The first lemon of the season from good ole Leo. Extremely bad casting and Clarence Brown must have been punch drunk when he directed this ...*

Walter Odom, Sr., Dixie Theatre, Durant, MS:

> *... Boys, please write to your producers who make pictures for us and beg them to make us pictures that will keep our patrons awake and keep them from walking out disgusted ...*

Looking Forward, for all its noble Depression intentions, took in a worldwide rental of only $475,000, losing MGM $5,726.93. *Peg O'My Heart*, incidentally, cost $608,550.85 (over twice as much as *Looking Forward*) and took in a worldwide rental of $979,000 (double the take on *Looking Forward*). *Peg O' My Heart's* profit: $32,449.15.

It's tempting to imagine that *Peg O'My Heart* might have nicely advanced Colin's film stardom. It did little or nothing for Onslow Stevens' career. Stevens, incidentally, would later contribute dynamically to Universal's Frankenstein saga: He'd play the doomed Dr. Edelmann in Universal's *House of Dracula* (1945), tending to Lon Chaney's Wolf Man, John Carradine's Dracula, and Glenn Strange's Frankenstein Monster.

A final note on *Looking Forward:* Colin's role was such a supporting one that his name didn't even appear on the film's posters.

While Colin was in Hollywood, Boris Karloff had taken a plane across the country to New York and sailed to England to star in *The Ghoul.* He was set for James Whale's *The Invisible Man* upon his return, but Whale couldn't imagine Karloff (who lisped) in the role, preferring his acquaintance from the London theater, Claude Rains. It was the scenario of *Frankenstein* all over again—Universal wanted a vehicle for its horror star, and Whale wanted an actor who, in this case, had never appeared in a Hollywood film.

As Whale and Junior Laemmle argued back and forth, Whale suggested Colin as *The Invisible Man.* Universal liked the suggestion. So did Colin, who told a reporter that the role was "down his street."

The Invisible Man would have revived Colin's stardom with a vengeance. Imagine him in "The Invisible One's" bandages and goggles, his pipe organ voice sounding the classic line:

> *"Even the moon's frightened of me! Frightened to death! The whole world's frightened to death!"*

However, Whale's heart was set on Claude Rains. Aware Colin was homesick for England, Whale persuaded him it was best to go home, and Rains came to Hollywood to star as *The Invisible Man.* He was the ideal man for the role. As good as Colin would have been, he'd have perhaps missed the sense of mad mischief Rains provided; when Clive's Invisible Man laughed, one might have imagined the crazy cackling would never stop.

So, in late May, Colin left Hollywood, leaving behind two solid performances in films that would lose money, having forfeited a romantic lead opposite Marion Davies, and having given up *The Invisible Man,* a role he'd have loved to have played. He sailed from British Columbia for London on the *Damsterdijk,* and while at sea, he suffered a vivid nightmare:

> *Coming home, I dreamt about the quake and woke up in my cabin, having forgotten I was safely at sea, and jumped out of bed to stand in the archway of the cabin.*
> *Then I woke up ... realized it was only a dream. You see, they are nasty things, earthquakes!*

Colin was back in his country cottage in Kent, with Jeanne, for their fourth wedding anniversary.

Saturday, July 8: The *London Times* reported Colin and Jeanne would attend a garden party at Cobham Hall, Kent, to raise money for the Rochester Theatre Company. Also in attendance were such theater personages as Lady Forbes-Robertson, Jean Forbes-Robertson, and Dame May Whitty. The *Times* reported that Rochester Repertory Company would "perform non-stop burlesque," that there'd be golf games, a Children's Corner conducted by "Uncle Robbie" (formerly of the B.B.C.), and "dancing on the lawn by floodlight."

Meanwhile, trouble had erupted at Universal City. On June 1, Boris Karloff had walked out after the studio refused to provide the raise his contract had promised—from $750 weekly to $1,250 weekly. His action had paved the way for James Whale to engage Claude Rains for *The Invisible Man,* but it had scuttled the studio's hope for a *Frankenstein* sequel. In that regard, Karloff was indispensable

Monday, July 10: The Los Angeles *Evening Herald Express* announced that Karloff and Universal had agreed to a new pact, that the studio would produce *The Return of Frankenstein,* and that the sequel "would probably entail the return of Colin Clive from London to play his original role." *Photoplay* magazine played the news up big:

Claude Rains as *The Invisible Man*, 1933. James Whale considered Colin for this role, and Colin would have loved to play it.

Well, what do you know about this!

"Frankenstein" is on his way back—but that isn't the half of it. Sex has reared its ugly head—and how ugly—Dear old "Frank" is to have a monster-mate after all.

Universal is busy on The Return of Frankenstein, *with Boris Karloff in his original role—and Colin Clive, whom you will remember was the scientist who constructed the Monster out of whole cloth, as it were, is building up a better half for him. In other words, when better monsters are made, Colin Clive will make them!*

The last remark was a take-off on Buick's slogan, "When Better Automobiles Are Made, Buick Will Make Them." The *Photoplay* news was premature—over a year would pass and various scriptwriters would come and go before the *Frankenstein* sequel would actually start production.

Right now, Colin was still on country retreat in England ... concerned with his own mate.

Jeanne's career was still flourishing, especially her "Mrs. Feather" radio performances. The 1933 British International Pictures film, *Radio Parade*, presented Jeanne's Mrs. Feather among its airwave attractions, driving her convertible automobile into a gas pump. She emerges, talking a blue streak about her car ... but, since she's referring to her auto as "her" and "she," risqué wordplay ensues:

> *You see, we couldn't get her going for quite a long time ... We'd tickle her various places, you know, the way you have to ... Then a little boy on a butcher's bicycle came and did it. And when he did it, she seemed to like it better, because she was trickling along quite nicely, when she suddenly saw this pump, and then she bolted!*

Later the petrol station manager asks if she's had any lessons—meaning driving lessons. Mrs. Feather's reply: "Oh, I've had a lesson or two, but the man said there was really nothing he could teach me!"

Jeanne's quite remarkable in the skit: attractive in her witchy way, playing with wicked comic timing. In Hollywood, Hal Roach might have cast her effectively as Stan Laurel's batty, oversexed sister—or wacky, transvestite brother. In great demand in theatre and radio, Jeanne was, in England, a more popular star than her husband, despite his Hollywood fame.

Indeed, strangely, London wasn't offering Colin the roles, in theater or film, that the star of *Journey's End* and *Frankenstein* deserved. He was in danger of becoming, for many Brits, Mr. Jeanne de Casalis.

Based on his constant anxiety as an actor, Colin was, in a way, perhaps relieved. Jeanne probably felt, deservedly, partially responsible for his stardom—a stardom he didn't always appear to appreciate—and she perhaps resented his seeming ingratitude. As Elsa Lanchester had noted, Colin was the "English gentleman," who preferred to relax with his pipe and his dogs; he was basically shy, retiring. Jeanne liked to dress up, and play the actress; she was, as always, ambitious, fearless.

Colin made a revealing remark at this time:

> *... the only life I really enjoy is away from London, pottering about in the garden at the cottage. I suppose it may sound a bit queer for a fellow to say that there is no spot on the earth to compare with England when you want the joys of the simple life. Well, I have yet to discover anything better than English country life.*

So, Colin and Jeanne spent this summer together in the country. Her ambition likely frightened him. His addictions, still under basic control, probably frightened her. And when a job offer arrived that he liked, it came from New York, not London.

For Colin and Jeanne, 1933 might well have been their own "haunted summer." He left England that fall, never returning to his beloved garden, his countryside ... or his wife.

From what can be determined, Colin and Jeanne never saw each other again.

Chapter Seventeen
Eight Bells,
The Lake with Katharine Hepburn, and
"Trying Again" in Hollywood

It was a wild and wicked 1933 All Hallow's Eve on Broadway.

At the New Amsterdam Theatre on 42nd Street, Bela Lugosi was playing "Sieben-kase," a mysterious red herring in *Murder at the Vanities*, Earl Carroll's racy musical. At the Fulton Theatre on 46th Street, Dwight Frye was portraying "Ah Sing," an aged Asian in *Keeper of the Keys*, a Charlie Chan thriller. And at the Hudson Theatre on 44th Street, Colin Clive was starring as Captain Dale, a drunken swine of a shipmaster in *Eight Bells*, advertised as "A Vivid Melodrama of the Sea."

"For Thrills and Entertainment," proclaimed the Halloween teaser in the *New York Times*, "See *Eight Bells.*"

Colin Clive's new Broadway play was by Percy G. Mandley, who'd written the star role especially for Colin. The play had been a success in London, where Reginald Tate had landed the role since Colin had been unavailable. Financing the Broadway version: Columbia Pictures, which also held the film rights.

The briny plot: It's the summer of 1914, and Colin's vile captain lords it over his fully-rigged ship, *The Combermere*, like a boozy Captain Bligh. Also on board in the tropic heat, about 500 miles out of Rio, are his wife, Marjorie (Rose Hobart, who'd played Jekyll's fiancée Muriel in Paramount's 1931 *Dr. Jekyll and Mr. Hyde*), the heroic first mate she loves (John Buckler), and a crew of Britishers and Germans. Captain and first mate are fighting it out over Marjorie in a furniture-crashing brawl as a passing steamer signals that England is at war against Germany. Captain Dale refuses to put the Germans ashore in Rio, they mutiny, and the Captain is murdered before the English sailors regain last act command.

Eight Bells' opening night, Saturday, October 28, had hardly proven a triumph. Brooks Atkinson critiqued in the *New York Times*:

> *In the last act* Eight Bells *runs amuck and ends in a ridiculous muddle of thunderstorms, pistol shots and desperate heroics, with the heroine trotting around the stage in yellow oilskins, looking like a trademark for cod liver oil. The program says that* Eight Bells *was written for Colin Clive ... (he) plays this bedraggled part with admirable bite, but he should think twice in the future about parts that are written especially for him. Captain Dale is not only a scoundrel, but he is murdered before the play is over.*

Variety's review was no better:

> *... judging from the mild reception at the premiere, will hardly make the grade ...*

This Is Colin Clive, Who Visits This Country Every Now and Again. The Present Occasion Is on Behalf of "Eight Bells," in Which He Is Now Acting at the Hudson Theatre. The Play Opened There Last Night.

A sketch of Colin as Captain Dale, boozy ship master of *Eight Bells*, his second Broadway play.

Colin Clive ... gives an excellent impersonation of a heat-harried, short-tempered skipper. But impression is that he is younger than the men popularly believed to be captains of fully-rigged sailing ships.

Rose Hobart is Marjorie. She is supposed to be seductive, but isn't ...

During the run, Colin made lasting friends with *Eight Bells'* John Buckler. Born in Cape Town, South Africa on April 1, 1906, Buckler was a tall, attractive matinee idol type with an excellent speaking voice. Colin and Buckler would resume their close friendship in Hollywood, where, ironically, Buckler would play Colin's role of Captain Dale in Columbia's 1935 film version of *Eight Bells*.

As to his leading lady, Rose Hobart, Colin was withdrawn. Ms. Hobart, living her final years at the Motion Picture Country House, remembered Colin Clive:

> *I found him a most sensitive actor, but a very private person who would not let you into his private world.*

HUDSON THEATRE

COLIN CLIVE, ROSE HOBART AND JOHN BUCKLER

EIGHT BELLS

The program for *Eight Bells*. Colin Clive, Rose Hobart, and John Buckler.

The run of *Eight Bells* was brief—it sank after only 17 performances. Dwight Frye's *Keeper of the Keys* also flopped, lasting 23 performances. As for *Murder at the Vanities*, the show would run well into 1934, but Bela Lugosi would leave in late 1933 and soon return to Hollywood.

Friday, November 17: Six days after *Eight Bells* closed, *The Invisible Man*, in which Colin had hoped to star, opened at Broadway's Roxy and broke a three-year box office record.

> Eight Bells ... *well, he laid an egg this time, hadn't he?*
>
> *Quite a bad streak, isn't it?* Lily Christine *caused British Paramount to shutter.* Christopher Strong *was grand, working with Hepburn, but no success.* Looking Forward—*silly little role in a flop. Now* Eight Bells *went under.*
>
> *Was* Journey's End *a fluke? He'd always said it was.* Frankenstein? *It belonged to Boris, deservedly so.*
>
> *He had to soldier forward. A drink always helped, yet he couldn't let it get out of control again. See here, no more wallowing. Keep the demons at bay. Soldier on ...*

"She runs the gamut of emotions from A to B," notoriously remarked Dorothy Parker of Katharine Hepburn's performance in 1933's *The Lake*.

The Lake was a play by Dorothy Massingham and Murray MacDonald. Massingham worked on the script while suffering from a nervous breakdown and influenza. Shortly

Colin as Captain Dale in _Eight Bells_.

after completing the play, and before seeing it produced on Broadway, she committed suicide, found dead March 30, 1933 after gassing herself in the London home of a friend. Massingham was 42-years-old.

The story of _The Lake_: Stella Surrege, wealthy society beauty, has a mother who wants to cut down some venerable trees on their property to create a lake. Stella also has a meddlesome aunt and a married lover. Nevertheless, she engages herself to a different

"One Man _Crazy_ ...!"

man, John Clayne, who marries her, fully believing she really doesn't love him. But—lo—after the wedding, Stella and John "open their hearts" to each other, and she realizes she truly *does* love him. In bliss, they leave the wedding in his car. But the new lake has overflowed, the road is wet, the car skids into the lake, and John dies. The final act sees Stella walking to the lake ...

Katharine Hepburn, having starred in Hollywood in *A Bill of Divorcement*, *Christopher Strong*, *Morning Glory*, and *Little Women*, selected *The Lake* to prove she was still a theater star. She even agreed to work with the brilliant but notoriously cruel Jed Harris, who enjoyed trying to destroy the confidence of many actresses he directed and became known as the "Big Bad Wolf" of the American theater of that era.

Hepburn must have approved the casting of Colin, and he was surely eager to work again with her. Normally, Actors Equity would have ruled that Colin, as a foreigner, could appear in only one New York play every six months. However, on November 21, only 10 days after *Eight Bells* had closed, the council of Actors Equity met and agreed that Colin could join the cast of *The Lake*. Frank Gillmore, president of Actors Equity, explained, "the employment of Mr. Clive would benefit the employment of 25 to 26 American actors." In other words, *The Lake* had a better chance of a long run with Colin in the cast.

It must have been reassuring to receive this vote of confidence from Actors Equity after the failure of *Eight Bells*. And it would be exhilarating to act with Hepburn again, this time on the stage.

Colin received more good news two weeks later: December 5, 1933 saw the repeal of Prohibition.

As scripted, *The Lake* had a trio of star parts: Stella, Stella's mother Mildred, and Stella's Aunt Lena. Frances Starr (whom film fans will remember as the suicide mother in Warner Bros.' 1931 *Five Star Final*) signed on as Mildred, and Blanche Bates joined the show as Aunt Lena. Both ladies had been once-upon-a-time stars for the late David Belasco. Colin's role of John Clayne was basically a featured one. That he took the part was testimony both to his desire to act with Hepburn again, and his lack of ego as an actor.

Monday, December 18, 1933: The *Lake* opened for a try-out at the National Theatre in Washington, D.C. It was a capacity audience, with many socially prominent Washingtonians and alumnae from Bryn Mawr, Hepburn's alma mater, turning out "in force." It was a big night for Katharine Hepburn.

" ...Miss Hepburn found a decidedly appreciative audience, which called her

MARTIN BECK THEATRE

THE LAKE

KATHARINE HEPBURN

Program for *The Lake*, Colin's third Broadway play, 1933.

Katharine Hepburn and Colin in *The Lake*.

back for repeated bows of acknowledgement once the curtain had fallen," reported the *New York Times*. "She appeared to enjoy it very much."

"Miss Hepburn Triumphs in a Play of Merit," headlined the December 19th review in the *Washington Post*. Critic Nelson B. Bell praised Hepburn, Starr, and Bates. Late in his review, under the heading of "Excellent Support," he got around to Colin:

"One Man Crazy …!"

Colin Clive, in the tragic role of the ardent lover whose dream of happiness is abruptly snapped off by the skidding of an auto wheel, has less to do than the feminine members of the cast, but executes such tasks as fall to his lot with earnestness and warmth.

Tuesday night, December 26: *The Lake* opened at New York's Martin Beck Theatre, with a spectacular advance sale of $40,000. The opening night audience included Judith Anderson, Nancy Carroll, Kay Francis, George S. Kaufman, Amelia Earhart, and Hepburn's parents.

Katharine Hepburn's infamous line in *The Lake*: "The calla lilies are in bloom again …"

Initially, the play wasn't the debacle the legend has made it out to be; Hepburn's reviews were divided. In Los Angeles, the *Evening Herald Express* reported that the actress had received "mingled emotional outbursts of joy and pain by New York critics." *The Hollywood Reporter* headlined, "Hepburn Saves *The Lake* …" and opined the actress was "no disappointment." As for Colin, the same review wrote:

… Colin Clive is the noble gent and sorry indeed are we for him. Mr. Clive's part is just about the vaguest piece of characterization that any two authors had to collaborate on and on top of that he is forced to speak mainly in un-finished sentences and assume awkward silences. Mr. Clive does nobly—if he hadn't, no one would have noticed him at all.

Stage reported:

As John Clayne, the quiet ex-soldier … Colin Clive turns out, artistically, to be the star of The Lake *… Mr. Clive is alive, authoritative, queerly moving.*

The Lake would last 55 performances, the final curtain falling Saturday night, February 10—Hepburn had paid Jed Harris $15,000 of her own money to close it. Through it all, Colin gallantly defended his leading lady: "Someday she will probably be one of the leading stars of the Broadway stage."

In 1978, aware that Katharine Hepburn never signed autographs or answered fan mail, I nevertheless wrote to her at her Connecticut home, hoping against hope she might respond to an inquiry about Colin Clive. They'd co-starred in *Christopher Strong* and *The Lake*, and he'd been such a vocal champion of her—might there have been more to the story? Katharine Hepburn's response, penned on my returned letter: "I played with Colin. He was a lovely actor. I did not really know him at all."

She signed it, "K. Hepburn." As terse a response as it was, the fact that she never answered such requests, but did this one, must certainly have been testimony to her admiration for Colin.

With the handwriting on the wall for *The Lake*, Colin decided he'd head back to Hollywood after the play closed. The January 26, 1934 headline in *The Hollywood Reporter* had stated the news none-too-flatteringly:

Colin Clive Tries Again

The report noted he'd signed with agent Leo Morrison and "was due from New York for another sally at pictures in two weeks."

Colin took a plane to Hollywood. The *Omaha World-Herald* reported his layover in Omaha:

> *"Have you any Bourbon, please?" Colin Clive, the British actor, on his way to Hollywood to begin work on a picture Monday morning, asked an astonished airport restaurant waitress Sunday night.*
>
> *The waitress shook her head in amazement and rattled off a few brands of beer.*
>
> *"I say, haven't you any whiskey?" he asked. "I've been riding since morning and I need a spot of whiskey to set me up."*
>
> *He was surprised to learn Nebraska is dry.*

Warner Bros. was the gutsiest of the studios, with a contract roster boasting James Cagney, Bette Davis, Paul Muni, Kay Francis, Edward G. Robinson, Dick Powell, Joe E. Brown, Joan Blondell, Pat O'Brien, and Ruby Keeler.

Famed for its sexy musicals and gangster sagas, all dressed up with racy Depression era atmospherics, Warners had also produced several notable melodramas: John Barrymore had starred as *Svengali* (1931) and Lionel Atwill had achieved horror stardom in the studio's Technicolor chillers, *Doctor X* (1932) and *Mystery of the Wax Museum* (1933).

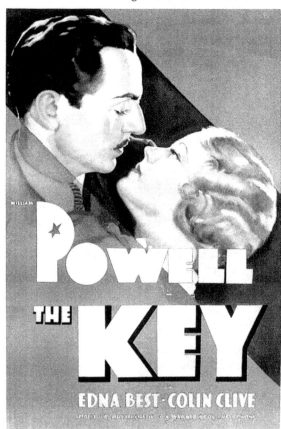

The Key, **Warner Bros., 1934.**

When Colin checked in at Warners—at $1,500 per week on a three-week guarantee—he found his new assignment, *The Key*, had started shooting February 9, and was in total disarray. Kay Francis, originally cast, was gone, and now Edna Best assumed the female lead. Colin himself was replacing Warren William as Captain Kerr. Archie Mayo was to direct, but the corpulent director was suffering stomach trouble, so Warners' top dog director, Michael Curtiz, replaced Mayo.

The story of *The Key*: It's 1920 Dublin, site of the Irish rebellion. Captain Andrew "Andy" Kerr (Colin), of British Intelligence discovers his best friend, Captain Bill Tennant (top-billed William Powell) dallying with Kerr's wife Norah (Edna Best, Colin's leading lady in 1930's *The Swan*). Kerr goes on a binge, is

"One Man *Crazy* ...!"

The Key. **Edna Best and Colin.**

captured by the Irish rebels—at which time Tennant, learning that Norah still loves her husband, forges a military document to rescue him. Powell, the forgery discovered, goes off a prisoner of the British Army, while Colin and Edna Best watch, eyes filled with gratitude for his noble self-sacrifice.

Columnist Grace Kingsley reported:

> *Colin Clive and Edna Best indulged in somewhat of a repast to make one scene for* The Key *at Warner Bros. The property man had to cook for them eight tender and juicy tenderloin steaks before the scene was approved. At the same time, they also finished four cans of peas, 18 cups of coffee and a loaf of bread. Everything for this particular meal had to be fresh.*

There was also a near-donnybrook on *The Key*'s set. To serve as a technical advisor, Warner Bros. hired Dr. Thomas McLaughlin, who'd been a staff surgeon in the Italian army during World War I, and a pathologist in the Leopold-Loeb murder trial case. McLaughlin was also a lawyer and a writer, and very persnickety in his work. Several small part actors in *The Key* decided to rebel and, as a prank, hooted with laughter one day at all of McLaughlin's suggestions. McLaughlin finally lost his temper and attacked his deriders, wildly swinging his fists until one detractor hit the floor.

According to the *Los Angeles Post-Record*, it was Colin who sympathetically led the nearly hysterical Dr. McLaughlin away from the set.

The Key wrapped up March 15. On March 16, Katharine Hepburn had a laugh on her *The Lake* naysayers—she won her first Academy Award, for *Morning Glory*.

Colin, director Michael Curtiz, and William Powell between scenes of *The Key*.

The same ceremony, Charles Laughton won the Best Actor prize for *The Private Life of Henry VIII*.

Neither Hepburn nor Colin's former classmate were in Hollywood that night. Colin was.

It was obvious to Warners, as it would be to audiences who'd see *The Key* after its summer release, that Colin gave the film's finest performance. He transcended his "other man" role of Captain Andy Kerr, giving a sharp, dynamic portrayal that became the true core of the film. Elinor Barnes would write a virtual ode to Colin in the *Boston Herald*:

> *Someday a really great mind in the cinema world will awaken to the fact that in the person of Colin Clive there is potential star material … While watching* The Key … *we were forcibly impressed once again with the emotional force and the seriousness which he can bring to a part that is even remotely in his line. He was not the star of this production, that honor being reserved for William Powell, but his performance was so far superior that as to leave the debonair Mr. Powell holding the short end of the stick.*
>
> *… he possesses an intangible something that distinguishes a fine actor from merely a competent one. A first sight of him and you are struck by the extreme mobility of his face; his mouth in particular is capable of any number of changes of expression, from a very winning smile to the extremities of bitterness and despair.*

It is, indeed, in essentially serious roles that he excels: his Captain Stan-hope in Journey's End *is already a classic both on the English stage and on the American screen, epitomizing in itself the futility and desperate courage of mankind when faced with utter disaster ...*

If there is any justice, or any common sense, for that matter, Colin Clive is going to be a name to be reckoned with ...

The justice and common sense would fail to be forthcoming. For one thing, *The Key*, which had a final cost of $246,000, would take in a worldwide rental of only $386,000, recording a loss of $16,500. For another, Hollywood was about to go into a mad panic, hysterically trying to save itself from a tornado of religious forces that threatened to destroy it.

For Colin Clive, one of the Pre-Code screen's most electrifying presences, the storm threatened to be catastrophic.

Chapter Eighteen
Holy War, Sex Beast, and Iris

The Black Cat, starring KARLOFF and Bela LUGOSI, as the posters proclaimed them, was shooting at Universal City in February and March of 1934, while Colin Clive was acting in *The Key* at Warner Bros.

The chiller presented a Black Mass, necrophilia, bastardized Poe, and a profane lulu of a climax—Lugosi skins Karloff alive. It's a wildly sensational vignette—Karloff, made up to look like Satan, hanging on a rack, stripped to the waist, yelping in agony.

The perverse imagery: Lucifer Crucified.

Joseph Breen, chief of the flexing Production Code Administration, had warned Universal about the skinning alive episode, along with approximately 20 (!) other points after he'd read the script for a censorship green-lighting. Producer Junior Laemmle and director Edgar G. Ulmer had spitefully thumbed their noses at most of Breen's objections, but Breen surprisingly gave *The Black Cat* a free pass. Perhaps he figured anyone who'd buy a ticket to such a movie deserved whatever he or she got.

The saga of the Production Code Administration and its 1934 blitzkrieg on Hollywood is far more complex than most historians care to present. The predominant portrait of Joe Breen, former Catholic seminarian, is one of a self-righteous bluenose, and Breen, early on, definitely had his prejudices.

"Sexual perversion is rampant," wrote Breen shortly after his arrival in Hollywood, "and any number of our prominent stars and directors are perverts."

Lugosi and Karloff in *The Black Cat*: Lucifer Crucified.

In fact, Breen was facing a critical challenge: a virtual Holy War. The Roman Catholic Church and its Legion of Decency, with its "Condemned" rating as its "big gun," was marching on the movies. It had Protestant and Jewish allies, but primarily it was a Catholic crusade, battling the Jews who dominated the film industry. The power of the Roman Catholic Church was easily able to scare filmgoers away—who wanted to go to Hell for seeing a movie?

"The pest hole that infects the entire country with its obscene and lascivious motion pictures," Joseph Breen had ghostwritten for Bishop John J. Cantwell in November of 1933, "must be cleaned and disinfected." The suggestive connotation was undeniable. Among the screen's racy sex symbols that would soon clean up their act was Jean Harlow—who'd even refine her hair color.

One More River poster, 1934.

For Colin Clive ... what would lie ahead for an actor who, as a Captain in the Great War, faced battle "doped with whiskey?" Or, as a mad scientist, orgasmically cried, "It's Alive!" over his blasphemous creation? Or, as a knighted adulterer, impregnated a young Amelia Earhart-type, bringing on her suicide and the death of their unborn child?

As if with a fanciful vengeance, the PCA "Purity League," as its enemies dubbed it, was about to chew up and spit out Colin Clive. In the majority of his films-to-come, the New Hollywood would cast Colin as the rampant pervert of Joe Breen's nightmares—or virtually castrate him.

First, he'd be a sex "beast," who ravages his wife with a riding whip ... directed by Jimmy Whale.

Diana Wynyard: *Father, did he tell you he used his riding whip on me?*
C. Aubrey Smith: *What? On you? The swine!*
Dialogue from *One More River*, 1934

One More River, based on the John Galsworthy novel, is basically the saga of Lady Clare Corven, gentle wife of Sir Gerald Corven. He's a sexual sadist ... and a rapist.

"He seems to be quite a beast!" says Dinny, Clare's sister—a line Joseph Breen will demand "looped" to say, "He seems to be quite a cad."

In a divorce trial climax that fills the final third of the film, Clare is too proud to tell the court how horrifically her vile spouse has victimized her. She's found guilty of

One More River: Colin Clive, as Sir Gerald, attacks Diana Wynyard, as his wife Clare.

adultery with her platonic admirer, Tony; Sir Gerald gets off scot-free. To add insult to injury, in the original ending, she attempts to seduce the loyal Tony—who, shocked, runs off into the night. The seduction scene would remain, but a new finale saw Tony returning for breakfast.

The script was by *Journey's End*'s R.C. Sherriff (who'd meanwhile scripted Whale's *The Invisible Man*). On April 10, 1934, Breen, having reviewed the script, had virtually told Universal there was no way *One More River* would ever see production:

> Under <u>Particular Applications</u> of the Code, Section 2 Subdivision 4, it is stated, "Sex perversion or any inference of it is forbidden" ... any story based upon sadism, or suggestive sadism, or inference of sadism, is, in its very nature, forbidden by the Code.

Whale tried charm on Breen, assuring him in a letter of May 5:

> We have actually secured for the picture the services of Diana Wynyard, Colin Clive, and Frank Lawton, to play the leading roles, and as they are all really gentle fools, I think our problem is already solved.

Diana Wynyard, who played Clare, was a sleek, towering British actress, borrowed by Universal from MGM. Her *One More River* deal paid $18,500 and provided a fashion parade of 19 costumes. Ms. Wynyard had already played a rape victim—violated by Lionel Barrymore's Mad Monk in MGM's *Rasputin and the Empress* (1932). Colin, of course, played the "beast" and "swine," Sir Gerald, signing on for four weeks at $1,500 per week. Frank Lawton, a charming (if diminutive) British actor, portrayed Tony, his deal calling for $7,500 plus a $1,000 bonus. Although Lawton was fine in the role, Ms. Wynyard loomed over him like an Amazon.

Friday, May 11: Whale, hell-bent on filming *One More River* his own way, began shooting on a $344,125 budget. The result, daring for its day, would be a handsome, uber-stylish romance/melodrama, sparked by Whale's dazzling stylistics, John J. Mescall's sparkling cinematography, and a superb featured cast: Jane Wyatt as Dinny, Clare's sister; C. Aubrey Smith as Clare's father; the legendary Mrs. Patrick Campbell (the original Eliza Doolittle in Shaw's 1914 *Pygmalion*) as Lady Mont; Alan Mowbray as Clare's lawyer; and—last but certainly not least—Lionel Atwill as Sir Gerald's lawyer.

In the shadowy presence of Colin's rapacious Sir Gerald, *One More River* is, at times, almost a horror film. Most of all, it survives as a Hollywood time capsule, the first film received by Joseph Breen's newly revised PCA ... to which Whale was defiantly throwing down the gauntlet.

Whale treats Colin to a *One More River* introduction worthy of Satan himself. "Sir Gerald Corven, My Lady" announces the heavyweight butler (Robert Greig), sinister music plays, and Colin slinks into the room, wearing a tux and mustache— receiving deluxe entrance close-ups, such as Whale had given Boris Karloff in *Frankenstein* and Claude Rains in *The Invisible*

The Roman Catholic Legion of Decency would give *One More River* its "Condemned" rating.

Man. Wynyard's Clare, at the news Gerald's in the house, has retreated behind a chair. Clive eyeballs her in her dark evening gown with plunging neckline and bare back:

> Wynyard: *What do you want?*
> Clive: *You!*
> Wynyard: *You can't have me.*
> Clive: *Don't be absurd!*
> He pounces, bends her back, tries to kiss her. She escapes.
> Colin: *Some women like rough- handling!*
> Wynyard: *You're a brute!*

The original line was "You're a beast!" Breen insisted it be changed to "brute." The scene escalates, Clive strutting, smoking a cigarette, saying he will not permit another man to have Clare, and admitting that divorce would be bad for his career.

> Wynyard: *Can't you understand? You've killed all the feeling I ever had for you. I'll never come back.*
> Colin: *And I say you will!*

The sadist strikes again, more viciously, bending her back, nearly yanking off her gown, almost exposing one of her breasts. He kisses her, laughs wickedly, and makes his exit.

"*Au revoir,*" says Colin's Sir Gerald, bowing. Undoubtedly, this "beast" belongs in a cage.

Unfortunately, Colin has little more to do in *One More River*, although his role runs throughout the 88-minute film. He has a soliloquy about his carnality, during a car drive with Jane Wyatt's Dinny, that Whale filmed despite Breen's objection:

> *What I want you to understand is that I'm two men. One, and the one that matters, has his work to do and means to do it. And the other man? Well, the less said about him the better.*

In fact, Colin and Diana Wynyard are both absent from the big, turning point rape scene, although he's the rapist and she's the victim. We see Sir Gerald accost Clare outside her apartment house and demand he go up with her to her flat. Based on scenes between that episode and the time Clare admits Dinny after Gerald has gone, the rapist has been having his wicked way with Clare for hours. And what does the freshly violated Clare say to her sister?

> Wynyard: *Have a cup of tea, I just made it ... Two lumps?*

Indeed, the stiff-upper-lip British cool that Whale personally emulated (usually) and admires in this film seems at times to play as satire. So do the highly mannered quirks of cast. There's a scene of Clare in her slip, calculated to be sexy, but becoming almost comical as Diana Wynyard tries valiantly all the while to keep her favored right profile facing the camera. And Whale surely should have noticed that Wynyard and Frank Lawton, while convincing as chums, totally lacked chemistry as potential lovers. As Jane Wyatt told film historian Tom Weaver:

> *I thought* One More River *was a very good picture, but they shouldn't have paired Frank Lawton and Diana Wynyard, because she looked like she could have been his mother ... She was never an ingénue, she was always a tall, wonderful-looking woman. And Frankie was tiny! So, there wasn't any romance, there wasn't any tension. Frankie Lawton could be very good, but in* One More River *he was so wimpy—and Colin Clive was so much more attractive! He was strong and masculine, a macho kind of guy.*

In fact, Wynyard *had* played Lawton's mother—in Fox's *Cavalcade*, 1933's Best Picture Academy Award winner. Wynyard (Oscar-nominated for Best Actress for *Cavalcade*, and losing to Katharine Hepburn for *Morning Glory*) had aged in *Cavalcade* from the years 1899 to 1933, and Lawton (two years older than Wynyard) had played her grown son, Joey, who dies in the Great War.

If Whale was trying, in his perverse way, to show that the Prince of Darkness was a more desirable lover than a cherub, he'd succeeded.

As *One More River* continued shooting at Universal, "macho" Colin moonlighted at Poverty Row's Monogram Studios, squeezing in *Jane Eyre*. He starred as Mr. Edward Rochester, he with the mad, screaming wife locked away in Thornfield Hall, in the first Talking version of Charlotte Bronte's 1847 novel.

Jane Eyre began shooting May 17, based at the General Service Studio and directed by Christy Cabanne. It was quite an auspicious "special" from Monogram, and blonde Virginia Bruce, who was divorcing John Gilbert, came over from MGM to play a picturesque Jane.

The result? A *Classics Illustrated* comic book of *Jane Eyre*, shot in eight (!) days, running 62 minutes, and scavenging the sets from Monogram's 61-minute *Oliver Twist* (1933). Still, the film has its charms. Colin's a dashingly Gothic Rochester, striking in his top hat, Victorian costume and sideburns, and impressive on horseback. He and Virginia Bruce strike limited chemistry—their kisses hardly set the screen afire—and while she appears a bit wilted at times, perhaps from the strain of the rapidly shot production, Colin never does.

Colin's Rochester makes a curious entrance in *Jane Eyre*: We see him (or most likely his

Jane Eyre **poster, 1934.**

double) in a horse fall—a reminder of the real-life accident that caused Colin to forsake the military for the theater. Also, one wonders if the character of Bertha, his lunatic wife (played by Claire de Brey), might have upset the sensitive actor in regard to his tragic Uncle Piercy. After Bertha sets Thornfield Hall on fire, and Rochester is blinded trying to rescue her, both Bruce and Colin do nicely with the Jane-and-Rochester Happy Ending, as snow falls outside and the music swells.

Monday, June 4: Variety reported: "Monogram has completed production of *Jane Eyre*, carrying heaviest negative cost of any picture made by the company in the past three years. Picture goes out as a special for the 1933-34 program ..." Monogram wasn't specific about its "heaviest negative cost," probably aware that the sum would cause producers at MGM and Paramount to roar with laughter. On June 29, *Jane Eyre* previewed at the Colorado Theatre in Pasadena. *Variety,* citing the current censorship hysteria, predicted

Jane Eyre: **Virginia Bruce and Colin Clive.**

that *Jane Eyre*'s box office chances depended on the sincerity of "the present campaigners who are calling for less hotcha subjects." The review tried to be as favorable as possible:

> *Virginia Bruce is an attractive "Jane," especially effective in the romantic parts calling for pathos. As "Rochester," Colin Clive is typical of the romantically-inclined story book Englishman of those days.*

"One Man *Crazy* ...!"

Colin as the blind Rochester.

Meanwhile, *One More River*, definitely a "hotcha" subject, was still shooting ... and Warner Bros. had offered Colin a contract.

Impressed by Colin's performance in *The Key*, Warner Bros. had prepared a pact for him. The terms, as they survive in the Warner archives:

> *Effective 5/15/34, or on the day following completion of artist's services for Universal in* One More River*:*

Service—Compensation:
Artist to render his services in two pictures during the period of one
year, and to be paid $1,500 per week for a period of at least four weeks in
each picture, and pro-rated thereafter.
Option for an Additional Picture
Company has option for a third picture in the first year on the same terms
and conditions. Applicable to each of the first two pictures in the first year.

The Hollywood Reporter announced the Warner Bros. contract on May 22, and Colin signed it on June 7. It was a good deal, in the sense that it allowed Colin freedom to work outside Warners, while affording him the prestige of being a contract star. However, the Warner Bros. lot in Burbank, under the rule of teeth-flashing, joke-cracking, ruthless Jack L. Warner, was always the site of explosive battles between the talent and the front office. Wilson Mizner, who'd written scripts for Warners such as *20,000 Years in Sing Sing* (1932) and who'd died in 1933, had quipped, "Working for Warner Bros. is like trying to fuck a porcupine. It's one prick against a hundred."

Colin would soon suffer quills in his hide at Warner Bros.

Meanwhile, there was personal news: Jeanne de Casalis was planning to sail from England and visit Colin in Hollywood! On June 11, both the *Los Angeles Examiner* and the *Los Angeles Evening Herald Express* announced the news, and there was word she, too, would sign for a film at Warner Bros.

Perhaps fortunately, Jeanne never made the trip. If she had—shades of that night during *Journey's End* in London when Tallulah Bankhead made her move on Colin—there might have been one hell of a catfight.

Colin had a lover.

The surviving Pre-Code glamour and cheesecake pictures of Iris Lancaster are an eyeful.

In one, the five foot, five inch 118-pound, red-haired leggy showgirl stands in her black high heels, holding a large bonnet that barely covers her breasts and pubis. Another shows her outside, in lingerie, hands on hips, smiling triumphantly, winning a contest as the "Perfect Physical Specimen of Girlhood," her competitors lined up and probably wishing they could scalp her. Perhaps the most startling shot is the one of Iris, seated at a table, staring at the camera with wild eyes and a rictus smile, holding a syringe needle, other syringes littering the table.

Born in Arcadia, Florida on February 3, 1915, Iris Idele Lancaster had moved to Los Angeles with her mother and sister Valerie, who was five years older than Iris and had been voted "Best Looking" girl in the St. Petersburg High School Yearbook of 1927. Iris attended Immaculate Heart School in Hollywood, and at age 18, she (along with sister Valerie) was on contract to Educational Films Corporation, which despite the name, specialized in racy comedy shorts. Among her films there: *Hot Hoofs* (1933), a George Moran and Charles Mack race track hilarity with Iris as "Rabbit's Foot, the good luck girl." She'd been one of the "200 Beauties!" in RKO's *Flying Down to Rio* (1933), presumably one of the scantily-clad chorus girls dancing on the wings of the soaring planes. She was also one of seven beauties (and the only redhead) Earl Carroll personally selected out of a pool of 760 applicants to festoon Paramount's *Murder at the Vanities* (1934). According

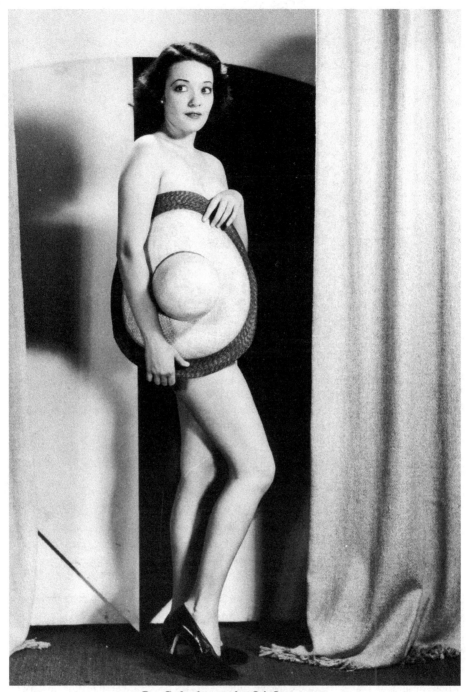

Pre-Code cheesecake: Iris Lancaster.

to a February, 1934 press release at the time of *Murder at the Vanities*, "Her chief diversion is riding horseback, her avocations are piano and guitar playing and painting."

Iris Lancaster, stripped to her lingerie, is named Hollywood's "Perfect Physical Specimen of Girlhood." The shot is publicity for *Flying Down to Rio* (RKO, 1933), in which Iris was a showgirl. Standing by are "Madame Sylvia, a famous masseuse and physical culture genius," various other contestants, and an RKO Associate Producer.

Iris took herself, her beauty, and her self-perceived talent quite seriously. In the spring of 1934, while providing publicity for Earl Carroll and her fellow *Murder at the Vanities* showgirls, Iris proclaimed:

> *I don't want to get married. I'll never marry! Not for a long, long time—if ever. It doesn't interest me. I want to be a dramatic actress, like Greta Garbo or Katharine Hepburn. They're my favorites. I want to do something fine—something hard—something worthwhile ... I don't suppose anything can be done about love. You have to take it if it comes to you, but I shan't let it stop me! I'm going to make my mark. You'll see!*

She moved on to MGM, where Iris was a showgirl in *Hollywood Party* (1934) starring Laurel and Hardy, Jimmy Durante, Lupe Velez, and Mickey Mouse. She also became Metro's stand-in for Joan Crawford.

Iris Lancaster was a spectacularly attractive 19-year-old, even by Hollywood standards, when she and 34-year-old Colin Clive became lovers. It's not clear when Jeanne de Casalis learned about her, but the fact that Jeanne cancelled her trip to Hollywood infers that she either discovered the truth about Iris, or Colin had persuaded Jeanne to stay in England.

Colin and Iris ... Dr. Frankenstein and the redheaded "Perfect Physical Specimen of Girlhood," who'd vowed to make her mark. Quite a couple they were. She'd be loyal to

Iris Lancaster and ... needles. In Pre-Code Hollywood, almost anything was possible!

him to the last, and late in his life, even claim to be his spouse, although he and Jeanne would never divorce. Yet some Clive fans have been over-eager to see the union as a storybook romance. David Lewis, James Whale's lover, who along with Whale, kept an eye on Colin at this time, referred to Colin as "a very sweet man who tended to be very badly used by women." While Lewis didn't mention Iris specifically, she was apparently Colin's steady lover the last three years of his life, so one can draw a conclusion.

One More River: **The climactic courtroom episode. Lionel Atwill plays Colin's dynamic lawyer. Seated behind Colin is E.E. Clive.**

Also, while Colin's "Hyde" side had been basically under control since 1930, his startling, soon-to-come, ultimately fatal plunge would coincide with his love affair with Iris Lancaster.

One More River went on at Universal, over schedule, Whale battling Breen. He even had to fight Diana Wynyard, who announced one day she'd play a scene in a sweater without her brassiere. Whale got so angry he closed down the set while he and Diana had it out. "I don't remember if he ever got her into a bra ...," recalled Jane Wyatt.

Most of the time, Jimmy Whale had fun, and even made a cameo: leading a cheer at a political rally. The climactic courtroom scene in the Old Bailey is a dazzler (although sadly lacking in a proper payoff), Diana Wynyard in her cocked hat and draped fur, duking with Lionel Atwill's preening "Mr. Brough." When Colin's "Gerald" takes the stand and claims he and Clare had resumed sexual relations—when, in fact, he'd raped her—*One More River* takes on a dark, perverse aura, rare in even the rawest Pre-Code films.

> Sir Gerald: *My wife and I were reunited.*
> Judge: *You mean that the marital relationship between you was reestablished?*
> Sir Gerald: *Yes, my lord.*

Breen had warned Universal to cut Sir Gerald's lie. Whale had shot it anyway. Meanwhile, censorship across America had become a firestorm.

"One Man *Crazy* ...!"

• June 8: Cardinal Dougherty announced his Philadelphia diocese would boycott all movies.

• June 18: 50,000 people took the pledge for the Catholic Legion of Decency in Cleveland.

• July 3: Whale completed *One More River*.

• July 7: Breen demanded over 30 cuts. Whale worked feverishly with retakes and new scenes.

Cut, spliced and patched together like a filmic Frankenstein's Monster, *One More River* played a preview in Santa Barbara July 27, underwent more revision and, after a week's delay for its opening, premiered August 9 at both the Hollywood Pantages Theatre and Radio City Music Hall. The negative cost was $366,842.24—more than $20,000 over budget. As such, it was Colin's most expensive film since *Frankenstein*. Reviews were raves, and *Literary Digest* saluted Colin's "properly savage" portrayal.

Nevertheless, despite all the cuts and revisions, The Roman Catholic Legion of Decency gave *One More River* the rating "Condemned."

21st century sensibility encourages abused women to fight back against their abusers. *Time* magazine's Person(s) of the Year for 2017 were "The Silence Breakers" of the MeToo Movement. As such, the pride of *One More River*'s Clare Corven seems pathetically vain and almost shocking to a modern audience, leaving her twisted husband free to romp and rape another night. As a director, James Whale largely reserved human emotion for his lost souls and his monsters. One wishes Diana Wynyard had screamed at the sight of Colin Clive in court in *One More River* the way Elsa Lanchester would shriek at the sight of Karloff in the laboratory in *Bride of Frankenstein*.

Times change, sometimes for the better. As such, *One More River* appears fated to become one of Golden Age Hollywood's most stylishly directed, best-acted fossils.

One More River was a milestone of sorts for Colin Clive. Even those who avoided the film out of fear of eternal damnation probably heard about it, and the "shocking" nature of the role Colin so convincingly played. In a country with a film industry, as some might say, ravaged by censorship, Colin's dashing Sir Gerald Corven was the pervert's pin-up boy. The man who made a monster had an all-new notoriety.

Meanwhile, just after *One More River* originally wrapped, Colin was at the Cocoanut Grove, enjoying Gus Arnheim's Orchestra. His date, of course: Iris Lancaster.

Chapter Nineteen
A *Journey's End* Reprise,
The Right to Live, and
"That Hard-Drinking Ancestor of Mine"

All was not well at Warner Bros.

In July of 1934, Colin was set to star in Warners' *The Firebird*. His sympathetic role-to-be was John Pointer, whose 18-year-old daughter (Anita Louise) kills an actor/Lothario (Ricardo Cortez) who's been dallying with her ... and now wants to dally with her mother (Veree Teasdale). William Dieterle was to direct. Then Colin was out—replaced by no less than Lionel Atwill.

Why? *The Hollywood Reporter* claimed it was because Colin was being saved for "a more important assignment"—which probably didn't sit well with Atwill! However, a July 31, 1934 memo from Warner producer Hal Wallis to an executive underling reveals the true reason, and the studio's rapid disillusionment with its new contractee:

> *Before we agree to exercise the option on Colin Clive for a third picture during the year, I think we should get [Leo] Morrison [Clive's agent] in and let him know the insistence on exercising the option for a third picture is unreasonable ... the principal reason we took Clive out of [The Firebird] was because his head was shaved, which we did not know when we signed him for the picture, and generally, he looked very bad for the part ... Don't do anything on an option for a third picture until you have battled with Morrison and, if you can't do anything with him, let me know.*

Why was his head shaved? A hot summer in Hollywood? A Samson and Delilah role-playing night with Iris?

It's possible Wallis was referring to Colin having a military haircut for a stage revival of *Journey's End,* set to open at the Hollywood Playhouse. However, publicity shots for the *Journey's End* revival don't show any severe trimming—certainly nothing to keep him out of movies, where wigs and hairpieces were always in use. In fact, it appears Colin might be wearing a toupee in shots from the 1934 *Journey's End,* although it's impossible to confirm.

At any rate, if Colin *had* shaved his head in mid-July of 1934, for whatever bizarre reason, it must have spooked Hal Wallis—whose memo suggests he was eager to scrap Colin's option for a third picture and get Colin off the lot as quickly as possible.

Thursday, August 9, 1934: On the date *One More River* opened at Radio City Music Hall and the Pantages, *Journey's End* opened at the Hollywood Playhouse, with Colin Clive reprising Captain Stanhope. *Variety* reported the curtain had gone up 15 minutes late and that the house wasn't full. Edwin Martin, who'd become a personal friend of Colin's and frequently name-dropped him in his column, handled the publicity for the revival and wrote the next day in the *Hollywood Citizen News:*

> *The Boulevard at 11:30 P.M ... breathing in gulps of fresh air after going over to see Colin Clive and an excellent company enact* Journey's End *...*

A revival of *Journey's End*, Hollywood Playhouse, August, 1934. Colin reprises Stanhope. Left in the shot is Forrester Harvey (memorable as the innkeeper in *The Invisible Man*) as Trotter. On the right is Reginald Sheffield as Hibbert.

and James Whale was kept busy ... running back and forth from the Play-house to the Pantages ... he was the original director of Journey's End, *and is very interested in the production ... but he is also director of* One More River *at the Pantages ... he'd see one show for five minutes and then sneak across and see how the other was doing ... and both were doing splendidly, thank you, he said.*

While Whale, of course, directed the original production of *Journey's End*, the actual director of the revival was E.E. Clive (no relation to Colin), who'd played Constable Jaffers in Whale's *The Invisible Man* and the snooping detective in *One More River*. E.E. Clive also appeared in this production as Mason, the comical cook.

Colin had approached the revival with all his intensity. At a dress rehearsal, in the showdown scene between Stanhope and the cowardly Hibbert, played by Reginald Sheffield, Colin threw Sheffield against a table so roughly that the table overturned and Sheffield badly cut his hand on glass from a broken bottle.

"The first thing Clive did after the scene was over," wrote Edwin Martin, "was to rush to Sheffield and apologize for being too rough in the scene."

Response to the revival was mixed. The *Los Angeles Examiner* wrote that Colin Clive "was warmly applauded on his entrance and after his poignant scenes, and his first appearance on the Los Angeles stage added another triumph to his career." The *Evening*

Herald Express, however, found the play's opening night "unsteady," wrote that Gerald Rogers (as Osborne), Forrester Harvey (as Trotter), and E.E. Clive were "superb," and that Colin Clive was among several cast members who would be seen to better advantage "when the play settles down to smoother staging."

It might be simply an impression, but Colin looks a bit startling in the publicity shots for this incarnation of *Journey's End*. He appears far older than he had in the film (perhaps due to the hairpiece, if it was a hairpiece) and somehow unhealthy, as if actually drunk. As noted, on the London stage and in the Hollywood film, he'd truly been drunk, at least part of the time. Here, he looks strange ... dissipated.

He'd always relied on alcohol to portray Stanhope. Was he doing it again?

Saturday, August 11: The *Hollywood Citizen News* noted Colin's starring in the *Journey's End* revival and called him "a frank young actor" because: "He admits that he is always broke—because he spends his money on books." The article continued:

> *Books are one of his three major interests—one is his wife, Jeanne de Casalis, a famous French actress; another is his own theatrical and film activity; and the third, his books.*

One suspects that if Iris Lancaster read this story, Colin caught hell for it.

Monday night, August 13: Colin guest-starred on KFI Radio's *The Show*, playing a scene from *Journey's End*. Stage fright was still a bugaboo for him. Three days later, Hollywood columnist Read Kendall reported:

> *Colin Clive played the lead for months in the stage production of* Journey's End. *He was starred in the filmization and is now reviving it on the stage here. And he got the jitters when he did a radio version.*

Clearly, Colin's Stanhope still had its haunting power—Ayn Rand thought so. After a *Journey's End* performance, E.E. Clive introduced Colin to Rand, who'd been in the audience that night. The 29-year-old Rand, destined to author *The Fountainhead* (1943) and *Atlas Shrugged* (1957), had written the courtroom play *Night of January 16*, which E.E. Clive would produce at the Hollywood Playhouse in October of 1934, and which would open on Broadway in 1935. Ms. Rand followed up her meeting Colin with a fan letter:

> *Dear Mr. Clive,*
> *I do not know whether you read 'fan mail,' but I hope you will read this, and I hope—most anxiously—that it will interest you ...*
> *I want to thank you for the little bit of rare beauty you have given me, a real spark of something which does not exist in the world today ... I am speaking of your achievement in bringing to life a completely heroic human being.*
> *The word heroic does not quite express what I mean. You see, I am an atheist and have only one religion: the sublime in human nature. There is nothing to approach the sanctity of the highest type of man possible and there is nothing that gives me the same reverent feeling, the feeling when one's spirit wants to kneel, bareheaded. Do not call it hero-worship, because it is more than that. It is a kind of strange and improbable white heat where*

"One Man *Crazy* ...!"

admiration becomes religion and religion becomes philosophy, and philosophy becomes—the whole of one's life.

I realize how silly words like these may sound today. Who cares about heroes anymore and who wants to care? ... [W]ho can still understand the thrill of seeing a man such as you were upon the stage? ... It was something in you, in the whole of the man you were, something not intended by the play at all, that gave me, for a few hours, a spark of what man could be, but isn't ... and that is an achievement for which one has to be grateful.

This is what I wanted to say to you, when I met you a few days ago, but I could not say it to you in person. That is why I am writing this. Perhaps it will only make you smile ...
Gratefully yours,
Ayn Rand
(In case you don't remember—as, of course, you don't—this is the Russian writer to whom Mr. E.E. Clive introduced you a few nights ago. The 'vodka' may remind you.)

In the 1997 *Letters of Ayn Rand*, editor Michael S. Berliner added that, "Clive responded that AR's letter meant a great deal to him and that he would always keep it. He told her that he'd toasted her play *Woman on Trial* (later retitled *Night of January 16th*) with vodka that night."

Between acts of a *Journey's End* performance, Colin joined Forrester Harvey (who played Trotter in the revival, and who'd portrayed Mr. Hall, the landlord in *The Invisible Man*) and columnist Edwin Martin for tea and told a funny story. Colin always gave autographs, and one young boy had asked him to sign his book again, even after Colin had signed it several times. **Ayn Rand: Future novelist of *The Fountainhead*, and a Colin Clive fan.**

"But I've signed your book before," said Colin, amused.

"Yes sir," said the boy, "but when I get 10 of yours I can swap them for one of George Arliss!"

Colin had taken up quarters, as he usually had during his trips to L.A., at "The Hollywood Tower," aka "La Belle Tour," 6200 Franklin Avenue. The hotel/apartment house overlooked the movie capital to the south and offered a view of the HOLLYWOODLAND sign to the north. In 2018, it still stands.

He remained a champion of Katharine Hepburn. Various folks sought his opinion of her, considering he'd starred with her in *Christopher Strong* and Broadway's *The Lake*.

The Hollywood Tower, where Colin lived off and on during the early 1930s. (Photo by author)

At one point, he handwrote a four-page letter on his "La Belle Tour" stationery in reply to a Hepburn inquiry:

> *She is charming to work with and not in the least conceited ... I met her before she was the great Hepburn and I met her after she was the great Hepburn. She hadn't changed in the least. Everyone has mannerisms and certainly she has but they are not put on. I don't think there's much more that I can say except that she played in* The Lake *under a <u>tremendous</u> handicap—There was too much ballyhoo before she opened and her nerve failed her on the first night. Had the critics seen her performance two weeks later, I think there would have been a different story.*
>
> *Finally, she possesses one of the most vital qualities in the "make-up" of an actor—she can take it on the chin and come back for more.*
>
> *I hope to God you can read this but I'm writing under difficulties.*
> *Sincerely,*
> *Colin Clive*

August 27, 1934: Colin wrote a letter to Jeanne:

> *I've been waiting and waiting for the promised copy of your play ...*
>
> *My next picture doesn't start for a few weeks so I am "in response to numerous requests etc. etc." playing* Journey's End *here. No money in it of course but great houses. Sherriff didn't even bother to come near us or even send the company a wire!*

"One Man *Crazy* ...!"

Colin on the rooftop of the Hollywood Tower and the HOLLYWOODLAND sign as a backdrop.

Well, Darling, all the luck and money you deserve and my God that's
a hell of a lot!
Bisto Loco
Colin

The view from the Hollywood Tower rooftop in 2016. The HOLLYWOOD Sign, long minus the LAND, still stands in the distance. (Photo by the author)

The letter's a curiosity. Colin was seriously involved with Iris Lancaster, Jeanne had cancelled her trip to Hollywood—yet he was still referring to Jeanne as "Darling." Perhaps Jeanne realized the truth—she apparently tore the letter in half. Nevertheless, she saved it with her correspondence, the only letter from her former husband found when her archive went up for sale at Heritage Auction Galleries in 2007.

As for "Bisto Loco"… "Loco" means crazy, but "Bisto Loco" eludes translation, even when shown to a veteran Spanish-to-English translator for the State of Pennsylvania. Perhaps it was an inside joke.

Colin departed the *Journey's End* revival early, *Variety* giving the reason that his status as a foreigner might have flagged immigration officials to his permit nearing expiration. He took off to Mexico to renew his quota extension, and John Warburton assumed his role for the last 10 days or so of the run.

The reason for the Mexican trip was no doubt authentic, but there was likely an additional attraction. During his visits to Hollywood, Colin's gambling addiction had intensified, both north and south of the border. The casino at Agua Caliente had great allure for him, as it did for such Hollywood gamblers as Carl Laemmle, Sr. and Jean Harlow.

Warners, meanwhile, was wondering what to do with Colin. Aware of his role in *One More River*, the studio had found a new part for him that seemed almost a belated come-uppance for rapist Sir Gerald Corven: a character paralyzed from the waist down.

The Right to Live, based on Somerset Maugham's play *The Sacred Flame*, dealt with this bizarre romantic triangle: Maurice Trent, hopelessly crippled in a plane crash, will never again have sexual relations with his young wife, Stella. Enter Maurice's dashing brother, Colin Trent, who comes at the news of his brother's accident and falls madly in love with Stella. They profess their love for each other—and Maurice dies.

Did Stella and Colin kill Maurice so they could run off together? If not, who did?

On August 21, 1934, Joseph Breen had responded to Warner Bros.' intention of producing *The Right to Live*, then titled *The Future Belongs to You*:

> *... The elements of the story, which deal with the frustrated sex life of Maurice and Stella are, at present, open to grave and serious objection. We feel, however, that these portions of the script might easily be changed ...*
>
> *What makes this story unacceptable from the point of view of the Production Code is the fact that Mrs. Trent [Maurice's mother] steps into a situation which is making the lives of three people permanently unhappy, and, as a* deus ex machina, *solves the situation by killing her crippled son. Such an immoral act is definitely a crime against human and Divine law, presented in such a manner that it throws sympathy toward the crime and the criminal.*
>
> *... We feel that the problems involved in the presentation of this story and the solutions effected for them do not present a satisfactory moral attitude for universal public consumption.*

The Right to Live, Josephine Hutchinson as a not-very-happy-looking bride, and Colin as her soon-to-be-crippled husband. C. Aubrey Smith stands behind Colin.

Two mornings later, Hal Wallis met with Breen, who wrote to Jack L. Warner about Wallis' proposed revamp of the story:

> *The new treatment, which Mr. Wallis has in mind, removes entirely from the story any suggestion of the condonation of murder ... in addition, it has been agreed between us that the relationship between the brother and the wife will be kept clean. There will be the suggestion, of course, that they have fallen in love—but there will be no suggestion of any sex relationship between them.*

Breen concluded by commending Warner and Wallis "for the very excellent way" they'd cooperated, opining that the new approach "improves the story both from a dramatic and entertainment standpoint, as well as its general acceptability."

Warner Bros. considered Genevieve Tobin and Barbara Stanwyck for Stella, but eventually set the studio's new contractee, the red-haired Josephine Hutchinson, formerly of Eva Le Gallienne's Civic Repertory Company. "Jo" Hutchinson's fee for *The Right to Live*: $12,000.

George Brent, strapping all-purpose Warner Bros. leading man, landed the role of Colin Trent, while Colin Clive took on the role of crippled Maurice Trent. Brent's salary for the picture: $4,000. Colin as Maurice Trent got his usual Warners payday—$1,500 per week, for a total of $6,000.

The new cause of Maurice's death: Suicide.

Monday, October 1: Shooting began, with William Keighley directing. Josephine Hutchinson recalled that Keighley shot economically, all set scenes and angles at a time, and regularly had gigantic meals served to him on the set. The featured cast included Henrietta Crosman as Mrs. Trent, C. Aubrey Smith as the Major, and Leo G. Carroll as Dr. Harvester. Peggy Wood was a standout as Wayland, the tall, blonde, rather spooky nurse who clearly falls into obsessive love with her patient, Maurice. ("I saw his naked, tortured, triumphant soul!")

As for Colin, Ms. Hutchinson said, "Colin was a good actor and a charming man. It is sad that his time came in his early years."

George Brent was considerably sharper in his opinion of Colin: "A maniac who might cut your head off one night and plunk it in the icebox!"

The Right to Live, Warner Bros., 1935.

"One Man *Crazy* ...!"

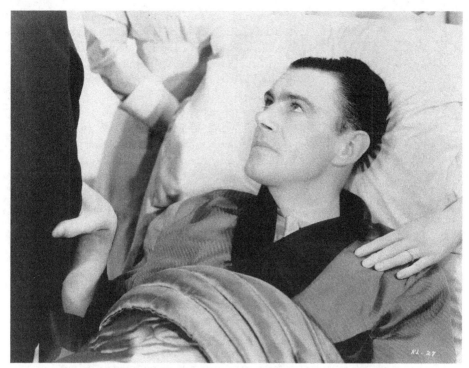

One of Colin's finest performances: Maurice Trent in *The Right to Live*.

Ironically, as Colin was playing a crippled pilot in *The Right to Live*, he was actually taking flying lessons in Hollywood. So was Iris Lancaster. On October 13, this item appeared in the *Los Angeles Examiner:*

> *Irene* (sic) *Lancaster and Colin Clive, the British actor, who are "thata' way" about each other, are rowing; not a lovers' battle but arguing over their air record; seems the red-haired actress beat her boyfriend to a goal of soloing by two days.*

Colin plays Maurice with great gallantry of spirit, a sense of bravery. Rarely did he look so pleasant in a film, even though the smiles are clearly a mask for the torment Maurice is suffering. His death scene is remarkably moving, as he dies slowly after his self-poisoning:

> *Free, not to be afraid anymore. Free, not to have to try anymore. Free, like the trees and the clouds and the streams. Not to have to set your will towards anything. But just to be carried on, unresisting, in the flow of things—down to the last, final, merciful sea.*

It's one of his finest showcases.

Colin finished his work on *The Right to Live* Monday, October 22, with an exterior shot of a church at Maurice's wedding to Stella (35 extras) and an interior shot in Maurice's bedroom. *The Right to Live* wrapped up October 24, and Warners toyed with the idea of a revised ending for British release, with the original revelation of the mother

poisoning her son. Joseph Breen responded that any such ending would be "a grave violation of both the spirit and letter of the Production Code," and that the studio was opening itself up to a fine of $25,000.

Warner Bros. retained the Breen-approved ending.

As for Josephine Hutchinson ... having played Colin's wife and widow in *The Right to Live*, she was destined to appear in Universal's 1939 *Son of Frankenstein*, playing Henry Frankenstein's daughter-in-law, Elsa, wed to Basil Rathbone's Dr. Wolf von Frankenstein. Colin wouldn't live to see her *Son of Frankenstein* performance.

Meanwhile, both significant ladies in Colin's life had made new films.

Jeanne de Casalis as the wicked, lascivious Duchess in England's *Nell Gwyn*, 1934.

England's sumptuous *Nell Gwyn*, produced by Herbert Wilcox and starring his wife Anna Neagle in the racy title role, co-starred Sir Cedric Hardwicke as Charles II, Nell's lover, and Jeanne de Casalis as the Duchess, Nell's rival for the King's bed. Censorship travails abounded. At one point, a maid refers to Jeanne's Duchess as a "dirty, wicked, shameless, scheming foreign whore."

Nell's reply: "We must be fair to her. She can't help being foreign."

Picture Play wasn't impressed:

> *Sir Cedric Hardwicke, who can't have won his title by acting, is a phlegmatic Charles II and Jeanne de Casalis—Mrs. Colin Clive—quaintly suggests a female impersonator as the stately, spiteful duchess ...*

Also, Monogram Studios released *The Trail Beyond*, one of John Wayne's "six-day wonders," from Lone Star Productions. Blonde Verna Hillie (who'd been a runner-up as the Panther Woman in *Island of Lost Souls*) was the heroine, and red-haired Iris Lancaster, hoping to ascend from showgirl to featured vamp, was the beret-sporting villainess, "Marie LaFleur." *The Trail Beyond* revealed Iris to be a beautiful woman and a dreadful actress, and it would be years before she landed another film role. Meanwhile, her steady pay gig continued at MGM, where Iris was the stand-in for Joan Crawford.

Clive of India, was a biopic about Robert Clive, from Darryl F. Zanuck's 20th Century Productions. Ronald Colman played the title role, Loretta Young played his wife Margaret, and Colin Clive—although third-billed—had a virtual bit as "Captain Johnstone." We meet Johnstone early in the film, in India, waging a pistol duel with Robert Clive, then a clerk of the East India Company. Robert Clive fires first and misses. Johnstone advances on him, his pistol at point blank range:

> Johnstone: *Do you still say I'm a cheat?*
> Robert Clive: *I still say you're a cheat! Get it over—shoot!*
> Johnstone: *The man's mad!*

Clive's Johnstone doesn't fire. We see him a few more times, including reprimanding Colman's Clive for leaving his post at the Battle of Trichinopoly. Then he vanishes until the climax of the film when Johnstone appears in the House of Commons, testifying against Robert Clive, claiming he accepted bribes in India.

Presumably Colin was supposed to epitomize the sinister forces that threatened Robert Clive's career. Obviously, *Clive of India* wanted Colin Clive for publicity; as noted, he later claimed it was only four days' work. It must have galled him, considering that one of his most cherished possessions was a gold medal awarded his alleged ancestor for his colonial adventures.

Richard Boleslawski directed *Clive of India*. Its best moments: the Battle of Plassey, with Robert Clive's army fighting the armored battle elephants of King Suraj Ud Dowlah (played by Mischa Auer), and a too-brief visit to the Black Hole of Calcutta.

An advertisement for *Clive of India* (1935).

Both *Clive of India* and *The Right to Live* were set for early 1935 release. More on them later.

On November 28, 1934, Colin attended the Screen Actors Guild Ball at the Biltmore Bowl, although he'd not yet joined the SAG. Among the many celebrities at the Ball: James Cagney, Joan Crawford, Fredric March, Jeanette MacDonald, Bill "Bojangles" Robinson, and one of the SAG's founders, Boris Karloff.

Meanwhile, James Whale had engaged William J. Hurlbut to write the final script for the Universal's *Frankenstein* sequel. Hurlbut's major success had been the 1926 Broadway play *Bride of the Lamb*, starring Alice Brady as a sexually hysterical Midwest housewife who murders her husband. Come the finale, the insane murderess dresses as a bride to marry an invisible Jesus Christ.

Whale had found his man. *The Return of Frankenstein* prepared production.

> *The restlessness was growing again ... the anxiety.*
> *Another Christmas time in Hollywood, as it had been during* Journey's End. *The Santa Claus Lane Parade down Hollywood Boulevard. He'd heard a rumor that Santa rode every night roaring drunk. Maybe St. Nick had stage fright. If so, he sympathized.*

Colin as Johnstone in *Clive of India*, 20th Century, 1935.

Sun-baked Hollywood, where they didn't know what the hell to do with him ... cast him as a rapist or a eunuch? Stick him in that Clive of India *whitewash. Still a puppet, dancing to a director's strings ...*

Iris in Hollywood ... Jeanne in London ... What to do? Keep moving. Drive fast. Buy books. Fly the biplane.

Drink.

"One Man *Crazy* ...!"

Yes, he was back where he'd been at Yuletide, 1929. Drinking again. Melting in a city of woolen snowmen. He'd read all the studios were sending their stars to the Shrine Auditorium for a Christmas benefit. Universal was sending Karloff to the festivity. Nobody had invited him. Just as well; he'd have been scared to death.

And what in bloody hell would he do to provide Yuletide entertainment—scream "It's Alive!"?

It reminded him—Jimmy finally had the Frankenstein *sequel in the works at Universal.* The Return of Frankenstein, *they were calling it. Of course, the "return" everybody anticipated was the Monster's, not Henry Frankenstein's. Still, he'd be glad to play God again, make a new monster ... but a very different one. How had the Bible put it, when the Jesuits at Stonyhurst had drilled it into them? Oh, yes.*

"Male and Female, created He them ..."

Part V
Bride of Frankenstein, Mad Love, and Other Grotesqueries

After coming in daily contact with Karloff as the misshapen monstrosity, there were nights when I went home dodging shadows. For no matter how practical or unimaginative a person may be, he is bound to react to some extent to the situations he helps develop in the blood-curdlers.

During the making of Mad Love, *when another's hands were supposedly grafted onto my own wrist stubs, hideous scars were so realistically faked that I involuntarily shuddered every time I looked at them.*

Aside from that, though, it has been interesting and lucrative work, and I'd rather have my sleep disturbed by dreams of imaginary monsters than the thoughts of real creditors!

Colin Clive, "Hollywood Parade," Los Angeles *Examiner*, October 29, 1935

"One Man *Crazy* ...!"

Chapter Twenty
1935

I began to be tortured with throes and longings, as of Hyde struggling after freedom. I once again compounded and swallowed the transforming draught. My devil had been long-caged; he came out roaring ...
Robert Louis Stevenson, *Dr. Jekyll and Mr. Hyde*

New Year's Day, 1935 ...

It would be one of Hollywood's most glorious years. The battle of the Film Industry vs. the Production Code Administration was escalating, creating a mad mix of piety and sadism—and making the movies a bloody Colosseum of martyrs and monsters.

1935's Best Picture Oscar winner: MGM's *Mutiny on the Bounty*, in which Charles Laughton's Captain Bligh flogs a corpse. 1935's Best Actor winner: Victor McLaglen for RKO's *The Informer*, which ends with McLaglen dying before a statue of Christ on the Cross. While McLaglen got the Oscar, Laughton won the New York Film Critics Award.

Basil Rathbone whipped little Freddie Bartholomew in *David Copperfield*. Douglass Dumbrille (as noted in Chapter One) inserted bamboo shoots under Gary Cooper's fingernails in *Lives of a Bengal Lancer*. Blanche Yurka, as Madame De Farge, ogled headless guillotine victims in *A Tale of Two Cities*.

Meanwhile, as Shirley Temple, number one box office star, put her prints into the cement at Grauman's Chinese Theatre, Hollywood prodigally produced a gaggle of classic horror films. Colin Clive starred in two of the most audacious.

He'd create a female monster in one; he'd be a *victim* of mad science in the other, amok with grafted-on knife-thrower's hands. His offscreen persona, in a very real sense, was at least as grotesque.

DeWitt Bodeen, who'd write the screenplay for *Cat People* (1942) and who was a fledgling writer in Hollywood in the mid-1930s, knew more about the movies and their actors than anyone I've ever met. "In the '30s," Bodeen told me, "everybody out here knew that Clive was brilliant, but also an alcoholic, and often unreliable." As such, as Bodeen sadly recalled, the gossip vultures were having a wickedly fun time, ripping away at Colin's private personality.

The Jekyll/Hyde persona infamy that had leeched onto Colin ever since *Journey's End* had festered in Hollywood, although he'd been, until late 1934, basically under control and on the wagon. If a Drew Friedman-like caricaturist had been around in 1935 to capture Colin Clive as the movie colony underbelly saw him, we'd have beheld a Colin a lá Goya, in Hyde top hat and cape, cigarette clenched in his twisted lips, recklessly joyriding in his biplane, flying over the HOLLYWOODLAND sign under a full moon, leaving a wake of tossed whiskey bottles and gambling debts.

"It's Alive!" he'd madly shriek from the plane—forever the hysterical Dr. Frankenstein.

Then, after a few loops over the Pacific, he'd land his plane ... and visit a male brothel. Yes, this was the new waxing rumor in Colin's warping reputation. Stories circulated increasingly that he was bisexual—and a "tormented" one at that. He was a prized "beast" (as *One More River* had referred to his character), a scary attraction in the Hollywood zoo, requiring a regular hosing-down in his cage to stay functional in the studios.

Colin and Iris Lancaster dining out in Hollywood. (Courtesy of Tracy Surrell)

How long until the big breakdown? How soon would the "maniac," as George Brent had called him, plunk that severed head in the icebox and get locked away in an asylum?

Was he drinking? Yes, sometimes catastrophically so. Was he out of control sexually? If so, he expertly covered his tracks. Despite decades of innuendo that Colin was gay, no information has come to light that he was ... or wasn't. "Nothing could be further from the truth," David Lewis, James Whale's companion, wrote to me regarding Colin's reputed homosexuality or bisexuality. If Colin were as wildly promiscuous as some would have us believe, Iris Lancaster would likely have deserted him. She didn't.

The drinking, the reclusiveness, the friendship with the openly gay James Whale, the roles he played ... all made Colin Clive a favorite target for grotesque rumors. Certainly, the torment was there, although in far more profound ways than Hollywood—pruriently, homophobically, and melodramatically—ever imagined it. Colin slept nights not only with Iris Lancaster, but with his deserting mother, his lunatic Uncle Piercy, and his first and dead wife Evelyn. He faced a stage fright that agonized him, nursed a worsening leg that threatened to cripple him, and suffered an alcoholism that deeply shamed him.

And although he'd made breaks with his military family and the Catholic church, there was the fearful awareness that what he'd traded it all in for was hardly worth a damn.

Seeing himself in a mirror, or unthinkably, on a movie screen, was a painful experience. What Hollywood reflected back at him, its image of him personally and professionally, was a growing torment. His 1935 screen performances, especially in *Bride of Frankenstein* and *Mad Love*, allowed moviegoers, more so than in his previous films, peeks at his pet devils.

The devils peeked back at his audiences.

Chapter Twenty-One
Anti-Christ

"While Heaven blasts the night without, open up your pits of Hell!"
Gavin Gordon as Lord Byron, Prologue to *Bride of Frankenstein*

As director of *Bride of Frankenstein*, James Whale was ringmaster of a crazy three-ring circus.

In the center ring, behold KAR-LOFF, as he's billed above the title, as the Monster ... savagely crucified by the bloodthirsty villagers, hanging on a pole, the cinema's most all-time outré Christ symbol. He talks, he laughs, he smokes a cigar, he drinks wine, he hiccups, he weeps ... and for a grand finale, he commits suicide.

In the left ring, see Ernest Thesiger, as the serpentine Dr. Pretorius, Whale's stand-in for Lucifer—although the frizzy-haired, witchy-nosed Thesiger looks and acts more like Lucifer's aging mistress. "Increase and multiply," he teases ... "You, alone, have created a MAN—now, together, we will create his MATE."

And, in the right ring, watch Elsa Lanchester as the prologue's Mary Shelley, her breasts coyly peeking above the bodice of her beautiful 19th-century gown ... and as the climax's vainglorious Bride, her red Nefertiti hairdo laced with

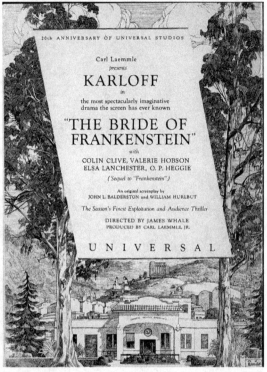

Trade advertisement for *Bride of Frankenstein*, 1935.

two silver streaks. She strikes poses like a spastic "Glam" model, screaming, hissing, and between scenes, lifting her gown, revealing to the company that she's truly a redhead.

This is the trio of *Bride of Frankenstein* attractions that Whale clearly prizes, but he's also offering a midnight carnival sideshow. There's 17-year-old Valerie Hobson as Elizabeth; she wears a flowing wig, looking so much like a Christmas Eve angel that one almost expects her, in this anything-can-happen fantasy, to sprout wings and fly. There's Dwight Frye as graverobber/village idiot Karl; he mugs merrily, sporting a hat that makes him evoke a baggy-pants comic from a Borgo Pass burlesque house. There's Una O'Connor as Minnie, the maid; she screeches, screams, does comic "takes," crosses her eyes ...

Among these outside-the-main-tent grotesqueries: Colin Clive, as Henry Frankenstein, seemingly reduced to a grim, twitchy romantic lead. Yet he too has his quirks.

KARLOFF, as the Monster.

I have been cursed for delving into the mysteries of Life. Perhaps Death is sacred—and I've profaned it ...

His "face of Christ," as Mae Clarke had described it in *Frankenstein*, appears a bit ravaged. He has his own dynamic going on here ... a bristly, disturbing quality. Firing up the performance will be his hang-ups, tragedy, and addiction.

In *Bride of Frankenstein*, Colin's Dr. Frankenstein, formerly with the "face of Christ," becomes the Anti-Christ.

214

Wednesday, January 2, 1935: *Bride of Frankenstein* began shooting. The budget: $293,750 (almost the precise cost of the original *Frankenstein*). The shooting schedule: 36 days. (The original was shot in 35 days.)

The Prologue takes us back to *Frankenstein*'s climax. The Monster, played of course by Boris Karloff—only this time billed as simply KARLOFF—rises from the burned windmill. The villagers bear Henry Frankenstein home to his fiancée, Elizabeth. One of the first scenes shot: Henry Frankenstein in his large Gothic bed:

> *I dreamed of being the first to give to the world the secret that God is so jealous of—the formula for Life!—Think of the power—to create a man—and I did it! I created a man! And who knows ... I could have bred a race. I might even have found the secret of eternal life.*

Elizabeth piously responds with her "Figure of Death" soliloquy:

> *Listen, Henry—while you have been lying here, tossing in your delirium ... a strange apparition has seemed to appear in the room—It comes, a figure like Death ... It seems to be reaching out for you, as if it would take you away from me ... There! It is coming for you ... !*

She becomes hysterical, and falls, laughing and crying, into Henry's bed. Teenager Valerie Hobson was nervous about this scene, especially as James Whale demanded a run-through with no introductions between her and Colin Clive. As Ms. Hobson told me 54 years later:

> *The first time I ever saw Colin Clive, I was dressed in a flimsy nightgown and had to climb into bed with him. And I was introduced as I arrived in the bed! Jimmy Whale: "Mr. Clive ... this is Miss Hobson. Now let's get on with the scene!"*
> *That was a bit far-fetched, even for Hollywood!*

Valerie Hobson and Colin, snuggling in *Bride of Frankenstein*.

It's a risqué joke to play on a 17-year-old, but typical of the high-spirited way Whale directs *Bride of Frankenstein*. It's also, probably in Whale's eyes, a necessary levity. Colin's personal decay is quickly and painfully clear to the *Bride* Company. Whale's fretful about the actor's drinking, as well as fearful what might happen if the self-destructive friend takes off in a plane, drunk, for a joyride into the Hollywood sky.

From the start of shooting, Colin spooks the company. As Ms. Hobson recalled:

> *Colin Clive was a strange, quiet, buttoned-up, saturnine sort of man. He reminds me of a very early James Mason—I played in one of James' first films. They had the same sort of quality. At least James Mason was a fighter, who gave the impression of being able to unravel his own emotional problems. But Colin Clive ... He had sort of a hounded, naïve quality, like a man who couldn't fight back—whatever his problems were.*

It soon becomes clear to the young Valerie that the problem, which Colin couldn't fight back against, is alcohol. She notes his "rather watery eyes," and a dresser who shadows Colin on the set—whom she suspects is a "keeper," hired to make sure he doesn't find a bottle and lose control during the shooting.

The clouds lessen as Karloff makes his entrance on the set. Ms. Hobson's memory:

> *Well, I remember that the very first time I saw Boris Karloff, he was in full gear as the Monster! I had been warned what he was going to look like, and I thought he was absolutely extraordinary ... I was totally amazed! And then to hear a very gentle, English voice coming out of this awful makeup—and with a pronounced lisp!*
>
> *It was Boris' kind eyes—he had the kindest eyes! Most monsters have frightening eyes, but Boris, even in makeup, had very loving, sad eyes ... The thing I remember best about him was his great gentleness ... He was a dear man.*

Ernest Thesiger, as Dr. Pretorius.

As with *Frankenstein*, Whale sees himself as the Monster, but he no longer sees himself as Henry Frankenstein. He does see himself, however, as Pretorius, toasting "A New World of Gods and Monsters!" Thesiger, too, amuses and delights Valerie Hobson: "a darling duck of a person ... sweet and terribly funny!"

Karloff is earning $2,500 per week; Colin, $1,500 per week; Thesiger, $1,000 per week. The Monster and Pretorius are having a skeleton's ball on the set, but Henry Frankenstein is restless, aside from the moments when, as Colin put it, "I nearly laughed myself to death ... every time I looked at Karloff!"

Colin Clive, as Henry Frankenstein.

Of course, Karloff is now a major star, as well as a founder of the Screen Actors Guild, so Whale no longer dares to torment him. On January 19, Kenneth Thomson, Executive Secretary of SAG, writes a letter to Karloff:

> *I don't suppose with that makeup you get much chance for conversation while you are working, but according to the* Reporter *the following members of your cast are not Guild members ...*

The letter lists Colin Clive, Valerie Hobson, Elsa Lanchester, O.P. Heggie, E.E. Clive, and Ernest Thesiger. The only actor who joins during the movie's shooting, and "right away" according to SAG records, is Colin, always eager to do the "heroic" thing. His membership number: 3,489.

While Whale's sadism is under control, his stylistics are amok. Meanwhile, rumors rustle again about the Whale/Clive relationship. Elizabeth Yeaman in the *Hollywood Citizen News* suggestively lays it between the lines:

> ... *something really should be said about the partnership of director James Whale and actor Colin Clive. At the moment Clive is making his fourth picture under Whale's direction,* The Return of Frankenstein. *The director-actor partnership began some years ago in London when Whale directed the stage production of* Journey's End *and cast Clive for the lead of Captain Stanhope. When Whale [directed] the screen version, he insisted upon sending to England for Clive to play his original role. Then Whale demanded Clive again for* Frankenstein. *And after that he obtained him for* One More River. *It rather naturally followed that Clive would be sought by Whale for* The Return of Frankenstein. *This record of a star-director team is probably topped only by the Dietrich–von Sternberg team ...*

The lavender insinuation has all the more innuendo via the mention of Marlene Dietrich and Josef von Sternberg, then working at Paramount on *The Devil Is a Woman*, and whose partnership had inspired all variety of kinky tales in Hollywood.

Karloff's Monster is marvelously amok—chasing townspeople through Universal's back lot village, haunting a splendidly stylized soundstage forest complete with a waterfall and a shepherdess (Anne Darling) he saves from drowning, toppling a giant statue of a bishop in a nighttime cemetery scene. He also talks. "Stupid!" says the star three decades later, feeling the Creature's mime was part of his charm.

Colin's also restless with Whale's approach, and apparently with Whale himself. In his biography, *James Whale: A New World of Gods and Monsters*, James Curtis quotes Jack Latham, an acquaintance of Whale who'd met the director during *Frankenstein* and visited his sets. Latham remembered Colin:

> *He was very excitable. Whale had to be careful so that Colin wouldn't shoot his mouth off—about Whale or anything else. He would go off to his own little dressing room and they'd call him and he'd come out and do the "It's alive" thing and then go back. We didn't see him very much.*

What Colin might "shoot his mouth off" about, Latham didn't say.

At any rate, James Whale was lucky to have such discreet and valiant "troupers" in starring roles. Karloff fell while rising from the windmill waters and damaged a hip, but he went to the studio infirmary, had the hip bandaged, and came right back to work! And Colin, for all his troubles, was also a great professional. *Variety* wrote January 30:

> *Colin Clive, who plays Frankenstein in Universal's* Bride *of* Frankenstein, *yesterday injured the ligaments of his knee in a fall on the set and was compelled to use crutches for close-ups.*
>
> *Boris Karloff is working with a dislocated hip in a cast. He slipped and fell with 62-pound makeup several days ago.*

Valerie Hobson (without her "Elizabeth" wig) and Colin. Note his crutches, following a fall on the set.

The Hollywood Reporter adds that Colin's fall had been down a flight of stairs. A couple of candids from *Bride* show Colin with crutches outside at Universal, with Valerie Hobson, who's wearing a leopard-skin coat, and apparently having just removed her "Elizabeth" wig (or had her own hair pinned and prepared for it). In one shot, Colin appears to be holding the smiling, unwigged teenager tightly and playfully, locking her into position as the photographer gets a quite unflattering candid shot. Colin was surely just trying to have fun with the girl, although over 50 years later, Valerie Hobson will still be a bit sensitive about how scalped she looks in these behind-the-scenes pictures.

Colin makes the most of his opportunities. One of his best *Bride* moments comes when the Monster, confronting Henry Frankenstein to demand a Mate, orders, "Sit—down!" and Colin, with a dash of comic timing, instantly sits. It's an echo from the original film, when Frankenstein first taught the Monster to "sit -down." At a 2012 theater

Elsa Lanchester as Mary Shelley and Gavin Gordon as Lord Byron in the prologue of *Bride of Frankenstein*.

screening of both films in Abingdon, Maryland, sponsored by Turner Classic Movies, the sequel's "Sit -down!" scene brought down the house.

Most of all, it's Henry Frankenstein unleashed in the spectacular creation episode. The tower laboratory, the Strickfaden machinery, the stormy night sky ... all captured by John J. Mescall's enchanted cinematography. Colin's Frankenstein, atop the tower, launching the kites to attract the lightning, is zealous, passionate ... a man on fire. The blackmail plan of the Monster and Pretorius—the Monster kidnapping Elizabeth and binding her in a mountain cave—had forced him to create the Bride, but here Frankenstein, back in the laboratory as the Bride's body ascends to the lightning, embraces his blasphemy. Whale mercilessly exploits Colin's haggard face as the Female Monster rises to the heavens, the director treating him to terrific, chilling close-ups. It's as if Frankenstein is wearing a Halloween mask of the Fallen Lucifer as he beholds his unholy miracle.

It's the Universal Bible, a chapter from the book of Jimmy Whale ... verse 1935.

The tower laboratory roars and flashes, the creation episode so spectacular that the Hollywood preview audience will applaud its daring and magnificence. Henry Frankenstein, now truly a man possessed, watches as the table lowers ... he removes the swath of cloth that covers the Bride's eyes ... and her eyes are open.

"She's alive! ALIVE!" exults Colin's Dr. Frankenstein.

In time, the Bride poses in her long white gown, and seems vainly proud, showing off the stitches in her neck. She also appears to have the hots for Henry, and since he's her creator, that's yet another kinky twist of *Bride of Frankenstein*. Then she gawks at the wooing Monster ... and screams.

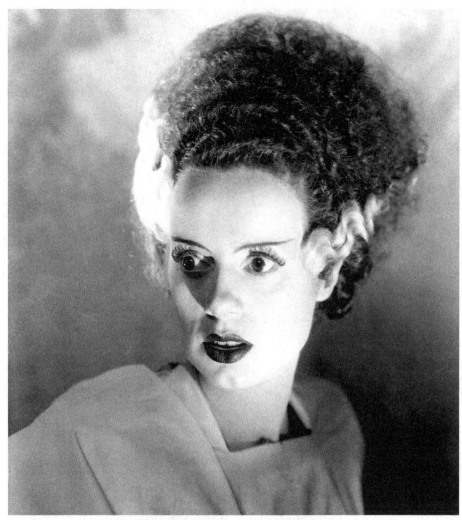

Elsa Lanchester, as the Female Monster.

She hate me—like others ...

Elizabeth, escaping her bondage, runs to the tower for Henry. The heartbroken Monster, a tear running down his face, grabs a lever. The Bride, a drama queen diva to the last, hisses like a swan Elsa Lanchester once fed at London's Regent's Park lake, hellishly spiteful in the face of her weeping bridegroom and Death itself. The tower explodes, blasting the Monster, the Female Monster, the devilish Pretorius, the angelic Elizabeth, and the Anti-Christ to Kingdom Come. Franz Waxman's magnificent musical score climaxes.

Henry Frankenstein had received the demise that Colin had fervently believed he'd deserved in the original film. Considering the character's frightening decay and horrific transformation, it appears, at the moment, the best possible finale.

Karloff and Colin, relaxing between scenes.

Colin appears to be gripping Valerie to pose and smile in this close-up candid.

"One Man *Crazy* ...!"

Colin and Valerie, enjoying a tea break.

Bride of Frankenstein shuts down in late February, as Whale awaits O.P. Heggie's availability to play the old blind Hermit in the only episode left to shoot. Colin, pleased that Henry Frankenstein has finally perished, says goodbye to his Monster Maker alter-ego. Or so he thinks.

Yes, so much for the Monster and the nasty, bitchy Bride he created for him.
Jimmy Whale has surely used him strangely—quite the scary puppet this time.

729-P.26

The magnificent laboratory set.

Imagine those pitiless close-ups of him that Jimmy so delighted in, thrown 25 feet-high on a movie screen—Crikey! Well, he always avoided his own films—no bloody desire to see this one.

The original Frankenstein *had been a duet—he and Karloff. This time, Jimmy's made it a bloody burlesque show. Indeed, with Elsa hissing, and Thesiger prancing, and Una shrieking, and that Frye fellow wearing that silly hat, and that teenager Valerie flouncing about in her virgin martyr wig,*

"One Man *Crazy* ...!"

On the tower rooftop, to launch the kites: Colin, Ted Billings and Dwight Frye.

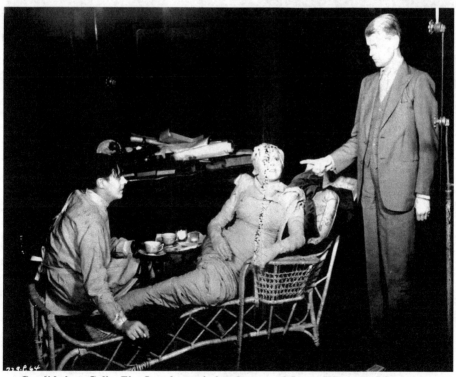

Candid shot: Colin, Elsa Lanchester in bandages, and James Whale, striking a pose.

A 1925 painting of Elsa Lanchester by Doris Zinkeisen, National Portrait Gallery, London. Ms. Zinkeisen, a British artist and designer, was allegedly engaged to James Whale in the 1920s.

reminding him of Saint Agnes back at Stonyhurst, and Karloff performing tricks like a circus gorilla in a tutu ... what in bloody hell was HE supposed to have done to vie for attention?

He'd done what he knew was right—play it as Henry Frankenstein, hooked on blasphemy. No Mickey Mouse for him. Amidst the flamboyance

"One Man *Crazy* ...!"

The Bride of Frankenstein!

that Whale teased from the other players, he'd brought his own dynamic to
Bride of Frankenstein.

  *All quite clever, really. A jittery addict, played by a jittery addict. As
an actor, you use what you've got.*

  *Anyway, Frankenstein's dead. Blown to bits. Jimmy had somehow
brought him back from the dead in the original film, but he couldn't do it
again ...*

  Could he?

Chapter Twenty-Two
A Monster's Absolution

As Colin had worked on *Bride of Frankenstein*, two of his previously completed films had seen release.

Thursday, January 17, 1935: *Clive of India* had its world premiere at Broadway's Rivoli Theatre. The negative cost had been $648,000; the worldwide rental would be $1,598,000; and the profit would tally $190,000. As such, *Clive of India*, the film in which Colin had the smallest part, was the one that, in original release, the most audiences saw.

Friday, February 15: Warners' *The Right to Live* opened on Broadway, also at the Rivoli. "Colin Clive, Famous star of the stage in his greatest role," advertised Warner Bros., and indeed, he'd win the laurels. As the *New York Times* wrote:

> *If* The Right to Live *catches you up in the neurotic anguish of a man who loves his wife too dearly to make her share his burden, it is because Mr. Clive succeeds so well in daubing his role with authentic emotions.*

The final negative cost of *The Right to Live* was a mere $153,000. Worldwide rentals would be $342,000; profit, $23,500.

By now, Colin is living at 3687 Fredonia Drive, close to Universal City. The Spanish house, storybook in style, has room for his garden, his dog, and Iris, on those nights she agrees to stay.

Wednesday, March 6: While Whale puts the finishing touches on *Bride*, Colin goes into his next film for Warner Bros.—*The Girl from 10th Avenue*. The star was Bette Davis, who'd been a sensation on loan-out to RKO for 1934's *Of Human Bondage* and would win the 1935 Best Actress Oscar for Warners' *Dangerous*. Colin's the third lead; the leading man is Ian Hunter. Originally titled *Outcast*, it's the fourth film version of the 1914 play of the same name, promoted thusly:

> *When West Side meets East Side, the battle royal begins. The man-wrecker in* Of Human Bondage *defies a Park Avenue husband-snatcher!*

The comedy/soap opera story: Factory worker Miriam Brady (Bette Davis, still a blonde) sooths drunken, broken-hearted Geoffrey Sherwood (Ian Hunter), as he stands outside a church, watching as his ex-fiancée, Valentine (Katharine Alexander, in a role so bitchy Genevieve Tobin refused to play it) marries John Marland (Colin). The comfort act goes too far—Davis and Hunter get drunk and wake up married. She offers an annulment, he decides to make the best of it, and soon they're in love. Later, John Marland—Colin, slickly costumed in dark suit, derby, and cane—sadly informs Ms. Davis that Valentine has jilted him too.

"Valentine's after your husband," he warns her. " ... get him away if you can."

The film goes on from there, with several highlights. One of them is Alison Skipworth, Davis' gone-to-seed Florodora Girl landlady, who coaches Davis on how to be a lady. Another is a showdown between Davis' Miriam and Alexander's Valentine in the

Colin's house, 3687 Fredonia Drive, North Hollywood. (Photo by author)

dining room of the Waldorf. There's a grapefruit on the table, and any fan of Warner Bros. classics wants Davis to smash the grapefruit into Alexander's lacquered face, à lá James Cagney's "citrus massage" of Mae Clarke in 1931's *The Public Enemy*. As it goes, Alexander throws the grapefruit at Davis, but misses.

The climactic highlight: Colin's Marland gets drunk. Riotously drunk. He sings (painfully!), *I'll String Along with You*, fouling up the lyrics:

> *I want to be an angel ...*

Colin's singing is so horrid that one suspects he would have made the same awful sounds if he were acting a man having a limb amputated. At any rate, in a crowd-pleaser finale, Colin takes Hunter at 3:00 a.m. to his home, arriving at Alexander's boudoir door, telling her he's brought Geoffrey with him.

"Well, I wouldn't have the impertinence to come alone!" he tells her, smiling and nudging Hunter.

Colin collapses on one of the twin beds, Hunter says good-bye to Alexander and returns to Davis—THE END.

In his book *Fasten Your Seat Belts: The Passionate Life of Bette Davis*, Lawrence J. Quirk describes Colin as "a tormented and confused bisexual [who] had humiliating homosexual episodes which left him demoralized." He also claims that Colin developed an attraction to Davis "that was more neurotic than genuine." Quirk quotes the late Ian Hunter:

> *Colin was a fine actor, but he made everyone around him nervous—nervous as hell! One didn't want to be in the vicinity for what seemed an inevitable blow-up, breakdown, or both.*

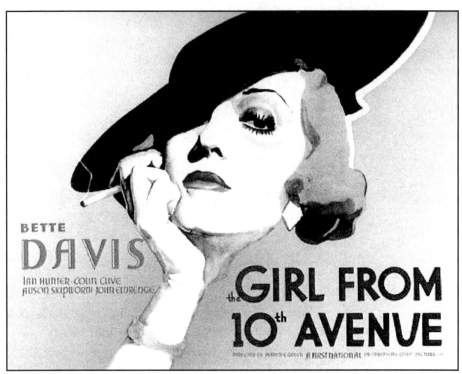

Title lobby card for Warner Bros.' *The Girl from 10ᵗʰ Avenue*.

Directed by Warner workhorse Alfred E. Green, *The Girl from 10ᵗʰ Avenue* had a negative cost of only $186,000. Quirk wrote that Bette Davis regretted never having Colin as her leading man in a worthy vehicle:

> *If some people called her a witch, then Clive qualified as a warlock. Their onscreen chemistry would have been mighty interesting.*

Warners owed Colin a good vehicle of his own. He wouldn't get one.

The rumors spread: the drinking, the gambling, the anxiety. It's decided he best try to put out the fires.

April Fool's Day, 1935: The Los Angeles *Illustrated Daily News* ran an interview with Colin, by Harry Mines. "His fellow workers on the lot know little if anything about him," wrote Mines, adding, " ... certainly Hollywood society sees him not ... Apparently Clive lives in a world of his own." However, the interviewer discovered, "that, for a man of mystery, Clive is a swell person with a grand sense of humor." To quote from the feature:

> *"I never go anywhere," Clive explained. "I loathe the night life of any kind—parties, night clubs and the rest of it. I never have enjoyed it. Mind you, it's not a pose. For heaven's sake, don't think that. It's just that when I get home at night I don't like to stir. I enjoy my own front room, my own society, my own few friends and my garden. While I'm working I see enough people to satisfy my social side.*

A candid shot from *The Girl from 10ᵗʰ Avenue*: Ian Hunter, Bette Davis, and Colin.

> *"Look at this!" here Colin proudly displayed a scarred hand. "Poison oak! Got it from my garden. I love to grow things—flowers, vegetables, anything. Somehow, I picked this up, though, from some green shrubbery.*
>
> *"Yes, my life away from the studio is very quiet. I live in a house in North Hollywood. My sole companion is a police dog. I have no neighbors on either side of me, so I can roam where I please without the fear that I'll have to indulge in some back-fence conversations.*
>
> *"I go for occasional walks on the boulevard and patronize all the book shops in Hollywood. In London, I have a valuable library. Buying books for this library is what keeps me working, or else I'd be broke."*

When the interviewer mentions to Colin that he was, notoriously, "the despair of American press agents, because of his intense dislike of publicity," the actor "laughed," but revealed a bit of asperity:

> *"I just don't go out for it. I won't indulge in stunts to get my picture in the paper, and I won't live sensationally. Why should I? I never dodge interviews, though. That's part of my business. I'm the last person in the world to say I dislike publicity, for that would make me a hypocrite and a liar. I suppose the reason one doesn't hear much more about me is there's really little of glamour about me to make an interesting story. I just work and go home at night and come to work the next morning."*

The interview, clearly calculated to quash any nasty circulating stories, mentions that Colin was married to Jeanne de Casalis ("who, because of her successful stage career, lives

The Monster: "Go ... You live ... We BELONG dead!"

in Europe"), that he'd achieved his success in *Journey's End*, and that "he loves Southern California." It plugs his recent film with Bette Davis, as well as *Bride of Frankenstein*. It concludes with Colin bidding good-bye to the interviewer with these words:

> *"Don't call me mysterious. Just call me quiet."*

Meanwhile, at Universal, James Whale is preparing *Bride of Frankenstein* for an official preview. On March 23, 1935, Joseph Breen, after seeing the completed film, writes to Universal that he's "gravely concerned:"

> *The finished picture seems to us definitely to be a violation of our Production Code because of its excessive brutality and gruesomeness. The shots early in the picture in which the breasts of the character of Mrs. Shelley are both exposed and accentuated, constitute also a Code violation ...*

Breen demands a dozen cuts; Whale, defiant, agrees to only six, including Elsa's breast shots, Dwight Frye strangling his Uncle Glutz, and a mother carrying her bloody child in her Holy Communion dress.

Saturday, April 6: Universal previews *Bride of Frankenstein*, with Franz Waxman's magnificent musical score, at the Warners Beverly Theatre. *Variety's* review raves, "This tops all previous horror pictures in artistry and popular entertainment values," and praises the cast:

> *Karloff does a striking job in keeping his role as the Frankenstein creation on the fantastic borderland between the ruthless laboratory Monster and*

"One Man *Crazy* ...!"

a bewildered pathetic being with human impulses ... The Dr. Pretorius creation by Ernest Thesiger is extraordinary in its cunning and power and intensity—a flawless piece of psychopathic characterization ... Colin Clive effectively plays Frankenstein, beset by the Monster he regrets creating as he plans to renounce his blasphemous meddling with life's secrets during his honeymoon with Valerie Hobson ...

The review all-hails James Whale ("an ace job of direction") and praises the climax in the exploding tower ("as awesome as a page from Genesis").

There's a mystery here: *Variety* clocks *Bride* at 90 minutes; *The Film Daily*, which attends the same preview, at 80 minutes. If 90 minutes is correct, Whale presumably treated the preview audience to everything he'd shot, including scenes he'd already agreed to cut. If so, it must have been quite a show.

Bride of Frankenstein is set to premiere the following week—Holy Week, leading to Easter. Despite the lavish reviews, Whale decides to trim the film, both to appease Breen and improve the pace. Meanwhile, Universal hosts at least one afternoon preview of *Bride of Frankenstein* at the studio. Attending is an 18-year-old horror film fan named Forrest J Ackerman who, 23 years later, will become the editor of *Famous Monsters of Filmland* magazine.

"As I was walking out," Ackerman will remember, "going through the door to leave the front office, Colin Clive came through, and our shoulders just touched. A little electrical spark flew into me. To think I was in the presence of Dr. Frankenstein!"

It's possible that Colin is coming to Universal that day to discuss, or perhaps even film, the new finale: Whale has decided again to spare Henry Frankenstein! With only days before the film's opening, Karloff, Colin, and Valerie Hobson return to the *Bride* set, where they receive the Monster's mercy:

Valerie Hobson and Colin, saved by the mercy of the Monster, in *Bride of Frankenstein*'s revised ending.

Half-sheet poster, *Bride of Frankenstein.*

Frankenstein (with Elizabeth): *But I can't leave them—I can't!*
Monster: *Yes! Go! You live! Go! (indicated toward Pretorius and the Female Monster). You stay. We BELONG Dead!*

The couple escapes the tower, the new shots spliced into the existing print. The master long shot of the exploding laboratory, previously filmed from high in the soundstage, had shown a glimpse of Frankenstein pressed against a wall as the blasts began. Whale gambles nobody will notice. Frankenstein and Elizabeth, safely outside the exploded tower, observe the deaths of the Monster, Female Monster, and Pretorius.

"Darling," says Colin soothingly as he hugs Valerie Hobson. "Darling."

Colin apparently never goes on record as to his feelings about the revised ending. It's a safe bet, however, that once again, as an actor who loves death scenes, he feels betrayed. Anyway, it's finally all over, the final cost documented by Universal as $397,023.79 ($103,273.79 over budget and 10 days over schedule). Valerie Hobson, for whom *Bride of Frankenstein* has been a wonderful adventure, says goodbye to her co-stars and her director.

"We all loved each other then," she'll recall in 1989.

Friday, April 19: On this Good Friday, the day Christians reverently observe the crucifixion of Jesus Christ, audiences at the Orpheum Theatre in San Francisco behold Karloff's crucified Monster in *Bride of Frankenstein*. The film breaks the Orpheum record.

Saturday, April 20: *Bride of Frankenstein* opens at the Hollywood Pantages Theatre, with special late showings for folks who want to go directly to the Hollywood Bowl's Easter sunrise service. Again, business is record-breaking.

"One Man *Crazy* ...!"

A sketch by the late artist Linda Miller, showing Colin Clive's Henry Frankenstein as he might have appeared as killed in the original ending.

Friday, April 26: Variety writes, "Colin Clive is taking his Scotties to Ventura for the dog show Sunday." (Does he now have Scotties in addition to, or instead of, his German shepherd?)

Monday, April 29: Variety reports, "Colin Clive has been carrying around a fan letter from Transylvania and no one can find out what language it's written in." (One wonders—did Colin ask Bela Lugosi?)

Bride of Frankenstein is on the loose. The film, for all its splashy success at its big openings, will suffer a fall-off in various cities; it's too quirky for some, not scary enough for others. It will also run into censorship trouble both in the U.S. (Ohio, for example, originally demands nine cuts) and abroad (Hungary, Palestine and Trinidad reject it outright, and China accuses the film of necrophilia!). By 1937, after around-the-world play dates, *Bride of Frankenstein* will have earned a profit of $166,000—very respectable, but a fraction of the amount realized by the original *Frankenstein*.

No matter. Today, the film is what it is—kinky, quirky, audacious, silly, at times ludicrous, but overall, brilliant. Often overlooked: The remarkable nature of the revised 11ᵗʰ hour ending, which is a duet between Karloff and Colin Clive.

Rather than vengefully destroy the man who created him, abandoned him, and only created a Mate for him out of threat of violence ... the *Creation* forgives his *Creator*. In what is perhaps *Bride of Frankenstein*'s supreme irony, <u>Man</u> forgives <u>God</u>. The smile of clemency in Karloff's face ... the anguish in Clive's as he realizes he's literally at his Monster's mercy ... unforgettable. The Anti-Christ, who's done little if anything to atone for his blasphemy, runs safely into the night with his angel bride, absolved by his Creature, while the Monster, in self-sacrifice, blows himself to pieces—or so it appears.

In the final revised, crazy, explosive minute of this mad, subversive, and ultimately profound movie, Karloff and Colin Clive perform this sacrament of forgiveness ... and in a skewered Passion Play finale, become the two major stars of *Bride of Frankenstein*.

Chapter Twenty-Three
Mad Love, Mad Actor

In the spring of 1935, Madeline Glass of *Picture Play* magazine interviewed Colin Clive.

She found him at home in North Hollywood, his hands bandaged, having suffered, as he put it, "some lively burns" due to a disinfectant a doctor had prescribed for that poison oak he'd previously mentioned in the *Illustrated Daily News* interview. Colin was in fine form, accompanied by Brenda, a Cairn terrier. (*Another* dog!)

"I'm no Clark Gable in the matter of looks," said Colin waggishly, "and I require a good dramatic play before my fatal charm is discernible."

He appeared to be flirting with Miss Glass throughout the interview, teasing her about her ideal choice for a pet ("Leopard?" he exclaims). She seemed taken by her subject, writing that he addressed her with "a wink and a grin," and penning, "For this actor, who portrays morbid, menacing or harried souls on the screen, is by nature addicted to humor, sports, gardening, and other quite normal pursuits." Fresh from *Bride of Frankenstein*, he joked about his horror notoriety:

> *Well, I noticed in this morning's newspaper—and it must be a mistake; such things can't happen even in Hollywood—that Bela Lugosi, Boris Karloff, Claude Rains, and myself are to appear in the same production. I can't imagine what a picture would be like with four horror actors running at large in it.*

The interview, titled "Clive of England," appeared in *Picture Play*'s July issue, but must have been conducted a couple months previous, when the publicists were trying to suppress the unsavory Clive rumors. By the time *Picture Play* hit the stands, Colin had completed another horror film. It hadn't co-starred Lugosi, Karloff, or Rains—and it had been no laughing matter. In fact, it was one of the most disturbing movies produced in 1930s Hollywood, playing a crucial role in jacking up censorship internationally. It also subjected Colin to a symbolic castration.

He'd bridle throughout *Mad Love*, protesting almost everything about it, loudly and bitterly.

Metro-Goldwyn-Mayer, at its peak in 1935, had always given its few horror films its best shot, letting loose a bevy of remarkable star monsters.

1932 had seen Olga Baclanova as the evil Cleopatra of *Freaks*, fated to be mutilated into a "Chicken Woman." Boris Karloff's "Yellow Peril" in *The Mask of Fu Manchu*, also in 1932, came with a menagerie of snakes and crocodiles, as well as Myrna Loy as his nymphomaniacal daughter Fah. More recently, in early 1935, Tod Browning had filmed *Mark of the Vampire*, featuring Bela Lugosi as Count Mora, flanked by his sexpot bloodsucker daughter Luna, expertly slinked by Carroll Borland.

Then came *Mad Love* ... with *two* star monsters.

Peter Lorre, in his U.S. debut, was Dr. Gogol, mad surgeon, his shaved head and pop-eyes suggesting a kinky Humpty Dumpty, serenading at the organ a wax statue of the actress he adores, going rhapsodically insane by the film's climax, trying to strangle the heroine with her hair.

Poster for *Mad Love*.

The second monster was virtually a Hollywood in-joke: Colin Clive as Orlac, now the <u>victim</u> of mad science—an agonized freak created in Gogol's laboratory. Formerly a concert pianist, whose compositions include a demonic boogie-woogie heard a number of times in the movie, Orlac now wears the transplanted hands of a guillotined knife murderer, sporting garish stitches on his wrists worthy of Frankenstein's Monster himself.

"They feel for knives ... they want to kill!" says Colin's Orlac of his new horrible hands.

Budget: $217,176.53. Shooting schedule: 24 days. As *Mad Love*'s shooting approached, *Variety* ran this notice on May 1, 1935:

> *Clive Wary*
> Colin Clive goes to Metro for featured spot in Mad Love, *which Karl Freund directs with Peter Lorre heading cast.*
> Picture is third horror thriller for Clive, who was in two Frankenstein features at Universal, and suffered injury while working each. Player is trying to anticipate what will happen on Metro picture.

Monday, May 6, 1935: Mad Love began filming. MGM's Leo the Lion roared as the new supercharged shocker dared to challenge such previously released 1935 horror shows as Universal's *Bride of Frankenstein* and MGM's own *Mark of the Vampire*.

Metro lovingly baked this crazed confection with what appeared to be all the top ingredients. The director was Karl "Papa" Freund, 300-pound Bohemian cinematographer of *Metropolis*, *Dracula,* and *Murders in the Rue Morgue*, and director of *The Mummy*. John L. Balderston, whose name appeared on the credits for *Dracula*, *Frankenstein*, *The Mummy*,

Colin Clive and Frances Drake in *Mad Love*.

and other horror classics, wrote the final draft of *Mad Love*'s script, stocking it with over a dozen in-joke horror homages (including May Beatty, as Gogol's housekeeper, screaming "It's come alive!" after the heroine Yvonne, posing as her own wax statue, moves).

The episode in the lab was to be *Mad Love*'s spectacular centerpiece: Lorre's Dr. Gogol re-attaching the head of the guillotined knife murderer Rollo (Edward Brophy) to its corpse. This was to cause the blood to flow again in Rollo's body, to make the amputation of his hands and their grafting onto Orlac's wrists scientifically plausible. It was fashioned to rival Universal's Frankenstein laboratory episodes.

Colin, regarding *Mad Love*, betrayed a bit of reluctance about the whole eerie enterprise, telling the *Los Angeles Times*, "Creating monsters is good fun in fiction, but scientists and biologists should thank their stars that it's never occurred in real life."

He'd soon wish *Mad Love* had never occurred in real life.

Mad Love began chaotically. Balderston was still refining the script. Freund, despite his soubriquet of "Papa," was a notorious sadist. During *The Mummy*, "Papa" Freund, directing a Christian martyr reincarnation episode cut from the release print, had ordered leading lady Zita Johann into an arena of lions, totally unprotected, while he himself directed the scene from inside a cage.

"A very large one," recalled Zita.

As for *Mad Love*'s leading lady, she was foxy Frances Drake, as Yvonne, the Grand Guignol's *Theatre des Horreurs* star actress. Adorned in flowing hair and white robe, she screams wildly on a rack, branded with a prop that realistically suggests a hot poker. Yvonne

A candid on the *Mad Love* set: Colin, Frances Drake, and director Karl "Papa" Freund.

is also Mrs. Stephen Orlac, and the target of Gogol's maniacal longings ... and perhaps the smartest, bravest, and most stylish heroine of all classic horror.

In 1986, Frances Drake, long retired from films and a very wealthy widow, relaxed in her Beverly Hills aerie, recalling the highs and lows of *Mad Love*.

> *Little Peter Lorre was charming, and so cute ... He had to meet me before he had his head shaved, to show me that he had hair. And lots of it ... But he was rather naughty. If your scene was going very well, he'd say, "Don't you know me? I'm your little Peter!" You know, he didn't want you to be too good!*

As for Freund ... MGM indulged him with two ace cameramen. Chester Lyons had been cinematographer of MGM's *Sequoia* (1934), with its beautiful nature and animal photography. Gregg Toland, borrowed from Samuel Goldwyn for *Mad Love*'s special effects, would win an Oscar for *Wuthering Heights* (1939) and be Orson Welles' cameraman on *Citizen Kane* (1941). Frances Drake recalled:

> *Director Karl Freund kept wanting to be the director and the cinematographer at the same time. And Gregg Toland was a marvelous cameraman! And he was such a dear little man, sort of slender, and he looked rather hunted when this wretched big fat man would say, "Now, now, we'll do it this way!"*
> *You never knew who was directing. The producer [John Considine, Jr.] was dying to, to tell you the truth, and of course he had no idea of directing.*

"One Man *Crazy* ...!"

Frances Drake with "Little Miracle" at the Santa Anita Race Track, CA, in 1935. How about that boa?

> *Finally, I did say, "Look here, we've got to have one director, because we're all going mad!"*

As for Colin ... Ms. Drake remembered that he was "a professional," and had his own way of escaping *Mad Love's* hothouse atmosphere:

> *That Englishman would go to sleep. He'd pay no attention to anybody—it was too sweet! Colin Clive—he just went to sleep. He didn't care who was*

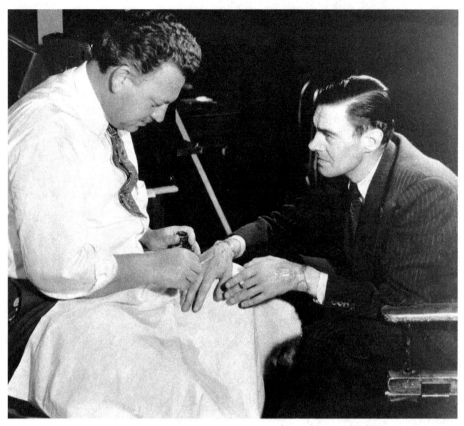

The strain shows: Colin submits his hands for what he called the "ghoulish" makeup on *Mad Love.*

> *directing, he didn't give a damn. He was such a good actor that he didn't need it, perhaps!*

The shoot went on, Freund throwing fits, Balderston sending in fresh script revisions. As for the laboratory scene, on May 29, *The Hollywood Reporter* wrote that MGM had borrowed an "ultraviolet ray diffuser" from the California Institute of Technology that would emit a 200-degree flash on the set. The company had to shield all camera and microphones from the light, and "all players with gold teeth were warned out of range."

Meanwhile, the role of Orlac gave Colin the creeps. Little wonder. At the time, Karloff was defending horror films as "just bogey stories" and "fantastic fairy tales," and comparing his horror roles to the Big Bad Wolf. After *Mad Love* wrapped, however, Colin harpooned the horror genre, giving an angry, rip-roaring interview to the Hollywood representative of England's *Film Weekly*.

The title of the interview: "I Hate Horror Films."

> *You may tell me that millions enjoy horror films and that, of those millions, thousands appreciate my work in them, and I will tell you that I still hate playing in them!*

"One Man *Crazy* ...!"

If a producer says to me: "Here you are Mr. Clive; another job of horror for you," what am I to do but play it? ... There is, however, one important point, which the actor who like myself, finds himself in a chain of such films, must be concerned. Not every producer approaches the job of producing a thriller in quite the same serious mood as he would a drama. This means that, from the word "Go," the writers, the art directors and even the directors themselves, strain every nerve, and stretch every shred of material to the utmost limits in order to produce shocks.

Questions of feasibility and good dramatic construction are apt to get thrown out the window while this process of sensationalisation is going on ... The danger of laughs in the wrong places is the greatest bugbear the actor must face in portraying screen horrors ...

Then, again, most horror pictures involve unpleasant and, in some cases, painful recourse to grotesque makeup. Karloff could tell you quite a lot about having his mouth and eyes drawn all shapes with fish-skin and glue ...

Colin had fun where he could. He had a number of passionate onscreen kisses with the beautiful Frances Drake; he likely enjoyed seeing such MGM stars as Jean Harlow around the lot, as well as the showgirls from *Broadway Melody of 1936;* and he probably ran into Stonyhurst classmate Charles Laughton, between scenes, as Captain Bligh on *Mutiny on the Bounty.* Iris Lancaster was there too, as Frances Drake remembered:

Colin Clive had a girlfriend, a fantastic, red-haired creature ... she was Joan Crawford's stand-in at MGM. She wanted to meet me ... and Colin took her up and introduced her to my wax dummy!

One of Colin's best scenes in *Mad Love* is Stephen Orlac's visit to his father's jewelry shop, desperately hoping to borrow money as his hands heal. Playing the father: Ian Wolfe, veteran character player, who was only slightly over three years older than Colin. The vicious older Orlac refuses his son's plea, and makes a lewd comment about Yvonne (" ... she could *supplement* her earnings!")—at which time Stephen hysterically throws a knife at his father. Fortunately, he misses, then comes out of the shop, pitifully dazed, walking into the street, car horns blaring at him.

"I remember that Colin Clive was a very talented and precise actor," Ian Wolfe told interviewer Roger Hurlburt in 1990, "but a noticeably high-strung and nervous one. Perhaps he was perfectly suited for the Orlac role."

There's a sinister sexual undercurrent in *Mad Love*. As Lorre's Gogol lusts after Drake's Yvonne, there's the definite suggestion that Colin's Orlac, having lost his hands, is sexually dysfunctional—Gogol's surgery having emasculated him. It hardly could have been a "fun" role, and living for weeks in Orlac's goosepimply skin must have taken a toll.

Mad Love's most famous scene: Orlac meets Gogol. The doctor, hoping to drive Orlac mad so he can have his wife, has killed Orlac's father, and suspicion falls on the former pianist. Gogol arranges for Orlac to come one night to a dark lodging to learn the truth about his hands. Gogol sits in disguise, in a dark cloak and large black hat. He reveals his hands ... shining steel prosthetic fingers. He sticks a large knife into the table.

Gogol: *Use it when they try to arrest you.*
Orlac: *Who are you?*

The Life and Death of Colin Clive Hollywood's Dr. Frankenstein   **243**

Colin as Orlac.

Gogol: *I am Rollo, the knife-thrower.*
Orlac: *No, no! Rollo died on the guillotine!*
Gogol (rising): *Yes. They cut off my head. But that Gogol—he put it back—here!*

Gogol, in dark glasses, shows his face, revealing a horrific steel and leather harness that appears to fasten the head to the neck. He bares his teeth, exploding into horrible laughter. Orlac runs away. Of course, it's all a masquerade to drive Orlac insane ... and it almost succeeds.

It's the highlight of the movie, brilliantly played by two superb actors.

Friday, May 10: Bride of Frankenstein opened big at Broadway's Roxy Theatre, complete with a musical stage show that included the acrobatic troupe, The Gretonas. *Variety* reports that one of the troupe, Eleta Dayne, "is shot from a cannon in a short white skirt and brassiere."

Wednesday, May 15: *The Mask of Virtue* opened in London. The costume play starred Jeanne de Casalis as a bitter, discarded mistress, whose wealthy former "keeper" (Frank Cellier) begins a romance with an enchanting young girl (Vivien Leigh). He falls madly in love with her, marries her, and then learns the truth—she's actually a vile prostitute, whom the rejected mistress has vengefully engaged to trap and torment her former lover. It was a triumph for Jeanne, and Vivien Leigh immediately received a film contract. (Leigh will say that one of the thrills of the play for her was nightly watching the "beautiful Jeanne de Casalis, holding the stage like its queen.") Colin, always interested in the London theater doings, surely heard about Jeanne's new success.

Friday, May 24: The Girl from 10ᵗʰ Avenue opened at Broadway's Capitol Theatre. The film will earn a worldwide rental of $428,000 and a profit of $55,000.

Meanwhile, *Mad Love* went on at MGM. Colin's most vehement ire, as expressed to *Film Weekly*, regarded the makeup for his knife-murderer hands:

> *Believe me, I was never more thankful in my life than when Karl Freund told me I was through with my part ... Clever makeup men experimented for some time before they succeeded in getting my hands to look sufficiently horrible to suit the director and his cameramen. By the time they were all satisfied they had elaborated a special hand makeup, which took two hours to fix. Two hours each morning; at the end of which my hands looked terrible, and felt much worse!*
>
> *The finger joints were built up; the hands had to be almost a quarter larger than normal size. Then around the wrists, where the surgeon had supposedly grafted them on to their new "foundation," ghastly scars were created ... I know that my hands were first stained with something green; then with something blue, and then with something white. Meanwhile, the knuckles and palms were built up and coarsened with some kind of wax, over which new skin was laid. The wrinkles in the joints were picked out with innumerable exaggerations traced with an ordinary lead pencil.*
>
> *The experience of viewing one's own hands in this condition was itself a shock. Often, I felt quite sick, and the real hands underneath this awful disguise ached with some unaccountable form of irritation. All day and every day, I felt that I would give almost anything to be able to wash away the whole ghoulish mess and forget the rest of the picture!*

"Whose hands are these?" demands Clive's Orlac of Lorre's Gogol.

"One Man *Crazy* ...!"

For all this misery with the makeup, *Mad Love* rarely dwells on Colin's hands.

The climax of *Mad Love* included a cockatoo, Drake posing as her own wax dummy, Lorre trying to strangle Drake with her hair, and the 11th hour Stephen Orlac-to-the-rescue as Colin, using the knife-thrower hands Gogol has given him, fatally throws a knife into the madman's back.

It is good melodramatic irony, but allows for a chillingly unresolved ending ... Will Orlac fulfill Gogol's prophecy, "Each man kills the thing he loves?" ... and will Yvonne be Orlac's tragic victim?

Saturday, June 8: Mad Love completed shooting, a week over schedule. The negative cost was $257,562.14, more than $40,000 over budget.

Friday, June 21: An assignee for New York agent Frank Zeitlin sued Colin in superior court for $20,000, claiming he had a three-year contract with the actor, during which time Colin had earned $200,000. It appears highly unlikely Colin earned anywhere near this sum between 1932 and 1935. There are no reports as to the settlement

Wednesday, June 26: MGM previewed *Mad Love* at the Alexander Theatre in Glendale, California. A reviewer for the *Los Angeles Post-Record* caught the show, reporting the film was "quite capable of scaring to death at least a few timid people."

What the critic saw was the 83-minute version. What audiences would see after *Mad Love*'s release had been trimmed by 15 minutes.

Cut from the film were the characters of Marianne, a woman of the streets, played by Isabel Jewell, and her Apache thief colleague, played by Harold Huber. Ian Wolfe's Henry Orlac tempts Marianne with a bracelet while the thief prepares to knock him out and rob the jewelry shop. Instead, Gogol arrives, throwing a knife into Henry Orlac's back. This had amplified Gogol making Stephen Orlac think he'd killed his own father.

Also ... out came the laboratory sequence! There's no indication that Joseph Breen and the Production Code demanded that MGM axe this showpiece—Metro presumably did so because it feared that *Mad Love* was already a horror overdose without it. This was damaging to the film—not only did it take away the spectacle of the laboratory transplants, but the scene had originally presented the steel and leather brace Gogol later wore, used in the lab to fasten Rollo's head during the operation.

Saturday, June 29: Variety wrote that Colin was "off to Arrowhead Springs for a few days" with John Buckler and Norman T. Shaw, Colin's business manager.

Friday, July 5: Joseph Breen gave *Mad Love* Certificate 1034, merely requesting the deletion of the shots of Rollo being tipped forward into the guillotine, which Breen found "unduly gruesome." MGM promoted this wicked witch's brew of Grand Guignol horror and surgical amputation as "The Screen's Strangest Sensation," and *Mad Love*'s trailer proudly heralded its star:

> PETER LORRE
> *Whom Charlie Chaplin Calls*
> *"The Greatest Living Actor"*

Over a minute-and-a-half later, the trailer proclaims:

> COLIN CLIVE
> *"Doctor Frankenstein"*

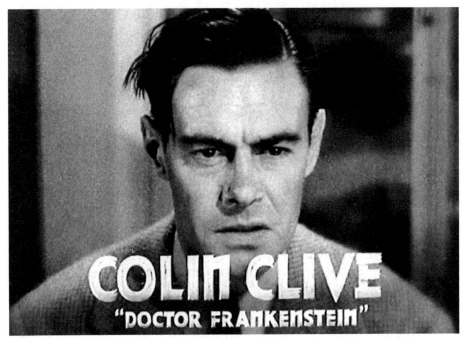

From the trailer for *Mad Love*. Colin Clive "Doctor Frankenstein."

And speaking of *Frankenstein*, MGM originally released *Mad Love* with a recorded warning, played before the credits, which went this way:

> *Ladies and Gentlemen, Metro-Goldwyn-Mayer feels that it would be a little unkind to present this picture without just a word of friendly warning. We are about to unfold a story which we consider one of the strangest tales ever told. We think it will thrill you. It may shock you. It might even horrify you. So, if any of you feel that you do not care to subject your nerves to such a strain, now is your chance to—well, we've warned you!*

Yes, with only a few adjustments, that's precisely the pre-credit speech that Edward Van Sloan delivered in *Frankenstein!* Presumably John L. Balderston added it to *Mad Love* as a satirical jab (or homage) to the 1931 shocker. At least two early reviews of *Mad Love* allude to the speech, but it's no longer part of the release print as we know it today, and likely long lost.

Friday, July 19: Colin was the guest star on KFI Radio's *Inside Stories*. An advertisement for the program billed Colin as the "Star of Metro-Goldwyn-Mayer's *Mad Love*."

Wednesday, July 24: Mad Love opened at the Hollywood Pantages, supported by *Manhattan Moon*, and a cartoon titled *Mouseland*. Described by *Time* as "one of the most completely horrible films of the year," *Mad Love* was a critical triumph for Lorre. However, following Universal's *Bride of Frankenstein* and the Karloff-and-Lugosi film *The Raven*, both of which had set off censorship gnashing of teeth in the U.S. and abroad, *Mad Love* was destined for trouble.

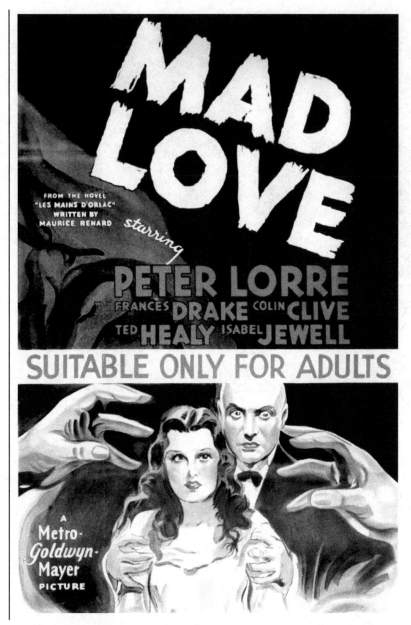

Mad Love advertisement. Note the "Suitable Only For Adults" warning.

Big trouble.

Pennsylvania made seven cuts. Quebec made 11 cuts, including the payoff shot of Orlac throwing the knife into Gogol's back. The worst trouble, however, was abroad—where England made *29* (!) cuts or alterations. Hungary, Finland, Austria, and Palestine rejected the film altogether.

The anti-horror vigilantes were lighting their torches.

Frances Drake as Yvonne in *Mad Love*. Her most vivid impression of Colin Clive was a tragic one.

Mad Love's worldwide rental: $364,000. *Mad Love*'s loss: $35,500.

Peter Lorre went on to become one of the movies' most distinctive character stars. Frances Drake soon signed up as the leading lady of Universal's Karloff and Lugosi *The Invisible Ray* (1936). Karl Freund never directed another film, returning to cinematography, winning an Oscar for MGM's *The Good Earth* (1937). The formidable "Papa" later oversaw all camera work on Desilu TV productions.

And as for Colin ... He had a neurotic's field day as Orlac, even if he hated every minute of it:

> *My only hope is that I may outlive this demand for horror pictures. Then I shall have more time and opportunity to play the kind of dramatic roles I like better.*

In some ways, it was too late. *Mad Love*, coming hot on the heels of *Bride of Frankenstein*, had canonized Colin Clive as Hollywood's Patron Saint of Lost Souls.

Two final reflections on *Mad Love*.

It's very probable that Colin despised the film for more reasons than the gruesome plot and the nasty hand makeup. After the horse fall at Sandhurst in 1919, the second horse fall in 1931, and the fall on *Bride of Frankenstein* earlier in 1935, he was increasingly.

suffering with his bad leg. His limp was more noticeable now, his body language onscreen sometimes affected by it. The leg trouble was growing quite serious ... and *Mad Love*, after all, was a film about amputations

The last reflection came from Frances Drake—her own real-life haunting memory of *Mad Love:*

> *Colin Clive was such a good actor, but a great drunk, you know. It was a pity. I remember once, at a party, about six or seven in the evening, Colin was in the garden, sitting on a little straight-backed chair. While we were all having a drink, the back of his chair sank slowly down. He just lay there, with his head in a flowerbed, drinking his drink.*
>
> *Nothing fazed him! Absolutely amazing!*

Chapter Twenty-Four
Libel!

Tuesday, August 20, 1935: Darryl F. Zanuck's newly formed 20th Century-Fox Studios began shooting *The Man Who Broke the Bank at Monte Carlo*. Suave Ronald Colman was the dapper exiled Russian prince who broke the bank; Joan Bennett was the blonde siren hired to lure him back to the casino; and a scowling Colin was her wicked accomplice, Bertrand Berkeley, Monte Carlo's avenger.

Directed by Stephen Roberts, and inspired by the 1890s British Music Hall song of the same title, *The Man Who Broke the Bank at Monte Carlo* is one of those movies considered "frothy" in 1935. It was then, and still is, a delight for devoted Ronald Colman fans. As for Colin, he makes his entrance on a train, enthusing to Joan Bennett about taking her to Switzerland:

> *"... Sunshine on the ice ... The mountains in the sky."*

Colman figures he's Bennett's husband; she later tells Colman that Colin's her brother. It appears Colin's a kink again, panting after his own sister. However, he's (presumably) not her brother, but her crooked partner, working for the casino. His only decent scene comes when, in a dressing gown, he realizes Bennett's falling for Colman and threatens her:

Colin and Ronald Colman share a lobby card for *The Man Who Broke the Bank at Monte Carlo*.

"One Man Crazy ...!"

Ronald Colman, Joan Bennett, and Colin in *The Man Who Broke the Bank at Monte Carlo*.

Colin: *You realize, of course, that you're throwing away 250,000 francs on a filthy Russian who'd kick you out in a second?*
Bennett: *That's not true!*
Colin: *Ah! So, you think he'd marry you, do you? You? A girl hired from a back-street music hall! Don't you realize what you are, and what he is?*

Publicity for *The Man Who Broke the Bank at Monte Carlo* claimed Colin was using his own "gambling paraphernalia gathered from all over the world" in the film:

> *Clive, who maintains he is one of the unluckiest gamblers existent, has in the past 10 years been so elated over rare winnings that he has purchased the apparatus, which proved lucky for him. It is this equipment he is using in the film. It includes a pair of dice from Caliente; two decks of cards from Cannes; a chuck-a-luck wicket and a faro box from Carson City, Nevada; and a roulette wheel ball from Monte Carlo. Clive also possesses a slot machine he bought in Tijuana, after it had showered quarters upon him.*

The acquisitions probably really existed, but the surviving print of *The Man Who Broke the Bank at Monte Carlo* has no scene of Clive with his casino memorabilia.

Completed September 19, *The Man Who Broke the Bank at Monte Carlo* would have a negative cost of $532,000, open in November, take in a worldwide rental of $984,200, and earn a profit of $138,600. The *New York Times* would whip up a fine pair of words to describe Colin's performance: "nicely acid."

Meanwhile, Warner Bros. exercised its option for Colin to act in a third film, tossing him into a comedy, *Meet the Duchess*, later retitled *The Widow from Monte Carlo* (and having nothing to do with *The Man Who Broke the Bank at Monte Carlo*). Produced by

Warner "B" unit chief Bryan Foy, it began shooting September 19, 1935, designed as a double-bill attraction. Warren William, usually the other man in films, was the male lead. Colin played Lord Eric, the silly ass fiancé of a sacredly photographed Dolores del Rio.

Colin is comically lily-livered in his proposal scene:

> Dolores del Rio: *Well—aren't you going to kiss me?*
> Colin: *Why, yes ... yes, I suppose it's done!*

The Widow from Monte Carlo also offers the spectacle of Colin in a bathing suit, bobbing on a raft with del Rio in the sea at Cannes. The curvaceous Dolores looks like she could snap her skeletal co-player in half with her thighs.

"And Colin Clive as her Cold-Storage Fiancé," proclaimed the trailer for *The Widow from Monte Carlo*. The film, which wrapped up October 8, runs a mere 60 minutes, has a great amusement park episode, and like most Warner "B" films, goes down easy. The negative cost was only $214,000; the worldwide-rentals, $353,000, which was even lower than the take for *Mad Love*. Loss: $19,250.

For his final Warner Bros. film, the studio had reduced Captain Stanhope and Henry Frankenstein to a virtual comic castrato.

By the way, two 1935 roles that Warners had considered for Colin: Oberon, King of the Fairies, in the spectacular *A Midsummer Night's Dream* (Victor Jory got the role); and Jeremy Pitt, faithful mate to Errol Flynn's *Captain Blood* (Ross Alexander played the part).

Colin and Dolores del Rio in *The Widow from Monte Carlo*.

"One Man *Crazy* ...!"

Universal had been toying with producing *Dracula's Daughter* since 1934, proceeding with censor-defying scripts by John L. Balderston and later, R.C. Sherriff. Junior Laemmle had tried unsuccessfully to entice James Whale to direct it. If he had, it's possible Whale would have considered Colin for the film, along with Karloff and Lugosi. None would ultimately appear in it.

By late summer, *Dracula's Daughter* was still flapping tentatively toward production. Considering Colin's warping reputation in Hollywood, some wags might have joked he'd play the film's title role.

Colin wanted no more to do with horror films, cinema colony innuendo, or movies at all. He needed to get out of Hollywood—fast—and he did. By the time *The Widow from Monte Carlo* opened at New York's Astor Theatre in January, 1936, Colin was enjoying a Broadway triumph.

On the night of November 14, 1935, in New York City—the same date that *The Man Who Broke the Bank at Monte Carlo* opened at Radio City Music Hall—Colin Clive was the guest star on Rudy Vallee's *The Fleischmann's Yeast Hour*. He starred in a short play titled *The Other Place*, written by John L. Balderston, formerly of *Frankenstein*, *Bride of Frankenstein*, and *Mad Love*.

"You've seen Mr. Clive most recently in *The Man Who Broke the Bank at Monte Carlo*," said Vallee in his introduction, "and as the Monster-making scientist in the *Frankenstein* pictures."

The story of *The Other Place*: A man dies in a car accident on a mountain road in Wales, finds himself in a place where his every desire for wealth and women is met by a perfect butler (Leo G. Carroll), and soon goes mad with boredom. The climactic dialogue:

> Colin: *I want to suffer ... I'm sick of Heaven ... I can't stand this confounded everlasting bliss ... Well, whatever the devils do to me can't be as bad as this. I want to go to Hell!*
> Leo G. Carroll: *Why, sir—wherever do you think you are? This is Hell, sir!*

The story later became *The Twilight Zone* episode titled "A Nice Place to Visit," telecast April 15, 1960, with Larry Blyden in the Clive role (revamped here to be a gunned-down hoodlum) and Sebastian Cabot in the Leo G. Carroll part. John Brahm directed and Charles Beaumont received credit for the script.

Colin had come east to star in the play *Libel!* It was a courtroom melodrama, directed by Otto Preminger—who went those days by the name of Otto Ludwig Preminger. The playwright was Edward Wooll, a *nom de plume* of an actual British barrister. The play had been a 1934 London success, starring Malcolm Keen.

The plot: Sir Mark Loddon (Colin), baronet, is a survivor of the Great War. Shell shock has caused amnesia and turned his hair stark white. Sir Mark wages a libel suit against a newspaper that claims that he is, in fact, an imposter—the real Sir Mark having perished in the war, and his identity assumed so flawlessly that the imposter has fooled the man's own wife, Lady Enid Loddon (Joan Marion). Sir Wilfred Kelling, K.C., M.P. (Ernest Lawford) represents Sir Mark, and Thomas Foxley, K.C. (Wilfrid Lawson), defends the newspaper. Courtroom fireworks ensue, exploding when a monstrous, deformed

Advertisement for the Broadway play *Libel!*

"One Man *Crazy* ... !"

being called "Numero Quinze" (Robert Simmons) enters the court. Is this the *real* Mark Loddon ... mutilated physically and mentally by his war wounds?

Colin starred as Sir Mark, a role that offered him a stab at a truly *tour de force* performance. He was so keen about the role, and so confident the play would enjoy a long run, that he refused to use a "wash" in his hair and actually dyed it white.

Monday, December 2, 1935: Libel! opened for a try-out at Philadelphia's Chestnut Street Opera House. *The Brooklyn Eagle* reported Colin's high spirits:

> "Mr. Clive, we'd like to take pictures of the show after the second night's performance in Philadelphia, if it's all right with you," the press representative of Gilbert Miller's production of Libel! said to the leading actor of the play recently. She spoke with some trepidation, since 11 o'clock at night, following a wearing performance and so soon after all the rush of opening the play, hardly seemed an hour calculated to please a star.
>
> Colin Clive regarded the speaker with unconcealed amazement, and some slight displeasure, and the speaker made hurried mental calculations as to just when, in the next hectic few days, pictures of the entire cast might be taken in the stage setting.
>
> "But I don't expect you to ask me if it's all right," said Mr. Clive mildly. "I expect you to tell me when you want me to appear for those pictures, and then I expect to be there, whether it's 7 o'clock in the evening and I miss my dinner, or 4 o'clock in the morning.
>
> "You see," he added kindly, as his interlocutor looked completely dazed at this un-Olympian reaction, "I've just come from Hollywood, where one does learn to expect that kind of deference to the star's wishes. But I think it's a very bad thing, and coming from the stage I was looking forward to returning to that tradition of theater discipline, which is one of the things that made the stage my first and real love, in preference to the screen.
>
> "Discipline is the very essence of the theater. Look at the way an actor is expected to be in the theater at the same hour every night, no matter what weather or traffic conditions are. No audience will sit around three-quarters of an hour after curtain time because the star's taxi got caught in a jam in Times Square. Nor will they put up with a poor performance if a player has a bad headache, or a couple of degrees of fever. The trouping tradition is one of the grandest things in the world. I can tell you, it's fine to be back." And with a charming smile, Colin Clive tipped his hat and walked briskly away.

It was a very telling conversation. Discipline ... the very essence of theater. Discipline was what his family had raised him to respect in the military. Discipline was what had held him together during the London run of *Journey's End.* Lack of discipline had contributed to his recent decay in Hollywood.

Libel! was more than a professional engagement for Colin Clive. It was, without exaggeration, a chance for personal and professional salvation.

The Philadelphia reviews were encouraging. "Colin Clive shows his versatility as Sir Mark Loddon," wrote the Philadelphia *Record.* "Playing a role which demands that he show constant emotional stress, he heightens the effect by delicate underplay and sharp contrast in mood."

Friday, December 20: Libel! opened at Broadway's Henry Miller's Theatre. Iris Lancaster was there for the opening, attracting eyes as she wore camellias in her red hair. Act III presented this showcase for Colin's brilliance as an actor:

> Sir Mark: *I did what I did in hot blood! ... (Pause)*
> Foxley: *What did you do, to that German of yours?*
> Sir Mark: (in tense agitation): *I've told you. I've told you. Leave me alone.*
> Foxley: *Have you? Have you? What are you keeping back?*
> Sir Mark: *The way I killed him.*
> Judge: *(interrupting—reading note) I have a note of what you said (Reading.) "I brought the butt down on his head. He dropped like a stone."*
> Sir Mark: *Yes—yes—*
> Foxley: *Is that all the truth? I want an answer. Have we got it all even now?*
> Sir Mark: *(reluctantly). No ... not all ... not all ... I'll tell you. My first blow smashed his arm. He gave a dreadful scream. More noises would have brought up some of his friends. He was down—helpless. I saw red. (Hysterically.) I had to finish him off ... I had to ... If I was to have a chance of getting away ... getting home ... seeing ...*
> Sir Wilfred: *Take your time, Sir Mark.*
> Foxley: *How many more blows?*
> Sir Mark (hysterically). *How can I tell? ... blow after blow ... blow after blow ... till the head was a pulp and the face was ... I can't think of it ... I won't think of it ... I've tried to forget it all these years ... I won't remember it ... I've never told my wife ... I couldn't tell my wife ... (relapses exhausted into chair) ... There was always that between us ... keeping us apart ... She told the truth ... it was the truth ... never since the war ... .never have I been the Mark Loddon she promised to marry!*
> Foxley: *So, we seem to be right. You are a man capable of brutal murder?*
> Sir Mark: *(rising in sudden passion). Did you ever serve in the war, Mr. Foxley?*

The curtain fell a few moments later. Colin's Sir Mark is indeed the real Sir Mark—winning £25,000, "the fullest possible apology and complete withdrawal of every allegation" ... and reconciliation with his wife.

"Colin Clive's baronet is a very model of blooded grace, poise, and personal sincerity," praised Brooks Atkinson in the *New York Times* the next day. The Christmas Day issue of *Variety* critiqued, "Colin Clive has no easy part ... He sits most of the time brooding but, on the witness stand, injects the dramatic power that makes *Libel!* something unusual."

It was a Yuletide Broadway gathering of the stars of the London *Journey's End*. On December 23, Maurice Evans opened at the Martin Beck Theatre in *Romeo and Juliet*, co-starring with Katharine Cornell. Playing Benvolio, incidentally, was a 21-year-old actor who, in 1936, would become a major film star—Tyrone Power. On December 26, George Zucco opened at the Broadhurst Theatre as Benjamin Disraeli in *Victoria Regina*, which starred Helen Hayes. Playing Prince Albert was a towering, 24-year-old Adonis named Vincent Price.

A *New York Times'* drawing of Colin for his star appearance in Broadway's *Libel!*

It was a happy time for Colin, personally as well as professionally. On January 3, 1936, Walter Winchell reported that "the girl with the camellias in her hair at the *Libel!* premiere is Colin Clive's sweetheart. They're engaged." It was big news, even though, as Winchell confessed, "I didn't get her name." Two weeks later, Winchell wrote, "I just heard the name of the lovely lady who is Colin Clive's bay-bee. It is Iris Lancaster ..." Reporting the news was rather indelicate, since Colin was still married to Jeanne de Casalis. Nevertheless, on February 3, Winchell's column confirmed:

Colin Clive of Libel! *and Iris Lancaster, an image of Joan Crawford, are secretly betrothed.*

One suspects that it was Iris herself who gave Winchell the scoop.

Libel! played on, Colin sounding as if he'd finally controlled his stage fright:

> *Being back on the stage is a lovely rest from the films. It's like a holiday, like returning to one's first love. The direct audience response is one of the most important things in the world for an actor. I believe the American audience—except the Thursday matinee women who swarm down the aisles in the middle of the first act—is the finest audience in the world.*

Colin spoke happily about the role he most desired to play—Raskolnikov of Dostoyevsky's *Crime and Punishment* (which Peter Lorre had just played in the Columbia 1935 film version, directed by Josef von Sternberg), and his dream of one day having his own theater, performing the works of Shaw, Galsworthy, and Shakespeare.

He was upbeat, exhilarated. Yet the strain of the discipline he was imposing on himself, the responsibility he felt for the performance, and at least a residue of the old bugaboo of stage fright were taking a toll. Once again, however, he was determined to conquer the anxiety ... to be the hero.

Meanwhile, Colin expressed at this time a rather whimsical and revealing admission of what he'd do if he had the "choice of any job in the world:"

> *It's always been my ambition to be the captain of a freighter, traveling between, let's say, San Francisco and Liverpool.*
>
> *Even now, as a matter of fact, I travel that way whenever I have the time. I'd make only one condition and enforce it strictly: No passengers.*
>
> *For many years I've thought about it in my few leisure moments, looking forward to the time when I could take my pilot's examination and learn every detail of handling such a craft.*
>
> *The absence of passengers would make it possible for me really to spend my time taking care of the vessel and taking it easy when I was off duty.*

Wednesday evening, March 11, 1936: Colin was "taken from his suite at the Hotel Algonquin soon after 5:00 p.m." as reported by the *New York Times*, and rushed to Harbor Sanitarium, 667 Madison Avenue, for an intestinal operation. The sudden illness was mysterious, although it was quickly noted that Colin (who'd admirably controlled his drinking during the run) had recently joined the cast of *Libel!* celebrating at a champagne party, toasting the play's 100th performance since the Philadelphia opening. The rumor was that he'd fallen catastrophically off the wagon. The truth was that he'd developed a serious ulcer.

His understudy, Colin Hunter, took over while the producers promised Colin's return within a week. However, he contracted pneumonia—and never returned. *Libel!* limped along without him for two more months, closing in May after 159 New York performances. Everyone agreed it would have run far longer had it not lost its star.

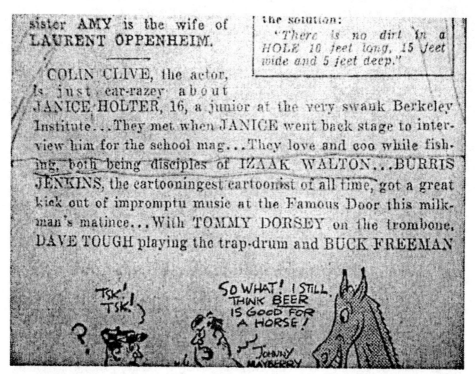

The 1936 clipping about Colin and Janice Holter, saved by Ms. Holter until her death. (Courtesy of Tracy Surrell)

Colin was heartbroken. He also felt guilty that his illness had ended *Libel!*'s run. He began drinking heavily again.

Worse was still to come.

On February 11, 2003, a woman named Janice Holter Judd died in Honolulu, Hawaii, at the age of 83. For the last eight years of her life, a pastor's wife cared for her. Mrs. Judd had no family, and when she died, she left everything to a woman who was a member of her pastor's church. Before her death, she made her heir promise she'd not throw away any of the possessions she'd especially prized during her lifetime.

Among those possessions were her 1936 diary and movie stills of Colin Clive.

The story was that during Colin's run in *Libel!* Janice Holter, then 16 years old and from a socially prominent New York family, came to interview him for her school magazine. Colin began a relationship with the underage Janice.

In 2012, the daughter of the woman who'd inherited her possessions persuaded her mother to sell the stills, but not the diary, which was apparently quite revealing. The daughter sold a number of the stills via eBay to Tracy Surrell, a devoted Colin Clive fan, and wrote to her:

"We'd assume from Jan's diary that most of the pictures that are listed came directly from Colin. Jan was a school girl in love and Colin had a passionate fan."

Among the material Janice Holter Judd had saved was a clipping from a newspaper or magazine, un-sourced, with this report:

> *COLIN CLIVE, the actor, is just car-razey about JANICE HOLTER, 16,*
> *a junior at the swanky Berkeley Institute ... They met when Janice went back*
> *stage to interview him for the school mag ... They love and coo while fishing,*
> *both being disciples of IZAAK WALTON ...*

This was seriously explosive—a famous, married, 36-year-old actor, "loving and cooing" with a 16-year-old girl. The published account is so repellant in its suggestively smarmy wording that one wonders what the reporter or editor was thinking by running so disturbing a story.

There are, of course, various interpretations open to this account. Janice Holter might have fantasized the affair and leaked it herself to the press. This, however, seems unlikely, as publicizing her sexual relationship with a famous man over twice her age would have created potentially catastrophic consequences, including the wrath of her family and expulsion from her school. (She'd graduate from Berkeley Institute in 1937.) No one can say what actually happened without access to the 1936 diary (and maybe even what's written there is fanciful) and the family of the heir has no plans to sell the diary or make it public.

The newspaper/magazine clipping served as the smoking gun. Colin was in serious trouble.

There's no comeback or redemption for a celebrity sexually involved with an underage lover, be it 1936 or 2018 (just ask any of the current crop of actors whose careers are in ruins due to such behavior). One of the very first facts of life any famous individual learns is to steer clear of precisely this sort of star-struck peril.

If Colin had actually become involved emotionally and sexually with Janice Holter, his behavior perhaps reveals just how tragically he'd fallen in his own mind, how much he'd forfeited his self-control, and how bewildered he'd become, trying to cope with his own escalating tragedy.

With this tornado forming, Colin fled New York in May, 1936, boarding *The Chief,* virtually escaping to Hollywood. The brewing scandal of the love saga of Colin Clive and Janice Holter fizzled in his absence, its evidence buried for over 65 years in Janice Holter Judd's personal belongings, and entombed another decade by her heir.

> *Riding across America on* The Chief. *A full moon.*
> *When he'd first come to Hollywood by train, he'd seen the prairie. He*
> *was seeing it again, in the moonlight. He'd been frightened when he'd gone*
> *west in 1929. In some ways he was more frightened now. Frightened by his*
> *failures; by how people saw him; by how he saw himself.*
> *Frightened to be heading back to the sideshow of the movies; ill, desper-*
> *ately unhappy, and realizing how terrible it would be to die in Hollywood.*
> *It would be rather like a geek dying in the pit ... wouldn't it?*

Part VI
The Jeering Tragic Mask

Think of all the topping fellows who've gone already.
It can't be very lonely there, with all those fellows.
Sometimes I feel it's lonelier here.

Captain Stanhope, *Journey's End*

Chapter Twenty-Five
Return to the Coast

Sunday, May 10, 1936: Colin Clive arrived in Los Angeles on *The Chief*.

It was a tail-between-his-legs return to the film colony. Movie producers knew a Broadway play had folded because Colin had become ill. The rumors of his potentially disastrous relationship with 16-year-old Janice Holter had likely reached gossip-loving Hollywood as well.

The hapless "homecoming" came at a significant time.

Monday, May 11: Universal released *Dracula's Daughter*. Gloria Holden starred in the title role, Lambert Hillyer directed, and neither Karloff nor Lugosi appeared. A wax dummy of Lugosi as Dracula was present, cremated by his faithful daughter, and Lugosi received $4,000 for the time he'd reserved for the film.

Tuesday, May 12: Universal celebrated the opening of James Whale's *Show Boat*, with a Hollywood Boulevard parade to the Pantages Theatre for the gala premiere. Irene Dunne and Allan Jones, both of whom had heartily disliked Whale during the shoot, were the stars. He'd worked more cordially with Paul Robeson, who'd been in the 1928 London stage production of *Show Boat* with Colin. The musical had cost almost $1,300,000—approximately the costs of *Journey's End, Frankenstein, One More River*, and *Bride of Frankenstein* combined. This was a gargantuan expense for Universal, and it had ultimately cost the Laemmles the studio. Indeed, on March 14, three days after Whale had completed *Show Boat*, "Uncle Carl" and "Junior," unable to pay a loan, lost Universal to new management.

"The New Universal" claimed *Show Boat* as its own, although the Laemmle regime had produced it. For Whale, this was his supreme night of triumph. For Colin, who surely wished his friend all the best, it must have stirred odd feelings. Here was the film of *Show Boat*, the show in which he'd first won real notice in London, his role of Steve played in the film by Donald Cook. The premiere was at the Pantages, where *One More River, Bride of Frankenstein*, and *Mad Love* had opened. And here was Whale, who'd basically discovered Colin, at the peak of his career, while Colin had come back to Hollywood with no offers.

He was, after all, hardly in a good bargaining position—and he was still very ill.

Friday, June 5: *Variety* reported that Colin was at Good Samaritan Hospital, suffering from pneumonia, his condition "not considered critical." In truth, he'd developed pulmonary tuberculosis.

Wednesday, August 19: *Variety* wrote that Colin had "checked out" of Hollywood Hospital. There was no specific mention of his ailment.

Meanwhile the film of *Show Boat* wasn't the only reminder to Colin of his past. On February 4, 1936, *St. Helena*, a play about the exiled Napoleon, had opened at the Old Vic Theatre in London. Kenneth Kent played Napoleon, and the two playwrights were R.C Sherriff, who'd written *Journey's End*, and Colin's estranged wife, Jeanne de Casalis. It was, as reported by the *New York Times*, a "triumph."

Plans evolved for a Broadway production. It must have stirred complex emotions for Colin that, as he'd just had to vacate a New York play that had folded without him, Sherriff and Jeanne were anticipating a new Broadway success. Additionally, Maurice Evans, who'd played Raleigh to Colin's Stanhope in London, signed to play Napoleon.

Jeanne de Casalis wrote of the play's early production adventures in a *New York Times* feature:

> *To write a play because one is in love with the subject matter, and then to have it published and handsomely bound on one's bookshelf accompanied by a sheaf of gratifying criticisms, is a highly comfortable state, but when it finds its way into the theater—then, as with an unholy passion, begin the fevers and the torments!*

Tuesday, October 6: St. Helena opened at Broadway's Lyceum Theatre. Brooks Atkinson, critic for the *New York Times*, found Evans an impressive Napoleon, but wrote:

> *... Mr. Sherriff and Miss de Casalis have made a faithful record of those inglorious years without giving them much significance ... [they] never let us know what they think of Napoleon or why they are writing such a methodical play about his dying years and* St. Helena *is diffuse biography.*

It proved to be, despite its London popularity, only a tepid success in New York, lasting 63 performances ... less than half the run chalked up by *Libel!*

Wednesday, October 21: After having been back in Hollywood for over five months, Colin finally landed a job: *Variety* reported that Walter Wanger had cast him in *History Is Made at Night.* The role: an insanely jealous husband.

He needed the work. On October 29, the *Omaha World Herald* reported that the income tax bureau had filed federal liens against several Hollywood figures for back taxes. They were nailing Colin for $1,951.

Then came another personal tragedy.

The legend stubbornly persists: Was Colin Clive bisexual?

Throughout his travails, Colin had Iris Lancaster, who was both his lover and, presumably, his caregiver as his health declined. He also had a good friend in John Buckler, the aforementioned actor who'd worked with Colin in Broadway's *Eight Bells* in 1933. In fact, Buckler had played Colin's stage role of Captain Dale in Columbia's 1935 film version of *Eight Bells*, while Ralph Bellamy had taken Buckler's role of the hero and Ann Sothern played Rose Hobart's part of the heroine.

Buckler and his parents, Hugh and Violet, had settled in Hollywood, father and son both working in films. Offscreen, Colin and John Buckler spent much time in each other's company. Rather dousing the homosexual partners innuendo, however, was that while Colin was romantically involved with Iris Lancaster, Buckler was reportedly engaged to an actress named Ulla Casanova. A July 12, 1936 photo in the *Los Angeles Times* showed John Buckler with his fiancée Ulla, father Hugh, actor Sir Guy Standing, and Iris Lancaster at the Victor Hugo Restaurant in Hollywood.

Horror fans might remember John Buckler for his vivid performance as Beran, the peasant who leads the revolt against Karloff's evil Baron Gregor in Columbia's *The Black Room* (1935). Also in 1935, MGM had Buckler on contract and cast him as Captain Fry, the villainous big game hunter who wants to trap Johnny Weissmuller's Tarzan and display him in a circus in *Tarzan Escapes.* The film was shot in the summer of 1935 (complete with the famous, long-lost flying vampire bats

John Buckler and Maureen O'Sullivan in MGM's *Tarzan Escapes*.

episode), underwent major revisions, and resumed shooting again in the summer of 1936.

During these rather frightening times for Colin Clive, John Buckler stayed a good and close friend, often joining Colin and Iris at their favorite corner table at Travaglini's, a Hollywood night spot, its proprietor a former officer in the Italian army.

Friday, October 30: On this eve of Halloween, 30-year-old John Buckler and 55-year-old Hugh Buckler (who, earlier in the week, had secured a divorce from his wife) were at Malibou Lake, where they had a summerhouse—and where, incidentally, James Whale had filmed the "Little Maria" episode in *Frankenstein*. Son and father decided to drive back to town late that night. As later theorized by investigators, a driving rainstorm made it impossible for them to see where they were going and swept their car off the road and into the lake.

The *Baltimore Sun* reported that the Bucklers "drowned at midnight" as Halloween arrived.

Come morning, residents at Malibou Lake saw the car floating in the water. There was an autopsy and inquiry, and John Buckler's death certificate reads: "Car he was in skidded on mud into lake and pinned him under it. Drowned."

The Shierry & Walling Funeral Parlor in Canoga Park handled the funeral arrangements. There was a joint funeral on Tuesday, November 3 (three days before MGM released *Tarzan Escapes*), followed by a joint cremation at Oakwood Cemetery in Los Angeles/Chatsworth.

"One Man *Crazy* ...!"

On the same day as the funeral and cremation of John and Hugh Buckler, shooting began on *History Is Made at Night*, featuring a deeply grieving Colin Clive.

Chapter Twenty-Six
History Is Made at Night

Colin Clive carves a new type of menace that gets a niche in the Hall of Cinema Fame.
The Film Daily review of *History Is Made at Night*, March 8, 1937

The late critic Andrew Sarris called *History Is Made at Night* "the most romantic title in the history of cinema."

The film is also a remarkable anomaly—it plays as a romantic screwball comedy, sexually attacked by a darkly sinister melodrama. Charles Boyer and Jean Arthur, as star-crossed lovers, supply the romance. Colin Clive, as a sado-masochistic psycho, provides the melodrama.

Very rarely has an actor so agonizingly performed such a spiritual striptease in a film. It's harrowing to watch.

History Is Made at Night was an independent production, produced by Walter Wanger and released through United Artists. The director was Frank Borzage, who'd won the first Best Director Oscar for 1927's *7th Heaven* (winning again for 1931's *Bad Girl*). Almost acrobatically, Borzage juggles the seemingly-at-odds parts of *History Is Made at Night* with seamless skill.

Boyer and Arthur, as Paul and Irene, have a sparkling chemistry, somehow making a scene where she removes her high heels to dance a late-night tango with him in her stocking feet incredibly erotic. And Colin is Lucifer-in-the-flesh as the insane Bruce Vail, a shipping tycoon and Irene's demon-lover husband.

Indeed, Colin's Vail is so maniacally jealous that he drives his wife to a lover, commits murder, knocks his wife to the floor, tries to sink his own ship in iceberg-haunted waters in a *Titanic*-style climax, and for a grand crowd-pleasing finale, shoots himself.

The frightening thing about the hysterically vile performance: It's so chillingly convincing.

What pet devils so agonizingly torment Bruce Vail in *History is Made at Night*?

Wanger, Borzage, and screenwriters Gene Towne and Graham Baker (who often wrote scripts on hot days while wearing bathing suits, and sometimes brassieres) played it close to the vest. Unlike Junior Laemmle and James Whale, who'd teasingly sent the sadism-scented script for *One More River* to Joseph Breen as a red cape dare, Wanger coyly played footsie with Breen, sending the *History Is Made at Night* script in two installments. Breen, responding to the first part on October 30, 1936, could find only minor troubles, such as making sure one of the leading lady's costumes would "avoid any exposure of her body." On December 1, Breen responded to the final installment, again concerned about Irene's costuming, the use of the word "lover," and this episode with Bruce Vail and Irene:

> *Page 68: Political censor boards will certainly delete the action of Vail knocking Irene to the floor. We suggest you change this.*

The rest of the scenario got by, with Wanger, Borzage, and the writers aware the dynamite was in the casting. Bruce Vail's mania, in the hands of Colin Clive—an alco-

"One Man Crazy ...!"

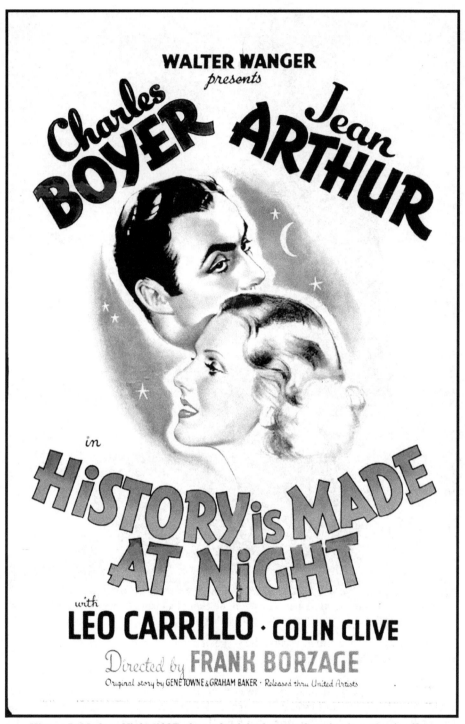

History Is Made at Night (1937), framed original poster, hanging in author's office.

"... a new type of menace that gets a niche in the Hall of Cinema Fame." Colin Clive as insanely jealous Bruce Vail in *History Is Made at Night*.

holic whom gossipers claimed was on the verge of a possibly violent breakdown—would explode onscreen like fireworks.

"No man is going to take Irene away from me!" Colin's Bruce Vail cries, already approaching the throes of hysteria early in the film. He arranges a sick trick for his wife, who's left him: He sends his smarmy chauffeur (Ivan Lebedeff) to rape Irene in her Paris hotel room. Vail and another witness will break in to watch her ravishment, and Vail's tale that she was having an affair will destroy her divorce suit.

The action rapidly establishes him as a pervert.

Paul (Boyer), witnessing the scene from another balcony, interferes, knocks out the chauffeur and, when Clive arrives, locks him in a closet. He "kidnaps" Irene—the romance begins, as they dance the tango at the restaurant where he's headwaiter. Meanwhile, Vail, escaping the closet, feeds his own torment: He adjusts his story, forcing the chauffeur to claim that the chauffeur broke in on Irene making love to Boyer. To frame Irene's "lover" for murder, Vail strikes the chauffeur with a poker.

He's now a murderer.

To save her lover from his pursuit, Vail blackmails Irene into dropping her divorce and sailing with him to New York. There follows a remarkable episode, where Clive's Vail, a bit tipsy, returns from dinner to his sulking wife in her ship's cabin. "Kiss me!" says Clive, grabbing Arthur, passionately, pathetically begging her for affection. She responds with total disdain.

"I see," says Colin. "Too soon from his arms, eh?"

Colin goes on, slyly taunting Arthur about the lover he thinks she's protecting:

> Colin Clive: *Wouldn't it be wonderful, Irene, if you were a magician, and could change me into him? Just think—you two alone, right now, in this room, on this boat, in the middle of the sea. What would you give, Irene? Well? What* would *you give?*
> Jean Arthur: *I'd give my* soul!

She laughs in his face, proud of her love affair. He grabs her throat. "I'll kill you!" he prophesies, throwing her to the floor—the action staying in the film despite Breen's objection.

He's now a frighteningly abusive husband.

The power, intensity, and fascination of the scene, and the performance, transcend the rather daring-for-1937 dialogue and action. There's more than the sadism and masochism, more than the almost palpable tinge of self-loathing.

In the role of Bruce Vail, Colin Clive, the actor himself, seems on the verge of a long, anguished scream.

History Is Made at Night has its ample share of comedy, much of it provided by the repartee of Boyer and Arthur, and especially in the presence of Leo Carrillo as a master chef known as "the Great Cesare." Carrillo is marvelous, tossing out malapropisms such as, "The females of the spices is a more-dead than the male."

Colin and Carrillo had no scenes together, and perhaps it's just as well. In 1933, when Carrillo was 52, he'd dated 18-year-old Iris Lancaster.

It was one of those quirky, magical casts that only existed in 1930's Hollywood. Charles Boyer, superb as Paul, was actually bald, short, and stout. It was remarkable how he transformed himself into a great screen lover each morning with toupee, lifts, and corset, although one might think his soulful eyes and seductive voice were all he really needed. Jean Arthur, charming as Irene was, as was her custom, a mass of nerves, suffering stage fright, convinced she was unattractive, even at this peak of her stardom.

Yet Jean Arthur's torments paled beside Colin's.

It was Yuletide again, Colin's fourth in Hollywood. The Santa Claus Lane parade every night down Hollywood Boulevard, lights and wreaths on every corner ... and here he was, playing a virtual Satan. He was gaunt, almost frighteningly thin, still ill from his bout with consumption, and drinking. Hollywood awaited word of the breakdown, and it finally came, although never publicized. DeWitt Bodeen remembered the shocking news:

> *On Colin Clive in* History Is Made at Night—*I'd heard that in his big scene he went all to pieces in hysteria; I think he must have been drinking. But the emotion he was showing and the scene he was playing got mixed up in his own private downfall, and he wept and sobbed bitterly.*

Bodeen wasn't certain which "big scene" it was, but Colin had several of them in the later part of *History Is Made at Night*. Particularly, as the climax nears, and Vail, back in Paris, learns that Paul and Irene have fled New York to Europe on the maiden voyage of his ship (which he'd christened *The SS Princess Irene*), he calls the ship's commodore. Vail spitefully demands that the commodore pursue the speed record by racing the ship through foggy, iceberg-infested waters. Vail hopes, of course, the ship will crash, sending the lovers—as well as all the other passengers, crew, and *The SS Princess Irene* itself—to the bottom of the frigid sea.

Vail is now, or so he expects, a catastrophic mass-murderer.

The ship indeed hits an iceberg. There follows screaming, wailing, and old men singing *Nearer My God to Thee*. However, the ship ultimately survives. In a climax that still gives chills today, Alfred Newman's rhapsodic music swells, and Boyer and Arthur have a triumphant fade-out kiss. However, moments before, Colin's Bruce Vail hears a radio report that prematurely claims the ship has sunk ... and all have died. The look on Colin's face as he hears the news is, for all his diabolics in the film, heartbreaking. The shattered man writes a confession and approaches his cherished oil painting of Irene. We see the painting from his point of view; for a moment *we* are Bruce Vail, with all his guilt, torment, and horror.

A shot fires. Smoke from the revolver rises up before the portrait, almost as a corpse's incense offering to the woman he believes he has killed, and whom he blames for destroying him.

History Is Made at Night completed shooting January 4, 1937, although there are indications that additional shooting took place in February. The final cost: $821,790.85. The star salaries of *History Is Made at Night* are telling regarding the "caste system" of Hollywood stardom:

> *Charles Boyer: $72,040.00*
> *Jean Arthur: $66,666.64*
> *Colin Clive: $13,816.08*

Released by United Artists, *History is Made at Night* previewed Friday, March 5, 1937 at the Village Theatre in Westwood. "Fine Combo of Romance and Thrills Has Unusual Appeal for Femmes with Novel Love Story," headlined *The Film Daily's* chauvinistic review. The carefully selected words only slightly inferred the wickedly kinky performance that Colin had delivered, but the review elaborated, giving him much of the glory:

Colin and Jean Arthur – *History Is Made at Night.*

... It has fascination for all the femmes in the contrast of a husband insanely jealous of his wife, and a lover sacrificing everything if necessary to make her happy. It has a rare hypnotic quality in the constant menace of Colin Clive, the husband. It should have every dame and damsel in a delightful dither of shudders, wondering what the lady's ball-and-chain is going to do to her next. This menace-shudder quality alone should sell the dames ...

A candid shot on *History Is Made at Night* – Ivan Lebedeff, Colin, director Frank Borzage, and Charles Boyer.

It did, considerably. *History Is Made at Night* opened Easter Eve, March 27, 1937, at New York's Rivoli Theatre, and would earn a worldwide rental of $1,410,877.26, making it one of Colin's most widely seen films. The movie emerged as a far more vivid case study of a sado-masochist—as well as a far more dynamic film—than Whale's highly mannered *One More River*. Frank Borzage directed with such stylish subtlety that the daring film faced relatively little censorship trouble.

There was some. The Irish Free State would reject the film, as would the Canton of Fribourg, a territory in Switzerland. Quebec excised several scenes of "kissing and embracing"; it also made a bizarre cut in Colin's suicide scene. As noted, we see Jean Arthur's oil painting from Colin's point of view, then hear the gun shot, then see the gun's smoke rising. Quebec cut the sound of the revolver.

The resulting impression: The villain was still alive, gazing at the portrait, and smoking in supernatural, devilish desire.

Colin had richly deserved a Best Actor Academy nomination for *Journey's End*, and arguably for *Frankenstein*. Had there been Best Supporting Actor Academy Awards in 1935, he'd have rated a nomination for *The Right to Live*. The Best Supporting prizes began for films released in 1936, and come 1937, Colin absolutely rated a nomination for *History Is Made at Night*. As it was, by the time the Academy selected its nominees for that year, Colin was dead.

Of course, how much of Colin's *History Is Made at Night* performance was acting and how much was raw emotion will forever be a mystery—but it likely was a toxic mix.

"One Man *Crazy* ...!"

Spanish poster, *History Is Made at Night*.

It's a passionately haunted, haunting portrayal, and his out-of-the-cage Bruce Vail has raised some eyebrows over the years.

"Clive is nearly as insanely obsessive here as in *Frankenstein*," wrote the UCLA Film and TV Archive. Dan Callahan, in a tribute to Colin in Online's *The Chiseler*, writes of Colin's "revoltingly personal and convincing" Bruce Vail:

> ... *Clive dives down very deep into this man's self-hatred and demented jealousy. He's ill-tempered and twitchy here, as if he's trying to control the shakes, and there's an enormous loss of control if you compare his work in this film to the precision of his performance in* Journey's End *just seven years earlier, but there has been no diminishment in intensity. The man in* Journey's End *was bound to crack at some point, just as Clive himself was a lit fuse ready to explode, and when he did in* History is Made at Night, *it's as if all kinds of bugs crawled out of him and bad smells and agonized sounds ...*

Perhaps Dorothy Manners put it most succinctly in her *Los Angeles Examiner* review of *History Is Made at Night,* after the film opened April 7, 1937 at Grauman's Chinese Theatre and Loew's State Theatre in Los Angeles.

"Colin Clive is so grim in this role," wrote Manners, "the audience applauded when he shot himself."

One-sheet poster for *The Woman I Love*.

Chapter Twenty-Seven
The Woman I Love

Before *History Is Made at Night* wrapped up, Colin had signed for another movie. It wasn't a horror picture, but its shooting was certainly horrific.

The Woman I Love, from RKO Studios, was a Lafayette Escadrille love saga. The star was a bearded, stoop-shouldered Paul Muni, likely the biggest male camera hog in Hollywood. He'd met his match in his leading lady, blonde, piggy-eyed Miriam Hopkins, whose diva temperament explosively clashed with Muni's egomania. The director was Anatole Litvak, who fell in love with Hopkins, married her later that year, and divorced her two years later.

The film went perilously over budget and schedule. Can-Can girls who worked in the film's opening came perilously close to causing an in studio scandal. RKO despaired the film might never finish.

And, most sadly, there was Colin Clive, looking like a skeleton in a Lafayette Escadrille uniform, literally falling down drunk on the set ... bravely giving what would be his final screen performance.

Budgeted at $618,807, *The Woman I Love* was a remake of the 1935 French film, *L'Equipage*. The story: Lt. Claude Maury (Muni), is a "Jinx" pilot in the Lafayette Escadrille. Along with carrying the curse of getting his flying partners killed, he has an unloving wife, Helene (Hopkins). Fevers rise as a young lieutenant named Jean (Louis Hayward) becomes not only Claude's new partner, but also Helene's lover—and she fears, rightly, Jean will die in the air with her undesirable husband to blame.

The leader of the Lafayette Escadrilles squadron was the gallant but doomed Captain Thelis, played by Colin. It was the type of heroic role he enjoyed, and even provided a great death scene.

The contracts for the four stars of *The Woman I Love* again show the giant gaps in Hollywood compensation:

· Paul Muni: Set for four weeks and four days—total $65,000.00
· Miriam Hopkins: Set for four weeks—total $65,000.00
· Louis Hayward: Set for $10,166.67
· Colin Clive: Set for a four-week guarantee at $1,500 per week—total $6,000.00

Frenchman Anatole Litvak had directed *L'Equipage*, and *The Woman I Love* was his first Hollywood film. (Salary: $35,000.) He signaled attention on the set by blowing a gold whistle. The film's title, which might have suited almost any film of the era, came from King Edward VIII's December 11, 1936 Abdication Speech as he announced he would wed the woman he loved, Wallis Simpson.

Monday, December 14, 1936: Shooting of *The Woman I Love* began on the RKO Ranch in the San Fernando Valley, with Hopkins, Hayward, and over 100 extras. Colin was still working on *History Is Made at Night*. His first day on *The Woman I Love* was Saturday, January 9, 1937, acting on the Captain Thelis Office set with Muni and Hayward.

The film rapidly became a "Jinx" itself—crashing and burning under the high-flying egos of the two stars. Muni, then riding the wave of *The Story of Louis Pasteur*, was a safe

Paul Muni and Colin, in *The Woman I Love*.

bet for Best Actor Academy Award winner of 1936 for that biographical film produced by his home studio, Warner Bros. His wife, Bella, as was her custom, sat on the set, nodding approvingly whenever her husband totally dominated a scene. If she shook her head no, all hell broke loose.

And break loose it did, whenever Muni acted with Miriam Hopkins ... perhaps best remembered as "bad girl" Ivy in Paramount's 1931 *Dr. Jekyll and Mr. Hyde*, strip-teasing down to garter and coyly-draped bed sheet. Hopkins terrorized *The Woman I Love*'s set with her tantrums and rabid scene-stealing. During her ingénue nights in stock, Hopkins had stolen focus by sitting with her legs provocatively parted. Joe Breen would never have allowed such antics, but she was nearly as ruthless now, even as a major film star.

Hopkins dared to rewrite Muni's dialogue while she had her lunch, and to advise him how to play his role. Muni finally demanded Hopkins get the heave-ho, and Albert Lewis, the film's producer and Muni's personal friend, decided to fire her. Litvak, in love with Miriam, refused to allow her to be fired.

"A disturbing element during the shooting," understated Albert Lewis regarding the tempestuous Hopkins

By this time, Colin was desperately ill, frightfully thin, and terribly addicted. He was only working because he desperately needed the salary, and his lack of ego might as well have placed him on another planet as on a film set with Muni and Hopkins. Tragically, he found his usual escape from the trauma: alcohol. In James Curtis' *James Whale: A New World of Gods and Monsters*, the author reported Louis Hayward's memory of the doomed film, and Colin's chillingly self-fulfilling prophecy:

"Get out of this business. It'll kill you ... " – A grim close-up of a failing, fatally ill Colin on
The Woman I Love.

*All Clive's scenes had to be shot in the morning, as he was drunk by noon.
He had to be held up for over-the-shoulder shots. "My dear sir," he told the
young actor, "get out of this business. It'll kill you, it'll kill you."*

As terrible as it was, for all his anxiety, despite the tuberculosis, and in spite of his
drinking, Colin was still being heroic. The RKO records indicate he was always on time.

Clive as the dead Captain Thelis. This scene of him as a corpse would be the last one moviegoers would see him play.

He never missed a day. Despite Hayward's recollection that Colin could only act before noon, the RKO production reports show that at times he worked into the night, sometimes very late. Possibly seated and held up, he nevertheless was there. He was giving an excellent performance. He was doing his duty.

As Stanhope had been in the dugout, so was Colin on the soundstage.

Monday, January 25, 1937: *The Woman I Love* began location shooting at seaside Point Mugu, about 40 miles up the coast from Santa Monica. This area served as the film's exterior flying field. Colin was there, as was Louis Hayward and the actors playing the pilots. There were six real-life soldiers, 10 mechanics, and four drivers.

Muni joined the company the next day, and the location site gave everyone a break from the wrath of Miriam Hopkins. The World War I fighter planes, flying above the Pacific, provided a nice splash of spectacle. Indeed, these visuals (along with flying footage lifted from *L'Equipage*) remain one of the strong points of *The Woman I Love*. However, rain soon had its wicked way on location, as did "bad roads and motor trouble." A typical day at Point Mugu would entail six sedans, three trucks, 120 lunches, and seven gallons of coffee.

How much of the coffee Colin drank, and needed, must have been estimable.

Location work at Point Mugu lasted until Thursday, February 4. The next day, the company was back in Hollywood, working on Stage 1A at RKO on the Barracks set.

Colin worked that night with Louis Hayward. On Monday, February 8, Colin put in a long day and night on Stage Four, from 1:30 p.m. to 11:00 p.m.

Thursday, February 11: Jimmie Fidler visited RKO and reported:

> *Miriam Hopkins and Colin Clive were enacting an intensely dramatic scene ... They rehearsed fully 20 times, then played the scene for 11 takes. Once, a fly on a camera lens spoiled a sequence. Then a mouse squeaked in the recording booth (most unusual, this was). Another scene was ruined when the recording scene required reloading. For each new take, the entire machinery was set in motion. At times like these, I wonder at the patience of directors and players and technicians.*

Fidler also noted that Litvak was "very much in love with Miriam Hopkins," who seemed in "a teary mood." He asked Hopkins if the dramatic scene "was getting to her." "It isn't that," she replied. "I have a cold in my head. Before the end of the day, we'll be making retakes because of my sneezes."

Meanwhile, a peculiar event happened. On December 23 and 24, 1936, 17 dancing girls had performed a Can-Can in a Paris nightclub scene that opened *The Woman I Love*. Now, Anatole Litvak recalled a bunch of these ladies, who'd dance on the set, presumably to perk up spirits. By Friday, February 12, *The Woman I Love* was 15 days behind schedule, and one imagines the lingering presence of the dancing girls was doing little to accelerate production. Rumor soon claimed the set of *The Woman I Love* was an RKO bordello.

By February 19, the film was *20* days behind schedule.

And so, it went. Miriam Hopkins had basically completed her role and gone her merry way, but *The Woman I Love* set was still coping with monster Muni, Mrs. Muni wildly shaking her head whenever her spouse failed to gobble up a scene, a frantic producer, and dancing girls performing the Can-Can ... and possibly other "dances."

Monday, February 22: Colin finally finished *The Woman I Love*, working 9:45 a.m. to 11:05 p.m. The film itself wrapped up 3:30 a.m. on Thursday, February 25. Muni and Hayward worked that last day; so did five of the indefatigable dancing girls.

The final cost: $724,974 ... more than $106,000 over budget. "It was a miracle that the picture was finished at all," said Albert Lewis. A rare pleasant moment during the shooting: Amelia Earhart visited the set.

For all the travails, Colin is superb as Captain Thelis—brave, gallant, popular with his men; a Stanhope without the drinking problem. Fatally wounded in an air battle, he pulls out of a spinning nosedive, lands his plane, and walks away from the wreckage, bleeding and finally collapsing.

It's here that *The Woman I Love* presents its most dramatic vignette: As the men fly off to avenge their leader's death, we see the corpse of Colin's captain, laid out in his uniform.

Ironically, it would be the last scene moviegoers ever saw Colin Clive play.

Thursday, March 4: Paul Muni won the 1936 Best Actor Academy Award for *The Story of Louis Pasteur*.

Friday, March 5: Reine Davies wrote in her "Hollywood Parade" column in the *Los Angeles Examiner* that Anatole Litvak had hosted a dinner party at Travaglini's "to honor the members of his company" of *The Woman I Love*. At this party (apparently given a night or two before the Oscars), the company presented Litvak with "a handsome desk set, a leather-bound volume of all the beautiful stills taken during the filming of the picture, and a caricature of the director in a scowling, worried mood, and inscribed with the words, 'The fog did this to me.'" The caption was apparently due to the fog at Point Mugu, as well as the fog machine Litvak used at the studio.

Davies reported that the party became raucous, complete, not surprisingly, with a can-you-top-this contest between Muni and Hopkins. Muni, a skilled violinist, played Schubert's *The Bee*. After he finished to applause, Hopkins, intimidated, ordered the band to play, and burst into a wild, thigh-flashing Charleston.

According to Davies' column, Colin was in attendance at Travaglini's. She didn't mention if *The Woman I Love* Can-Can girls were there as well. It's hard to imagine they weren't.

Friday, April 9: Colin joined Miriam Hopkins and Louis Hayward in a radio version of *The Woman I Love* on Louella Parsons' *Hollywood Hotel* show. In lines likely scripted, Hopkins spoke admirably of Colin's performance in the film.

"Of course, Clive's good," added Hayward—"but then you can always depend upon him to steal the show."

The Woman I Love opened at New York's Radio City Music Hall April 15, 1937, and at the Pantages and RKO-Hillstreet Theatres in Los Angeles on April 27. For all of Colin's woes on the set, *Variety* and *The Film Daily* both rated him "excellent," *The Hollywood Reporter* called him "especially fine," and even the Women's University Club chimed in, hailing Colin's performance as "perfection."

Yet his reviews were of little help to *The Woman I Love*. The film earned worldwide rentals of $783,000, losing $266,000 at the box office.

20th Century-Fox signed Colin for what was to have been his final film work, *Lancer Spy*. The star was George Sanders, in a dual role as a World War I officer and the British agent who doubles him. The espionage melodrama also starred Peter Lorre as a Teutonic villain; the leading lady was originally Germaine Aussey, a French stage and screen actress, who was replaced during the shoot by Dolores del Rio. Gregory Ratoff made his directorial debut with *Lancer Spy*, and filming began May 10.

Colin's role: Col. Fenwick, who engages the agent for the masquerade and who, over two decades later, tells the story on a plane in flashback to his daughter (Lynn Bari). It was a good, sympathetic part and would present him in age makeup for the film's opening and closing sequences. However, according to Fox legal files, Colin, by now very ill, lasted only "a couple days" before having to relinquish the role. The May 20th edition of *Variety* reported that Lionel Atwill had joined *Lancer Spy*, and he inherited Colin's part. Atwill had previously replaced him on *The Firebird*.

Colin's address now was 2520 Nottingham Avenue, up in the hills of the Los Feliz colony, east of the HOLLYWOODLAND sign, near the Griffith Observatory. A Spanish-style house, built in 1927, it still stands, with a pool behind it and a current estimated value of $3,023,248.

Adolphe Menjou and his actress wife Veree Teasdale lived a short way up the hill. Basil Rathbone resided below on Los Feliz Boulevard, his English Tudor house the site of many elegant parties. Cecil B. DeMille lived south of the Boulevard in Laughlin Park.

"One Man *Crazy* ...!"

Colin's final home, 2520 Nottingham Avenue, high in the Los Feliz colony of the Hollywood Hills. (Photo by author)

James Whale had rented several Los Feliz area homes, but in 1936, had moved west to Pacific Palisades, living with David Lewis at 788 Amalfi Drive.

2520 Nottingham Avenue provided Colin a spectacular night view of the lights of Hollywood. It was also a hideaway, where he reclusively faced what he must have realized were the closing days and nights of his life. *The Los Angeles City Directory* of the time lists Colin residing there with his spouse, "Iris." Of course, he and Iris Lancaster weren't married—Colin was still legally wed to Jeanne de Casalis—but they were "living in sin," as the saying went, although Iris also kept an address on the Sunset Strip.

By this date, "sin" was only part of what bonded the couple. Iris, at age 22, was trying to take care of a dying man. He wouldn't accept her help, or anyone's. Colin was wearing the "tragic mask" David Manners had seen him hide behind over seven years ago on *Journey's End.* He was, as Manners had remembered, jeering at his own softness. It was all too late now for help.

They must have been terrifying days and nights for him ... and for Iris Lancaster.

Chapter Twenty-Eight
The Final Act

Saturday morning, May 1, 1937: A despondent 22-year-old named Myrtle Ward threw her three-year-old daughter Jeanette Louise off the aforementioned 170 foot-high Colorado Bridge in Pasadena, then jumped herself. Witnesses hurrying to the scene found a miraculous sight: Little Jeanette was alive and unhurt, crawling toward her dying mother, crying "Mommy, Mommy." The branches of a tree had broken the child's fall and she had no broken bones. Myrtle Ward died two hours later in Pasadena Hospital.

"God sent his angels and saved me," Jeanette said years later.

Sadly, there weren't enough angels in Los Angeles in 1937 to save all who needed them.

1937 had been one of Hollywood's most tragic years. In January, 1937 alone, there'd been three celebrity deaths. Warners star Ross Alexander, who'd won the role of Jeremy Pitt in *Captain Blood* over Colin Clive's competition, shot himself on his ranch the night of January 2, 13 months after his wife had fatally shot herself. Alexander was 29. Richard Boleslawski, who had directed *Clive of India*, died of a heart attack January 17. Boleslawski was 47. And on January 21, authorities found the corpse of former star Marie Prevost, alone in her apartment, dead from alcohol poisoning. Prevost was 37.

The year had proceeded with more movie colony tragedies. One of the most macabre was that of Arthur Edmund Carewe, featured in the horror films *The Phantom of the Opera* (as "The Persian"), *Doctor X*, and *Mystery of the Wax Museum*. On April 20, Carewe, age 52, had checked into Bowman's Auto Court at 2520 Santa Monica Boulevard and fired a .45 caliber bullet into his head. He left a note with $31.00 in cash to cover "payment for damages to the cabin."

The 1937 tragedies seemed to hit an apex Monday morning, June 7, when Jean Harlow died at Good Samaritan Hospital from kidney failure. She was only 26-years-old. For the viewing, the corpse wore a blonde wig; doctors had shaved Harlow's head prior to an operation to relieve the pressure on her brain due to retained waste fluid, but she became too weak to endure the operation. She wore a pink silk negligee from her unfinished film *Saratoga;* MGM would complete the film with two doubles, one for her body and one for her voice. After Harlow's 9:00 a.m., 20-minute funeral on June 9, fans overran the grounds of Forest Lawn's Wee Kirk of the Heather, where the rites had taken place, and made off with many of the flowers.

There was another funeral that day at Forest Lawn. 1:00 p.m. saw services in the cemetery's Little Church of the Flowers for Monroe Owsley, who often played "the other man" in movies. The obsequies followed Harlow's epic funeral like a "B" film on a double feature.

Owsley was 36. Cause of death: A heart attack, due to alcoholism.

There'd been other troubles in Hollywood in 1937, and one might have fancied they were targeting movers-and-shakers of the horror genre. Universal dropped Boris Karloff on April 16, after he'd been on contract to the studio, in one form or another, for almost six years. Fortunately, he now also had a contract with Warner Bros., where he'd starred in *The Walking Dead* (1936), one of his finest performances.

James Whale, meanwhile, had been in a bitter battle with "the New Universal," directing *The Road Back*, the long-awaited sequel to *All Quiet on the Western Front* (which had been directed by Lewis Milestone). The studio, under the new leadership of Charles Rogers, bowed to Nazi pressure and eviscerated the film. Whale demanded Universal release him from his contract, but they refused. He did sign for an outside film with Warners, *The Great Garrick*, a comedy based on the famed 18th-century British actor, which began shooting June 14.

Junior Laemmle, ousted at Universal, had joined MGM, but was caught in a web of studio politics. He'd soon resign and never produce another picture. Bela Lugosi was playing the third lead in the West Coast production of *Tovarich*; his film career was at a standstill, and when Republic offered him the villain role in the serial *SOS Coast Guard* in June, he was glad to get it ... especially since he and Lillian were now expecting a baby.

Also, England had slapped horror films with the "H" certificate.

For some of Colin's *Journey's End* London stage colleagues, life was happy and prosperous. George Zucco, "Osborne," had moved west after his Broadway run in *Victoria Regina*, settling in Pacific Palisades with his wife Stella and daughter Frances. He was busy as a character player at MGM; in fact, he'd played Jean Harlow's doctor in *Saratoga*.

"People teased him about it—you can imagine!" laughed Stella Zucco. "They said that George had killed her!"

Melville Cooper, "Trotter" in *Journey's End*, was also living in the movie colony, and active at Warner Bros., where he was playing in *The Great Garrick* for James Whale. Zucco and Cooper saw each other socially but were wary of a reunion with Colin Clive.

"We'd heard he'd gone completely wild," said Stella Zucco.

As if life hadn't turned dark enough for Colin, he was now facing another trauma. His horse fall at Sandhurst had caught up with him, horrifically, as Mae Clarke remembered:

> *James Whale told me that Colin Clive had suffered a leg injury in his cavalry training. After many years of agony as he "trod the boards" of England and New York, the old leg wound worsened ... There was a chance they would amputate—and it broke his spirit.*

For a man as hypersensitive as Colin, and for one so fond of sports, this was his latest real-life nightmare.

He had to keep working, although he was dying. Colin landed a radio job—signing for the June 21, 1937 broadcast of "Monsieur Beaucaire" on Cecil B. DeMille's *Lux Radio Theatre*. The stars were Leslie Howard and Elissa Landi, and Colin was to play the villain, Lord Winterset. Stella Francis Zucco had a small role on the show.

For Colin, Fate intervened.

Friday, June 18: "Colin Clive Ill," headlined the *Seattle Times*, writing he "was seriously ill of a chest ailment."

Saturday, June 19: "Colin Clive Near Death," reported *The Canton Repository*, noting he was at Hollywood's Cedars of Lebanon Hospital and "suffering from a pulmonary ailment that failed to respond to treatment."

Monday, June 21: Denis Green played Lord Winterset on *Lux*'s "Monsieur Beaucaire." The show had an additional tragedy associated with it, although nobody foresaw it: DeMille promised listeners that Amelia Earhart, then on her around-the-world airplane flight, would be a guest on his June 28 show, or, if delayed, the July 5 broadcast. Of course, Earhart never returned.

Cedars of Lebanon Hospital, Los Angeles.

Tuesday, June 22: "Film Actor Slightly Better," headlined the *Riverside Daily Press*, writing that Colin had "passed a comparatively restful night."

Thursday, June 24: "Colin Clive, Screen Actor, Believed near Death in Hollywood," headlined the *Riverside Daily Press*, reporting that "he took another turn for the worse last night" and now had developed intestinal trouble. Dr. Frederick Bergstrom described Colin as "much weaker," and the article concluded that, "grave fears were felt for the actor."

Iris Lancaster kept a deathwatch.

On the night of June 24, a full moon had risen over the glowing HOLLYWOOD-LAND sign. Word always spread quickly through the film colony whenever an actor was ill, especially if he or she were young.

At Travaglini's, Edwin Martin, Colin's friend and a reporter for the *Hollywood Citizen News*, was seated at what had been Colin's favorite table. Martin, as he wrote, "had known [Colin] for many years—liked him and admired him since they first brought him from England to star in the picture version of the same play he had made famous on the stage." He'd also handled the publicity for Colin's stage revival of *Journey's End* in Hollywood in 1934.

Colin had planned a radio interview with Martin, and come his hospitalization, had sent a note: "Must have this old pump repaired a bit. Sorry we'll have to postpone our interview until I come out. Keep the corner warm at Travaglini's."

Martin sat in the corner round-table. He was talking with Mr. Travaglini, reminiscing about the latter's days as a young officer in the Italian army. Tony Travaglini, Jr. reviewed a radio script planned for Harry Langdon. Other men were gathered at the table as well. As Martin wrote, Iris Lancaster arrived:

"One Man *Crazy* ...!"

Into this crowd of men came a saddened figure—a lovely woman who had been a friend of Colin. She was the last member of that gay trio who often occupied this same table together ... from which another splendid young British actor, John Buckler, had left one night only to meet his journey's end in Malibou Lake in a tragic auto accident.

She was the last one left—and she dragged her weary self up to the bar and ordered a double brandy.

Everyone wanted to ask about his condition, but Larry Kent was the only one who had the courage ... "How is he?" he asked.

"He is going," the woman said. "When I left he was already in an oxygen tent. They wouldn't let me see him."

Meanwhile, at Cedars of Lebanon Hospital, Colin Clive, alone but for hospital staff, spent his final night.

The death of a movie star. A bloody, awful, alcoholic movie star.

Probably best they'd sent Iris away ... wouldn't let her see him now. He must look a horror.

Yes, it was all better this way. If they took his leg, maybe he'd have played Captain Ahab in Moby Dick. *Jimmy could have directed it as a horror movie ...*

Heaven? What will it be? Maybe those Stonyhurst favorites, Saint Barbara and Saint Agnes, waiting for him without their heads? Now, now ... no time to be irreverent.

One more show to play—these Yanks enjoy gawking at the dead. They'd paint him up and lay him out, and everyone could have a weepy last look. He'd talked with poor Iris about the funeral service. He'd requested what music to play, including Danny Boy. *Pretty. Always good for a nice cry.*

No, he'd never been a Bengal Lancer. Never had even played one in the movies. Too busy making monsters.

He'd always wanted to die in his movies. They'd provided him 11th-hour escapes in Frankenstein *and* Bride of Frankenstein, *but there'd be no life-saving retakes now.*

Yes, almost over. What did Stanhope say ... "Think of all the topping fellows who've gone already. It can't be very lonely there, with all those fellows. Sometimes I feel it's lonelier here."

No more clanging, no more cacophony. Just a solitary bell. The night's ending. Light's coming. What film was he in where somebody reached up to the light? Oh, yes ... that one ...

Friday, June 25, 1937: It was a fair day in Los Angeles, with some morning cloudiness. At 10:05 a.m. Colin Clive died. He was 37 years old.

Some papers reported that he'd died alone. Others noted Iris Lancaster was with him at the end, and at least one claimed Iris' sister Valerie was there too. The widely reported cause of death: "Intestinal and pulmonary ailments." The death certificate listed the cause(s) of death as Pulmonary Tuberculosis, with a date of onset of June 1936; Tuberculosis Pneumonia, dated to June 11, 1937; and Tuberculosis of the Intestines, with an onset date of "?"

Iris Lancaster was informant for the death certificate. The data she did provide, and didn't, was a bit startling. She gave his name as "Colin Clive," with no "aka" of his birth

Clive Reaches Journey's End

COLIN CLIVE
Shown in scene from "The Life of a Lancer Spy," his last picture, from which illness compelled him to withdraw.

Noted British Actor Succumbs Following Year's Illness

Colin Clive reached Journey's End yesterday.

The well-known English actor who made famous the role of hard-drinking Captain Stanhope in the stage play and picture production of "Journey's End" died at 9:40 a. m. at the Cedars of Lebanon Hospital following illness of more than a year.

Death was caused by pulmonary and intestinal tuberculosis. He was only 37 years old.

LINE RECALLED

"won India for England." One of his picture roles in Hollywood was a featured part in the production of "Clive of India."

BORN IN FRANCE

Born January 20, 1900, in St. Malo, France, Mr. Clive was the son of Capt. Colin Clive Craig, of the British army. He received his early education at Stoneyhurst College. Later he attended the Royal Military College at Sandhurst.

He received his early training

This Los Angeles newspaper obituary for Colin Clive used this very rare picture of Colin in *Lancer Spy*, on which he'd worked very briefly at 20th Century-Fox. Lionel Atwill had replaced him due to Colin's illness.

name, Colin Glennie Greig. She knew St. Malo had been his birthplace, but for "Name" and "Birthplace" of his father and mother, Iris gave one word: "Unknown." Either she

"One Man Crazy …!"

couldn't remember such details in her grief or, more likely, Colin had never discussed his father or mother with her, even near the end of his life.

For the "Married, Widowed or Divorced Name of Husband or Wife" information, Iris did give the name, "Jeanne de Clive." Although Iris had been living with Colin, she gave her own address as 9006 Sunset Boulevard.

Iris also announced plans to arrange the funeral.

The night of June 25, 1937 was the sold-out world premiere of 20th Century-Fox's *Wee Willie Winkie*, starring Shirley Temple and directed by John Ford. 15,000 fans cheered the celebrity arrivals at the Carthay Circle Theatre, and the Mutual Network broadcast the ceremony,

As Colin Clive's body lie that night in a mortuary, searchlights swept the Hollywood sky.

Chapter Twenty-Nine
"Mortuary Row"

The irreverent Los Angeles sobriquet "Mortuary Row" referred to a number of stately funeral parlors, some of them on Washington Boulevard, all in basic proximity to each other.

The Edwards Brothers Colonial Mansion Mortuary was located at 1000 Venice Boulevard, parallel to Washington Boulevard, and as such merited membership in "Mortuary Row." Established in 1930, it was a large, white, two-story (as the name said) Colonial mansion, complete with towering front pillars. As Colin had been so ill, he required master morticians to prepare him for his final viewing. Iris Lancaster entrusted her lover to the skills of Edwards Brothers.

Hollywood mortuaries at the time vied with each other as to how best present the deceased. In Jean Harlow's case, two-and-a-half weeks earlier, the Pierce Brothers Mortuary on Washington Boulevard had placed her negligee-clad corpse on a chaise lounge for the viewing. Harlow had languished on such a lounge, and in the same negligee, when George Zucco, as her doctor, had examined her in *Saratoga.*

As for Colin, the Edwards Brothers undertakers garbed his body in a dressing gown and placed him in a large bed, as if he were asleep.

Meanwhile, Colin had listed his "Next of Kin" as Leslie L. Landau, of Rodeo Drive, Beverly Hills.

Who was Leslie Landau? He was a 32-year-old Britisher who had just produced 20th Century-Fox's *The Lady Escapes,* directed by Eugene Forde and starring Gloria Stuart, Michael Whalen, and George Sanders. It was Landau's first film as a producer for Fox and apparently his last. Was Landau a relative of Colin's? Or was he an intimate friend—perhaps even more intimate than Iris Lancaster, considering that Colin had named him, not her, his "Next of Kin"?

Jeanne de Casalis, in London, promptly sent an inquiry as to funeral plans. Norman Tucker Shaw, Colin's manager, responded that it was "certain" the funeral would proceed in Hollywood. Iris had apparently made this "certain" and, with Leslie Landau's blessing, had taken control of the funeral arrangements. She also arranged for cremation, claiming it was Colin's wish.

However ... Reese Edwards, of Edwards Brothers, and Norman Shaw quickly found themselves in the indelicate position of informing Leslie Landau that, if "Mr. Clive had expressed the wish to be cremated," permission had to come from Jeanne. Landau cabled Jeanne, who responded by telegram June 26:

> *Thank You Dear Leslie Proceed According to Colin's Wishes Your Cable Very Comforting Love Jeanne*

For years, some Clive fans have severely criticized Jeanne de Casalis for staying in London and not traveling to Los Angeles for the funeral. In actuality, she must have realized that Colin's lover had taken charge and that Jeanne's presence might have sparked nasty funeral theatrics.

A postcard of the Edwards Brothers Colonial Mansion, the funeral parlor where Colin Clive's viewing and funeral took place.

Considering how Jeanne had reacted to Tallulah Bankhead eight years before in London, her absence was a discreet choice. It would have been indecently scandalous to have two ladies in black, having a catfight next to Colin Clive's funeral bed. And although Jeanne was more than 20 years older than Iris, she likely still could be, if provoked, a force of nature.

Edwards Brothers opened its doors to the public to pay tribute to Colin Clive. One fan who did was 20-year-old Forrest J Ackerman, who'd seen Colin alive in 1935 after the *Bride of Frankenstein* preview at Universal City. Now Ackerman visited the funeral parlor:

> *Do you remember in the beginning of* Bride of Frankenstein, *when Clive's recuperating and he's sitting up in bed with a nice dressing gown on? Well, in those days, it was possible to walk into the funeral parlor and into the room where he was just lying in bed. He looked very much like that scene in* Bride. *As I recall, he had a dressing gown on and was calmly lying there. I just stood by his side and thought my thoughts about him—I liked him immensely.*

I asked Ackerman if there were many other mourners at the time he viewed the body. "Just me, as I recall," he said.

For three days and nights, Colin's body rested in the funeral bed at Edwards Brothers. *Tuesday, June 29, 2:00 p.m.:* The funeral for Colin Clive took place at the chapel at Edwards Brothers Colonial Mansion. It was a fair day in Los Angeles, although the afternoon became overcast at times. Hollywood funerals were always picturesque—women in black dresses with bonnets and veils, men in somber suits, and cascades of flowers. The press would report that 250 to 300 mourners attended the Colin Clive funeral.

Iris Lancaster, of course, was there. So was Billie Burke, who'd played Colin's wife in *Christopher Strong*. There were floral tributes from Charlie Chaplin, Virginia Bruce Gilbert (Colin's leading lady in *Jane Eyre*, and the widow of John Gilbert, who'd died in 1936), Brian Aherne, Slim Summerville, Leo Morrison (Colin's agent) ... and James Whale who was not in attendance.

It might seem odd that Whale, so dynamic a presence in Colin's life and career, wasn't present at the funeral. For all his cinema forays into horror, Whale was uneasy at funerals; he avoided them, refusing to make an exception, even for Colin. On June 29, according to Warner Bros. records, Whale put in an 8:30 a.m. to 6:30 p.m. day on *The Great Garrick* at Warners. Stars Brian Aherne and Olivia de Havilland were off that day, and Whale directed such featured players as Edward Everett Horton, Melville Cooper, and Albert Dekker,

A photograph of the old Edwards Brothers building, almost 70 years after Colin's funeral, taken at night in 2006. In recent years the building served as a PTA center and a dental clinic. (Photo by author)

starlets Lana Turner, Linda Perry, and Marie Wilson, and 16 extras.

Whale should have told Warner Bros. to go to hell and, despite being outside his comfort zone, attended the funeral.

As for Jeanne de Casalis, still in London ... she sent a spray of red roses.

The pallbearers were Peter Lorre (who'd tried to drive Colin crazy in *Mad Love*), Alan Mowbray (who'd appeared with Colin in *One More River*), Norman Shaw (Colin's business manager), Robert George, H. Hadley, and Jack Dunn. The Rev. Philip A. Easley of St. Stephen's Episcopal Church officiated. The musical selections were Colin's personal favorites: Rachmaninoff's *Concerto No. 2, Second Movement*; Tchaikovsky's *None But the Lonely Heart*; and *Londonderry Air*, aka *Danny Boy*.

After the funeral, a hearse drove the body the short distance to Rosedale Cemetery for cremation.

On the day of the funeral, Iris Lancaster signed an "Authorization and Receipt for Delivery of Cremated Remains" form, noting that she was "the legal custodian of the cremated remains of said Deceased." She directed Rosedale Crematory to deliver "the said remains to Edwards Brothers."

AUTHORIZATION AND RECEIPT FOR DELIVERY OF CREMATED REMAINS

Date June 29, 1937

To Rosedale Crematory CALIFORNIA

THIS IS TO CERTIFY THAT Miss Iris Lancaster, a m
(I or We)
the in charge funeral arrangements of Mr. Colin Clive,
(relationship to deceased)

Deceased, and I a m the legal custodian of the cremated remains of said Deceased, and I do hereby re-
(I or We) (I or We)
quest you to deliver the said remains to Edwards Brothers, for the purpose of interment in

(Place of Interment) and I hereby promise and agree to hold Rosedale Crematory harmless,
(I or we)
and to indemnify it or its assigns from any and all claims, demands or damages which may be made or declared
against said company or its assigns, by reason of delivery of said remains as above requested, and further declare

that a the surviving, of the above named
(I or We) (Husband, Wife, Brother, Daughter, Son, Cousin)
Deceased.

June 25, 1937 9006 Sunset Blvd. Los Angeles
Date of Death Address

hereby acknowledge receipt of said cremated
(I or We)
remains for the purpose set forth above.

Receipt for Cremated Remains

Office of Cemetery
1831 W. Washington Street

Los Angeles, California, July 8 - 37

Received of the Rosedale Cemetery Association, Ltd., the cremated
remains of Colin Clive
cremated June 29 - 37

Signed Edwards Bros. By N. N. Page
Address 1000 Venice Blvd.

The Rosedale Cemetery Association, Ltd.
Los Angeles, California

Forms related to Colin's cremation. Note that the place of interment is blank.

As for "Place of Interment," she left it blank.

Also on June 29, Rosedale Cemetery completed a "Cremations" form, noting Edwards Brothers as the undertaker, Leslie L. Landau as Next of Kin and, beside "Disposition of Ashes," the code, "TN 884." It also noted the "consideration" as $50.00.

The *San Francisco Chronicle* reported that same day that "Interment was to be arranged later."

Wednesday, June 30: The *Hollywood Citizen News* reported that "Mr. Clive's ashes will be sent to England for interment."

One suspects that Jeanne de Casalis and Iris Lancaster, over 5,000 miles apart from each other, gave a considerable amount of regretful thought to Colin, and each other,

Frankenstein, 1938 re-release poster. Boris Karloff now has the star-billing.

during the ensuing sad days and nights. They had known him more intimately than anyone. Each lady likely felt a nagging guilt that she hadn't succeeded in reversing Colin's path to an early, tragic death.

Thursday, July 8: The last surviving recorded evidence of the ashes of Colin Clive found by this author appeared on a Rosedale Cemetery "Receipt for Cremated Remains" form, signed by an Edwards Brothers Colonial Mansion representative. The ashes came this day, nine days after the funeral and cremation, to Edwards Brothers.

Were the ashes ever sent to England? More on this sad mystery later.

And so, it was over.

Colin Clive's acting career had lasted a little less than 18 years. Fewer than nine of those years had seen him as a celebrity. His early death naturally still inspires accusations and blame, even 81 years after the fact.

"He should never have gone to *Hollywood*," a Clive fan said recently, as if saying Colin should never have danced naked with a snake in a Weimar Berlin cabaret. Hollywood produced *Journey's End, Frankenstein, History Is Made at Night* and at least a half-dozen other films that provided Colin excellent showcases. The film colony also afforded him steady work, beautiful homes, a red-haired, long-legged lover, James Whale's watchful eye (professionally, if not always personally), and plenty of sports and games. It inflicted scars, of course, in its typecasting and by its garish rumor mill, but Hollywood scarred most people who worked there in the 1930s. It was the nature of the beast. Colin Clive, sad but true, was already a ticking time bomb when he first arrived there.

"One Man *Crazy* ...!"

Son of Frankenstein: **Lionel Atwill and Basil Rathbone regard the portrait of Colin Clive's tormented Henry Frankenstein.**

England, conversely—where, presumably, this fan prefers he'd stayed—left him at the mercy of a London theater establishment that never offered him a worthy follow-up to *Journey's End*, and a British film industry that never provided him anything worthy at all. Had he stayed in London, he'd have had his country garden, but he'd also have dealt with an estranged family, an estranged wife, reminders of Evelyn Taylor, a lousy climate, and a history of very bad luck with horses.

Iris Lancaster in an early glamour pose.

Years ago, a Clive fan phoned me, angry that neither James Whale nor Boris Karloff ever apparently did anything to help Colin during his downfall. The British, for all their prowess in the arts, can be a stoical lot; if a man doesn't have what Karloff called "the fire in the belly" to be an actor, well, then the feeling is that he bloody well shouldn't be an actor. Also, such a charge against Colin's acquaintances misses the heartbreaking nature of addicts and alcoholics, who too often insist on handling their problems their own way, even as the world catastrophically crashes down around them.

And Iris Lancaster? Why didn't *she* save him? Why, in fact, did she, based on all evidence, *enable* him to die this way? To be fair, Iris was a 22-year-old in awe of a world-famous man almost old enough to be her father. Could she have been expected to rescue him from an eight-years-in-the-making self-destruction?

The truth is difficult to accept, and in cases such as this one, terribly sad. More agonizingly than anything else, it was the private pet devils, taking deadly aim at their victim's hypersensitivity, which had taken the life of Colin Glennie Clive Greig.

1937, as noted, was a very tragic year in the Hollywood film colony. Al Boasberg, comedy writer, had died June 18, age 44, from a heart attack. Musical maestro George Gershwin died on July 11, age 38, from a brain tumor. The September 1936 loss of 37-year-old Irving Thalberg, MGM's certifiable genius, was still deeply felt as well. On July 15, 1937, *Radio Daily* offered a florid but touchingly sincere tribute to talents the movies had recently lost:

> *Yesterday at lunch someone said a few words which impelled silence in the noisy room ... They were: "The Almighty will cast His biggest show with Jean Harlow as leading lady and Colin Clive as leading man ... Al Boasberg will write the script and George Gershwin the music, with the entire production under the personal supervision of Irving Thalberg."*

For those who'd known Colin intimately, life went on.

September 2, 1937: *The Hollywood Reporter* wrote that MGM was testing Iris Lancaster this day for a contract. Her publicity claimed she'd left pictures four years ago to study "Voice" in New York and had been playing in "legit" theater. It sounded better than she'd been Joan Crawford's stand-in and the mistress of a now-dead movie star. She didn't get the contract.

September 9: Edwin Martin, who'd often joined Colin at Travaglini's, wrote in the *Hollywood Citizen News*: "And in the ranks, we find: Iris Lancaster, exotic actress, who used to be the late Colin Clive's companion, going places with her perky Scotty."

Two days later, Jeanne de Casalis was in the news, having attended a literary luncheon in London, where she and other actresses talked about an "Ideal Man." Jeanne's opinion:

> *The really nice women like a man who is either a little bit of a bounder or a weak, pathetic little creature. A woman likes someone she can either reform or someone she can stand behind and hold up.*

One could certainly slice and dice Jeanne's choice of words. Her expression, "stand behind and hold up" was particularly unfortunate, considering the crew had to hold up Colin on *The Woman I Love*.

1937 remained grimly eventful in Hollywood, with the September death of serial queen Ruth Roland and the December demise of comic Ted Healy, former head of The Three Stooges and Colin's co-star in *Mad Love*. Healy's death, following a brutal beating (and just days after the birth of his son), caused a frenzy of gossip, garishly ringing down the curtain on an unusually tragic year.

In 1938, Iris Lancaster, now billing herself as "Russette," landed a gig at the Seven Seas Restaurant in Los Angeles, singing in seven different languages. On May 26, columnist Harrison Carroll wrote, "Dennis O'Keefe, recently separated from his wife, is calling at the Seven Seas these evenings to take Iris Lancaster home."

Also in 1938, Jeanne de Casalis married Cowan Douglas Stephenson. They'd remain wed for the rest of her life.

Meanwhile, a show business miracle happened: *Dracula* and *Frankenstein*, after a smash hit August 1938 booking at the Regina Theatre in Los Angeles, began a late summer double-bill nationally. The censors had attacked both films—among the cuts from *Frankenstein* were Colin's "In the name of God! Now I know what it feels like to BE God!" and the shots of Marilyn Harris' Little Maria thrown into the lake. The new posters for *Frankenstein* gave first-billing to Karloff. The double-bill broke records across the country.

Friday, January 13, 1939: A new Monster saga opened in Hollywood: Universal's *Son of Frankenstein*. The stars were Basil Rathbone as Dr. Wolf von Frankenstein (son of the "Maker of Monsters"), Boris Karloff as the Monster (his third and final appearance in the role), Bela Lugosi as broken-necked old Ygor, and Lionel Atwill as Inspector Krogh—whose right arm had been "torn out by the roots" in a childhood encounter with the Monster. Rowland V. Lee produced and directed.

Early in *Son of Frankenstein*, Rathbone's "Wolf" stands in the library of Castle Frankenstein on a stormy night. Above the blazing fireplace is a magnificent full-length portrait of Colin Clive as Henry Frankenstein, illuminated by the fire and the flashes of lightning. The thunder roars, just as it had that magical night when Colin's Frankenstein triumphantly cried, "It's alive!" over the quivering hand of Karloff's Monster. And as the storm wickedly rages, Rathbone's "Wolf" reads his father's will—words that conjure up the tragedy of Colin Clive:

> *My son ...*
> *Even though the path is cruel, and tortuous, carry on ... You have inherited the fortune of the Frankensteins. I trust you will not inherit their fate.*

The Life and Death of Colin Clive Hollywood's Dr. Frankenstein   **297**

Chapter Thirty
Legacy

Frankenstein's Monster, of course, stomped about Universal City during the World War II years, a perennial moneymaker for the studio, along with Deanna Durbin and Abbott and Costello. Boris Karloff was on Broadway, making a fortune as the star (and one of the owners) of Broadway's super hit, *Arsenic and Old Lace*, while others took over as the Monster.

In 1942, Universal released *The Ghost of Frankenstein*. Lon Chaney, Jr. fresh from *The Wolf Man*, was a mute, stolid Monster, and top-billing went to Sir Cedric Hardwicke, Colin's colleague from London's *Show Boat*, as Dr. Ludwig von Frankenstein, "the second son" of Henry Frankenstein. The plot revolved around Ludwig's intention to restore (disastrously) the family's good name. Erle C. Kenton directed, and the film featured Lionel Atwill as a very mad doctor, Bela Lugosi as Ygor, and a nostalgic bonus: As Ludwig's daughter Elsa (Evelyn Ankers) read her grandfather's diary of how he created the Monster, *The Ghost of Frankenstein* featured flashbacks of Colin Clive and Dwight Frye from *Frankenstein*, and Colin from *Bride of Frankenstein*.

Universal's Frankenstein series went on, nose-diving into *kitsch* and abounding with twists and ironies. *Frankenstein Meets the Wolf Man* (1943), atmospherically directed by Roy William Neill, starred Chaney as the Wolf Man and a desperate Bela Lugosi as a blind and speaking Monster. Post-production editing cut the Monster's blindness and dialogue, making Lugosi's performance an epic misfire. It seemed to be the Monster's revenge on Lugosi for having denounced the role so bitterly in 1931.

Come *House of Frankenstein*, Universal's 1944 Christmas release, Karloff, back in the fold, starred as a Mad Doctor, referred to as a "would-be Frankenstein." He's wildly insane, with none of the Prometheus heroics of Colin Clive's Henry Frankenstein or any apparent curiosity about "what lies beyond the clouds and the stars." As in the 1931 film, the Mad Doctor's assistant is a hunchback (J. Carrol Naish), but the motivation is bloodthirsty vengeance, as crazy Karloff revives and unleashes the Wolf Man (Chaney), Dracula (John Carradine), and the Monster (cowboy heavy Glenn Strange). Portraying the traveling chamber of horrors proprietor whom Karloff and Naish murder: *Journey's End*'s George Zucco, now a horror star. Erle C. Kenton directed.

Karloff's agonizing back trouble on *House of Frankenstein* was at least partially due to the awful night on *Frankenstein* during which James Whale had made him carry Clive over his shoulder and up a back lot hill all night long. Nevertheless, "Dear Boris," always game, willingly sank with Strange's Monster into a pit of "quicksand" on Universal's cold back lot at 3:00 on the morning of April 25, 1944. It was Karloff's farewell to the series.

House of Dracula, Universal's 1945 Christmas release and also directed by Kenton, scripted the "Mad Doctor" as a humanitarian who wants to help Chaney's Wolf Man, Carradine's Count, and Strange's Monster, but due to the treacherous Dracula, becomes himself a foul thing of the night. The showy role was designed for Karloff who, unhappy with what had happened to his "dear old Monster," refused it. His replacement: Onslow Stevens, who'd claimed Colin Clive's role in *Peg O' My Heart* in 1933. This time, the hunchback was starlet Jane Adams, who played her role with a false hump, as well as false eyelashes.

"One Man Crazy ...!"

Iris Lancaster, now billing herself as Iris Clive, holding a black cat in Universal's *The Cat Creeps* (1946). Also left to right: Noah Beery, Jr., Douglass Dumbrille, and Paul Kelly. (Courtesy of John Antosiewicz)

Curiously, shortly after World War II ended, a ghost from Colin's past came slinking to Universal City—Iris Lancaster. In the studio's final "horror" film of the era, *The Cat Creeps* (1946), starring Noah Beery, Jr. and Lois Collier and featuring Rose Hobart (Colin's leading lady in Broadway's *Eight Bells*), Iris had a juicy featured role as "Kyra Goran," an alluring, cat-cradling mystic in an old dark house. The film shot January 3 to January 17, 1946, was budgeted at $144,060, and Iris' contract called for $250 per week and a week-and-a-half of work—total, $375. Iris was still no great shakes as an actress, but it didn't matter—"Kyra" turns out to be a Follies showgirl, posing as a mystic to help catch the killer.

The Cat Creeps was a far cry from *Frankenstein*, but it placed Iris on the same hallowed ground where Colin had cried, "It's Alive!"

Also, significantly, she signed her contract and billed herself as "Iris Clive."

In 1948, Universal (then Universal-International) produced *Abbott and Costello Meet Frankenstein*. Bela Lugosi was Dracula, Lon Chaney, Jr. the Wolf Man, and Glenn Strange the Monster. Director Charles T. Barton treated the trio with respect, and the film dropped the curtain on the studio's Frankenstein saga. Although *Abbott and Costello Meet Frankenstein* was a terrific hit, Karloff refused to see it. One wonders what Colin Clive's reaction would have been.

Thursday, March 16, 1950: Lt. Col. Colin Philip Greig, Colin Clive's father, died at St. Mary St. Abbot's Hospital in London. He was 79 years old and had been living at 25 Holland Park Avenue, London with his daughters, 48-year-old Cicely Margaret Lugard Greig and 46-year old Noel Audrey Greig. In 1939, London's Burns, Oates & Washborne, Ltd. ("Publishers to the Holy See") had published *My Sisters Pass By*, by Marie Rene-Bazin, "Translated from the French by Lt. Col. C. P. Greig." The book included a photograph of Mother St. Francis of Borgia on her deathbed.

Lt. Col. Greig's probate date was June 13, 1950 and he left his "spinster" daughters his estate— £889, 18s. 2d. Likely due to the threat of inherited lunacy, as evidenced by their Uncle Piercy, neither daughter ever married. It would be the end of the Greig line.

Summer, 1952: Iris Lancaster got her picture in the newspapers again as she fought for a divorce and settlement. She'd married Adolph John Dietel, a 44-year-old lumberman, in Santa Barbara on July 24, 1950, and they'd parted July 12, 1952. Iris, now 37 (and claiming to be 33), charged Dietel with cruelty, accusing him of "threatening to take her life" and asking he be "restrained from annoying and molesting her." She claimed Dietel owned community property exceeding $500,000 and had an annual income of $75,000, and she demanded $1,000 per month alimony, pending trial of her suit for separate maintenance. She also wanted the house.

Dietel volleyed that his worth wasn't "much more than $50,000" and that his income was only $991 per month. He also argued that, since Iris was continuing to live in the family home, 5320 Hermitage Avenue in North Hollywood, she could get along nicely on $197 per month. Superior Judge William P. Haughton, reviewing the evidence of Dietel's worth, cut Iris' alimony to $250 a month.

By now, Iris was referring to herself alternately as Iris Lancaster and Iris Clive.

Although she was no household name by either billing, Iris and her divorce got attention as far away as Bradford, Pennsylvania, where *The Bradford Era*, reporting the proceedings on August 28, 1952, ran a picture of Iris. Its caption: "Sounds Difficult."

Wednesday, May 29, 1957: James Whale, 67-years-old, drowned in the pool behind his home, 788 S. Amalfi Drive, Pacific Palisades. Whale, following a stroke, had feared the same horror that had haunted Colin Clive—insanity. He left a touching suicide note, addressed "To ALL I LOVE," reading, in part:

> *Do not grieve for me. My nerves are all shot and for the last year I have been in agony day and night—except when I sleep with sleeping pills … I have had a wonderful life but it is over and my nerves get worse and I am afraid they will have to take me away …*

It read like a note that might have been written in the trenches by Colin Clive's Captain Stanhope.

Whale had spent time early in 1957 at Las Encinas Sanitarium, in Pasadena. His final companion had been Pierre Foegel, whom Whale had met abroad, and to whom Whale left his home. His final estate was valued at $556,764.21 and he provided generous bequests to former lover David Lewis, and such actress friends as Una O'Connor and Doris Lloyd. Gates, Kingsley and Gates cremated the body and his ashes are interred in niche 20076, the Columbarium of Memory at Forest Lawn Memorial Park, Glendale.

Had Whale lived only several more months, he'd have witnessed a remarkable, if unholy, resurrection.

Tuesday, October 1, 1957: Los Angeles, California.

It was a frightening time in U.S. history. On this first day of October, B-52 bombers began a full-time flying schedule in the face of U.S.S.R. aggression. Appropriately, on this same date, the words "In God We Trust" first appeared on United States paper currency. Sputnik would launch in three days.

On this night of October 1, KTLA in Hollywood presented the L.A. TV premiere of 1931's *Frankenstein*.

9:30 p.m. *Nightmare Theatre*, as KTLA titled the package of old Universal melodramas, began. The hostess was "The Old Lady," played by 68-year-old character actress Ottola Nesmith as a crazy crone, living in squalor. She showed *Frankenstein*, imagining all the while she was the film's leading lady, Mae Clarke. At one point, she "prances about" in a wedding veil, remembering when Karloff's Monster crept up behind Clarke's Elizabeth in her bridal boudoir:

> *"Oh, we had such a time making the scene! When dear Boris jumped in that window, how I screamed and carried on! I carried it off with such flair ... such style ... "*

Within 48 hours, the *real* Mae Clarke, mortified, filed suit against KTLA and Ottola Nesmith. Meanwhile, during the showing of *Frankenstein*, "The Old Lady" never once said the name of the star-billed actor playing Henry Frankenstein.

Yet L.A. viewers took notice. The flashing lightning, roaring thunder ... a virtual spectacle of blasphemy ...

"It's alive, it's alive ... *IT'S ALIVE!*"

Within weeks, *Shock! Theatre*, as the 52-film package would be heralded, was a national phenomenon. In San Francisco, KRON-TV's ratings jumped 807% the night it showed *Frankenstein*. Along with Elvis' new single *Jailhouse Rock*, and the dog Laika who rode in space in Sputnik 2 (and whom the Russians knew would never return alive), the old horror films were a '57 sensation.

Karloff and Lugosi (who'd died in 1956 and was buried at Los Angeles' Holy Cross Cemetery in his Dracula cape) headlined a *Shock!* repertory company boasting Lon Chaney, Jr., Claude Rains, and the late Lionel Atwill (who'd died in 1946). Colin Clive appeared only in *Frankenstein*. *Bride of Frankenstein* would be part of the *Son of Shock!* package, airing in late 1958. So would *The Ghost of Frankenstein*, which included flashbacks of Clive from *Frankenstein* and *Bride of Frankenstein*. Indeed, the only other glimpse horror disciples caught of Colin Clive on the original *Shock! Theatre* was in *Son of Frankenstein*, in which we see the life-size painting of Colin as Henry Frankenstein above the ancestral castle's fireplace.

Colin Clive seemed a ghost, forlornly haunting the shadows of *Shock! Theatre*.

Meanwhile, on May 24, 1958, Colin's uncle, the Reverend Father John Glennie "Jungly" Greig, of Milford-on-Sea, died. He was 86 years old. He had become a Roman Catholic priest in the mid-1930s and in 1947, had become honorary Canon of the diocese of Portsmouth. He'd also received the Companion of the Order of the Indian Empire Award from King George VI. John Glennie Greig's

A later picture of Jeanne de Casalis.

effects totaled £340.14s.11d. He left his estate to the Roman Catholic bishop of Portsmouth.

Three days after Fr. Greig's death, May 27, 1958, Jeanne de Casalis Stephenson, almost 21 years after Colin Clive's death, finally settled her ex-spouse's estate in England. The value: £75.11s.9d.

The approximate value in 1958 American currency: $209.57.

"One Man *Crazy* ...!"

Friday, August 19, 1966: Jeanne de Casalis died, survived by her husband. She was in her early 70s, her precise age a mystery she'd guarded since her early days of stardom. She'd authored a 1953 book, *Things I Don't Remember*. It made no mention of Colin Clive, but it wasn't a biography—it was a collection of random stories and memories. Her personal letters mysteriously turned up at a garage sale in New York approximately 40 years after her death and were auctioned by Heritage Galleries in 2006. I catalogued the archive and its letters from many giants of the British theater—Sir Laurence Olivier, Vivien Leigh, Maurice Evans, and so on. The one aforementioned letter she'd saved from Colin, written in 1934 in Hollywood, had been torn in half. Jeanne de Casalis' ashes are at Golders Green Crematorium in England.

Sunday, February 2, 1969: Boris Karloff died at King Edward VII Hospital in London, at the age of 81, beloved internationally and worth over $2,000,000. He worked almost to the very end, as he'd wished. Karloff said very little about Colin Clive in his late years— frankly, the interviewers never asked. Karloff was cremated at Guildford Crematorium in Surrey, his ashes buried outside the chapel and unmarked. Among the memorials: his widow Evelyn restrung the bells of St. Mary the Virgin church in Bramshott, near the cottage where they spent Karloff's last years. The church dates to 1220 and the countryside is reputedly one of the most haunted in all of England.

As for the remains of Colin Clive ...

As previously noted, Iris Lancaster had directed the cremains go back to the Edwards Brothers Colonial Mansion, leaving the "Place of Interment" space blank. The ashes went there July 8, 1937. Maybe Edwards Brothers sent the ashes to England. Perhaps Iris Lancaster or Leslie Landau eventually claimed them.

Or maybe the ashes stayed at Edwards Brothers for over 30 years.

In 1969, the State of California revoked Edwards' license. In 1973, the mortuary reopened as The Abbott & Hast Colonial Mansion, and in 1980, Mr. Ronald A. Hast responded to my inquiry about Colin Clive's cremains:

> *At the time of purchase, we inherited many of the old Edwards Brothers records, however the business had been closed for four years. In 1975 we had a major fire in the building, and at that time elected to dispose of all former records for a number of reasons.*
>
> *We do know that, when the State of California took the license of Edwards Brothers, there were numerous cremated remains in the basement. At that time, the State Board recovered all cremains, about 300 in number, and placed them in a community grave in the Los Angeles County Crematorium Grounds.*

Mr. Hast suggested that I contact the State of California Board of Funeral Directors in Sacramento to see if they had any relevant information. A letter came back, "We regret we can't help you ..." and "We have no information ..." Either the agency genuinely had no information, or they didn't want to admit they did. Informing a fan of an actor who died in 1937 that the actor's ashes were in a community grave might, in their eyes, have caused bizarre complications.

Colin Clive's name on a cenotaph at the Chapel of the Pines Crematory in Los Angeles. (Photo by author)

As for The Los Angeles County Crematorium Grounds, they are in Boyle Heights, in East Los Angeles. The Crematorium Grounds are part of the old Evergreen Cemetery and date back at least to the early 1920s. The establishment cremates unclaimed bodies, holds the ashes for a time and, if they are never claimed, buries them in mass graves marked by the year-of-burial date. Considering the size of Los Angeles, and the fact that these burials have been taking place there for over 90 years, the number of cremains interred there must be staggering. In 2010, a news story reported that the Grounds was about to bury the cremains of another 1,400 people.

Basically, to use an age-old euphemism, the Grounds are a Potter's Field.

In 2017, I wrote to the Los Angeles County Crematorium Grounds, noting the 1969 communal burial cited by Mr. Hast and asking for any specific information on Colin Clive, or Colin Glennie Clive Greig. The reply, from C. Garnette, crematory operator, was prompt, but hardly encouraging:

> *There are no records of abandoned remains at that time in our ledger. I am not certain how abandoned remains were handled at that time.*

Nobody knows … or nobody admits they know.

So, since the records of Edwards Brothers no longer exist, the mystery goes unsolved. In a macabre scenario, Iris Lancaster's desire to retain legal custody of Colin's ashes vs. Jeanne de Casalis' intention to return his remains to England had possibly placed the cremains in a virtual Limbo—namely, the Edwards Brothers basement.

The true expert on these matters is historian Scott Wilson, author of the 2016 two-volume *Resting Places: The Burial Sites of More Than 14,000 Famous People*, now in its third edition. Wilson, a Clive admirer, has done extensive research on this subject. "It sounds like the ashes went to Edwards Brothers," says Wilson, "and after that is anybody's guess." He adds, "If the ashes were not taken by Lancaster or Leslie Landau, they likely ended up in the Los Angeles Crematorium Grounds."

The one person who might have solved the mystery: Iris Lancaster. Instead, she became a mystery herself.

Wednesday, September 26, 2001: Iris Lancaster died at the Rancho Springs Medical Center in Murrieta, California. She was 86. The cause of death: Cardiopulmonary Arrest. In her late years, Iris went by the name of Paula Iris Markus. If she were aware of the interest in her days and nights in Old Hollywood as an actress or as Colin Clive's lover, she apparently did nothing to emerge from her basic anonymity. Her final address was 38246 Via De Largo in Murrieta; if one does an Internet search for that address today, you will see an upscale mobile home. The death certificate notes that she was widowed and that her occupation had been an "Actress," having spent "5" years in "Motion Pictures." She'd actually been an actress for about 13 years and presumably hadn't acted for 55 years. Her informant on the death certificate was her attorney.

Wednesday, October 3, 2001: The Cremation Society of Riverside County cremated the body of Iris Lancaster, aka Iris Clive, aka Paula Iris Markus, and the ashes were scattered at sea off the Coast of Orange County.

Colin Clive does have a memorial in Los Angeles, thanks to the heartfelt generosity of a very devoted fan.

In May of 1998, Denise Fetterley paid to have Colin's name added to a cenotaph in the rose garden at the Chapel of the Pines. Ms. Fetterley had visited Los Angeles from her home in Florida to arrange a proper tribute. She first visited Rosedale Cemetery, aware that Colin had been cremated there, but wasn't pleased with what the cemetery had to offer. As Ms. Fetterley explains:

> *I started looking for something nicer. A friend reminded me of the English fondness for roses. I visited Forest Lawn, Glendale, which had nothing, and Hollywood Forever Cemetery, which required that I buy an entire full-sized plot and marker. Westwood Cemetery had a rose garden, but theirs just didn't seem like Colin. Then I saw the rose garden at Chapel of the Pines. It was close to Rosedale, the cenotaph was much nicer, and with Lionel Atwill and Helen Chandler being there, I thought it might be the best choice.*

Lionel Atwill's ashes were at the Chapel of the Pines, in "Vaultage"—an area below the building, not open to the public—until 2003, when his son Tony removed them and buried them with Tony's mother's ashes in Vermont. Helen Chandler's ashes are still in "Vaultage." As Ms. Fetterley says:

> *I didn't know that anyone but myself and a few friends would even know that Colin's name was at the Chapel of the Pines. Unfortunately, I haven't been there in years. The rose garden used to be pretty. I hope it still is.*

Chapter Thirty-One
The Fans and the Ghost

Colin Clive fans are a devoted lot. After all, he provides many obsessive aspects—addiction, early death—as well as an iconic performance and wildfire talent. As this book nears its conclusion, here are just a few stories about several Clive fans that, in my experience, have gone above and beyond the call of duty.

After my book *It's Alive! The Classic Cinema Saga of Frankenstein* was published in 1981, a young artist and sculptor named Kevin McLaughlin phoned me. Kevin was a Colin Clive fan and told me he was planning to create a bust of Clive in his workshop. A short time later, he left his home in upstate New York late one night, driving his motorcycle to my home in southern Pennsylvania, arriving the next morning ... and giving the superbly-done Clive sculpture to me. It was an incredible honor.

Kevin and I unfortunately lost touch. If he reads this book, hopefully he'll contact me again in care of the publisher.

Then there's Bryan Moore, a superb artist and sculptor. In 1997, Bryan became friends with Sir Ian McKellen while the celebrated star was playing James Whale in the film *Gods and Monsters*. Bryan kindly managed to get me on the laboratory set one evening while they were filming the flashback of Whale directing *Bride of Frankenstein*. There was McKellen, as the 1935 red-haired "Jimmy" Whale, as well as "the Monster" (Amir AboulEla) and "the Bride" (Rosalind Ayres). What a sight to see!

Author Greg Mank with a bust of Colin Clive, as sculpted by Kevin McLaughlin, 1984. (Photo by Ellis J. Malashuk, *Baltimore Sun*)

"One Man *Crazy* ...!"

The "Crazy Am I?" Colin Clive model kit, sculpted by Bryan Moore, 1997.

There were delays, as there often are on a film set. Meanwhile, Bryan presented me with a gift: He'd created his own Colin Clive model kit, titled "Crazy, Am I?"—Colin as Dr. Frankenstein, a startlingly incredible likeness. I was delighted and proudly carried it around the set with me, in its box with a picture of the glowering Clive and the words "Crazy, Am I?" emblazoned on it. Only later did it occur to me that McKellen and the others I met that night, all of whom were remarkably gracious, perhaps figured I was some wacky Clive "groupie" who, considering where I was visiting, had brought my model kit along with me. Maybe, they thought, I took it everywhere I went.

At any rate, I was too pleased by the surprise gift to worry about these matters. Bryan and I stay in touch, and I strongly suggest you see his amazing art at his Arkham Studios webpage.

A drawing of Colin Clive by the late Linda Miller.

The late Linda Miller was a sweet, gentle, and very gifted artist whose beautiful work appears elsewhere in this book. Linda and I became friends on the Internet and she generously sent copies of her drawings. Aware I traveled to do research, she gave me a surprise gift: an exquisitely done portrait of Colin Clive in a small frame.

Colin Clive at sea, 1932.

"You can take this along on your research trips," Linda wrote.

In 2004, my wife Barbara and I met her at the Monster Bash Convention near Pittsburgh. It wasn't very long afterwards that Linda died suddenly. Missed by many, the Classic Horror Film Board annually presents an art award in her honor. The Clive portrait she generously gave me sits prominently on a bookshelf in my den, a daily reminder of what a kind, talented lady Linda Miller was.

The aforementioned *Gods and Monsters*, released in 1998 and based on the novel by Christopher Bram, featured Matt McKenzie as Colin Clive, seen briefly in the *Bride of Frankenstein* flashback, appearing a bit testy and restless as Whale and Ernest Thesiger (Arthur Dignam) joke about having done the Female Monster's hair. (Neither McKenzie nor Dignam were on the set the night I visited; McKenzie might have been especially interested in my Colin Clive kit). Incidentally, Bill Condon, who directed and wrote the screenplay for *Gods and Monsters*, won an Oscar for Best Writing, while Ian McKellen received a Best Actor Academy nomination for playing Whale, and Lynn Redgrave garnered a Best Supporting Actress Oscar nomination as Whale's housekeeper.

Colin Clive had a brief but marvelous showcase at the 2018 Oscar Ceremony. His voice introduced the "90 years of Motion Pictures" montage, as he delivered *Frankenstein's* "Have you ever wanted to look beyond the clouds and the stars ... " soliloquy. Seconds later, the montage showed a glimpse of him saying the memorable words. It was a wonderful moment.

"One man crazy ...!"

As the reader has hopefully realized, the "One Man *Crazy*" of the title refers not only to a classic line of dialogue delivered by Colin Clive in *Frankenstein*. It also relates to Colin's ill-fated Uncle Piercy Greig, whose death in the Public Lunatic Asylum on the island of Jersey in 1924 was possibly one of the most taunting of Colin's pet devils. There were other torments, of course. The mother that abandoned him; the first wife who died tragically. The agonizing stage fright that had never eased up. He even had every right to be haunted by horses.

We can only conjecture, because he never talked publicly about these things. To do so would have been non-heroic.

Colin Clive was valiantly determined to be a hero.

Like his heartbreaking Stanhope of *Journey's End*, he was bravely determined to conquer his demons. As with Stanhope, Colin required the crutch of alcohol; but as did the doomed Captain he so vividly played, he accomplished his mission nobly. Indeed, he indelibly made his mark in cinema history, and as Henry Frankenstein, in popular culture.

It came at a terrible personal price. As Shakespeare wrote, "We are such stuff as dreams are made on; and our little life is rounded with a sleep." The dreams Colin Clive inspired as Frankenstein were nightmares, and his real life virtually became one as well.

Yet he's beyond all that now.

In the most moving scene of *Frankenstein*, Colin Clive's renegade scientist opens the laboratory roof, revealing the light to Karloff's Monster, who heartbreakingly reaches to grasp it.

"Man looking at God!" said Mae Clarke emotionally.

The episode remains powerful, the metaphor still profound. After a life of often-insidious sadness, in which darkness prevailed and tragedy had far too major a role, Colin Glennie Clive Greig now plays in a very different pageantry. The nightmare's over. He's out of the torment.

He now exists in the Light.

Colin Clive portrait, circa 1929.

"One Man *Crazy* ...!"

Appendices

Appendix One: Select Theater Credits

Journey's End. By R.C Sherriff. Produced by Maurice Browne. Directed by James Whale. Scenery designed by James Whale. Costumes designed by John Hyman.

Opened at the Savoy Theatre, London, January 21, 1929. Moved to the Prince of Wales' Theatre, June 3, 1929. 593 performances.

The Cast: David Horne (Captain Hardy), George Zucco (Lieutenant Osborne), Alexander Field (Private Mason), Maurice Evans (2nd Lieutenant Jimmy Raleigh), Colin Clive (Captain Dennis Stanhope), Melville Cooper (2nd Lieutenant Trotter), Robert Speaight (2nd Lieutenant Hibbert), Reginald Smith (Company Sergeant Major), H.G. Stoker (Colonel), Geoffrey Wincott (German soldier), John Fernald, John Curtis, Geoffrey Clarke, Frank Prebble (Private soldiers).

As noted in the biography section, *Journey's End* originally opened at the Apollo Theatre in London on December 9, 1928, directed and designed by James Whale. The principal players were the same as above, except that Laurence Olivier had played Stanhope and Percy Walsh played the Company Sergeant Major.

James Whale also directed the New York production, which opened at Henry Miller's Theatre March 22, 1929, starring Colin Keith-Johnston as Stanhope, Leon Quartermaine as Osborne, Derek Williams as Raleigh, and Jack Hawkins as Hibbert; and a company at the Adelphi Theatre in Chicago, opening September 9, 1929, starring Richard Bird as Stanhope, Reginald Mason as Osborne, and Edwin Woodings as Raleigh. The play re-opened in New York at Henry Miller's Theatre August 4, 1930, again directed by Whale, with Richard Bird as Stanhope, William Sauter as Osborne, and Maury Tuckerman as Raleigh, then went on tour.

Colin Keith-Johnston, Clive's rival for the Stanhope role in London, not only starred in the original New York production, but also reprised the role in a Broadway revival of *Journey's End* (Empire Theatre, September 18, 1939). He had a long, distinguished career on stage and theater and film and died in 1980 at the age of 83.

Incidentally, Laurence Olivier played Stanhope again in a special performance of *Journey's End* at London's Adelphi Theatre on November 12, 1934. It commemorated the end of the war in 1918. George Zucco again played Osborne and Derek Williams portrayed Raleigh.

A revival *of Journey's End* opened at Broadway's Morosco Theatre February 22, 2007. It was directed by David Grindley and starred Hugh Dancy as Stanhope, Boyd Gaines as Osborne, and Stark Sands as Raleigh. The play ran 125 performances and won the Tony Award and Drama Desk Award for the season's Best Revival of a Play. Boyd Gaines won the Drama Desk Award for Best Featured Actor.

R.C. Sherriff (1896-1975), born Robert Cedric Sherriff in England, would superbly adapt *The Invisible Man* (1933) for James Whale, and also did un-credited work on *The Old Dark House* (1932) and *Bride of Frankenstein* (1935). He also worked un-credited on an early script for Universal's *Dracula's Daughter* (1936) when Whale was considering directing it (Lambert Hillyer eventually directed the film). Sherriff wrote the original script for Whale's ill-fated *The Road Back* (1937) and received an Oscar nomination for Best Screenplay (shared with Eric Maschwitz and Claudine West) for MGM's *Goodbye Mr. Chips*, directed by Sam Wood. Among Sherriff's later credits: *That Hamilton Woman* (1941), *Odd Man Out* (1947), *No Highway in the Sky* (1951), and *The Dam Busters* (1955).

Finally, as for George Zucco, who so memorably co-starred with Colin Clive in London's *Journey's End*: He died at Monterey Sanitarium in South San Gabriel, California on May 27, 1960. He was 74 years old. Cause of death: pneumonia. Zucco had suffered a severe stroke on the set of 20th Century-Fox's *The Desert Fox* in 1951 and had spent most of the time since at the Sanitarium, his condition such that he always recognized his wife Stella and daughter Frances, but he recognized fewer and fewer of his friends and colleagues. Zucco's ashes are interred at Forest Lawn, Hollywood

Hills. In 1962, his daughter Frances died after an overdose of radiation for cancer of the throat. Her ashes are with her father's. His wife Stella died in 1999 at the age of 99.

Overture. By William Bolitho. Produced and directed by Bela Blau. Settings designed by Donald Oenslager. Production built by Frank Dwyer, Inc. and painted by Robert W. Bergman Studios. Electrical Equipment by Century Lighting Company. Costumes by Eaves Costume Co. Furniture by W.J. Birns, Inc. Company Manager, L.S. Leavitt. Stage Manager, Royal C. Stout. Assistant Stage Manager, Anthony Pawley.

Opened at the Longacre Theatre, New York City, December 6, 1930. 41 performances.

The Cast (In order of their appearance): Lois Arnold (Mrs. Lopper), Armand Cortes (Peters), George Bollmer (Attendant), William Foran (Thomas), Pacie Ripple (Jung), Frederick Roland (The Mayor), Daniel Makarenko (Kraus), Richard Freeman (Felder), Martin Malloy (Lindermann), Colin Clive (Karl Ritter), Barbara Robbins (Katie Tauler), Pat O'Brien (Maxim), Maurice Cass (Doctor Levy), Joseph Robison (Rubens, a blacksmith), N.R. Cregan (Pepper, a miner), Ward Vernon (Hans), J.P. Gould (Paul), Lee Burgess (A Girl), Royal C. Stout (Lieutenant of Police), Frederick Backus (Heiber), William Boren (Peter Hessel), Bjorn Koefoed (A Delegate), Daniel Hamilton (A Corporal), John Hoysradt (Lieutenant Hoffman), Carlos Zizold (General Von Hoeffer), Harry Selby (Another Corporal), Bjorn Koefoed (Chaplain) and "Soldiers and Townspeople."

The program for *Overture* noted that Clive appeared "by permission of Maurice Browne, Inc." It was Browne, of course, who'd produced the stage *Journey's End* and had allowed Clive permission to make the film *Journey's End* in Hollywood.

Pulitzer Prize-winning playwright Marc Connelly (1890-1980) worked with William Bolitho on writing *Overture*, but did not officially receive credit.

Pat O'Brien (1899-1983), who played Maxim, enjoyed a lengthy career, best remembered for his work at Golden Age Warner Bros., where he starred in such films as *San Quentin* (1937), *Angels With Dirty Faces* (1938), and *Knute Rockne All American* (1940).

Eight Bells. By Percy G. Mandley. Produced by A.C. Blumenthal. Directed by Frank Gregory. Settings constructed by Cleon Throckmorton. Miss Hobart's frocks by Sonya Rosenberg. Men's uniforms by R.K.O. Tailor. Shoes by La Ray Boot Shop. Lighting equipment and effects by Century Lighting Equipment Inc. Furniture covers by I. Weiss. Stage Manager Edison Rice. Assistant Stage Manager, Richard Hughes.

Opened at the Hudson Theatre, New York City, October 28, 1933. 17 performances.

The Cast: (in order of appearance) Philip Tonge (Collister, Second Mate), Alfred Kappeler (Carol, Steward), Rose Hobart (Marjorie, the Master's Wife), John Buckler (Ormrod, Mate), Siegfried Rumann (Gerhardt, Sailmaker), Colin Clive (Dale, Master), Harrison Brockbank (Ashworth, Bos'n), Henry von Zynda (Zimmerman, Seaman), Richard Hughes (Schill, Seaman), Joseph Singer (Klotz, Seaman), Wayne Nunn (Pancho, Seaman), Carleton Young (Rastello, Seaman), David Hughes (Snider, Seaman), Eric West (Pedro, Seaman), Donald Bruce (Yetts, Seaman), S.B. Pink (Nalo, Seaman), Paul Dietz (Volotsky, Seaman), Walter Dressel (Oscar, Seaman).

In his "Who's Who in the Cast" section in the program for *Eight Bells*, Clive's entry includes this fact: "*Eight Bells* was written for him, but motion picture contracts prevented his opening in the play in London, where Reginald Tate is currently playing the role of the master of the windjammer." It was gracious of Colin to mention Tate's name. Unfortunately, *Eight Bells* did not duplicate its London success on Broadway.

Rose Hobart (1906-2000) had starred in the original 1929 New York production of *Death Takes a Holiday* and had played Muriel to Fredric March's *Dr. Jekyll and Mr. Hyde* (Paramount, 1931). She played featured roles in Universal's *The Mad Ghoul* (1943) and *The Cat Creeps* (1946), as well as Columbia's *The Soul of a Monster* (1944). Blacklisted in the late 1940s due to leftist politics, she made a modest "comeback" in the 1960s and was a regular on TV's *Peyton Place* (1966-1969). Rose Hobart spent her final years as a feisty resident of the Motion Picture Country House and Lodge.

Siegfried Rumann (1884-1967), aka Sig Rumann and Sig Ruman, had been a solider in the Imperial German Army in World War I. In Hollywood, he became a favorite foil for the Marx Brothers, and was memorable as "Concentration Camp Ehrhardt" in *To Be or Not to Be* (1942) and as Sgt. Shulz in *Stalag 17* (1953). Horror fans will recall him as the Burgomaster, killed by John Carradine's Dracula in *House of Frankenstein* (1944).

As noted in the biography section, Columbia Pictures had financed the Broadway version of *Eight Bells*. Despite the play's failure, Columbia proceeded with a film version, originally set to star Jack Holt in Colin's role of Captain Dale, Marian Marsh as Marjorie, and John Buckler in his stage role of Ormond. As things evolved, Buckler played Captain Dale, Ralph Bellamy played Ormond (here renamed "Steve Andrews"), and Ann Sothern played Marjorie (here called "Marge*)*. *Eight Bells'* director, Roy William Neill, later directed Universal's *Frankenstein Meets the Wolf Man* (1943) and 11 of the 12 films in the studio's Sherlock Holmes series.

The Lake. By Dorothy Massingham and Murray MacDonald. Produced and Directed by Jed Harris. Scenic Design by Jo Mielziner.
Opened at the Martin Beck Theatre, New York City, December 26, 1933. 55 performances.
The Cast: Frances Starr (Mildred Surrege), J.P. Wilson (Williams), Blanche Bates (Lena Surrege), Lionel Pape (Henry Surrege), Roberta Beatty (Marjorie Hervey), Katharine Hepburn (Stella Surrege), Esther Mitchell (Ethel), Geoffrey Wardwell (Cecil Hervey), Colin Clive (John Clayne), Mary Heberden (Maude), Edward Broadley (Stoker), Philip Tonge (Stephen Braite), Wendy Atkin (Dolly Braite), Audrey Ridgwell (Jean Templeton), Vera Fuller-Mellish (Anna George), Rosalind Ivan (Mrs. George), Florence Britton (Miss Kurn), Elizabeth Townsend (Miss Marie), Douglas Gordon (Mr. Hemingway), Eva Leonard-Boyne (Mrs. Hemingway), O.Z Whitehead (Dennis Gourlay), Constance Pellisier (Lady Stanway), Reginald Carrington (Sir Philip Stanway), James Grainger (Captain Hamilton), Lucy Beaumont (Miss White), Elliott Mason (Lady Kerton).

Katharine Hepburn (1907-2003) won Best Actress Oscars for *Morning Glory* (1933), *Guess Who's Coming to Dinner* (1967), *The Lion in Winter* (1968), and *On Golden Pond* (1981). As noted in the biographical section, she and Colin Clive had memorably co-starred in the 1933 film *Christopher Strong*. In 1999, the AFI rated Hepburn as the #1 Woman in its "50 Greatest Movie Legends."

Jed Harris (1900-1979), born in Austria, made the cover of *Time* magazine September 3, 1928, after he'd produced and directed the historic Broadway hit, *The Front Page*. Among his famous productions: *Broadway* (1926), *The Royal Family* (1927), and *Our Town* (1938). He later directed *The Heiress* (1947) and *The Crucible* (1953). Harris was legendary not only for his talent, but also for his abusive temperament—so much so that Sir Laurence Olivier made himself up as Shakespeare's diabolic *Richard III* to resemble Harris.

Frances Starr (1886-1973), had been a star for David Belasco, appearing in such plays as *Tiger! Tiger!* (1918) with Lionel Atwill. She was notable in the film *Five Star Final* (1931) and later did TV work in the 1950s.

Blanche Bates (1873-1941) was also a Belasco star, having created the title role of *The Girl of the Golden West* (1905). *The Lake* was her final Broadway appearance.

Journey's End. By R.C. Sherriff. Directed by E.E. Clive.
Opened at the Hollywood Playhouse, Hollywood, CA, August 9, 1934.
The Cast: Colin Clive (Captain Stanhope), Gerald Rogers (Osborne), John Warburton (Raleigh), Forrester Harvey (Trotter), Reginald Sheffield (Hibbert), E.E. Clive (Mason), Henry Mowbray, Desmond Roberts, Robert Adair, Burt Miller.

E.E. Clive (1883-1940), who directed this revival of *Journey' End* and played Mason, was born in Wales, and was the impresario of the Hollywood Playhouse. A prolific character player, he appeared in a number of films for James Whale: *The Invisible Man* (as Constable Jaffers, 1933), *One More River* (1934), *Bride of Frankenstein* (1935), *Remember Last Night?* (1935), *Show Boat* (1936), *The Road Back* (1937), and *The Great Garrick* (1937).

Libel! By Edward Wooll. Produced by Gilbert Miller. Directed by Otto Ludwig Preminger. Scenic Design by Raymond Sovey.
Opened at Henry Miller's Theatre, New York City, December 20, 1935. 159 performances.
The Cast: Colin Clive (Sir Mark Loddon, Bart., M.P.), Joan Marion (Lady Enid Loddon), Ernest Lawford (Sir Wilfred Kelling, K.C., M.P), Wilfrid Lawson (Thomas Foxley, K.C.), Frederick

Leister (Mr. Justice Tuttington), Arthur Vinton (Patrick Buckenham), Boris Marshalov (Emile Flordon), Helen Goss (Sarah Carleton), Charles Francis (William Bale), Colin Hunter (George Hemsby), Neville Heber-Percy (Major Brampton), Edward Oldfield (General Winterton, C.B), Emily Gilbert (Lady Agatha Winterton), Robert Simmons (Numero Quinze), Robert Benjamin (Admiral Fairfax Loddon), Lewis Dayton (Associate), Larry Johns (Captain Gerald Loddon), Robert Le Sueur, Charles Wellesley (Ushers).

Otto Preminger (1905-1986) would direct such films as *Laura* (1944*)*, *Anatomy of a Murder* (1959), *Exodus* (1960), and *Advise and Consent* (1962). He was also a memorable film Nazi in such movies as *Stalag 17* (1953). His sadism on film sets won him the nickname of "Otto the Ogre."

Wilfrid Lawson (1900-1966), who scored a personal success as Foxley, *Libel!*'s bullying prosecutor, also worked extensively in movies, playing Doolittle in the British film version of *Pygmalion* (1938) and the crazy lighthouse keeper in *Tower of Terror* (1941). He worked until the end of his life, despite severe alcoholism.

Libel! became a 1959 film, produced in England, starring Dirk Bogarde as Sir Mark and Olivia de Havilland as Lady Loddon. Anthony Asquith directed. There'd also been a 1948 British TV version, starring Michael Hordern as Sir Mark and Elizabeth Tyrrell as Lady Loddon.

Appendix Two:
Film Credits

Journey's End. Tiffany Productions/Gainsborough Studios/Gaumont British. Supervising Producer, George Pearson. Director, James Whale. Screenplay, Gareth Gundrey and Joseph Moncure March, based on the play by R.C. Sherriff. Cinematographer, Benjamin H. Kline. Editor, Claude Berkeley. Art Director, Hervey Libbert. Sound, Buddy Myers. Assistant Director, Millard K. Wilson. Technical Advisor, George Magee. Running Time, 120 minutes.

New York Premiere, Gaiety Theatre, April 8, 1930. Los Angeles Premiere, Mayan Theatre, April 10, 1930.

The Cast: Colin Clive (Captain Dennis Stanhope), Ian Maclaren (Lt. Osborne), David Manners (2nd Lt. Jimmy Raleigh), Billy Bevan (2nd Lt. Trotter), Anthony Bushell (2nd Lt. Hibbert), Robert Adair (Captain Hardy), Charles K. Gerrard (Pvt. Mason), Tom Whiteley (Sergeant Major), Jack Pitcairn (Colonel), Werner Klinger (German Prisoner), Leslie Sketchley (Cpl. Ross), Gil Perkins (Sgt. Cox).

British-born Ian Maclaren (1875-1952) deserved a finer film career. He played Cassius in DeMille's *Cleopatra* (1934) and Sir Charles in *The Hound of the Baskervilles* (1939), but many of his roles were small and un-credited, such as the Priest in Karloff's *The Man They Could Not Hang* (1939). Maclaren's final film role was as the Harmonica Player in *The Grand Escapade* (1947), in which he billed himself as Sydney Shaw.

David Manners (1900-1998), born Rauf de Ryther Daun Acklom in Nova Scotia, became Golden Age Horror's famed romantic hero in three Universal horror classics: *Dracula* (1931), *The Mummy* (1932), and *The Black Cat* (1934). He was starred in *The Death Kiss* (Worldwide, 1932, with Bela Lugosi) and played the ill-fated title character in *The Mystery of Edwin Drood* (Universal, 1935). He also acted with some of the era's top female stars: Loretta Young (*Kismet*, 1930), Ruth

***Journey's End.* Billy Bevan and Colin Clive. (Courtesy of Neil Pettigrew)**

Chatterton (*The Right to Love*, 1930), Barbara Stanwyck (*The Miracle Woman*, 1931) Katharine Hepburn (*A Bill of Divorcement*, 1932), Carole Lombard (*From Hell to Heaven*, 1933), Elissa Landi (*The Warrior's Husband*, 1933), and Claudette Colbert (*Torch Singer*, 1933). His favorite leading lady: Helen Chandler, with whom he starred in three films: *Mothers Cry* (1930), *Dracula* (1931). and *Last Flight* (1931). A hyper-sensitive man, Manners left Hollywood in 1936, helped develop a guest ranch, "Yucca Loma," in the Mojave Desert, wrote novels, did some late 1940s stage work (including replacing Henry Daniell in a 1946 Broadway revival of *Lady Windermere's Fan*, in which he also toured), and spent his golden years living in Pacific Palisades and later Santa Barbara, writing about metaphysical topics. On December 23, 1998, David Manners wheeled himself into the dining room at his nursing home, stopped eating, and died peacefully. He was 98 years old.

Journey's End featured two other actors whose film credits included notable horror films. Australian Billy Bevan (1887-1957), who played Trotter, was formerly a Mack Sennett comic, and appeared in such melodramas as *Dracula's Daughter* (1936), *Dr. Jekyll and Mr. Hyde* (1941), and *The Picture of Dorian Gray* (1945). Irishman Charles K. Gerrard (1883-1969), who played the cook Mason, appeared in *Dracula* (1931) as Martin the sanitarium guard, who memorably delivers the line, "They're *ALLLLL* Crazy!"

A remake/revamp of *Journey's End* was *Aces High* (1976), directed by Jack Gold, with the action moved to the Royal Flying Corps. Malcom McDowell had the "Stanhope" role (here called "Gresham"), Christopher Plummer the Osborne part (here named "Sinclair"), and Simon Ward the Raleigh role (here called "Crawford").

A 1983 U.S. TV film of *Journey's End*, directed by Kent Gibson and Steven Schachter, starred Maxwell Caulfield as Stanhope, Ken Letner as Osborne, and Andrew Stevens as Raleigh. A 1988 British TV film of *Journey's End*, directed by Michael Simpson, starred Jeremy Northam as Stanhope, Edward Petherbridge as Osborne, and Mark Payton as Raleigh. The 2018 *Journey's End*, produced by England's Fluidity Films and directed by Saul Dibb, starred Sam Claflin as Stanhope, Paul Bettany as Osborne, and Asa Butterfield as Raleigh. *Rolling Stone* magazine called the new *Journey's End* "a bleak, sobering experience that puts audiences through a wringer. It's also an emotional powerhouse you will not forget."

The Stronger Sex. Gainsborough Pictures, 1931. Producer, Michael Balcon. Director, Gareth Gundrey. Screenplay, Gareth Gundrey, based on a play by J. Valentine. Cinematographer, William Shenton. The Cast: Colin Clive (Warren Barrington), Adrianne Allen (Mary Thorpe), Gordon Harker (Parker), Martin Lewis (John Brent), Renee Clama (Joan Merivale), Elsa Lanchester (Thompson).

Michael Balcon (1896-1977), *The Stronger Sex's* producer, co-founded Gainsborough Pictures in 1924, headed MGM-British from 1936 to 1938 and Ealing Studios from 1937 to 1959. He was knighted in 1948. Balcon was the grandfather of actor Daniel Day-Lewis.

Gareth Gundrey (1893-1965) had received co-author credit on the screenplay of *Journey's End*. His film career as a producer/director/writer appears to have ended with Gainsborough's 1931 version of *The Hound of the Baskervilles*.

Adrianne Allen (1907-1993) starred in the original 1930 London production of *Private Lives*. In 1939, Allen divorced her husband, Raymond Massey, and married her divorce lawyer, William Whitney. Massey married Whitney's divorced wife Dorothy. Both marriages lasted.

Elsa Lanchester (1902-1986) had already appeared in at least 10 features and short films by the time she played in *The Stronger Sex*. For more about Ms. Lanchester, see the entry for *Bride of Frankenstein*.

Filmed in 1930 and released in 1931, *The Stronger Sex* has not turned up for viewing.

Frankenstein. Universal 1931. Producer, Carl Laemmle, Jr. Associate Producer, E.M. Asher. Director, James Whale. Screenplay, Garrett Fort and Francis Edward Faragoh (Robert Florey and John Russell, un-credited), based upon the composition by John L. Balderston, adapted from the play by Peggy Webling, from the 1818 novel by Mary Wollstonecraft Shelley. Cinematographer, Arthur Edeson. Editor, Clarence Kolster. Supervising editor, Maurice Pivar. Sound, C. Roy Hunter and William Hedgcock. Art Director, Charles D. Hall. Set designer, Herman Rosse. Makeup, Jack

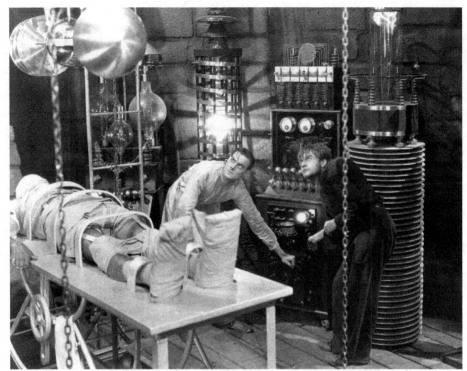

Frankenstein. **Boris Karloff, Colin Clive and Dwight Frye.**

P. Pierce. Special Effects, John P. Fulton. Special Electrical Effects, Kenneth Strickfaden. Music, Bernhard Kaun. Assistant Director, Joseph A. McDonough. Wig maker, Pauline Eells. Medical consultant, Dr. Cecil Reynolds. Running time, 70 minutes.

New York opening, RKO-Mayfair Theatre, December 4, 1931. Los Angeles opening, Orpheum Theatre, January 1, 1932.

The Cast: Colin Clive (Henry Frankenstein), Mae Clarke (Elizabeth), John Boles (Victor Moritz), Boris Karloff (The Monster), Edward Van Sloan (Dr. Waldman), Frederic Kerr (Baron Frankenstein), Dwight Frye (Fritz), Lionel Belmore (The Burgomaster), Marilyn Harris (Little Maria), Michael Mark (Ludwig), Arletta Duncan, Pauline Moore (Bridesmaids), Francis Ford (Extra at lecture/ Wounded villager in mountains), William Dyer (Gravedigger), Paul Panzer, Mary Gordon, Soledad Jimenez, Margaret Mann (Mourners), Ted Billings, Jack Curtis, Robert Milasch, Inez Palange, Rose Plumer (Villagers), Mae Bruce, Cecilia Parker (Maids), Carmencita Johnson, Seessel Anne Johnson (Little Girls), Cecil Reynolds (Waldman's secretary), Elinor Vanderveer (Medical Student), Robert Livingston (Double for Colin Clive in final scene).

Carl Laemmle, Jr. (1908-1979) was one of Golden Age Hollywood's most adventurous and courageous producers, although posterity has largely slammed him as a hypochondriacal Frankenstein's Monster created by rampant nepotism. In addition to producing the Best Picture Academy Award Winner *All Quiet on the Western Front* (1930) and unleashing the horror genre with *Dracula* and *Frankenstein* (both 1931), he headed a daredevil Universal regime that created such films as *Back Street* (1932), *Counselor-at-Law* (1933), *Imitation of Life* (1934), and *Show Boat* (1936). He never produced another film after leaving Universal in 1936, despite various announcements, and his late life saw him crippled and shamefully forgotten by the industry. "Junior" died at his home, 1641 Tower Grove Drive, atop Beverly Hills, on September 24, 1979, the 40th anniversary of the death of his father, Universal's founder Carl Laemmle, Sr. "Junior" never married and left no detailed interview about his legendary years at Universal City.

Mae Clarke (1910-1992) climaxed her Hollywood career in 1931: Mollie in United Artists' *The Front Page*, Kitty in Warner Bros.' *The Public Enemy*, and at Universal for James Whale, Myra in *Waterloo Bridge* and Elizabeth in *Frankenstein*. Her third film for Whale, 1932's *The Impatient Maiden*, was forgettable. Ms. Clarke sadly suffered mental illness that caused sanitarium stays and compromised her career, but nevertheless kept acting, tallying an impressive number of film and TV credits. She married three times (no children), and in her final years, was a famous (and at times formidable) resident of the Motion Picture Country House.

Edward Van Sloan (1882-1964) won Classic Horror celebrity status via three notable performances: Professor Van Helsing in *Dracula* (having created the role in the 1927 Broadway play), Dr. Waldman in *Frankenstein*, and Dr. Muller in The *Mummy*. He reprised Van Helsing in Universal's *Dracula's Daughter* (1936). Van Sloan also appeared with Karloff in *Behind the Mask* (1932), *The Black Room* (1935), and *Before I Hang* (1940), all for Columbia, and with Lugosi in *The Death Kiss* (1932), for Worldwide.

Dwight Frye (1899-1943), hailed as a brilliant and versatile 1920s Broadway actor, became a horror legend (and a victim of typecasting) due to his indelible portrayals of Renfield in *Dracula* and Fritz in *Frankenstein*. Whale would cast Frye as a reporter in *The Invisible Man*. For more on Frye, see the appendix entry for *Bride of Frankenstein*.

Marilyn Harris (1924-1999) was seven years and one month old when she played "Little Maria." Her mother had adopted her as a baby with hopes of raising a child star, and Marilyn's memories of her often-sadistic mother were nightmarish. Marilyn acted for James Whale again in *Bride of Frankenstein* (as a child the Monster encounters after his idyll with the Hermit—Marilyn had totally forgotten she was in the film), *Show Boat* (1936), and *The Road Back* (1937).

Russian-born Michael Mark (1886-1975), who played Ludwig, Little Maria's mournful father, went on to act in such horror films as *The Black Cat* (1934), *The Black Room* (1935), *Mad Love* (1935), *Son of Frankenstein* (1939), *Tower of London* (1939), *The Mummy's Hand* (1940), *The Ghost of Frankenstein* (1942), *House of Frankenstein* (1944), *Attack of the Puppet People* (1958), *Return of the Fly* (1959), and *The Wasp Woman* (1959).

Arthur Edeson (1891-1970) had many impressive cinematography credits, including *The Lost World* (1925), the first film to use stop-motion animation; *In Old Arizona* (1929), the first film shot entirely outdoors; and *All Quiet on the Western Front* (1930), which won Universal Studios a Best Picture Academy Award. (Karl Freund photographed that film's butterfly ending, added at the last minute.) Besides *Frankenstein*, Edeson was James Whale's cameraman on *Waterloo Bridge* (1931), *The Impatient Maiden* (1932), and *The Invisible Man* (1933); he also did un-credited work on *The Old Dark House* (1932). Edeson was cinematographer on such classics as *Mutiny on the Bounty* (MGM, 1935) and later joined Warners, where he captured the ambience of *The Maltese Falcon* (1941) and *Casablanca* (1943), receiving an Oscar nomination for the latter. He was also nominated for *In Old Arizona* and *All Quiet on the Western Front*. Incidentally, Edeson lived for many years in a home overlooking Malibu Lake, where he'd filmed the Monster meets Little Maria episode in *Frankenstein*.

Jack P. Pierce (1889-1968) created the legendary (and copyrighted by Universal) makeup designs for Frankenstein's Monster, the Mummy, the Wolf Man, and all of the studio's other creatures from 1930 to 1947. He later freelanced and ended his career as makeup man on TV's *Mister Ed* (1961-1964). Parts of his scrapbook were sold at auction by Heritage Galleries in 2008.

Kenneth Strickfaden (1896-1984) created the electrical paraphernalia for *Frankenstein* and the sequel *Bride of Frankenstein*. He was an electrician on MGM's *The Mask of Fu Manchu* (1932), doubling Karloff in that film in an electrical effect that gave Strickfaden a walloping shock that literally shot him through the air. Years later he was back at Universal City to contribute special effects to an episode of *The Munsters* ("Just Another Pretty Face," January 13, 1966), and still later contributed to *Dracula vs. Frankenstein* (1971) and *Blackenstein* (1973).

Dr. Cecil Reynolds (1880-1947) was Charlie Chaplin's physician in Hollywood and worked on *Frankenstein* as both an offscreen medical consultant and an onscreen secretary to Dr. Waldman. The scene with Reynolds, Mae Clarke and John Boles was shot but cut before release. Reynolds later appeared in *A Study in Scarlet* (1933, with Reginald Owen as Sherlock Holmes) and as a Minister in Chaplin's *Modern Times* (1936).

Among the many memorable Frankensteins of the screen: Peter Cushing in the Hammer series; Leonard Whiting of *Frankenstein: The True Story* (TV film, 1973); Kenneth Branagh of *Mary Shelley's Frankenstein* (Branagh also directed, and Robert De Niro was "the Creature," 1994). Jonny Lee Miller and Benedict Cumberbatch alternated playing Frankenstein and the Creature in the National Theatre Live production, released as a film (actually two films, to allow for the change of roles) in 2011. James McAvoy played Frankenstein in *Victor Frankenstein* (2015).

Lily Christine. Paramount British Pictures, 1932. Producer, Walter Morosco. Director, Paul L. Stein. Screenplay, Robert Gore Brown (based on the novel by Michael Arlen). Cinematography, Rudolph Mate. Set Designer, R. Holmes Paul. Running Time, 82 minutes.
Royal World Premiere, Plaza Theatre, Piccadilly Circus, London, April 28, 1932.
The Cast: Corinne Griffith (Lily Christine Summerset), Colin Clive (Rupert Harvey), Margaret Bannerman (Mrs. Abbey), Miles Mander (Ambatriadi), Jack Trevor (Ivor Summerset), Anne Grey (Muriel Harvey), Barbara Everest (Hempel), Freddie Bartholomew (Child).
　　Corinne Griffith (1894-1979), "The Orchid Lady" of the Silent Screen, achieved her greatest film success in *The Divine Lady* (1929), in which she played Lady Hamilton. At the time of *Lily Christine*, she was married to the film's producer, Walter Morosco, the second of her four husbands. In her later years, she was an ardent Christian Scientist, an outspoken Republican, and a fervent opponent of the U.S. Income tax system. A few tidbits about Ms. Griffith: She wrote 11 novels, including *Papa's Delicate Condition*, which became the 1962 film starring Jackie Gleason; her third husband, George Preston Marshall, owned the Washington Redskins Football Team; and she appeared in a featured role in the 1962 curio *Paradise Alley*, a film about Hollywood directed, written, and starring Hugo Haas. Corinne Griffith's final estate tallied $150,000,000.
　　Freddie Bartholomew (1924-1992), born in London, became the famous child star of such MGM films as *David Copperfield* (1935) and *Captains Courageous* (1937).

Lobby card from *Lily Christine*.

Director Paul L. Stein (1892-1951), born in Vienna, would be perhaps best remembered as the director of the 1934 British film *April Blossoms*, about the life of Franz Schubert.

Cinematographer Rudolph Mate (1898-1964) holds a record for cameramen with five consecutive Oscar nominations—*Foreign Correspondent* (1940), *That Hamilton Woman* (1941), *The Pride of the Yankees* (1942*), Sahara* (1943), and *Cover Girl* (1944). Unfortunately, he never won.

Christopher Strong. RKO-Radio, 1933. Producer, David O. Selznick. Associate Producer, Pandro S. Berman. Director, Dorothy Arzner. Screenplay, Zoe Akins, from the novel by Gilbert Frankau. Cinematography, Bert Glennon. Music, Max Steiner. Editor, Arthur Roberts. Set Decorations, Charles Kirk. Costume Design, Howard Greer, Walter Plunkett. Makeup, Mel Berns. Art Department, Van Nest Polglase, Thomas Little. Sound Department, Hugh McDowell, Jr., John Aalberg, Murray Spivack. Special Effects, Slavko Vorkapich, Vernon L. Walker. Technical advisor, Sir Gerald Grove. Alternate Title: *The Great Desire*. Running time: 78 minutes.
New York opening, Radio City Music Hall, March 9, 1933. Los Angeles opening RK0-Hillstreet Theatre, May 12, 1933.
The Cast: Katharine Hepburn (Lady Cynthia Darrington), Colin Clive (Sir Christopher Strong), Billie Burke (Lady Strong), Helen Chandler (Monica), Ralph Forbes (Harry Rawlinson), Irene Brown (Carrie Valentine), Jack La Rue (Carlo), Desmond Roberts (Bryce Mercer), Margaret Lindsay (Autograph seeker), Gwendolyn Logan (Bradford), Paul Ralli (Tango dancer), Agostino Borgato (Fortune teller), Zena Savine (Maid), Sherry Hall (American radio announcer), Miki Morita (Japanese radio announcer), Tiny Jones (Woman with organ grinder).

Katharine Hepburn: See the appendix entry for *The Lake*.

Billie Burke (1884-1970), the daughter of a circus clown, had been a superstar of stage and screen when she married legendary showman Florenz Ziegfeld in 1914. When Ziegfeld died on July 22, 1932, he'd lost his fortune, and Billie Burke went back to work, becoming one of the screen's unique presences. Notable films: *Dinner at Eight* (1933), *Topper* (1937) and its sequels, *Merrily We Live* (1938, for which she received a Best Supporting Actress Academy nomination), and, of course, *The Wizard of Oz* (1939), as Glinda the Good Witch. Her final release: *Pepe* (1960), in which she appeared as herself.

Helen Chandler (1909-1965) was a great stage star of Roaring 1920s Broadway (among her roles: a flapper Ophelia in a 1925 modern dress *Hamlet!*) and was impressive in Hollywood in Warners' *Outward Bound* (1930) and Universal's *Dracula* (1931). The victim of an aggressive stage mother, Helen became an alcoholic at an early age; her film career was over in 1937, her stage career by the early 1940s. She wed three times: to writer Cyril Hume, actor Bramwell Fletcher, and Merchant Mariner Walter Piascik. The last had shipped out in November of 1950 when Helen was caught in a fire in her Hollywood apartment. Investigators found liquor and sleeping pills; Helen survived, but the fire had badly scarred the left side of her face. Her brother Lee eventually committed her to DeWitt State Hospital in the California desert, where Helen spent at least five years. The end of her life saw her living in Santa Monica and taken care of by the Motion Picture Relief Fund. Helen Chandler's ashes are in "Vaultage" at the Chapel of the Pines, Los Angeles, where Colin Clive's name appears on a cenotaph in the garden.

Dorothy Arzner (1897-1979), the famed "Woman Director" of Hollywood's Golden Age, had her most notable successes directing women: Clara Bow in *The Wild Party* (1929), Ruth Chatterton in *Anybody's Woman* (1930), Anna Sten in *Nana* (1934), and Joan Crawford in *The Bride Wore Red* (1937). Arzner later directed World War II training films for the WACS, taught filmmaking at the Pasadena Playhouse and UCLA, and directed TV documentaries. Her friend Joan Crawford, during her tenure as a spokeswoman for Pepsi-Cola, recruited Arzner to direct Pepsi commercials. She spent her late years in the desert colony of La Quinta, California.

Bert Glennon (1893-1967), *Christopher Strong's* cameraman, received three Oscar nominations: For *Stagecoach* (1939), *Drums Along the Mohawk* (1939), and *Dive Bomber* (1941).

Max Steiner (1888-1971) won Oscars for his scores for *The Informer* (1935), *Now, Voyager* (1942), and *Since You Went Away* (1944). Two milestone Steiner scores: *King Kong* (1933) and *Gone With the Wind* (1939). He's among the film composers honored in 1999 by a series of $.33 stamps.

Colin Clive, in a movie star pose in kimono circa 1933.

Walter Plunkett (1902-1982), who designed Hepburn's remarkable "Moth" costume in *Christopher Strong*, would, among many other credits, design the costumes for 1939's *Gone with the Wind*. He'd win an Oscar for his creations for MGM's 1951 *An American in Paris*.

Looking Forward. MGM, 1933. Producer and Director, Clarence Brown. Associate Producer, Harry Rapf. Screenplay, Bess Meredyth and H.M. Harwood, based on the play *Service* by C.L. Anthony (aka Dodie Smith). Cinematographer, Oliver T. Marsh. Editor, Hugh Wynn. Music, William Axt. Art Director, Cedric Gibbons. Gowns, Adrian. Recording Director, Douglas Shearer. Sound Mixer, Robert Shirley. Assistant Director, Charles Dorian. Music Orchestrator, Paul Marquardt. Running Time, 83 minutes.

New York opening, The Capitol Theatre and Loew's Metropolitan Theatre, April 28, 1933. Los Angeles opening, Loew's State Theatre, May 25, 1933.

The Cast: Lionel Barrymore (Tim Benton), Lewis Stone (Gabriel Service, Sr.), Benita Hume (Mrs. Isobel Service), Elizabeth Allan (Caroline Service), Phillips Holmes (Michael Service), Colin Clive (Geoffrey Fielding), Alec B. Francis (Mr. Birkenshaw), Doris Lloyd (Mrs. Lil Benton), Halliwell Hobbes (Mr. James Felton), Douglas Walton (Willie Benton), Viva Tattersall (Miss Elsie Benton), Lawrence Grant (Philip Bendicott), George K. Arthur (Mr. Tressitt, salesman), Charles Irwin (Mr. Burton, clerk), Billy Bevan (Mr. Barker, night watchman), Marion Clayton Anderson (Gertie), Rita Carlyle (Mrs. Kentish), Alan Edwards (Gray Mortimer), Ethel Griffies (Miss Judd), Eily Malyon (Mrs. Munsey), Edgar Norton (Mr. Elliott), Harry Allen (Cab Driver), Leonard Carey (Employee talking to Miss Judd), Elspeth Dudgeon (Old Servant), Grayce Hampton (Woman buying dog basket), Tempe Pigott (Woman looking for Plumbing department).

Lionel Barrymore (1878-1954), MGM's super character star of the 1930s, won an Oscar for *A Free Soul* (1931), and was unforgettable as Kringelein of *Grand Hotel* and the Mad Monk in *Rasputin and the Empress* (both 1932). His horror credits included Metro's *Mark of the Vampire* (1935) and *The Devil-Doll* (1936), both directed by Tod Browning. Later wheelchair bound, he stayed on at MGM, playing Dr. Gillespie in the *Dr. Kildare* series, Gramps in *On Borrowed Time* (1939), and, loaned to RKO, the unspeakable Mr. Potter in Frank Capra's *It's a Wonderful Life* (1946). He also directed films, including MGM's *Madame X* (1929) and John Gilbert's disastrous *His Glorious Night* (1929).

Lewis Stone (1879-1953) was, like Barrymore, an MGM fixture, having joined the studio at its inception in 1924. He appeared with Garbo, Harlow, Crawford, and Helen Hayes. Stone was memorable as the scarfaced Dr. Otternschlag in *Grand Hotel*, and later played Judge Hardy in Metro's popular Andy Hardy series. Horror fans perhaps recall him most vividly in MGM's *The Mask of Fu Manchu* (1932), in which Karloff's Fu had Stone tied to a seesaw and dipped into a pit of crocodiles (he escapes).

Benita Hume (1906-1967), born in England, is maybe best remembered as Rita, Jane's cousin, in MGM's *Tarzan Escapes* (1936). Her second husband was Ronald Colman (from 1938 to his death in 1958; they had a daughter) and her third spouse was George Sanders (from 1959 until her death in 1967).

Elizabeth Allan (1910-1990), born in England, had a nice run at MGM in such roles as David's gentle mother in *David Copperfield* (1935), and Lucie Manette in *A Tale of Two Cities* (1935). She acted with a number of horror stars: Lionel Atwill in *The Solitaire Man* (1933), Bela Lugosi in *Mark of the Vampire* (1935), and Basil Rathbone in *David Copperfield* and *A Tale of Two Cities*; her final film was England's *The Haunted Strangler* (1958), in which Karloff strangled her. Ms. Allan's tempestuous time in Hollywood climaxed when she sued MGM; the studio had announced her for star roles in *The Citadel* (1938) and *Goodbye, Mr. Chips* (1939), both filmed at Metro's British studio, but replaced her respectively with Rosalind Russell and Greer Garson. She won her suit, but MGM appealed and blackballed her in Hollywood. Thereafter Ms. Allan acted in England, and was named Great Britain's Top Female TV personality of 1952 for her appearances on England's equivalent of *What's My Line?* Her final credit: British TV's *The Very Merry Widow* (1967-1968). Incidentally, Ms. Allan's marriage to agent Bill O'Bryen, who later worked as an executive for Alexander Korda and Michael Balcon, lasted until O'Bryen's death in 1977. She did not remarry.

Phillips Holmes (1907-1942), born in Michigan, starred as the doomed protagonist of *An American Tragedy* (1931). His sensitive, pretty-boy image, a lá David Manners, was a bit passé by the late 1930s, and his final film was the British-made *Housemaster* (1938). Holmes joined the Royal Canadian Air Force in 1941. A plane carrying him and six classmates collided with another plane mid-air over Ontario on August 12, 1942, killing all onboard.

Clarence Brown (1890-1987), a mainstay of Metro-Goldwyn-Mayer, holds the dubious record of most Best Director Oscar nominations without a win: *Anna Christie* (1930), *Romance* (1930), *A Free Soul* (1931), *The Human Comedy* (1943), *National Velvet* (1944) and *The Yearling* (1936). He was a fighter pilot in World War I, maintained his pilot's license in later years, and donated money to his alma mater, The University of Tennessee, to build its Clarence Brown Theatre. He left the college an additional $12,000,000 after his death.

The Key. Warner Bros., 1934. Producer, Robert Presnell, Sr. Director, Michael Curtiz. Screenplay, Laird Doyle, based on the play by R. Gore Brown and J.L. Hardy. Cinematographer, Ernest Haller. Editor, Thomas Richards. Art Director, Robert M. Haas. Gowns, Orry-Kelly. Music Director, Leo F. Forbstein. Props, Tom More. Dialogue Director, Frank McDonald. Technical Advisor, Thomas MacLaughlin. Running time, 71 minutes.

New York opening, Strand Theatre, May 29, 1934. Los Angeles opening, Warner Bros. Hollywood and Downtown Theatres, July 4, 1934.

The Cast: William Powell (Captain Bill Tennant), Edna Best (Norah Kerr), Colin Clive (Captain Andrew "Andy" Kerr), Hobart Cavanaugh (Homer, Tennant's aide), Halliwell Hobbes (General C.O. Furlong), Donald Crisp (Peadar Conlan), J.M. Kerrigan (O'Duffy), Henry O'Neill (Dan), Phil Regan (Young Irishman killed by Andrew), Arthur Treacher (Lt. Merriman, Furlong's aide), Maxine Doyle (Pauline O'Connor), Arthur Ayelsworth (Kirby), Gertrude Short (Evie, a barmaid), Anne Shirley (billed as Dawn O'Day, Flower Girl), Edward Cooper (Lloyd), Robert Homans (Patrick, a bartender), Pat Somerset (Laramour), Charles Irwin (Master of Ceremonies), John Elliott (Padre), Ralph Remley (Mack, Rivoli bartender), Lowin Cross (Dispatch Rider), Douglas Gordon (Telegraph operator), Luke Cosgrave (Man praising Conlan), Sam Harris (British officer), Lew Kelly (Angular man), Dixie Loftin (Irish woman), Mary MacLaren (Street walker), James May (Driver), Wyndham Standing (Officer), Dorothy Vernon (Woman on street), Olaf Hytten, Desmond Roberts, David Thursby (Regulars), Aggie Herring, Kathrin Clare Ward (Flower women).

William Powell (1892-1984) acted on the New York stage, was on contract to Paramount and later Warner Bros., but found his major stardom at MGM, in *The Thin Man* series with Myrna Loy and the title role in *The Great Ziegfeld* (1936). His legendary status in Hollywood includes having been married to Carole Lombard (1931 to 1933, divorced) and having been in love with Jean Harlow at the time of her 1937 death. Powell's last film was *Mr. Roberts* (1955) and he retired to Palm Springs with his third wife, actress Diana Lewis, avoiding any temptations of a comeback.

Edna Best (1900-1974) was a great star of the London stage. *The Key* was her only Hollywood film of the mid-1930s. She had a featured role in Alfred Hitchcock's British-filmed original *The Man Who Knew Too Much* (1934), and later had a nice showcase as Leslie Howard's scorned wife in *Intermezzo: A Love Story* (1939). Another memorable film role: Martha the housekeeper in *The Ghost and Mrs. Muir* (1947).

Michael Curtiz (1886-1962), Warner Bros.' legendary, Budapest-born director, won an Oscar for *Casablanca* (1943) and received Academy nominations for *Captain Blood* (1935), *Four Daughters* (1938), and *Yankee Doodle Dandy* (1942). He could direct anything and everything, including horror films: the early Technicolor chillers *Doctor X* (1932) and *Mystery of the Wax Museum* (1933), both starring Lionel Atwill, and *The Walking Dead* (1936), starring Boris Karloff.

Ernest Haller, *The Key's* cameraman, would win an Oscar for Best Color Cinematography (shared with Ray Rennahan) for *Gone With the Wind* (1939).

Jane Eyre. Monogram, 1934. Vice president in Charge of Production, Trem Carr. Producer, Ben Verschleiser. Director, Christy Cabanne. Screenplay, Adele Comandini, based on the novel *Jane Eyre* by Charlotte Bronte. Technical Director, E.R. Hickson. Cinematographer, Robert Planck. Sound, Ralph Shugart. Editor, Carl Pierson. Music Composer (stock music), Mischa Bakaleinikoff. Musical Director, Abe Meyer. Costume Jeweler, Eugene Joseff. Running Time, 62 minutes.

Release Date: October 1, 1934.

The Cast: Virginia Bruce (Jane Eyre), Colin Clive (Edward Rochester), Beryl Mercer (Mrs. Fairfax), David Torrence (Mr. Brocklehurst), Aileen Pringle (Blanche Ingram), Edith Fellows (Adele Rochester), John Rogers (Sam Poole), Jean Darling (Jane Eyre as a child), Lionel Belmore (Lord Ingram), Jameson Thomas (Charles Craig), Ethel Griffies (Grace Poole), Claire Du Brey (Mrs. Rochester), William Burress (Minister), Joan Standing (Daisy), Richard Quine (John Reed), Desmond Roberts (Dr. John Rivers), Gretta Gould (Miss Temple), Anne Howard (Georgianna Reed), Gail Kaye (Mary Lane), Edith Kingston (Lady Ingram), Clarissa Selwynne (Mrs. Reed), Hylda Tyson (Bessie), William Wagner (Halliburton), Olaf Hytten (Jeweler).

Virginia Bruce (1910-1982) married Sound Films casualty John Gilbert August 11, 1932. They had a daughter and divorced May 25, 1934, just as Virginia was shooting *Jane Eyre*. She later wed director J. Walter Ruben (one son) and married twice (and also divorced twice) Turkish producer/director Ali Ipar, who later entered a shipping business that eventually put him in jail. Bruce was a knockout in *The Great Ziegfeld*, MGM's 1936 Best Picture Academy Award winner, as "Audrey Dane," based on Ziegfeld's real-life mistress, Lillian Lorraine. Horror fans likely recall Ms. Bruce in MGM's *Kongo* (1932), in which she's pulled through a swamp by a wire inserted into her tongue, and Universal's *The Invisible Woman* (1940), in which she played the title role.

Christy Cabanne (1888-1950) directed over 160 films. He also worked as an actor in early silent films and as a writer throughout his career. A few Cabanne favorites: *Another Face* (RKO, 1935), in which gangster Brian Donlevy crashes the movies after plastic surgery; *The Mummy's Hand* (Universal, 1940), in which Tom Tyler's Mummy carries off Peggy Moran; and *Scared to Death* (Golden Gate Pictures, 1947), in which stars Bela Lugosi and George Zucco appear in a cheap two-color process called "Cinecolor."

Other Versions of *Jane Eyre* include: 20th Century-Fox's 1944 *Jane Eyre* starring Joan Fontaine and Orson Welles; the British 1971 TV movie, starring Susannah York and George C. Scott (who won an Emmy as Rochester); the BBC's 1983 TV mini-series, starring Zelah Clarke and Timothy Dalton; the British 1997 TV movie, starring Samantha Morton and Ciaran Hinds; the BBC's 2006 TV mini-series, starring Ruth Wilson and Toby Stephens; the BBC's 2011 feature film starring Mia Wasikowska and Michael Fassbender.

One More River. Universal, 1934. Producer, Carl Laemmle, Jr. Director, James Whale. Screenplay, R.C. Sherriff (William J. Hurlbut, un-credited), based on the novel by John Galsworthy. Cinematographer, John J. Mescall. Art Director, Charles D. Hall. Music, W. Franke Harling. Editor, Ted Kent. Supervising Editor, Maurice Pivar. Special Effects, John P. Fulton. Makeup, William Ely. Hairdresser, Margaret Donovan. Gowns, Vera West. Sound, William Hedgcock, Gilbert Kurland. Assistant Directors, Harry Mancke, Joseph A. McDonough. Second cameraman, Alan Jones. Script Supervisor, Helen McCaffrey. Jeweler, Eugene Joseff. Running Time, 88 minutes.
New York opening, Radio City Music Hall, August 9, 1934. Los Angeles opening, Hollywood Pantages Theatre, August 9, 1934.
The Cast: Diana Wynyard (Clare Corven), Frank Lawton (Tony Croom), Colin Clive (Sir Gerald Corven), Mrs. Patrick Campbell (Lady Mont), Jane Wyatt (Dinny), Lionel Atwill (Mr. Brough), Alan Mowbray (Mr. Forsyte), Reginald Denny (David Dornford), C. Aubrey Smith (The General), Henry Stephenson (Sir Lawrence Mont), Kathleen Howard (Lady Charwell), Gilbert Emery (Judge), E.E. Clive (Mr. Chayne), Robert Greig (Blore the Butler), J. Gunnis Davis (Benjy), Tempe Pigott (Mrs. Purdy), Snub Pollard (George), Billy Bevan (Cloakroom Attendant), Reginald Sheffield (Tommy), Doris Llewelyn (Vi), Arthur Hoyt (Perkins), Mary Gordon (Cook), J.C. Fowler (Sir John), Harold Nelson (Jury Foreman), Alfonso Corelli (Orchestra Leader), James Whale (Cheerleader at Political Rally).

Diana Wynyard (1906-1964) had starred with the three Barrymores in *Rasputin and the Empress* (1932) and was Oscar-nominated for Fox's *Cavalcade* (1933), which won the Best Picture Academy Award for 1933. As ballyhoo for that acclaimed film, Ms. Wynyard placed her high-heel prints in the forecourt of Grauman's Chinese Theatre on January 26, 1933. She was the first British actress to do so. Leaving Hollywood after *One More River*, Wynyard had an outstanding success as the nearly hysterical heroine of the British film *Gaslight* (1940), unforgettable in the role that won Ingrid Bergman an Oscar for the Hollywood 1944 version. Her true passion, however, was the classical stage. She received the Commander of the Order of the British Empire in 1953. In October of 1963, seven months before her death, Wynyard played Queen Gertrude to Peter O'Toole's Hamlet in the inaugural National Theatre production at the Old Vic in London, directed by Laurence Olivier. Lady Diana Wynyard was married and divorced twice; her first husband was the distinguished British director, Sir Carol Reed.

Frank Lawton (1904-1969), born Frank Lawton Mokeley in London, played the grown David in MGM's *David Copperfield* (1935), was the romantic lead in Universal's Karloff and Lugosi *The*

Invisible Ray (1936) and MGM's *The Devil-Doll* (directed by Tod Browning,1936). He worked on the London and Broadway stage and was married to the famed British actress Evelyn Laye, from 1934 to his death in 1969. Lawton served with distinction in France during World War II.

Lionel Atwill (1885-1946), born in England, was one of Broadway's major stars of the 1920s, a top Hollywood character player of the 1930s, and a legendary star of the horror genre. He married four times and his colorful life included a lurid sex scandal in the 1940s that eventually found him guilty of perjury and temporarily out of the movies. He was fatally ill (cancer) while playing the villain in Universal's *Lost City of the Jungle* (1946), and the studio completed his scenes with a double (George Sorel).

Alan Mowbray (1896-1969), also British-born, was a prolific character actor, as well as a member of "The Bundy Drive Boys"—John Barrymore, Errol Flynn W.C. Fields, John Carradine, Thomas Mitchell, Anthony Quinn, and the artist John Decker, all hard-drinking roisterers. As noted in the text, Mowbray was one of the pallbearers at Colin Clive's funeral.

As for James Whale's cameo in *One More River* ... He appears at a political rally in a dark overcoat and hat, removes the hat, turns his back to the camera, and yells, "Now, let's have a big cheer for David Dornford, MP for Condaford. Hip-hip ... " And the crowd shouts," Hooray!"

Clive of India. 20th Century Pictures, 1935. Producer, Darryl F. Zanuck. Associate Producers, William Goetz, William Griffith. Director, Richard Boleslawski. Screenplay, W.P. Lipscomb, R.J. Minney. Cinematographer, J. Peverell Marley. Music, Alfred Newman. Editor, Barbara McLean. Art Director, Richard Day. Costume Designer, Omar Kiam. Sound, Roger Heman, Sr., Vinton Vernon. Running time, 94 minutes.

New York opening, Rivoli Theatre, January 17, 1935. Los Angeles opening, Grauman's Chinese Theatre and Loew's State Theatre, February 22, 1935.

The Cast: Ronald Colman (Robert Clive), Loretta Young (Margaret Maskelyne), Colin Clive (Captain Johnstone), Francis Lister (Edmund Maskelyne), C. Aubrey Smith (Prime Minister), Cesar Romero (Mir Jaffar), Montagu Love (Gov. Pigot), Lumsden Hare (Sgt. Clark), Ferdinand Munier (Admiral Charles Watson), Gilbert Emery (Mr. Sullivan), Leo G. Carroll (Mr. Manning), Etienne Girardot (Mr. Warburton), Robert Greig (Mr. Pemberton), Mischa Auer (King Suraj Ud Dowlah), Ferdinand Gottschalk (Old member), Doris Lloyd (Mrs. Nixon), Edward Cooper (Clive's butler), Eily Malyon (Mrs. Clifford), Joseph Tozer (Sir Frith), Phyllis Clare (Margaret's friend), Leonard Mudie (General Burgoyne), Phillip Dare (Captain George), Ian Wolfe (Mr. Kent), Wyndham Standing (Col. Townsend), Neville Clark (Mr. Vincent), Phyllis Coghlan (Betty, Margaret's maid), Bruce Cook (Johnny, boy bugler), Herbert Bunston (First director), Lionel Belmore (Official at reception), Ted Billings (Old soldier), Vernon Downing (Mr. Stringer), Olaf Hytten (Parson at Hustine), Peter Shaw (Mr. Miller), Ann Shaw (Lady Lindley), Pat Somerset (Lt. Walsh), Charles Irwin (Officer), Barbara Lee (Clive's daughter), David Wade (Clive's son), Connie Leon (Ayah), D'Arcy Corrigan (Merchant), Mary Maclaren (Nurse), Murdock MacQuarrie (Sneering Man), Beatrice Griffith, Etta Lee (Slave girls), Don Ameche (Prisoner in the Black Hole of Calcutta), John Carradine (Drunken-faced clerk).

Ronald Colman (1891-1958) starred in such classics as *A Tale of Two Cities* (1935), *Lost Horizon* (1937), *The Prisoner of Zenda* (1937), and *Random Harvest* (1942), and won a Best Actor Oscar for *A Double Life* (1947). Nate D. Sanders Memorabilia auctioned his Oscar in 2012 and it fetched $206,250.

Loretta Young (1913-2000) also began her career in 1917 as a child actress. She won a Best Actress Oscar for *The Farmer's Daughter* (1947), the same year Ronald Colman won his Oscar. She's also well remembered for TV's *The Loretta Young Show* (1953-1961) and *The New Loretta Young Show* (1962-1963).

Richard Boleslawski (1889-1937), formerly of the Moscow Art Theatre, directed great stars in superb films: John, Ethel, and Lionel Barrymore in *Rasputin and the Empress* (1932, replacing Charles J. Brabin and directing most of it, including the episode where John's Prince assassinates Lionel's Rasputin); Clark Gable and Myrna Loy in *Men in White* (1934); Greta Garbo in *The Painted Veil* (1934); Fredric March and Charles Laughton in *Les Miserables* (1935); Marlene

Dietrich and Charles Boyer in *The Garden of Allah* (1936); and Irene Dunne in *Theodora Goes Wild* (1936).

Alfred Newman (1901-1970), who provided *Clive of India*'s music, would also be the musical director of *History Is Made at Night*. He'd win nine Oscars during his career, and he too is one of the composers honored in 1999 with his appearance on a $.33 stamp

By the way, Don Ameche's appearance as a prisoner in the Black Hole of Calcutta is unconfirmed. Also, in the print recently shown on TCM, John Carradine wasn't in evidence as a clerk, drunken-faced or otherwise.

The Right to Live. Warner Bros., 1935. Director, William Keighley. Screenplay, Ralph Block, based on Somerset Maugham's play, *The Sacred Flame*. Cinematographer, Sid Hickox. Editor, Jack Killifer. Art Director, Esdras Hartley. Gowns, Orry-Kelly. Music, Bernhard Kaun. Sound, Dolph Thomas. Hair Stylist, Ruth Pursley. Props, William L. Kuehl. Production Manager, Robert Fellows. Running time, 69 minutes.

Los Angeles opening, Warners Downtown Theatre, February 7, 1935. New York City opening, Rivoli Theatre, February 15, 1935.

The Cast: Josephine Hutchinson (Stella Trent), George Brent (Colin Trent), Colin Clive (Maurice Trent), Peggy Wood (Nurse Wayland), Henrietta Crosman (Mrs. Trent), C. Aubrey Smith (The Major), Leo G. Carroll (Dr. Harvester), Phyllis Coghlan (Alice), Claude King (Mr. Pride), Nella Walker (Mrs. Pride), Halliwell Hobbes (Sir Stephen Barr), J. Gunnis Davis (Harvey, gardener), John J. Richardson (John, chauffeur), Forrester Harvey (English Bobby), Bill Elliott (Wedding Guest), Vesey O'Davoren, Alexander Pollard (Waiters).

Josephine Hutchinson (1903-1998) had been an acclaimed star of Eva Le Gallienne's Civic Repertory Company, enjoying a special triumph in the title role of Le Gallienne's legendary 1932 *Alice in Wonderland*. (Ms. Hutchinson was 29 years old when she played Alice.) Signed by Warner Bros., she was impressive in such films as *Oil for the Lamps of China* (1935) and *The Story of Louis Pasteur* (1936). However, she was too genteel to engage in the battles for roles that regularly erupted on the Warner lot, and departed. She was a classy and attractive Elsa von Frankenstein in Universal's *Son of Frankenstein* (1939), with a smashing fur hat and a terrific scream, and later had a long career as a film and TV character actress. She wed three times: her second husband was her agent, James Townsend; after his death, she married actor Staats Cotsworth (1908-1979). "Jo" spent her late years residing in Cotsworth's penthouse on East 55th Street in New York City, a lovely, gracious lady.

George Brent (1904-1979) was an all-purpose leading man at Warner Bros., with a stolid presence that belied his true personality. Born in Ireland, he reportedly served as an assassin and messenger for Sinn Fein in the early 1920s, later was a licensed pilot, supposedly had a "tumultuous" two-year affair with Bette Davis (with whom he co-starred in 11 films). He married six times (his second wife was Ruth Chatterton; his fourth, Ann Sheridan). George Brent retired from the screen to raise racehorses.

Peggy Wood (1892-1978) had several distinctions in her long career: Noel Coward wrote two stage roles especially for her, the musical *Bitter Sweet* (1929) and the comedy *Blithe Spirit* (1941); she starred in the title role of the early TV series *Mama* (1949-1957); and she played the Mother Abbess, singing "Climb Every Mountain" in Rodgers and Hammerstein's *The Sound of Music* (1965), for which she received a Best Supporting Actress Oscar nomination.

William Keighley (1889-1984) was a prominent director at Warner Bros., where he directed such studio stars as Edward G. Robinson and Humphrey Bogart (*Bullets or Ballots,* 1936), Errol Flynn (*The Prince and the Pauper,* 1937), and James Cagney and Bette Davis (*The Bride Came C. O.D.,* 1941). Keighley was co-director of *The Adventures of Robin Hood* (1938), directing the location work in Chico, California before Michael Curtiz replaced him. His second wife was actress Genevieve Tobin, whom he wed in 1938 and to whom he remained married until his death.

Warners' earlier version, 1929's *The Sacred Flame,* starred Pauline Frederick as Stella, Conrad Nagel as Maurice, and Walter Byron as Colin. Archie Mayo directed.

Bride of Frankenstein. **Colin, Elsa Lanchester, Ernest Thesiger.**

Bride of Frankenstein. Universal, 1935. Producer, Carl Laemmle, Jr. Director, James Whale. Screenplay, William J. Hurlbut, from an adaptation by Hurlbut and John L. Balderston, suggested by the 1818 novel *Frankenstein* by Mary Wollstonecraft Shelley. Cinematographer, John J. Mescall. Editor, Ted Kent. Music, Franz Waxman. Art Director, Charles D. Hall. Makeup, Jack P. Pierce. Special Effects, John P. Fulton. Special Electrical Properties, Kenneth Strickfaden. Sound Recorder, Gilbert Kurland. Assistant Directors, Harry Menke and Joseph McDonough. Shooting Title: *The Return of Frankenstein.* Running Time, 75 minutes.

Los Angeles opening, Hollywood Pantages Theatre, April 20, 1935. New York opening, Roxy Theatre, May 10, 1935.

The Cast: Boris Karloff (The Monster), Colin Clive (Henry Frankenstein), Valerie Hobson (Elizabeth), Ernest Thesiger (Dr. Septimus Pretorius), Elsa Lanchester (Mary Wollstonecraft Shelley/The Monster's Mate), Gavin Gordon (Lord Byron), Douglas Walton (Percy Shelley), Una O'Connor (Minnie), E.E. Clive (The Burgomaster), Lucien Prival (Albert, Chief Servidor), O.P Heggie (The Hermit), Dwight Frye (Karl), Reginald Barlow (Hans), Mary Gordon (Hans' Wife), Anne Darling (Shepherdess), Ted Billings (Ludwig), Gunnis Davis (Uncle Glutz), Tempe Pigott (Auntie Glutz), Neil Fitzgerald (Rudy), John Carradine (A Hunter), Walter Brennan (A Neighbor), Helen Parrish (Communion Girl), Edwin Mordant (The Coroner), Lucio Villegas (Priest), Brenda Fowler (A Mother), Sara Schwartz (Marta), Arthur S. Byron (Little King), Joan Woodbury (Little Queen), Norman Ainsley (Little Bishop), Peter Shaw (Little Devil), Kansas DeForrest (Little Ballerina), Josephine McKim (Little Mermaid), Billy Barty (Little Baby), John Curtis, Frank Terry (Hunters), Rollo Lloyd, Mary Stewart (Neighbors), Frank Benson, Ed Piel, Sr., Anders Van Haden, John George, Grace Cunard, Maurice Black, Peter Shaw (Villagers), Marilyn Harris (Little girl in forest), Monty Montague, Peter Shaw (Doubles for Thesiger), George DeNormand (Double for Barlow).

Valerie Hobson (1917-1998) appeared in several Universal melodramas of the era, including *Werewolf of London* (1935). She became a major star of British cinema in such films as *Great Expectations* (1946), and starred as Anna in the 1953 London production of Rodgers and Hammerstein's *The King and I* at Theatre Royal, Drury Lane. (Herbert Lom played the King.) Her first husband was film producer Anthony Havelock-Allan, with whom she had two children; her second was politician John Profumo, who eventually became Secretary of State for War, and with whom she had one child. Profumo's brief affair with showgirl Christine Keeler (who was at the same time sleeping with a Russian military attaché) became in 1963 the most explosive political scandal in England's history, and Hobson won worldwide admiration for how graciously she stood by her husband. Profumo subsequently devoted himself to helping the poor in London; he died in 2006. Valerie spent her final years doing charitable work for mentally handicapped children and lepers.

Ernest Thesiger (1879-1961), a major figure of the London stage, had appeared with Boris Karloff in *The Old Dark House* (1932) and *The Ghoul* (1933). Later film appearances included playing "the Silk-Stocking Strangler" in *They Drive by Night* (1938), the Undertaker in *A Christmas Carol* (1951), and Emperor Tiberius in *The Robe* (1953). He died January 14, 1961, the eve of his 82nd birthday. In his unpublished memoir, Thesiger writes little about *Bride of Frankenstein*, focusing on his dislike of Jack Pierce for the misery he caused Thesiger while making him up.

Elsa Lanchester (1902-1986) received Best Supporting Actress nominations for *Come to the Stable* (1949) and *Witness for the Prosecution* (1957), winning a Golden Globe Award for the latter. She and Charles Laughton were married from 1929 until Laughton's death in 1962.

Una O'Connor (1880-1959), born in Ireland, was also uproarious as Mrs. Hall in James Whale's *The Invisible Man* (1933). Her final film: *Witness for the Prosecution* (1957). Whale left her $10,000 in his will.

O.P. Heggie (1877-1936), born in Australia, had a similar role to the Hermit as "Abbe Faria" in 1934's *The Count of Monte Cristo*. He died February 7, 1936, about a week before the Hollywood premiere of his final film, John Ford's *The Prisoner of Shark Island*.

As for Dwight Frye ... Whale actually combined two roles for him in *Bride of Frankenstein*: "Fritz," Pretorius' gallows bird ghoul, and "Karl," the village idiot who kills his Uncle and Auntie Glutz and blames it on the Monster. The combined character was called simply "Karl" and the subplot of his robbery and murders cut before release. Frye would be cut altogether from *Son of Frankenstein* (reportedly as an angry villager, 1939), and showed up (as a villager) in *The Ghost of Frankenstein* (1942) and *Frankenstein Meets the Wolf Man* (1943). On Sunday night, November 7, 1943, Frye suffered a fatal heart attack on a bus as he, his wife and his 12-year-old son were returning home from a double feature at the Hollywood Pantages Theatre. Dwight Frye was only 44 years old. Frye's son, Dwight David Frye (1930-2003), collaborated with this author and James T. Coughlin on the biography *Dwight Frye's Last Laugh* (Midnight Marquee Press, 1996).

John Carradine (1906-1988), born in New York City, was, at the time of *Bride of Frankenstein*, less than a year away from winning fame in the aforementioned *The Prisoner of Shark Island*, in which he played the vicious jailer.

John J. Mescall (1899-1962) began his career in 1920, was cinematographer of *The Black Cat* (1934), and was James Whale's cameraman on *By Candlelight* (1933), *One More River* (1934), *Show Boat* (1936), and *The Road Back* (1937). A later credit: *Not of This Earth* (1957). Mescall was an alcoholic who allegedly ended up on Skid Row.

Franz Waxman, who composed the *Bride of Frankenstein*'s magnificent score, won two Oscars—for *Sunset Blvd.* (1950) and *A Place in the Sun* (1951). Waxman was one of six film composers—Bernard Herrmann, Erich Wolfgang Korngold, Alfred Newman, Max Steiner, and Dimitri Tiomkin were the others—to appear on $.33 commemorative postage stamps in 1999.

Bride of Frankenstein was the only one of Universal's classic horror films to receive an Academy Award nomination: Gilbert Kurland for Best Sound. Kurland lost to Douglas Shearer (brother of actress Norma Shearer) for *Naughty Marietta*.

A remake of *Bride of Frankenstein*, more or less: *The Bride* (1985), directed by Franc Roddam, starred Sting as Frankenstein, Clancy Brown as the Monster, and Jennifer Beals as "Eva," the Bride.

Bride of Frankenstein is so acclaimed that it's almost refreshing to find a nay-sayer among the 1935 critics. Consider this review from the *London Times* (July 1, 1935): "It is fortunate that the film has its moments of unconscious (*sic*) humor, for otherwise it would be an intolerably morbid affair ... What period, for instance, does the director imagine he is in? As Frankenstein, the creator of the Monster, Colin Clive looks, and is dressed, like the kind of nice modern young man who is the pillar of his local tennis club; the peasants have a definitely medieval air about them; and Mary Shelley (Miss Elsa Lanchester) was early 19th century ... It is sad to see such personalities as Mr. Thesiger and Miss Lanchester, to say nothing of Mr. Boris Karloff himself, wasted in a production with so ignoble a motive."

The Girl from 10th Avenue. Warner Bros./First National, 1935. Producers, Henry Blanke and Robert Lord. Director, Alfred E. Green. Screenplay, Charles Kenyon, from a play by Hubert Henry Davies. Cinematographer, James Van Trees. Editor, Owen Marks. Music, Heinz Roemheld. Musical Director, Leo F. Forbstein. Composer, main and end title music, Bernhard Kaun. Composer, love theme, Allie Wrubel. Art Director, John Hughes. Gowns, Orry-Kelly. Costume Jeweler, Eugene Joseff. Running Time, 69 minutes.

New York opening, The Capitol Theatre, May 24, 1935. Los Angeles opening, Warners Downtown Theatre, June 27, 1935.

The Cast: Bette Davis (Miriam Brady), Ian Hunter (Geoffrey Sherwood), Colin Clive (John Marland), Alison Skipworth (Mrs. Martin), John Eldredge (Hugh Brown), Phillip Reed (Tony Hewlett), Katharine Alexander (Valentine Marland), Helen Jerome Eddy (Miss Mansfield), Gordon Elliott (James, College Club clerk), Edward McWade (Art clerk), Adrian Rosley (Marcel), Andre Cheron (Max, Waldorf headwaiter), Charles Fallon (George, Waldorf waiter), Edgar Norton (Valentine's butler), Mary Treen (Secretary), Matty King (Taxi Driver), Tom Mahoney (Public Library janitor), Eddie Lee (Geoffrey's servant), John Quillan (Hotel Bellboy), Heinie Conklin (Waiter at Marchand's), Jack Hatfield (Reporter), John J. Richardson (Elevator Operator), Bess Flowers (Valentine's Dinner Party guest), James Donlan, Davison Clark (Detectives), Sam Ash, Jack Norton, Bruce Warren (College Club Guests outside bar), Brooks Benedict, Wedgewood Nowell (Waldorf Diners).

Bette Davis (1908-1989), a Warner Bros. contractee, had scored a hit as the vile Mildred on loan-out to RKO for *Of Human Bondage* (1934). She ran as a write-in-vote candidate for the Academy's Best Actress, losing to officially nominated Claudette Colbert of *It Happened One Night*. Davis won the Oscar for *Dangerous*, her final Warner Bros. release of 1935, likely to compensate for the *Of Human Bondage* slight. She won a second Oscar for Warners' *Jezebel* (1938). She'd receive eight additional Oscar nominations, for such films as *All About Eve* (1950) and *Whatever Happened to Baby Jane?* (1962).

Ian Hunter (1900-1975), British and born in South Africa, was on contract in Hollywood to Warner Bros., where his best-remembered role might be Richard the Lion-Heart in *The Adventures of Robin Hood* (1938). Later at MGM, he was notable as the Christ-like "Cambreau" in *Strange Cargo* (1940) and as Dr. Lanyon in *Dr. Jekyll and Mr. Hyde* (1941). Another excellent Hunter performance: King Edward in Universal's *Tower of London* (1939), co-starring with Basil Rathbone and Boris Karloff. Hunter spent the post-Word War II years and afterwards acting in England.

Alison Skipworth (1863-1952), co-starred three times with W.C. Fields at Paramount: *If I Had a Million* (1932), *Tillie and Gus* (1933), and *Six of a Kind* (1934). Of note: In Warners' *Satan Met a Lady*, a 1936 version of *The Maltese Falcon*, Ms. Skipworth played "Madame Barabbas," a female version of "The Fat Man" played by Sydney Greenstreet in the 1941 *The Maltese Falcon*.

Katharine Alexander (1898-1977) appeared in such film roles as Madame de Lys in *The Hunchback of Notre Dame* (1939), and was an accomplished stage actress, whose credits included co-starring with Paul Muni in the 1949 London production of *Death of a Salesman*.

Alfred E. Green (1889-1960) had a directing career dating back to 1916. At Warners, he directed Bette Davis in her Oscar-winning performance in *Dangerous* (1935), later directed Columbia's box office smash *The Jolson Story* (1946), and directed 46 episodes of TV's *The Millionaire* (1955-1958).

The play *Outcast* opened in New York in 1914, and there were three other film versions (all titled *Outcast*) that pre-dated *The Girl from 10th Avenue*: 1917, 1922, and 1928 (this version starring Corinne Griffith, who acted with Colin in 1932's *Lily Christine*).

A by-the-way for horror fans: Edgar Norton (1868-1953), who played Valentine's butler, portrayed Jekyll's butler Poole in *Dr. Jekyll and Mr. Hyde* (1931) and Wolf von Frankenstein's butler Benson in *Son of Frankenstein* (1939).

Another by-the-way for horror fans: Heinz Roemheld (1901-1985), credited with "Music" for *The Girl from 10th Avenue*, assembled the classical score for *The Black Cat* (1934); and Bernhard Kaun (1899-1980), who composed *The Girl from 10th Avenue*'s main and end title music, composed the main credit music for *Frankenstein* (1931).

Mad Love. Metro-Goldwyn-Mayer, 1935. Producer, John W. Considine, Jr., Director, Karl Freund. Screenplay, P.J. Wolfson and John L. Balderston, based on an adaptation by Guy Endore, from Florence Crewe-Jones' translation/adaptation of Maurice Renard's novel, *Les Mains d'Orlac*. (Leon Gordon, Edgar Allan Woolf, Gladys Von Ettinghausen, Leo Wolfson, un-credited contributing writers). Cinematographers, Chester Lyons and Gregg Toland. Music, Dimitri Tiomkin. Musical Director, Oscar Radin. Organ music composer, David Snell. Editor, Hugh Wynn. Art Director, Cedric Gibbons (William A. Hornig and Edwin B. Willis, Associates). Wardrobe: Dolly Tree. Recording Director, Douglas Shearer. Makeup, Norbert A. Myles. Assistant Director, Dolph Zimmer. Dialogue Director, John Langan. Running Time, 68 minutes. Alternate Titles: *The Mad Doctor of Paris* and *The Hands of Orlac*.

Los Angeles opening, Hollywood Pantages Theatre, July 24, 1935. New York opening, Roxy Theatre, August 2, 1935.

The Cast: Peter Lorre (Dr. Gogol), Frances Drake (Yvonne Orlac), Colin Clive (Stephen Orlac), Ted Healy (Reagan), Sarah Haden (Marie), Isabel Jewell (Marianne), Edward Brophy (Rollo), Henry Kolker (Prefect of Police Rosset), Harold Huber (Thief), Keye Luke (Dr. Wong), Ian Wolfe (Henry Orlac), May Beatty (Francoise, Gogol's housekeeper), Charles Trowbridge (Dr. Marbeau), Robert Emmett Keane (Drunk), Clarence Hummel Wilson (Piano man), William "Billy" Gilbert (Man on train with dog), Murray Kinnell (Charles), Edward Lippy (Pierre, Henry Orlac's Clerk), Sarah Padden (Mother), Cora Sue Collins (Child patient), Edward Norris (Man outside horror show), Mary Jo Mathews (Woman outside horror show), Frank Darien (Lavin, waxworks proprietor), Rollo Lloyd (Varsac, fingerprint expert), Nell Craig (Nurse Suzanne), Maurice Brierre (Taxi Driver), Julie Carter (Nurse), Hooper Atchley (Conductor), Sam Ash, Christian Frank, Robert Graves, Roger Gray (Detectives), George Davis (Chauffeur), Otto Hoffman (Blind Man), Mark Loebell (Prince in horror act), Ramsay Hill (Duke in horror act), Carl Stockdale (Notary in horror act), Al Borgato (Doorman), Harvey Clark (Station Master), Alphonz Ethier (Fingerprint man), Russ Powell (Gendarme), Earl M. Pingree (Detective), Jacques Vanaire (Police broadcaster), Matty Roubert (Newsboy), Rolfe Sedan (Gendarme directing traffic), Michael Mark (Official at guillotine).

The silent film version, *The Hands of Orlac* (1924), starred Conrad Veidt as Orlac and was directed by Robert Wiene, who'd directed Veidt in *The Cabinet of Dr. Caligari* (1919). Alexandra Sorina played Yvonne and Hans Homma had the Gogol role, here named Dr. Serral. The doctor's role was definitely a featured one; it was Veidt's show all the way.

Peter Lorre (1904-1964), born Laszlo Lowenstein in Austria-Hungary, won worldwide fame as the child killer in Fritz Lang's *M* (1931). Shortly after his U.S. debut in MGM's *Mad Love*, he joined 20th Century-Fox, headlining the *Mr. Moto* series. Many of his best-remembered performances came from Warner Bros: *The Maltese Falcon* (1941), *Casablanca* (1942), *Arsenic and Old Lace* (1944), and *The Beast With Five Fingers* (1946). He wrote, directed and starred in Germany's *Der Verlorene* (1951). Late in his career, he starred in the AIP horrors *Tales of Terror* (1962), *The Raven* (1963) *and The Comedy of Terrors* (1964), and joined Boris Karloff and Lon Chaney Jr. on the famous *Route 66* TV episode, "Lizard's Leg and Owlet's Wing" (October 26, 1962). Lorre wed three times and was supposed to have finalized a divorce from his third wife on the day he died. Catherine Lorre, his only daughter, died in 1985. Lorre, as noted in the text, was a pallbearer at Colin Clive's funeral.

Frances Drake (1912-2000) began her career as a nightclub dancer in London. In addition to *Mad Love*, she won a special place in Golden Age Horror as Diane, unloving wife to Karloff's Mama's boy mad scientist in Universal's *The Invisible Ray* (1936), also co-starring Bela Lugosi. Among her Hollywood highlights: performing a censor-shocking rumba in *The Trumpet Blows* (Paramount, 1934); vamping Robert Montgomery to jilt Joan Crawford at the altar in *Forsaking All Others* (MGM, 1934); playing a great death scene as Eponine in *Les Miserables* (20th Century, 1935); and catfighting with Claudette Colbert in *It's a Wonderful World* (MGM,1939). She made her last film in 1942 (MGM's *The Affairs of Martha*), giving up her career at the demand of her husband, Cecil John Arthur Howard, who was British royalty. Frances Drake lived wealthily high in Beverly Hills, was a passionate champion of animal rights, and maintained her glamour, as proved when she met my wife and me for lunch at the Beverly Hills Hotel in 1987. What an entrance!

Ted Healy (1896-1937) was the star of "Ted Healy and His Stooges," namely, The Three Stooges. Healy's drinking and poor treatment of Moe Howard, "Curly" Howard and Larry Fine contributed to the break-up of the act; the Stooges went to Columbia, while Healy stayed at MGM. His official cause of death (despite the stories of a brutal beating): alcoholism and kidney disease.

Karl Freund (1890-1969), born in Bohemia, was cinematographer of many legendary films: *Der Golem* (1920), *The Last Laugh* (1924), *Variety* (1925), and *Metropolis* (1927); in the U.S., *All Quiet on the Western Front* (shooting the butterfly ending, 1930), *Dracula* (1931), and *Murders in the Rue Morgue* (1932). He became a director for Universal with *The Mummy*, starring Karloff (1932), and later such films as *The Countess of Monte Cristo* (starring Fay Wray, 1934) and the "all-star" musical *Gift of Gab* (with Karloff and Lugosi in cameo appearances, 1934). Freund joined MGM as a director, but only directed *Mad Love* before returning to cinematography, winning an Oscar for his camerawork on *The Good Earth* (1937). He later was on contract to Warner Bros. (*Key Largo*, 1948, etc.) and, creating the "three-camera technique," became a pioneering TV cameraman on such shows as *I Love Lucy* and *Our Miss Brooks*.

John L. Balderston (1889-1954) wrote the famed fantasy play *Berkeley Square* (which became a 1933 film from Fox) and contributed to the scenarios of an amazing roster of Universal Horror classics: *Dracula* (1931), *Frankenstein* (1931), *The Mummy* (1932), *The Mystery of Edwin Drood* (1935), and *Bride of Frankenstein* (1935); he also wrote an especially spicy early version of *Dracula's Daughter* (1936). He was an un-credited writer on MGM's *Mark of the Vampire* (1935) and wrote screenplays for such films as *The Lives of a Bengal Lancer* (Paramount, 1935) and *The Prisoner of Zenda* (Selznick/US, 1937). A later credit: *Red Planet Mars* (1952).

Oscar Wilde, incidentally, is the author of *Mad Love's* credo, "Each man kills the thing he loves." It's from Wilde's *The Ballad of Reading Gaol*.

Other versions include the 1960 French-English *The Hands of Orlac*, co-starring starring Mel Ferrer as Orlac and Christopher Lee as an evil magician. Donald Wolfit played the supporting role of the surgeon and Edmond T. Greville directed.

The Man Who Broke the Bank at Monte Carlo. Producer, Darryl F. Zanuck. Associate Producer, Nunnally Johnson. Director, Stephen Roberts. Screenplay, Nunnally Johnson, Howard Ellis Smith, based on the play by Ilia Surgutchoff and Frederick Albert Swann. Cinematographer, Ernest Palmer. Editor, Harold Schuster. Art Director, William Darling. Sound, Joseph Aiken, Roger Heman, Sr. Costumer, Gwen Wakeling. Music, Cyril J. Mockridge. Assistant Director, Ad Schaumer. Running time, 71 minutes.

New York city opening, Radio City Music Hall, 14 November 1935. Los Angeles opening, Four Star Theatre, December 7, 1935.

The Cast: Ronald Colman (Paul Gallard), Joan Bennett (Helen Berkeley), Colin Clive (Bertrand Berkeley), Nigel Bruce (Ivan), Montagu Love (Director), Frank Reicher (Second Assistant Director), Lionel Pape (Third Assistant Director), Ferdinand Gottschalk (Office man), Andre Cheron (Dealer), E.E. Clive (Waiter), Lynn Bari (Flower Girl), Alphonse Martell (Chasseur), John George (Hunchback), Christian Rub (Gallard's guide), Vladimar Bykoff (Helen's guide), George Davis (Taxicab driver), George Sorel (Hotel clerk), Shirley Aaronson (Telephone girl),

General Lodijensky (Captain of waiters), Dennis O'Keefe (Onlooker at casino), John Carradine (Despondent casino gambler).

Joan Bennett (1910-1990) is perhaps best remembered as "Kitty," the uber-bitch of *Scarlet Street* (1945). She was later the star of TV's *Dark Shadows* (1966-1971).

Nigel Bruce (1895-1953) will forever be "Dr. Watson" to Basil Rathbone's Sherlock Holmes; they were together in *The Hound of the Baskervilles* and *The Adventures of Sherlock Holmes*, both for 20th Century-Fox in 1939, and the 12-film series produced by Universal 1942 to 1946. Bruce also appeared in a respectable number of classic major releases: *The Charge of the Light Brigade* (1936), *Rebecca* (1940), and *Lassie Come Home* (1943). One of Bruce's final credits: the 3-D *Bwana Devil* (1952).

Stephen Roberts (1895-1936) had a directing career that dated to 1923. At Paramount, he directed the notorious Pre-Code shocker *The Story of Temple Drake* (1933), starring Miriam Hopkins. His final film was *The Ex-Mrs. Bradford* (1936), starring William Powell and Jean Arthur. He died of a heart attack at age 40.

Of interest to horror fans might be the passing glimpse of John George (1898-1968), who appears as a hunchback—according to the film, a sign of luck for gamblers. The 4-foot, 2-inch tall George had an impressive array of classic horror credits—"Cojo" in Lon Chaney Sr.'s *The Unknown* (1927), a beast man in *Island of Lost Souls* (1932), one of Karloff's cultists in *The Black Cat* (1934), a villager in *Bride of Frankenstein* (1935), a waiter in Karloff's *The Black Room* (1935), and more. He played hunchbacks in at least two other films—*Don Juan* (1926) and *The Picture of Dorian Gray* (1945). John George was active in films from 1916 to 1962 and did a large amount of TV work.

The Widow from Monte Carlo. Warner Bros., 1936. Producer, Bryan Foy. Director, Arthur Greville Collins. Screenplay, Charles Belden, George Bricker and F. Hugh Herbert, based on a play by Ian Hay and A.E.W. Mason. Cinematographer, Warren Lynch. Editor, Thomas Pratt. Art Director, Hugh Reticker. Gowns, Orry-Kelly. Sound, Everett Alton Brown. Music, Howard Jackson, Bernhard Kaun, Heinz Roemheld. Assistant Director, Drew Eberson. Costume Jeweler, Eugene Joseff. Running time, 60 minutes.

New York City opening, Astor Theatre, January 21, 1936. Los Angeles opening, Orpheum Theatre, March 4, 1936.

The Cast: Warren William (Major Allan Chepstow), Dolores del Rio (Inez, Duchess of Rye), Louise Fazenda (Rose Torrent), Colin Clive (Lord Eric Reynolds), Herbert Mundin (John Torrent), Olin Howland (Eaves), Warren Hymer (Dopey Mullins), Eily Malyon (Lady Maynard), E.E. Clive (Lord Holloway), Mary Forbes (Lady Holloway), Viva Tattersall (Joan, Inez' secretary), Herbert Evans (Evans, Inez' butler), Billy Bevan (Police Officer Watkins), Ann Douglas (Joan), Alphonse Martell (Emil, Hotel clerk), May Beatty (Dowager), Norman Ainsley (Englishman), Andre Cheron (Croupier), Charles Coleman (Torrent's butler), Gino Corrado (Torrent's cook), Ferdinand Schumann-Heink (Torrent's chauffeur), Charles Fallon (Foreigner), Olaf Hytten (Englishman at casino), Boyd Irwin (Desk sergeant), John Graham Spacey (Kilted man), Forrest Taylor (Surprised costume ball guest), Larry Steers (Costume ball attendee).

Warren William (1894-1948) won distinction as the star seducer in Pre-Code films such as *Skyscraper Souls* (MGM, 1932). On contract to Warners, his perhaps most memorable role was on loan-out to Paramount for Cecil B. DeMille's s *Cleopatra* (1934), in which he played Julius Caesar to Claudette Colbert's Queen of the Nile. Horror fans remember him as Dr. Lloyd in Universal's *The Wolf Man* (1941). Contrary to his predatory screen image, William was married only once (his widow died several months after he died). He was also an accomplished inventor.

Dolores del Rio (1904-1983), of an aristocratic Mexican family, was nicknamed "the Female Valentino" and left a legacy of exotically glamorous performances: *Bird of Paradise* (RKO, 1932), *Flying Down to Rio* (RKO, 1933), *Wonder Bar* (Warner Bros., 1934), and *Journey into Fear* (RKO, 1942, directed by Orson Welles, her lover at the time). Marlene Dietrich thought her "the most beautiful woman in Hollywood." Ms. del Rio was also noted for her charitable work on behalf of orphaned children.

Louise Fazenda (1895-1962) had a career as a slapstick comedienne that dated back to 1913. She flourished as a country bumpkin comic for Mack Sennett and in 1927, married Hal B. Wallis, who became the dynamic producer at Warner Bros. Louise worked at Warners in the mid- and late-1930s and had the dubious distinction of starring in what Humphrey Bogart considered his all-time worst picture: Warners' *Swing Your Lady* (1938), with Bogart as a promoter and Louise as a female wrestler in the Ozarks.

Arthur Greville Collins (1896-1980), born in London, began at Warner Bros. as a dialogue director. He'd direct only two films for Warners, moving on to direct such "B" films as *Thank You, Jeeves!* (20th Century-Fox, 1937) and *Saleslady* (Monogram, 1938). Trivia for horror buffs: Collins was married to Betty Ross Clarke, who Erik the Ape shoves feet first up a chimney in Universal's *Murders in the Rue Morgue* (1932).

History Is Made at Night. United Artists, 1937. Producer, Walter Wanger. Director, Frank Borzage. Screenplay, Gene Towne and C. Graham Baker; Additional dialogue by Vincent Lawrence and David Hertz; Frank Borzage (un-credited). Cinematographer, David Abel (Gregg Toland, un-credited). Editor, Margaret Clancey. Music, Alfred Newman. Art Director, Alexander Toluboff. Costume Designer, Bernard Newman. Sound, Paul Neal. Special Effects, James Basevi. Assistant Director, Lew Borzage. 2nd Unit Director, Arthur Ripley. Dialogue Director, Joshua Logan. Running Time, 97 minutes.

New York Premiere, Rivoli Theatre, March 27, 1937. Los Angeles Premiere, Grauman's Chinese Theatre and Loew's State Theatre, April 7, 1937.

The Cast: Charles Boyer (Paul Dumond), Jean Arthur (Irene Vail), Leo Carrillo (Cesare), Colin Clive (Bruce Vail), Ivan Lebedeff (Michael Browsky), George Meeker (Mr. Norton), Lucien Prival (Private Detective), George Davis (Maestro), John Marston (Captain Alden), Harvey Clark (Victor), Joseph E. Bernard (Headwaiter at Victor's), Georges Renavent (Inspector Millard), Barlowe Borland (Clumsy Waiter at Cesare's), Byron Foulger (Vail employee reading from newspaper), William Stack (Vail's Attorney), Pierre Watkin (Commodore Eldridge), Charles Williams (Room Service Waiter on ship), Edward Earle (Ship Officer), Adele St. Mauer (Hotel Maid), Tom Ricketts (Old Man on ship), George Humbert (Ship's Chef), Russ Powell (Chef with Mustache), Louis Mercier (Cab Driver), Jeanette Kerner (Hat Check Girl), June Preston (Little Girl with dog), Dennis O'Keefe (Restaurant patron), Tim Holt, Tetsu Komai (SOS radio operators), Bobby Barber, Franklyn Farnum, Jack Mulhall, James Sheridan (Waiters).

Charles Boyer (1899-1978) received four Best Actor Academy nominations: *Conquest* (1937), *Algiers* (1938), *Gaslight* (1944), and *Fanny* (1961). He received a special 1943 Academy certificate for "his progressive cultural achievement in establishing the French Research Foundation in Los Angeles as a source of reference." The famed screen lover, who co-starred with such legends as Greta Garbo, Marlene Dietrich, Bette Davis, Claudette Colbert, Irene Dunne, and Ingrid Bergman, was married only once, to Pat Paterson, and for over 44 years. Days after her death, he killed himself with an overdose of barbiturates.

Jean Arthur (1900-1991) replaced originally-cast Madeleine Carroll in this film. Arthur's perhaps best remembered for her appearance in the Frank Capra classics *Mr. Deeds Goes to Town* (1936), *You Can't Take It with You* (1938), and *Mr. Smith Goes to Washington* (1939). She received a Best Actress Oscar nomination for *The More the Merrier* (1943). Arthur had a 1950 Broadway success as *Peter Pan*, co-starring Boris Karloff as Mr. Darling and Captain Hook. Her stage fright and nervous temperament led her to leave films after the memorable *Shane* (1953); she came back in TV's short-lived *The Jean Arthur Show* (1966) and tried for a Broadway comeback in 1967's *The Freaking Out of Stephanie Blake*, which closed during disastrous previews. Jean Arthur spent her final years in virtual seclusion in Carmel, California.

Leo Carrillo (1881-1961) is well remembered for playing "Pancho" to Duncan Renaldo's *The Cisco Kid*, the TV series that ran from 1950 to 1956. Carrillo was related by blood and marriage to various distinguished California personages—his father was the first mayor of Santa Monica—and traced his lineage to the conquistadores. Carrillo the actor served on the State

Park and Recreation Commission, and California has both a Leo Carrillo State Beach and a Leo Carrillo State Park.

Walter Wanger (1894-1968) was an independent producer of such films as *You Only Live Once* (directed by Fritz Lang, 1937), *Stagecoach* (directed by John Ford,1939), and *Foreign Correspondent* (directed by Alfred Hitchcock, 1940), all released by United Artists. He also is notorious for having shot Jennings Lang, the paramour of Wanger's wife, actress Joan Bennett, in the groin; Lang survived, and Wanger spent four months at the County Honor Farm outside Los Angeles. Wanger later produced such films as *Riot in Cell Block 11* (1954) and *Invasion of the Body Snatchers* (1956) and ended his career with the disastrous *Cleopatra* (1963). His final estate reportedly amounted to only $18,000.

Frank Borzage (1894-1962) won Best Director Oscars for *7th Heaven* (1927) and *Bad Girl* (1931). He was also a producer, actor and writer, his career dating back to 1913. His final official directorial credit: *The Big Fisherman* (1959), produced by Rowland V. Lee. Borzage received the Directors Guild of America Lifetime Achievement Award in 1961; in 1962, the year of his death, he received the D.W. Griffith Award for "outstanding contributions in the field of film direction."

David Abel (1883-1973) was best noted for his cinematography on the Fred Astaire and Ginger Rogers musicals *The Gay Divorcee* (1934), *Top Hat* (1935), *Follow the Fleet* (1936), *Swing Time* (1936) and *Shall We Dance* (1937).

James Basevi (1890-1962) was an Art Director/Set Decorator/Special Effects creator. He masterminded the earthquake in *San Francisco* (1936) and the title disaster in *The Hurricane* (1937), and received an Oscar for his Black and White Art Direction/Interior Decoration for *The Song of Bernadette* (1943).

A special by-the-way for horror fans: Tetsu Komai (1894-1970), born in Japan, and who appears in *History is Made at Night* very briefly as an SOS radio operator, memorably played "M'ling," the "dog-man" of *Island of Lost Souls* (1932).

Radio's *Screen Guild Theatre* presented a 30-minute version of *History Is Made at Night*, broadcast November 10, 1940. Charles Boyer reprised his screen role, Greer Garson played Irene, and Lionel Atwill portrayed Vail. The revised adaptation eliminated Vail's suicide, and had a finale in which Atwill's Vail contritely gave his blessing to the lovers. Atwill had previously replaced Clive in *The Firebird* (1934) and *Lancer Spy* (1937).

The Woman I Love. RKO Studios. Producer, Albert Lewis. Director, Anatole Litvak. Screenplay, Mary Borden, based on a novel by Joseph Kessel. Cinematographer, Charles Rosher. Editor, Henri Rust. Art Director, Van Nest Polglase. Costumes, Walter Plunkett. Special Effects, Russell A. Cully, Vernon L. Walker. Musical Director, Roy Webb. Music, Arthur Honegger, Maurice Thirier (Roy Webb, uncredited). Stunt Pilot, Paul Mantz. Running time, 85 minutes.
New York Opening: Radio City Music Hall, April 15, 1937. Los Angeles Opening: Hollywood Pantages and RKO-Hillstreet Theatres, April 27, 1937.
The Cast: Paul Muni (Lt. Claude Maury), Miriam Hopkins (Mme. Helene Maury), Louis Hayward (Jean), Colin Clive (Captain Thelis), Minor Watson (Deschamps), Elisabeth Risdon (Mme. Herbillon), Paul Guilfoyle (Bertier), Wally Albright (Georges), Mady Christians (Florence), Alec Craig (Doctor), Owen Davis, Jr. (Mezziores), Sterling Holloway (Duprez), Vince Barnett (Mathieu), Adrian Morris (Marbot), Don "Red" Barry (Michel), Joe Twerp (Narbonne), William Stelling (Pianist), Richard Lane (Florence's Boyfriend), Richard Tucker (General), "Doodles" Weaver ("Chopin" pianist).

As noted in the text, *The Woman I Love* was a remake of *L'Equipage*, a 1935 French film also directed by Anatole Litvak. Charles Vanel played Lt. Maury, Annabella was Helene, Jean-Pierre Aumont was Jean, and Jean Marat played Captain Thelis.

Paul Muni (1895-1967) won the Academy Award for *The Story of Louis Pasteur* (1936) and the New York Film Critics Award for *The Life of Emile Zola* (1937), both for Warner Bros., where he was one of the studio's most powerful stars. He won a Tony Award for his "comeback" Broadway performance in *Inherit the Wind* (1955). Of note: Muni, in his early film stardom days in 1929, was promoted as "The New Lon Chaney," due to his use of makeup. He'd also tested for the title role in *Dracula* (1931).

Miriam Hopkins (1902-1972) was superb as Ivy in Rouben Mamoulian's *Dr. Jekyll and Mr. Hyde* (1931) and as Lily in Ernst Lubitsch's *Trouble in Paradise*, both from Paramount. She received an Oscar nomination for *Becky Sharp* (1935). Fans remember her best for her tempestuous Warner Bros. teamings with Bette Davis in *The Old Maid* (1939) and *Old Acquaintance* (1943). Ms. Hopkins married four times and Anatole Litvak, director of *The Woman I Love*, was her third spouse. The inscription on her marker at Oak City Cemetery, Bainbridge, Georgia paraphrases *Hamlet*: *Good night sweet princess, and flights of angels sing thee to thy rest.*

Louis Hayward (1909-1985) is perhaps best remembered for his title role performance as *The Man in the Iron Mask* (directed by James Whale, 1939) and the hero in *And Then There Were None* (1945). He also starred as *The Son of Dr. Jekyll* (1951), and headlined two TV series, the 1954/1955 *The Lone Wolf* and the 1961/1962 *The Pursuers*. The first of his three wives was Ida Lupino. Also, as a Marine

Rare wartime poster for *The Woman I Love*.

Corps Captain of a photography unit, Hayward bravely filmed World War II's three-day Battle of Tarawa, receiving a Bronze Star for courage under fire. (Most cast lists give Hayward's character's name as "Herbillion," but a shot in the film of his travel trunk spells it "Herbillon.").

Anatole Litvak (1902-1974) had directed in France the international hit *Mayerling* (1936). He was based from 1937 to 1941 at Warner Bros., where he directed the excellent 1941 *noir* film *Blues in the Night*. Litvak was Oscar-nominated for directing *The Snake Pit* (1948) and *Decision Before Dawn* (1951), both from 20th Century-Fox.

Roy Webb (1888-1982) received seven Oscar nominations for his musical work and is well remembered for his superb contributions to the Val Lewton horror films at RKO.

Paul Mantz (1903-1965) was the most famous stunt pilot of Hollywood's Golden years. Among his credits: *Hell's Angels* (1930), *Only Angels Have Wings* (1939), *I Wanted Wings* (1941), *Twelve O'Clock High* (1949), and *It's a Mad Mad Mad Mad World* (1963). On July 8, 1965, while working on *The Flight of the Phoenix* as the stunt double for James Stewart, Mantz died in a plane crash.

Appendix Three:
Select Radio Credits

Variety Show. December 14, 1929. Colin Clive and James Whale guested together, talking about *Journey's End.* The emcees were Fred Niblo, Will Irwin and Jack Oakie and additional guests included D.W. Griffith, Anita Page, Sally Blane, John Boles, and Inez Courtney. Broadcast by three California stations—KHJ, KFWB, and KNX.

Mrs. Feather. April 20, 1931, Colin appeared with Jeanne de Casalis in the episode "Mrs. Feather's Fire." Broadcast over England's National Programme Radio.

The Show. August 13, 1934. Colin guest-starred, playing a scene from *Journey's End.* Broadcast from Hollywood.

Inside Stories. July 19, 1935. Colin was the guest star. Broadcast from Hollywood.

The Fleischmann's Yeast Hour. November 14, 1935 Host, Rudy Vallee. Colin Clive starred in a playlet titled *The Other Place*, with Leo G. Carroll. Broadcast from New York City.

Hollywood Hotel. April 9, 1937. Louella Parsons, hostess. Colin Clive joined Miriam Hopkins and Louis Hayward in a radio version of *The Woman I Love.* Broadcast from Hollywood.

Colin Clive portrait.

End Notes

Prologue Notes:

2320 Bowmont Drive—The author visited and photographed this house in 2007.

a ghost haunted ... Charles Higham, *Kate: The Life of Katharine Hepburn* (Signet, 1976), pages 46, 47.

Top hat and skimpy elastic swim trunks—See Cynthia Lindsay's *Dear Boris*, (Knopf, 1975), p. ix. A snapshot of Karloff in this apparel, appearing in this *Prologue*, was among the Karloff memorabilia the author reviewed for auction by Heritage Galleries, Dallas, TX, in 2008.

Violet—Author's interview with Marian Marsh, Palm Desert, CA, 14 May 1983. Ms. Marsh, Karloff's leading lady in *The Black Room* (Columbia, 1935), visited the Karloff home and met Violet personally.

Water Cricket—*Variety*, 3 September 1935, p. 3.

Nigel Bruce ... "bottoms up"—Basil Rathbone, *In and Out of Character* (Doubleday, 1962; Second Limelight edition, 1991) p. 181.

Screen Actors Guild—Thanks to Valerie Yaros, Screen Actors Guild historian, who made it possible for me to review Karloff's SAG file.

Alan Mowbray ... risqué jokes—See James Curtis, *James Whale: A New World of Gods and Monsters* (Faber & Faber, 1998), p. 230.

"the face of Christ"—Personal letter to author from Mae Clarke, Woodland Hills, CA, post-marked 2 March 1984.

"the voice of a pipe organ"—Author's interview with Mae Clarke, Woodland Hills, CA, 11 May 1983.

"cinema's greatest sado-masochist ..."—Joel Hirschhorn, *Rating the Movie Stars* (by the Editors of *Consumer Guide*) (Beekman House New York, 1983), pgs. 85, 86. With Four Stars being the book's highest possible rating, Clive received a score of 3.22 stars, higher than Boris Karloff (3.17 stars) and Bela Lugosi (1.90 stars).

"I nearly laughed myself to death ..." Madeline Glass, "Clive of England," *Picture Play* magazine, July, 1935, p. 55.

... soloed as a pilot ... *Los Angeles Examiner*, 13 October 1934.

"Don't call me mysterious ..."—Harry Mines, *Illustrated Daily News*, Los Angeles, 1 April 1935.

"a blow-up"—Lawrence J. Quirk, *Fasten Your Seat Belts: The Passionate Life of Bette Davis* (Signet, 1990), p. 116.

"a maniac ..."—Quirk, *ibid*, p. 117.

Clive frequently starts drinking at night—Author's interviews with Frances Drake, Beverly Hills, CA, 7 June 1986 & 13 July 1987.

Danny Boy—"Services for Colin Clive," *Hollywood Citizen News*, 30 June 1937.

Chapter One Notes:

"It appears I am destined ..." This well-known quote is cited in many compilations of famous quotes. The circumstances surrounding Robert Clive's utterance of these sentences is re-counted in the "Robert Clive: Tearaway to empire builder" section of the BBC website: (www.bbc.co.uk/shropshire/content/articles/2005/03/29/robert_clive_feature.shtml).

"Adwaita"—"Clive of India's Tortoise Dies," *BBC News*, March 23, 2006.

"unstable sociopath"—Willian Dalrymple, "The East India Company: The original corporate raiders," *The Guardian*, 4 March 2015.

... stabbed himself in the throat with a pen knife—Scott Wilson, *Resting Places: The Burial Sites of More Than 14,000 Famous Persons* (Third Edition, McFarland and Co., Jefferson, NC, 2016), p. 141. Wilson includes Robert Clive's burial location: St. Margaret's Church, Moreton Say, Salop Shrewsbury, England.

"I would have liked an opportunity ... " Madeline Glass, "Clive of England," *Picture Play* Magazine, July 1935, p. 55.

"One Man Crazy ...!"

"I am afraid ..."Personal Letter to Scott Wilson from the Seventh Earl of Powis, 20 June 1990. Thanks to Scott Wilson for providing a copy.

Birth of Piercy Greig in 1868—FamilySearch.org.

Colin Philip Greig—The information on the Greig and Clive families in this chapter come from: India Births and Baptisms, 1786-1947; The England and Wales census of 1881, 1901, and 1911; the England and Wales Marriage Index, 1837-1915; UK, Hart's Annual Army List, 1908; UK, British Army Lists, 1882-1962. Thanks to Frank Dello Stritto and Scott Gallinghouse for providing copies of this material.

John Glennie "Jungly" Greig—See D.B. Deodhar's "'Jungly' Greig: India's First Little Master," at the Cricket Country Internet site (www.cricketcountry.com). The phrase "little master" perhaps refers to Greig's very short stature; Deodhar referred to him as "a white Pygmy."

Sierra Leone—*The Colonies and India* (London, Greater London, England), 4 January 1896.

The Hut Tax War of 1898—See military.wikia.com/wiki/Hut_Tax_War_of_1898. For a comprehensive account, see: Harris, David, *Civil War and Democracy in West Africa: Conflict Resolutions, Elections and Justice in Sierra Leone and Liberia* (I.B. Taurus, 2012).

The British Vice-Consulate—Colin Philip Greig gave the impression of having been a Roman Catholic, based on the schools he selected for his children and his later translation of a 1939 book regarding Catholic saints. That he married Daisy Clive at the British Vice-Consulate's office would indicate he wasn't a Roman Catholic, or at least a practicing one, in 1898. Perhaps his Roman Catholic faith came, as it did with his brother John, at a later time. On the other hand, he might have married Daisy at a Catholic wedding Mass at some time after their marriage at the British Vice-Consulate's.

The Second Boer War—For a comprehensive account see: Thomas Pakenham, *The Boer War* (Cardinal, 1991).

Caroline Margaret Lugard Clive Greig ... born October 29, 1881— "India Births and Baptisms 1786-1947" FamilySearch.org.

The daughter of British parents—Daisy's parents, Henry Somerset Clive and Ellen Lizzie Lugard, wed November 19, 1879 in North Petherton, Somerset, England. (See *England's Marriages, 1583-1973*, database familysearch.org). Thanks to Frank Dello Stritto.

Saint Vincent—The last agony was possibly borrowed from Saint Lawrence, who while being roasted alive, supposedly quipped, "Turn me over, I'm done on this side." Lawrence is the patron saint of comedians. His feast day is August 10.

1:51 a.m.—"Astrology: 26742 Famous People's Birth Charts," *Astrotheme*. The chart notes that the Sun was 29/35 Capricorn, the Moon 16/27 Virgo. Thanks to Tracy L. Surrell for sending this information.

"You see, my country was engaged ..." Glass, *ibid*, p. 18.

Billy Pratt—See Stephen Jacobs' biography, *Boris Karloff: More than A Monster* (Tomahawk Press, 2011).

Jimmy Whale—See James Curtis' biography, *James Whale: A New World of Gods and Monsters* (Faber and Faber, 1998).

Cicely Margaret Greig and Noel Audrey Greig—Divorce Court File: 1760. Appellant: Colin Philip Greig. Respondent: Caroline Margaret Lugard Greig. Co-respondent: Cecil A. Johnson. Type: Husband's Petition for Divorce. The British National Archives, Supreme Court of Judicature, Reference J 77/1047/1760. Thanks to Scott Gallinghouse for locating this document and providing a copy. The birthdates of Cicely and Noel are noted in this Petition for Divorce.

Captain Greig, meanwhile, had departed ... "Husband's Petition. Greig v. Greig And Johnson," The *London Times*, 1912.

September 19, 1907 ... "Husband's Petition ...," *ibid*.

Convent of the Cross—1911 England Census.

The Lives of a Bengal Lancer—The film also starred Franchot Tone and Richard Cromwell and was directed by Henry Hathaway. The villainess was Kathleen Burke, who'd played the Panther Woman in Paramount's *Island of Lost Souls*. The film received a 1935 Best Picture Academy nomination, losing to MGM's *Mutiny on the Bounty*.

"I like this film ..." Ivone Kirkpatrick, *The Inner Circle: Memoirs* (St. Martin's Press, 1959).

A sensational divorce—Divorce Court File: 1760, The British National Archives, *ibid.*

44 Bessborough Gardens ... 1911 England Census.

The Corinthian ... crossing into the U.S.A.—U.S. Border Crossings from Canada to the US., 1895-1956.

In the wake of the scandal ... Caroline also had a half-brother, Edward Archer Clive (1867-1952), and a sister, Phyllis Clive (1890-1981). Email to author from Frank Dello Stritto, 19 February 2017.

Cecil A. Johnson—He served in the British Expeditionary Forces during World War I. On April 14, 1919, Johnson married Harriet Brien in New York (New York, New York Marriage Certificate Index, 1866-1937, Ancestry.com). The 1920 U.S. Federal Census shows Cecil living in District 9 of Manhattan, working as an "artist," and living with 29-year-old wife Harriet, her 63-year-old mother Kate, her 35-year-old sister Anna, and her 22-year-old brother Harry. In the 1940 Census, Cecil A. Johnson, age 61, is now a naturalized U.S. citizen, and a draftsman living on E. 9th Street in New York City. His marital status: "Widowed." A Cecil Arthur Johnson died in Pinellas, FL in August of 1956; presumably it was "our" Cecil A. Johnson.

Sam Morris—England and Wales Marriage Registration Index, 1837-2005—FamilySearch.org.

Captain Greig would remarry ... If Captain Greig had been a practicing Catholic by 1920, the time of his remarriage, the Catholic Church, considering his divorce, would not have allowed him to remarry unless the divorced wife was deceased. If this were the case, it indicates that, by 1920, Caroline Margaret "Daisy" Lugard Clive Greig Johnson Morris was dead.

Chapter Two Notes:

"The Hermitage"—Records of Colin Glennie Greig, Stonyhurst Preparatory School. Thanks to Mr. David Knight, curator of Stonyhurst's Archives, for his generous and expert personal attention to my requests for information. The information provided me by Mr. Knight include a package of archival material on Colin Glennie Greig (postmarked 2 March 2016), as well as emails to the author, dated 1 March 2016, 3 March 2106, and 8 March 2016. All information related to Stonyhurst in this chapter comes from that correspondence.

Island of Lost Souls—Produced by Paramount Studio, based on H.G. Wells' novel *The Island of Dr. Moreau*, and released in December of 1932, *Island of Lost Souls* starred Charles Laughton as Moreau, whose surgery transforms animals into semi-human monsters. His "most nearly perfect creation": Lota, "the Panther Woman," a character not in the novel, and played by Kathleen Burke in the movie. In the film, Moreau hopes to mate Lota with a sailor (Richard Arlen); the movie, also featuring Bela Lugosi as "the Sayer of the Law," was directed by Erle C. Kenton. Its censorship troubles included Great Britain banning it for 25 years.

patron saints—Knight, David, "Stonyhurst Patron Saints and Guardian Angels," the *Stonyhurst Record*, 2017. Thanks to Mr. Knight, who emailed me a PDF copy 7 February 2017.

Charles Laughton ... cosmic guilt—Charles Higham, *Charles Laughton: An Intimate Biography* (Doubleday, New York 1976), pgs. 4, 5.

Sports—David Knight, Stonyhurst Archives, *ibid.*

Stonyhurst—After Colin's death in 1937, the Stonyhurst magazine, in its obituary, wrote that "an accident ... badly damaged his knee in his last year at school ... he spent the greater part of his last term laying in a chair before the Infirmary ... " It's possible that Colin hurt his knee during Sports Day, but unlikely he'd have been so shaken by it that he'd leave the school only five days later. Also, this doesn't fit with the account that he spent "the greater part of his last term" incapacitated

1915 films—April 1, 1915 was the release date of Britain's *The Lure of Drink*, produced by Ealing Studios, directed by A.E. Coleby, and described over a century later by the British Film Institute as "a lurid temperance tale warning of the evils of wicked women and demon drink." The lug of a hero, Ned (Roy Travers), has sworn off booze and happily weds Peggy (Blanche Forsythe), a widow with a daughter. However, Hell hath no fury like Ned's jealous ex-mistress, "Flash Kate" (Maud Yates). She sneaks into his house, gets him to drink again, and as the title card reads, "Kate Awakens Ned's Dormant Demon." The 37-minute shocker was "a surprisingly violent piece of temperance propaganda" and significant in early British cinema. Considering the later tragedy of Colin Clive, one wonders: By some slim chance, did 15-year-old Colin Glennie Greig see *The Lure of Drink*?

D.J. Cowles School—An advertisement for the school appears in the *London Times*, 4 September 1893, p. 12.

Major Hugh Irwin Greig—livesofthefirstworldwar.org/lifestory/1465192. For additional details on Major Greig, thanks to Scott Gallinghouse (email to author, 23 July 2018).

Sandhurst—The information regarding Colin Glennie Greig at Sandhurst comes from an email to the author dated 5 April 1916 from Dr. Anthony Morton, DPS/ARM, Curator Sandhurst Collection, Royal Military Academy Sandhurst, Camberley, Surrey, England.

Two knees were broken ... Madeline Glass, "Clive of England," *Picture Play* Magazine, July 1935.

"My family did not object ... " Elisabethe Corathiel, "How I Began" No. 12.- Colin Clive," *Theatre World*, July 1931, p. 39.

Chapter Three Notes:
"I do not want you to think ... " Corathiel, *ibid.*
" ... where angels fear to tread ... " Corathiel, *ibid.*

1919—At Yuletide of 1919, James Whale appeared in *The Merry Wives of Windsor* at the Gaiety Theatre in Manchester, where he met an actor who'd achieve offbeat distinction by playing female roles in drag—Ernest Thesiger, who'd later play the wicked Dr. Pretorius in Whale's *Bride of Frankenstein*. "Across the pond," on the U.S. vaudeville circuit, a diminutive actor named Dwight Frye, destined to play the hunchbacked Fritz in Whale's *Frankenstein*, was touring in a sketch titled *Magic Glasses*, sharing the stage with such attractions as "the DeWolf Girls."

John B. Mason—"John Mason Seriously Ill: Actors Suffers a Breakdown and His Recovery is Doubtful," *New York Times*, 12 January 1919; also, "Death of John Mason: Actor Famous on American Stage Expires Suddenly at Stamford," *New York Times*, 13 January 1919.

Maude Adams—"Maude Adams Must Rest; Actress at Home of Boston Friend Has Nervous Breakdown," *New York Times*, 13 January 1919.

Henry Brodribb Irving—"Henry B. Irving, Actor-Manager, Dies: Late Sir Henry's Eldest Son Succumbs in London After a Nervous Breakdown at 49 Years," *New York Times*, 18 October 1919.

"With the audacity of a beginner ... " Corathiel, *ibid.*
"I believe I had one line ... " Corathiel, *ibid.*
"Charles Hawtrey's kindness ... " Corathiel, *ibid.*

Annie Horniman—See "Annie Horniman; Rebel with a Cause," by Sharon O'Connor, *The Dulwich Society*, 17 September 2012 at the Dulwich Society Internet site (www.dulwichsociety.com/2012-autumn/745-annie-horniman).

"starting the modern theater movement"—Janet Sullivan Cross, "A Brief Biography of Colin Clive, Part 1," on the *Journey's End* Internet site (www.journeysendproject.com/2013/06/18/a-brief-biography-of-colin-clive-part-1/).

"I took part ... " Corathiel, *ibid.*

Colin Clive wed Evelyn Taylor—Divorce File: 9041. Appellant: Colin Glennie Clive Greig. Respondent: Evelyn Taylor. Co-Respondent: Carl Harbord. The National Archives—Supreme Court of Judicature: Divorce and Matrimonial Flies 1925-1928. Reference J 77/2540/9041. This file has information regarding the date and place of the wedding, the couple's addresses, and the divorce details. Most sincere thanks to Neil Pettigrew for visiting the National Archives in London and providing me a copy of this important document.

Evelyn Taylor—In early 1921, an actress named Evelyn Taylor earned a certain notoriety when William Henshall, described by the *London Times* as "the owner and producer of plays," was charged by his wife of having committed adultery with Evelyn in October, November, and December of 1918. Henshall had "posed" as Evelyn's husband, living with her in a flat at Ridgmont Gardens, Gower Street, Bloomsbury. The story became increasingly strange and salacious, claiming 1.) Evelyn had previously been married to a "Mr. Hargreaves," 2.) Evelyn had born "Mr Hargreaves" a child on February 1, 1915, 3.) William Henshall had named one of his racehorses "Mrs. Hargreaves," in Evelyn's honor, 4.) Come 1921, Henshall was living in Golders Green with Evelyn, whom he referred to as "the mother of my children." Was this the same Evelyn Taylor who wed Colin Clive? Highly unlikely. If she were, she'd have been a child bride of "Mr. Hargreaves," giving birth when she was only 14 or 15 years old. It would also have made Colin the overnight father of "children," who had at least two different biological fathers. Perhaps the most telling evidence against Colin's bride having been *the* "notorious" Evelyn Taylor is that they married in the Roman Catholic Church, which would never have sanctioned Colin's marriage to a woman with this past.

"The Public Lunatic Asylum, Jersey"—Thanks to Scott Gallinghouse for finding and sending me these documents.

St. Saviour's Asylum—The Jersey Archive theislandwiki.org.; also, BBC—Domesday Recorded: St. Saviour's Hospital.

A blog spot ... "St Saviours Mental Hospital—Much To Answer For" 5 May, 2011 (https://therightofreply.blogspot.com/search?q=st.+saviour%27s+mental+hospital).

Administration passed on the effects ... England & Wales, National Probate Calendar (index of Wills and Administrations), 1858—1966.

Chapter Four Notes:

Hull Repertory Company—Janet Sullivan Cross, "A Brief Biography of Colin Clive, Part 1," (http://journeysendproject.fileswordpress.com/2013/06/clive-b1.jpg.g).

Ronald Culver, *Not Quite a Gentleman* (Kimber, 1979).

Attending a performance—Cross, *ibid.*

"a terror-stricken brother"—"Before the Footlights," *Hull Daily Mail*, 22 September 1924.

"a father"—"Hull's Little Theatre," *Hull Daily Mail*, 29 September 1924.

"a vigorous brother"—"Effect of Wireless," *Hull Daily Mail*, 6 October 1924.

"Of very great value"—Elisabethe Corathiel, "How I Began," No. 12.—Colin Clive," *Theatre World*, July 1931, p. 39.

"...wife of Colin Clive ..."—"Bid for Popularity," *Hull Daily Mail*, 10 August 1925.

"My big scene ..." Noel Barber, *Fires of Spring* (Geoffrey Bles, 1952).

The Q Theatre—cinematreasures.org.

Rose-Marie—There were three versions of *Rose-Marie* from MGM. The 1928 silent film starred Joan Crawford as Rose-Marie, James Murray as Jim Kenyon, and House Peters as Sgt. Malone; Gertrude Astor was Wanda, and Lucien Hubbard directed. This version eliminated the score and is considered a lost film. The 1936 *Rose-Marie* is the most famous one; it starred Jeanette MacDonald as Rose-Marie, Nelson Eddy as the Mountie, and was directed by W.S. Van Dyke. MGM's 1954 *Rose-Marie* stared Ann Blyth in the title role, and Howard Keel as the Canadian Mountie. Wanda was back in this one, having been absent in the 1936 version, and was played by Joan Taylor; Bert Lahr and Marjorie Main were the comic relief, Mervyn LeRoy directed, and MGM released the film in Eastmancolor. Colin's stage role of Edward Hawley didn't exist in any of the three film versions.

Chapter Five Notes:

"in contact with her leprous, saintly bosom ..." John Corbin, "The Play," *New York Times*, 25 December 1922, p. 22.

Fata Morgana—For data on this play and other London stage productions noted in this book, I'm grateful to J.P. Wearing, author of volumes *The London Stage, 1910-1919* and *1920-1929*. (The Scarecrow Press, Metuchen, N.J. and London, 1982).

Evidence she was actually four or five years older—When Jeanne de Casalis sailed from Southampton to New York City on the *Homeric* in October of 1922, she gave her age to the authorities as 30, which would mean her year of birth was 1892. See List or Manifest of Alien Passengers for the United States, *The Homeric*, October 1922. Miss de Casalis' first marriage had occurred in mid-1913.

"... a far line of distant hills ..." Jeanne de Casalis, *Things I Don't Remember: Short Stories and Impressions* (William Heinemann Ltd., Melbourne, London, Toronto, 1953), pgs. 2, 3.

"Cass"—de Casalis, *ibid*, p. 154.

her sexiest lingerie—de Casalis, *ibid*, p. 24.

"London Is Shocked by *Potiphar's Wife*"—*New York Times*, 19 August 1927, p. 20.

"less risqué pajamas"—"Actress Alters Criticized Pajamas," *New York Times 20 August 1927*, p. 8.

The Witch—The play, written by Hans Wiers-Jenssen, had first played New York in 1910. A revival had opened at New York's Greenwich Village Theatre November 18, 1926 and had run 28 performances. Alice Brady was the star and featured in the cast was Maria Ouspenskaya.

"Incidentally ..." Madeline Gray, "Our Interview," *The Magazine Programme*, 23 September 1929. Thanks to Ms. Tracy L. Surrell.

"That from about the first day ..." Divorce File: 9041. Appellant: Colin Glennie Clive Greig. Respondent: Evelyn Taylor. Co-Respondent: Carl Harbord. The National Archives—Supreme Court of Judicature: Divorce and Matrimonial Flies 1925-1928. Reference J 77/2540/9041. Most sincere thanks to Neil Pettigrew for visiting the National Archives in London and providing me a copy of this very important document.

Show Boat—In September of 1928, Colin played the Hon. Anthony Deering in *Yellow Streak* (Embassy Theatre); and in November of 1928, portrayed James Haviland in *The Dark Path* (Savoy Theatre). In the latter, he appeared with Laurence Olivier. These were presumably showcase productions, which Colin did moonlighting from *Show Boat*.

Chapter Six Notes:

A large memorial—Neil Pettigrew, "Into the Black Country," *The Dark Side*, Issue 183, 2017, pages 28-33. Pettigrew provides an excellent tour of Whale's birthplace in Dudley. He notes that Dudley Castle might have been the inspiration for the tower laboratory in *Frankenstein* and *Bride of Frankenstein*. Pettigrew also points out that the windmills that stood in the Dudley countryside at the time of Whale's youth possibly influenced Whale's decision to retain the windmill climax written by Robert Florey in *Frankenstein*'s original script.

"The camp held enough ... "—"German Prison Taught Briton Dramatic Lore," *Los Angeles Evening Express*, 5 April 1930.

"a faun"—"Mr. Ernest Thesiger Writes ..." the *London Times*, 31 May 1957, p. 12.

"a face rather like a nice-looking monkey"—Author's telephone interview with Elsa Lanchester, Hollywood, CA, 10 June 1979.

"There was always a touch of the macabre ..." Author's interview with Alan Napier, Pacific Palisades, CA, 15 May 1983.

A Man With Red Hair—Neil Pettigrew, "James Whale On Stage," *The Dark Side*, Issue 189, 2018, pages 48, 49.

"Come in pajamas ..." Napier, *ibid*.

"Did you know ..." Napier, *ibid*.

R.C. Sherriff—R.C. Sherriff, *No Leading Lady: An Autobiography* (Victor Gollancz LTD, London 1968).

"As a slice of life ... "—Sherriff, *ibid*, p. 45.

"mostly skin and bone ... "—Author's telephone interview with Stella Zucco, Santa Monica, CA, 22 May 1991.

"I reached the end ..." W.A. Darlington, *Theatre Arts Monthly*, July, 1929.

"George Zucco, as Osborne, was perfect ..." Darlington, *ibid*.

Dorothy Elmhirst—Hannen Swaffer, "London as It Looks," *Variety*, 12 February 1930, p. 61.

"He could have played God!"—Author's telephone interview with Charles Bennett, Beverly Hills, CA, 29 October 1992.

Beau Geste—The production directed by Basil Dean, opened January 30, 1929 at His Majesty's Theatre in London and closed March 4, after only 39 performances.

It was Jeanne de Casalis ... R.C. Sherriff, who collaborated with Jeanne de Casalis on the 1936 play *St. Helena*, wrote that Jeanne "had been engaged to Colin Clive when *Journey's End* was in the making, and it was through her that Colin was given a trial which got him the part of Stanhope and made his name." (*No Leading Lady*, p. 298)

The audition, at any rate ... Sherriff, *ibid*, p. 75.

"Keith-Johnston's got it here ..." Sherriff, *ibid*, p. 75.

"It was difficult, of course ..." Sherriff, *ibid*, p. 77.

"Stanhope, I told him ..." Sherriff, *ibid*, p. 77.

"He was no longer ..." Sherriff, *ibid* p. 78.

A solitary "Bravo!" ... Sherriff, *ibid*, p. 86.

"George Zucco, the most modest ..."—Sherriff, *ibid*, p. 87.

"No young actor ..." Sherriff, *ibid*, p. 97.

Chapter Seven Notes:

"The success of *Journey's End* ..."—Robert Speaight, *The Property Basket: Recollections of a Divided Life* (Collins & Harvill press, 1970), pgs. 104, 105.

Maurice Browne—Speaight, *ibid*, p. 105.

30 pounds a week—James Curtis, *James Whale: A New World of Gods and Monsters* (Faber and Faber, 1998), p. 98.

"Women have been coming ..."—"No Woman, But Great Woman Interest"—by Colin Clive. Thanks to Neil Pettigrew, who found this newspaper clipping (unsourced and undated) in the Victoria and Albert Theatre Archive, London, England.

"I didn't know him that well ..." Author's telephone interview with Stella Zucco, Santa Monica, CA, 22 May 1991.

"Well, Tallulah and Jeanne ..." Zucco, *ibid*.

Evelyn Taylor Greig—"Death of a Film Actress: An Open Verdict," The *London Times*, 15 April 1929, p. 11. Accessed at the Johns Hopkins Library, Baltimore, MD, August 2017. Thanks to Sally Stark for bringing this article to my attention.

The Pigeon—J.P. Wearing, *The London Stage, 1920-1929* (The Scarecrow Press, Metuchen, N.J. and London, 1982).

"A very nice, gentle man ..." Scott Gallinghouse.

Shall We Join the Ladies?—Wearing, *ibid*.

Saturday, June 29 ... "Miss De Casalis. Marriage at a Country Register Office", The Observer, 30 June 1929.

Chapter Eight Notes:

Cheer Up Little Girl ... *Profiles in History* sold this letter on eBay, August 2012. The "Buy It Now" price listed was $9,500.

Wolf's Lair—Greg Williams, *The Story of Hollywoodland* (Papavasilopoulos Press, 1992), p. 27. The owner of Wolf's Lair was Milton (Bud) Wolf.

707 Film Releases—Gene Brown, *Movie Time* (Macmillan, New York, 1995), p. 95.

The top stars—Brown, *ibid*, p. 95.

First Academy Awards ceremony—Mason Wiley and Damien Bona, *Inside Oscar: The Unofficial History of the Academy Awards* (Ballantine Books, New York, 1987), p. 8.

" ... I saw it as ..."—Wiley and Bona, *ibid*, p. 10. Frances Marion later won Best Writer Oscars for MGM's *The Big House* (1930) and *The Champ* (1931).

Jean Harlow—The best book on Harlow is David Stenn's *Bombshell: The Life and Death of Jean Harlow* (Doubleday, 1993).

Coyotes—1929/Deranged LA Crimes, derangedlacrimes.com.

"Suicide Bridge"—Hadley Meares, "A History of L.A.'s Suicide Hot Spots, from the Colorado Street Bridge to the Hotel Cecil," *LA Weekly*, 10 April 2017.

Witch-Woman—"Sobs Shocking Tale of Weird Attack: Boy Beaten By 'Witch' Kidnaper," *Los Angeles Times*, 14 November 1929, p. A1. According to this article, the "Witch-Woman" had already beaten the same boy earlier that day, having taken him to a vacant house, and used the promise of candy to trap him again. Finally apprehended in 1934, and accused of three recent beatings, the "Witch-Woman" was revealed to be Betty Kocalis, an obese mother of six children, all of whom sat in court at her trial. She was convicted in June of 1934 and sentenced to three years at Tehachapi Women's Prison. (See "Child Case Terms Given: Court Denounces Mrs. Kocalis," *Los Angeles Times*, 16 June 1934, p. A10). Her husband would be faithfully waiting for her upon her release.

"A public display of hysteria"—Scott Wilson, *Resting Places: The Burial Sites of More Than 14,000 Famous Persons, Third Edition, Vol. 2* (McFarland, 2016). Alma Rubens died January 21, 1931, due to pneumonia. She'd been released from Patton State Hospital but, shortly before her death, had been arrested for smuggling morphine from Agua Caliente. She was 33 years old.

Hardly a love match—See Stenn, *ibid*, pages 44, 45.

$7.000 bonus from Hughes—James Curtis, *James Whale: A New World of Gods and Monsters* ((Faber and Faber, 1998), p. 90.

"Not only was he a very fine ..." Unsourced clipping, Colin Clive File, Billy Rose Library for the Performing Arts, Lincoln Center, New York.

" ... wait until Hollywood ..."—"Will Hays and a Code of Ethics, What Hollywood will do to *Journey's End*, Little exhibitors in New Orleans Get Worst of It," *The Film Spectator*, Hollywood, CA, 1 June 1929, p. 10. Editor, Welford Beaton.

"I suggested that we ..." Grace Kingsley, "*Wild Party* Story Will Be Filmed," *Los Angeles Times*, 16 February 1930, p. A9.

"I had to send for Colin Clive ..." Hannen Swaffer, *Sunday Express*, 20 April 1930.

cut-throat terms—George Pearson, *Flashback: An Autobiography of a British Film Maker* (George Allen & Unwin LTD, London, 1957), p. 168.

"au revoir" performance—Doris Denbo, *Hollywood Daily Citizen*, 5 December 1929.

Chapter Nine Notes:

The *Homeric* hit wicked weather ... "Storms Delay *Homeric*," *New York Times*, 29 November 1929, p. 26.

"New York' sky line ... " Colin Clive, "Filming *Journey's End*." This un-sourced newspaper clipping, dated 18 May 1930, comes from a file that Richard Gordon, producer of such films as *The Haunted Strangler* (1958), kept on *Journey's End* in his personal archive. Thanks to Tom Weaver, a personal friend of Mr. Gordon who worked with him on several book and DVD projects, for providing copies of these pages.

A bottle of Bass at lunch—Mollie Merrick, "Movieland," *Richmond Times Dispatch*, 6 December 1929.

"While being rushed ... "—"Britisher 'Bowled Over' By Speed Of 'The States,'" *The Detroit Free Press*, 15 December 1929.

" ... until we came to the prairie ... "—"*Journey's End*: Famous Play as Talkie," *Sunday Times*, Perth, Western Australia, 16 February 1930.

"Everything was done ..." Colin Clive, *ibid*.

"There were rehearsals ..." Colin Clive, *ibid*.

"I had actually decided ... " Author's interview with David Manners, Pacific Palisades, CA, 30 July 1976.

"As part of the Merlin-like atmosphere ... "—Clive, *ibid*.

"Colin's entry on the set ... " George Pearson, *Flashback: An Autobiography of a British Film Maker* (George Allen & Unwin LTD, London, 1957), p. 168.

"To me, his face ..." Manners, *ibid*.

John Barrymore—The best and most honest depiction of Barrymore can be found in Margot Peters' *The House of Barrymore* (Alfred A. Knopf, Inc., 1990).

Alma Rubens—Rubens died January 21, 1931 at the age of 33. The cause of death was pneumonia. Shortly before her death, she was arrested for smuggling morphine from Agua Caliente. See Scott Wilson, *Resting Places: The Burial Sites of More Than 14,000 Famous Persons* (McFarland and Co. Inc., North Carolina, 2016), Volume Two, p. 649.

"There was a blank feeling ..." Colin Clive, *ibid*.

"Christmas Day arrived ... " George Pearson, *Flashback: An Autobiography of a British Film Maker* (George Allen & Unwin LTD, London, 1957), pages 171, 172.

"They tried to steal his luggage ..." *Sunday Express*, 20 April 1930.

"I knew Colin Clive ..." Letter to author from David Lewis, Los Angeles, CA, 24 January 1983.

Chapter Ten Notes:

"a nice guy ..." Author's interview with Gil Perkins, Los Angeles, CA, 25 August 1991.

" ... ice water ..."—"His 'Journey's End'," *New York Times*, 12 January 1930, p. 113.

"The proudest person there ..." Hannen Swaffer, "London as It Looks," *Variety*, 12 February 1930, p. 61.

"Sherriff made a very poor speech ..." Swaffer, *ibid*.

$280,000—Swaffer, *ibid*.

"excellently staged ..."—"New Irish Drama Given," *New York Times*, 4 February 1930, p. 32.

"One almost forgets ..." Mordaunt Hall, "The Screen," *New York Times*, 9 April 1930.

"When Stanhope stumbles ..." William Bolitho, *New York World*, 30 April 1930. From the collection of the late Richard Gordon.

A number of the cast—Thanks to G.D. Hamann, who included an un-sourced Los Angeles newspaper opening night advertisement for *Journey's End* on page 67 of his book *James Whale in the 30's* (Filming Today Press, 2013).

He'd never willingly ... Hubbard Keavy, "Screen Life in Hollywood," *San Antonio Express*, 15 January 1933. In this article, Keavy quotes Colin as saying, "The director knows what's best—I let him tell me what to do. If I saw myself, I might freeze up."

Junior's End—Norman Zierold, *The Moguls* (Coward-McCann, Inc., New York, 1969), p. 111.

The Embassy Club Dinner—Rachel Rubin, "Society in Filmland," *Hollywood Daily Citizen*, 23 April 1930.

"sounds a bit like Glynis Johns ..." Dan Callahan, The Chiseler website: (http://chiseler. org/post/23947765431/highly-strung-colin-clive).

"powerful, subtle..." William K. Everson, "Rediscovery," *Films In Review* January 1975, p. 34.

Chapter Eleven Notes:

Ernest Thesiger—Some elucidation about Thesiger. The skeletal actor was the delight of London gossipers, in 1917, after returning wounded from the Great War as a rifleman in Queen Victoria's Rifles. ("Oh, my dear, the noise!" said Thesiger of the war. "And the people!") He wed Janette Ranken, sister of artist William Ranken, who'd painted Thesiger's portrait. The scoop was that Thesiger was actually in love with William, who took the news of the marriage so badly that he spitefully shaved his head and, for a time, went off to live in a cave. Popular in drag, Thesiger had made his film debut in 1916's *The Real Thing at Last*, a spoof of *Macbeth*, with Thesiger as one of the Witches. He'd scored in Noel Coward's 1925 play *On With the Dance*, also playing in drag. See the chapter on Thesiger in James T. Coughlin's *Forgotten Faces of Fantastic Films* (Midnight Marquee Press, 2015).

"so powerfully romantic" Charles Morgan, "Notes on the Acting of Comedy," *New York Times*, 27 July 1930, p. 95.

Twelve Against the Gods: Among the 12: Alexander the Great, Columbus, Isadora Duncan, and Woodrow Wilson.

October 17, 1930—"Colin Clive Arrives," *New York Times*, 18 October 1930, p. 25.

"Next to the thrill ...!" Mason Wiley and Damien Bona, *Inside Oscar* (Ballantine Books, New York, 1987), p. 25.

"unassertive pride of character ..."—J. Brooks Atkinson, "The Play," *New York Times*, 8 December 1930, p. 28.

"made but little ..." John Mason Brown "Overture," *New York Post*, 8 December 1930.

"what the trade calls ..." Pat O'Brien, *The Wind at My Back* (Avon Books, New York, 1967), p. 120.

"This is a play ..."—"Plays You Should See," *Theatre World*, July 1931, p. 8.

Sealyham terriers—"Clive of *Frankenstein*," the *New York Times*, 15 November 1931, p. 6x.

"Charles and I ..." Author's telephone interview with Elsa Lanchester, Hollywood, CA, 10 June 1979.

"There is only one thing ... "—Elisabethe Corathiel, "How I Began" No. 12.—Colin Clive," *Theatre World*, July 1931, p. 39.

"Why haven't you ... ?"—"The Strange Case of Colin Clive," *The Picturegoer*, 1931.

"One Man *Crazy* ...!"

Chapter Twelve Notes:

"Queer family ..." Mollie Merrick, *New Orleans Times Picayune*, 10 September 1931.

The Spanish-style house—The author visited this house (and climbed those steps) in October 2007. Thanks to Carolyn Sirof, XLC Realty, Hollywood CA, who was showing the house that day and graciously allowed me to explore it.

Villa Sophia—The author visited this house on September 30, 2016. Thanks to Constantine Timothy Vlahos for his wonderful courtesy in showing my wife and me the property.

"I don't float ..." Email from David Colton, 24 April 2016. Colton, moderator of the Classic Horror Film Board, was present at Malibou Lake for the ceremony. I first visited Malibou Lake in July of 1997 and my article about it appears in *Midnight Marquee*, Issue No. 60, Summer/Fall 1999, pages 33-35.

May 15, 1967—"$1 Million Worth of Sets Destroyed by Fire at Studio," *Los Angeles Times*, 16 May, 1967, p. 1.

Stage 12—See the Internet's theSTUDIOtour.com.

A shepherd, complete with a bell on a crook—Author's interview with DeWitt Bodeen, Woodland Hills CA, 8 December 1981.

Standing on a box—Author's telephone interview with Pauline Moore, Tucson, AZ, 26 September 1991; published as "The Hollywood Adventures of Pauline Moore," *Films in Review*, July/August 1994, p. 26. Ms. Moore recalled Junior Laemmle standing on a box when he interviewed her in New York for her contract.

Modern astronomers ... Donald Olson, of Texas State University in San Marcos, based his *Frankenstein* date on Mary Shelley's Introduction to the novel's third printing and her reference to the moonlight. Professor Olson, with two colleagues and two students, visited Villa Diodati in August, 2010 to investigate. Olson has also used astronomy and geographic tables to date such events as Caesar's invasion of Britain in 55 B.C., and the Battle of Marathon in 490 B.C.

The Golem—"Great Horror Figure Dies," *Famous Monsters of Filmland*, No. 31, December 1964, p. 50. Forrest J Ackerman, the magazine's editor, wrote that the interview took place the day after Thanksgiving, 1963, at Edward Van Sloan's home in San Francisco, and that Ackerman's wife Wendayne and a 15-year-old fan named G. John Edwards were present at the interview. In recent years, the historic revelations have come under scrutiny, as Edwards has claimed that Ackerman made no recording of the interview and took no notes, and that Edwards has no memory of Van Sloan describing the Golem-style makeup. The inference: Ackerman made up Van Sloan's account (published after Van Sloan's death). To this author, at least Edwards' claim seems unlikely.

"I was a star in my country ..." Al Taylor, "The Forgotten Frankenstein," *Fangoria*, No. 2, p. 40.

"like something out of *Babes in Toyland*."—"Great Horror Figure Dies," *ibid*.

June 16—See Brian Taves, *Robert Florey, the French Expressionist* (BearManor Media, 2014).

It was *his* picture ... !" Author's interview with Mae Clarke, Woodland Hills, CA, 11 May 1983.

"I laughed like a hyena!" Rick Atkins, *Let's Scare 'Em!* (McFarland, 1997).

"He talked about the fact ... " James Curtis, *James Whale: A New World of Gods and Monsters* (Faber and Faber, Boston, London, 1998), p. 133.

The last *Frankenstein* clipping ... Thanks to John Antosiewicz, who formerly owned this Lugosi scrapbook and provided me photocopies of the *Frankenstein*-related pages.

Two days of additional scenes ... *Waterloo Bridge*, Universal Collection, USC Performing Arts Library. Production had originally closed June 26, 1931. The two additional days of shooting were July 3 and July 6, 1931.

"queer, penetrating personality"—"James Whale and *Frankenstein*," *New York Times*, 20 December 1931, p. 4X.

"That dame's poison!" *Graft* was part of a Karloff triple-feature, along with *The Guilty Generation* (1931) and *The Raven* (1935), at a theater in New York in February, 2006.

July 12—*Graft* production end date cited in "Original Print Info" at Turner Classic Movies Internet site (www.tcm.com/tcmdb/title/76787/Graft/original-print-info.html).

"For a damned awful Monster!"—Denis Gifford, *Karloff: The Man, The Monster, the Movies* (Curtis Books, 1973), p. 39.

"Don't eat starchy foods, Sidney"—Jimmy Starr, "Strictly Dishonorable," *Los Angles Evening Express*, 7 November 1931.

Saturday, August 8—UK, Outward Passenger Lists, 1890-1960, Ancestry.com.

Meanwhile, as Colin crosses the Atlantic ... "Dinner Given at Laemmle Estate," *Los Angeles Examiner*, 16 August 1931.

August 14—"Holds Cuba Revolt, With No Issue, Fails," *New York Times*, 15 August 1931, p. 7.

"I am sending you herewith ..."—*Frankenstein* Finished," *The New York Times*, 11 October 1931.

"Disgraced"—*Variety*, 18 August 1931, p. 27.

"I chose Colin Clive ..."—"James Whale and *Frankenstein*," *ibid*, 20 December 1931, p. 4X.

"Karloff's eyes mirrored ... " Denis Gifford, *Movie Monsters* (E.P. Dutton & Co. Inc., New York, 1969). P. 12.

Chapter Thirteen Notes:

Monday, August 24, 1931—*Frankenstein*, Universal Collection, USC Performing Arts Library. All shooting dates in this chapter come from that source.

The previous day ... "Heat Causes Beach Rush," *Los Angeles Times*, 24 August 1931, p. A1.

Today is fair ... "Weather Report," *Los Angeles Times*, 24 August 1931, p. 16.

The approved final budget—*Frankenstein*, Universal Collection, *ibid*.

Similar "Method' approach—Mae Clarke described Frye's working methods on *Frankenstein* to her friend Doug Norwine, who shared them with me. Josephine Hutchinson, Frye's leading lady in Broadway's *A Man's Man* (1925), gave me a vivid account of Frye's startling intensity during the run of that play (interview, New York City, October 12 1994).

Dr. Jekyll and Mr. Hyde—Paramount Collection, Margaret Herrick Library, AMPAS.

a notoriety she'll despise ... "Mae Clarke: Cagney's Citrus Caress Made Her a Joke," *People* magazine, 9 February 1987. The article quotes Ms. Clarke, "I did about 90 films after this one, but this *thing* that took 10 seconds to do has taken notoriety over my whole career. I might as well never have lived."

"The producer hereby employs ..." *Profiles in History* catalog, Hollywood Auction 13, December 17, 2002, p. 33. The catalog described this item as "possibly the single most important principal actor contract ... to come up at auction."

" ... conduct himself with due regard ... "—*Profiles in History, ibid*.

Oh crikey! ... "—"Clive of Frankenstein," *New York Times*, 15 November 1931, p. 6X.

"Colin Clive was the dearest, kindest man ..." Author's interview with Mae Clarke, Woodland Hills, CA, May 11, 1983.

Mae's fragile emotionally ... "Mae Clarke, Actress, Is in Sanitorium," *Los Angeles Herald*, 5 March 1932. She was also in a sanitorium two-and-a-half years later—see "Mae Clarke Recovering," *Los Angeles Examiner*, 17 August 1934.

"One great and special Fourth of July! ... " Clarke, *ibid*.

"I hoped that no one up there ... " Arlene and Howard Eisenberg, "Memoirs of a Monster," *The Saturday Evening Post*, 3 November, 1962.

Cut for the late 1930s reissue ... David J. Skal, *The Monster Show* (W.W. Norton and Company, 1993), p. 137.

The Los Angeles premiere of *Waterloo Bridge*—"Gala Event Due Tonight at Orpheum," *Los Angeles Times*, 3 September 1931; also, Margaret Nye, "Society of Cinemaland," *Los Angeles Times*, 6 September 1931, p. B8.

"The most heartrending aspect ... " Robin Bean, "My Life of Terror, An Interview with Boris Karloff," *Shriek!* Magazine, *October 1965*.

"I thought Karloff was magnificent ... "—Clarke, *ibid*.

" ... a pussy cat!"—Mae Clarke wrote this sentiment while autographing a still from *Frankenstein*, in the author's collection.

Whale addresses the actors ... Tony Hutchinson, *Horror and Fantasy in the Movies* (Crescent Books, New York, 1974), p.19.

Stark naked ... splendid natural endowment—Author's interview with DeWitt Bodeen,

Woodland Hills, CA, 8 December 1981.

"Naturally, I like everything ..." Mollie Merrick, *New Orleans Times Picayune*, 10 September 1931.

"In transit ..." Merrick, *ibid*.

Colin Clive—Half-British, half-French ..." Merrick, *ibid*.

"I dreamed *Frankenstein*"—J. Eugene Chrisman, "Masters of Horror," *Modern Screen*, April, 1932, p. 121.

" ... this fiend is the embodiment ..." Donald Kirkley, "Screen: *Frankenstein*, with Boris Karloff, Colin Clive, Mae Clarke, and John Boles, at Keith's," *The Baltimore Sun*, 27 November 1931.

"He was the handsomest man I ever saw ... "—Personal letter to author from Mae Clarke, Woodland Hills, CA, postmarked 2 March 1984.

"Boris Karloff was funny ..." Author's telephone interview with Pauline Moore, Tucson, AZ, 26 September 1991. See also Mike Fitzgerald, "An Interview with Pauline Moore," *Western Clippings*. Westernclippings.com/interview/Pauline Moore_interview.shtml.

"Everyone on the set had his own cup and saucer ..." Clarke, *ibid*.

"Boris Karloff was a very sweet, wonderful man ..." Author's telephone interviews with Marilyn Harris, San Gabriel, CA, May 9, 11 and 30, 1991; interviews, San Gabriel, CA, July 20, 1997 and July 26, 1998.

"You see, it's all part of the *ritual*"—Hutchinson, *ibid*, p. 42.

"Throw her in again ... !"—Harris, *ibid*.

"It was wanton brutality ..." Burt Prelutsky, "Karloff, 80, Happy With Horror Trademark," *Los Angeles Times-Washington Post Service*, 4 June, 1968.

Jimmy Whale tortures Boris Karloff—Jack P. Pierce, who witnessed this event, told this story on Boris Karloff's *This Is Your Life* TV tribute (November, 1957), but didn't mention Whale's name. Cynthia Lindsay, a personal friend of Karloff's, gave Karloff's account of Whale's behavior in her book *Dear Boris* and wrote that Karloff believed Whale was jealous and punishing him for having snared all the attention during *Frankenstein*'s production. Karloff's fifth wife Evelyn, his widow, told the story to David James Smith of London's *TVTimes* in March of 1990, saying that Karloff's "back was never the same again." Evelyn, who died in 1993, had married Karloff in 1946 and clearly had heard the story from her husband.

"Queen of the Flippin May" and ... pee in a bucket—Email to author from Tatiana Ward, England, 3 May 2001. Ms. Ward was a neighbor of Karloff in London when she was a child and visited him at his home. Her family was also friendly with Bela Lugosi. Ms. Ward is an actress and heard this story from a theater acquaintance.

vacations at Lake Arrowhead and Palm Springs—"Clive Spurns Offers, "*Variety*, 27 October 1931, p. 2.

"Don't mention the name of James Whale ..." Harry Mines, *Los Angeles Illustrated Daily News*, 4 December 1931.

"I think *Frankenstei*n ..."—"Clive of *Frankenstein*," *New York Times*, 15 November 1931, p. 6X.

Chapter Fourteen Notes:

"*Frankenstein* 100% Shocker"—*The Hollywood Reporter*, 3 November 1931.

The final cost ... Universal Collection, USC.

Junior Laemmle ... ill since late October ... Elizabeth Yeaman, *Hollywood Daily Citizen*, 21 October 1931; also Elizabeth Yeaman, *Hollywood Citizen News*, 2 November 1931.

"Karloff has truly created a Frankenstein Monster"—Leo Meehan, *Motion Picture Daily*, 13 November 1931.

... vacationing in Paris ... *The Light that Failed*—*Variety*, November 17, 1931.

"The most remarkable performance ... "—Nelson B. Bell, "The New Cinema Offerings," *The Washington Post*, p. 14.

"The Monster is perfectly played ..." Donald Kirkley, "Screen: Frankenstein, with Boris Karloff, Colin Clive, Mae Clarke, ad John Boles, at Keith's," *The Baltimore Sun*, 27 November 1931.

" ... a terrible THING!"—Mae Tinee, "Horror, Thrills Compose Plot of *Frankenstein*," *Chicago Tribune*, 4 December 1931.

"Looks like a *Dracula* plus ..."—*Variety*, 8 December 1931.

The horse falls, throwing him—"Mr. Colin Clive," the *London Times*, 8 December 1931, p. 12.

Colin and Jeanne meanwhile travel again to Paris ... "Chatter," *Variety*, 29 December 1931, p. 27.

"And there is where ..." Relman Morin, "*Frankenstein*," *Los Angeles Record*, 2 January 1932.

"While a big crowd clamored outside ..."—"*Frankenstein* Gala Premiere," *Today's Cinema*, 27 January, 1932, p. 1.

The same night ... Un-sourced Los Angeles newspaper advertisement, 25 January, 1932.

$1,400,000—"Big Sound Grosses," *Variety*, 21 June 1932, p. 62. Even V*ariety* made the usual error—they wrote "grosses" when the numbers given are actually "rentals." *Dracula's* figure, by the way, was noted as $1,200,000.

"Dear Mr. Clive ..."—"Actors Never Know What Kind of Gift Next Mail Will Bring," *New York Herald Tribune*, 8 March 1936.

Chapter Fifteen Notes:

The author photographed this house in the Summer of 2010.

"A white flame"—Author's telephone interview with Gloria Stuart, Brentwood, CA, 19 May 1986.

"A Jean Harlow dress"—Stuart, *ibid*.

... Paramount Studios to scrap making films in England—"Lily Christine," *Variety*, 20 September, 1932.

"scanty attire"—*Variety, ibid*.

"Miss Griffith very nearly succeeds ..." the *London Times*, 2 May 1932, p. 12.

"There is something about the Talkie business ..."—"Acting's My Job," Says—Colin Clive," *Picture Show* magazine, 28 May, 1932, p. 22.

"Hollywood's real Woman of Mystery ..." DeWitt Bodeen, "Corinne Griffith: The Orchid Lady of the Screen," *Films in Review*, November 1975, p. 513.

"opened nicely"—"Colin Clive's $1,100," *Variety*, 29 March 1932, p. 61.

The Kiss Before the Mirror—Whale had envisioned Colin and Charles Laughton co-starring in the film, with Claudette Colbert as the lawyer's errant wife. There was indication Laughton would play the murderer—hence, Colin the lawyer. Considering the lawyer was by far the dominant role, however, it seems likely Laughton would have been the lawyer, and Colin the killer. At any rate, Laughton decided to go back to England, where he'd deliver his soon-to-win-an-Oscar performance in *The Private Life of Henry VIII*. Colin did *Christopher Strong*. So, Frank Morgan played the lawyer and Paul Lukas the murderer. Whale couldn't get Claudette Colbert, so Nancy Carroll took the role of the lawyer's wife. *The Kiss Before the Mirror* boasts cinematography by Karl Freund (who'd recently directed *The Mummy* but returned here as cameraman out of respect for Whale). Although Morgan and Lukas are very good, it's easy to imagine Laughton and Colin in their respective roles. In fact, Lukas plays on such a high note of hysteria that he seems almost to be doing a Colin Clive impersonation. The film began shooting on or around January 11, 1933. Colin's decision to do *Christopher Strong* instead apparently didn't damage his friendship with Whale.

Christopher Strong—"Clive Goes Radio, Not U," *Variety*, 13 December 1932.

Christopher Strong, Ann Harding, Leslie Howard—Homer Dickens, *The Films of Katharine Hepburn* (Citadel Press, Secaucus New Jersey, 1973), p. 10. Harding and Howard had co-starred in RKO's *The Animal Kingdom* (1932).

literally skin Hepburn alive—Charles Higham, *Kate: The Life of Katharine Hepburn* (Signet, New York, 1975), p. 41.

"Katharine Hepburn is a grand girl ..." *Picturegoer Weekly*, 29 July 1933.

"Miss Arzner is a clever technician ..." *Picturegoer Weekly, ibid*.

Good Samaritan Hospital—"Katharine Hepburn To Hospital, Must Rest," *The Hollywood Reporter*, 27 January 1933,

worried terribly about her health—Higham, *ibid*, p. 42.

Christopher Strong ... cost and worldwide rental—Thanks to Karl Thiede.

Helen Chandler—Thanks to the late Geraldine Chandler, Helen's sister-in-law and closest friend, for the candid telephone interview she provided me 14 May, 2003. Thanks too to Kevin Chandler, who arranged the interview and also provided important information.

Chapter Sixteen Notes:
Hearst and Marian wanted Leslie Howard ... "Leslie Howard's Tilt," *Variety*, 7 February 1933, p. 4.

On February 1 ... "Clive Wanted for 'Peg,'" *The Hollywood Reporter*, 2 February 1933, p. 1.

Helen Mack—"Rambling Reporter," *The Hollywood Reporter*, 25 February 1933, p. 2.

"I have never met an actor ..." John Gliddon, "The Woman Who Thrilled Me, by Colin Clive," *Picturegoer Weekly*, 29 July 1933.

Elizabeth Allan ... "bad reputation" Author's telephone interview with Carroll Borland, Los Angeles, CA, 7 June 1988.

"It's a grand break ..." Gliddon, *ibid.*

"I was sitting in my hotel room ..." Gliddon, *ibid.*

"Fox yesterday dusted off ... "—"'My Dear' On Again," *The Hollywood Reporter*, 23 March 1933, p. 3.

"The first lemon of the season ..." Walter H.E. Potamkin, Cedar Theatre (Lessy Amusement Co.), Philadelphia, PA, *Motion Picture Herald*, 2 September 1933.

"Boys, please write to your producers ..." Walter Odom, Sr., Dixie Theatre, Durant, MS, *Motion Picture Herald*, 17 June 1933.

Looking Forward, Peg O'My Heart—For costs and worldwide rental figures on these two films, thanks to Karl Thiede.

"Down his street" Gliddon, *ibid.*

On June 1, Boris Karloff ... *Variety*, 6 June 1933.

"Well, what do you know about this! ... "—"Cal York's Monthly Broadcast from Hollywood," *Photoplay*, October, 1933, p. 88.

"Coming home, I dreamt ..." Gliddon, *ibid.*

"The only life I really enjoy ..." Gliddon, *ibid.*

Chapter Seventeen Notes:
Eight Bells—including Gerhardt, a warm-hearted sail-maker, played by later Hollywood character actor Sig Rumann.

"In the last act ... " Brooks Atkinson, "Mutiny on Board the *Combermere* in a Nautical Play Entitled *Eight Bells*," *New York Times*, 30 October 1933, p. 14.

" ... judging from the mild reception ..."—"Plays on Broadway," *Variety*, 31 October 1933, p. 52.

John Buckler—Buckler had acted in over a dozen Broadway plays. In 1925, he'd made his New York debut in *The Green Hat*, starring Katharine Cornell and Leslie Howard. In 1932, he'd played Orestes to Blanche Yurka's *Electra*. Buckler and his father, Hugh Buckler, had both acted in the 1933 Broadway play *Late One Evening*.

"I found him a most sensitive actor ..." Personal letter to author from Rose Hobart, Woodland Hills, CA, 25 April 1985.

"She runs the gamut of emotions ... " Dorothy Parker later denied ever saying this, at least in a public forum. Katharine Hepburn however, thought Parker's assessment "extremely accurate and funny."

"The employment of Mr. Clive ... "—"Clive to Act in *The Lake*: Equity Makes Exception Because 25 Americans Will Benefit," *New York Times*, 22 November 1933, p. 23.

"Miss Hepburn found a decidedly appreciative audience ... "—"Katharine Hepburn Wins Ovation As Star: Her Debut in Leading Stage Role with *The Lake* Is Acclaimed in Capital," *New York Times*, 19 December 1933, p. 26.

Opening night audience—Homer Dickens, *The Films of Katharine Hepburn* (The Citadel Press, NJ, 1973), p. 11.

"Mingled emotional outbursts ... "—"Critics Divided on Katharine Hepburn in English Tragedy," EHE, 27 December 1933.

" ... Colin Clive is the noble gent ... "—"Hepburn Saves *The Lake*; First Apple Is Mediocre," *The Hollywood Reporter*, 2 January 1934, p. 3.

"The calla lilies are in bloom again ... " Hepburn used the line again, as a satirical self-homage, in *Stage Door* (RKO, 1937).

$15,461.67 ... Dickens, *ibid*.

"I played with Colin ... " Personal letter to author from Katharine Hepburn, postmarked 5 April 1978.

"Have you any bourbon ..."—"Say No Bourbon! Clive Surprised at 'Drouth' Here," the *Omaha World Herald*, 12 February 1934.

$1,500 per week on a three-week guarantee—Warner Bros. Archives, Los Angeles. The author accessed this material 17 July 1997. All information in this chapter regarding Clive's salaries, etc., at Warners comes directly from the Warner Bros. Archives.

"Colin Clive and Edna Best indulged ... " Grace Kingsley, *New Orleans Times Picayune*, 6 March 1934.

Dr. Thomas McLaughlin ... George Lewis, "Cinematters," *Los Angeles Post-Record*, 16 March 1934.

"Someday a really great mind ... " Elinor Barnes, "Colin Clive Has More Ability Than Most Young Film Players," *The Boston Herald*, 17 July 1934.

Chapter Eighteen Notes:

Joseph Breen ... *The Black Cat* ... *The Black Cat*, Motion Picture Association of America, Production Code Administration Records (AAMP File), Margaret Herrick Library, Academy of Motion Picture Arts & Sciences, Los Angeles, CA.

"Sexual perversion is rampant ..." Scott Eyman, *Lion of Hollywood: The Life and Times of Louis B. Mayer* (Simon and Schuster, New York, 2005).

"The pest hole that infects ... " Mark Vieira, *Sin in Soft focus: Pre-Code Hollywood* (Harry N. Abrams, New York. 1999), pgs. 342, 343.

"Under Particular Applications of the Code ..." *One More River* file, AAMP, *ibid*.

One More River—Financial figures on this film, including its budget, salaries, and final cost, come from the Universal Collection, USC.

"I thought *One More River* ... "Tom Weaver, interview with Jane Wyatt, *Starlog*, 1990.

May 17—"Cabanne Using Rehearsal Plan for Monogram," *Variety*, 15 May 1934, p. 6.

Shot in eight (!) days—Read Kendall, "Around and About in Hollywood," *Los Angeles Times*, 2 July 1934, p. 13.

"Monogram has completed production ..."—"Jane Eyre In at Top Budget for Mono," *Variety*, 4 June 1934 p. 7.

"Virginia Bruce is an attractive Jane ... "—"Film Previews," *Variety*, 30 June 1934, p. 3.

"Effective 5/15/34 ..."Warner Bros. Archives, Los Angeles. The author accessed this material 17 July 1997. All information in this chapter regarding Clive's salaries, etc., at Warners come directly from the Warner Bros. Archives.

"Working for Warner Bros. is like trying to fuck a porcupine ..." Bob Thomas, *Clown Prince of Hollywood: The Antic Life and Times of Jack L. Warner* (McGraw-Hill Publishing Company, 1990), p. 89.

Iris Lancaster—Special thanks to Scott Gallinghouse for information on Ms. Lancaster's early years.

"I don't want to get married ... "—"Career vs. Marriage, the *Lincoln Star*, Lincoln Nebraska, 8 April 1934, p. 3.

"A very sweet man who tended ..."James Curtis, *James Whale: A New World of Gods and Monsters* (Faber and Faber, Boston and London, 1998), p. 185.

"I don't remember if he ever got her into a bra ..." Curtis, *ibid*, p. 230.

June 17: 50,000 people ... Gene Brown, *Movie Time* (MacMillan, 1995), pgs. 1118, 119. $366,842.24—Universal Collection, USC.

Chapter Nineteen Notes:

"Before we agree to exercise ..." Warner Bros. Archives, Los Angeles. The author accessed this material 17 July 1997. All information in this chapter regarding Clive's salaries, etc., at Warners come directly from the Warner Bros. Archives.

The Boulevard at 11:30 P.M ... Edwin Martin, "Cinemania," *Hollywood Citizen News*, 10 August 1934.

... the showdown scene ... Edwin Martin, "Cinemania," *Hollywood Citizen News*, 9 August 1934.

"warmly applauded on his entrance ..." Florence Lawrence, "*Journey's End* Revival Colorful at Playhouse," *Los Angeles Examiner*, 10 August 1934.

"unsteady" W.E. Oliver, "One More River," *Los Angeles Evening Herald Express*, 10 August 1934.

"Colin Clive played the lead ..." Read Kendall, "Around and About in Hollywood," *Los Angeles Times*, 16 August 1934, p. 19.

Ayn Rand—*Letters of Ayn Rand*, Michael S. Berliner, editor, (NAL Reprint Edition, 1997).

"But I've signed your book before ..." Edwin Martin, "Cinemania," *Hollywood Citizen News*, 16 August 1934.

The Hollywood Tower—The author visited this site in September 2016. Thanks to Danny Brown, the Assistant Property Manager, who allowed my wife Barbara and me to go up on the rooftop, where Clive had posed for publicity photos.

"She is charming to work with ..." Thanks to the letter owner who graciously provided me a photocopy.

"Before we agree to exercise ..." Warner Bros. Archives, Los Angeles. The author accessed this material 17 July 1997. All information in this chapter regarding Clive's salaries, etc., at Warners come directly from the Warner Bros. Archives.

I've been waiting and waiting ... This letter written to Jeanne de Casalis was part of The Jeanne de Casalis Archive, auctioned by Heritage Galleries, Dallas Texas, in October of 2006. The author catalogued the letters, from such British stage luminaries as Sir Laurence Olivier, Vivien Leigh, and Noel Coward.

... flagged immigration ... "Colin Clive Flits into Mexico for Quota Digit," *Variety*, 11 September 1934, p. 1.

The elements of the story ... MPAA/PCA Archive, Margaret Herrick Library, Academy of Motion Picture Arts and Sciences, Los Angeles, CA. Thanks to Kristine Krueger.

$12,000—Salaries for the stars of *The Right to Live* come from the Warner Bros. Archives, Los Angeles.

"Colin was a good actor ..." Author's interview with Josephine Hutchinson, New York City, 17 August 1978; also, 12 October, 1994.

"A maniac who might cut off ..." Lawrence J. Quirk, *Fasten Your Seat Belts: The Passionate Life of Bette Davis* (Signet, 1990), p. 117.

A fine of $25,000—MPAA/PCA Archive, *ibid.*

"Sir Cedric Hardwicke ..." Norbert Lusk, "The Screen in Review," *Picture Play.* October 1934, p. 41.

Chapter Twenty Notes:

"In the '30s ..." Author's interview with DeWitt Bodeen, Woodland Hills, CA, 8 December 1981.

"Nothing could be further ..." Personal letter to author from David Lewis, Los Angeles, CA, 24 January 1983.

Chapter Twenty-One Notes:

...she's truly a redhead... David Del Valle, "Curtis Harrington on James Whale," *Films In Review*, January/February 1996, p. 5.

A flowing wig ... *Bride of Frankenstein*, Universal Collection, USC Performing Arts Library. The budget pages set the cost of Ms. Hobson's wig at $125.00.

The budget ... The shooting schedule ... Universal Collection, USC.

"The first time I ever saw ..." Author's telephone interview with Valerie Hobson, Basingstoke, Hampshire, England, 19 April 1989. All quotes from Ms. Hobson in this chapter come from this interview.

$2,500 per week ... The salaries listed here are from USC's Universal Collection, *ibid*.

"I nearly laughed myself to death ..." Madeline Glass, "Clive of England," *Picture Play* magazine, July, 1935, p. 55.

"I don't suppose ..." Todd Amorde, "Organizing: Past Efforts Blazed A Trail for the Future," *Screen Actors Guild Magazine*, Spring 2007, p. 30.

" ... something really should be said ..." Elizabeth Yeaman, *Hollywood Citizen News*, 10 January 1935.

"Stupid!" Mike Parry and Harry Nadler, "*COF* Interviews Boris Karloff," *Castle of Frankenstein*, No. 9, 1966, pages 10, 12.

"He was very excitable ..." James Curtis, *James Whale: A New World of Gods and Monsters* (Faber and Faber, Boston and London, 1998), p. 240.

"Colin Clive, who plays Frankenstein ..."—"Colin Clive Injured, Works on Crutches," *Variety*, p. 1, 30 January 1935.

Chapter Twenty-Two Notes:

"If *The Right to Live* ..." Andre Sennwald, "The Screen," *New York Times*, 16 February 1935, p. 9.

"Colin was a fine actor ..." Lawrence J. Quirk, *Fasten Your Seat Belts: The Passionate Life of Bette Davis* (Signet, 1990), p. 116.

"The finished picture ..." Letter from Joseph I. Breen to Harry Zehner, Universal Studio, 23 March 1935.

"This tops all previous horror pictures ..." "Film Previews!" *Variety*, 8 April 1935, p. 3.

"As I was walking out ..." Lee Harris, "Uncle Forry: First and Last Fan," *Cult Movies*, No. 11, 1994, p. 27.

The final cost ... 10 days over schedule ... Universal Collection, USC.

"We all loved each other then" Author's telephone interview with Valerie Hobson, Basingstoke, Hampshire, England, 19 April 1989. All quotes from Ms. Hobson in this chapter come from this interview.

Colin Clive is taking his Scotties ... "Chatter!" *Variety*, 26 April 1935, p. 2.

"Colin Clive has been carrying ..."—"Gals & Gab!" *Variety*, 29 April 1935, p. 3.

Ohio, for example ... Ohio originally insisted on nine "eliminations." Six of them were scenes Breen had warned Universal about prior to release.

Chapter Twenty-Three Notes:

"Clive Wary ..." *Variety*, 1 May 1935.

"Creating monsters is good fun in fiction ... " "Dr. Frankenstein Loaned Out for Another Thriller," *Los Angeles Times*, 13 May 1935, p. 19.

"A very large one" ... Author's interview with Zita Joann, West Nyack, NY, 27 December 1979.

"Little Peter Lorre ..." Author's interview with Frances Drake, Beverly Hills, CA, Al quotes from Ms. Drake in this chapter come from that interview, as well as correspondence and a telephone interview.

"You may tell me that millions enjoy ..." "I Hate Horror Films," *Film Weekly*, 16 August 1935.

"I remember that Colin Clive ...," email to author from Roger Hurlburt,

Eleta Dayne "Among the Women," *Variety*, 15 May 1935.

"Beautiful Jeanne de Casalis ..." Kendra Bean, *Vivien Leigh: An Intimate Portrait*, Running Press, Philadelphia/London, 2013), p. 27.

... Frank Zeitlin sued Colin ... "Zeitlin After 20 Grand from Colin Clive," *Variety*, 22 June 1935 p. 2.

"Quite capable of scaring to death ..." *Los Angeles Post-Record*.

"Ladies and Gentlemen ..." The speech appears in the script files for *Mad Love*, MGM Collection, USC.

"One of the most completely horrible films of the year" *Time*, 22 July, 1935

Chapter Twenty-Four Notes:

"Clive, who maintains ... "—"Actor Will Use Lucky Apparatus in New Picture," *Los Angeles Times*, 31 August 1935, p. 4.

"Mr. Clive, we'd like to take ... " "Reintroducing Colin Clive," *Brooklyn Daily Eagle*, 15 December 1935.

"Colin Clive shows his versatility ..." Peter Stirling, *The Philadelphia Record*, December 1935.

"Colin Clive's baronet ..." Brooks Atkinson, "The Play: "Libel," or Is It Possible that Sir Mark Loddon is a Couple of Other Fellows?" *New York Times*, 21 December 1935, p. 10.

"Colin Clive has no easy part ..." "Plays on Broadway: *Libel*," *Variety*, 25 December 1935, p. 48.

"Being back on the stage ... " "His Stage Life is So Serious, And Clive Has a Funny Streak," *New York Herald Tribune*, 2 February 1936.

"It's always been my ambition ..." Un-sourced clipping.

"was taken from his suite ..."—"Colin Clive Operated On," *New York Times*, 12 March 1936, p. 18.

Janice Holter Judd ... Her death date appears at FindaGrave.com.

Janice Holter Judd ... The author corresponded during the summer of 2012 with the eBay seller, who preferred to remain anonymous. Thanks to Tracy Surrell, who shared her emails with the seller and her experiences on this subject in emails to the author, 3 November 2017 and 7 November 2017.

Berkeley Institute, "To Greet Berkeley Class," *New York Times*, 10 June 1937, p 17.

Chapter Twenty-Five Notes:

Sunday, May 10, 1936—"Colin Clive via Chief," *Variety*, 11 May 1936, p. 1.

Dracula's Daughter ... $4,000, Universal Collection, USC.

Show Boat ... $1,300,000, Universal Collection, *ibid*.

Pneumonia—"Ill in Pix!" *Variety*, 5 June 1936, p. 6.

Hollywood Hospital—"Ill in Pix!" *Variety*, 19 August 1936, p. 3.

"a triumph"—"New Sherriff Play Succeeds in London," *New York Times*, 5 February 1936, p. 13.

"To write a play ..." Jeanne de Casalis, "On the Origins and History of St. Helena," *New York Times*, 4 October 1936.

" ... Mr. Sherriff and Miss de Casalis ..." Brooks Atkinson, "The Play", *New York Times*, 7 October 1936, p. 82.

A newspaper photo shows John Buckler ... *Los Angeles Times*, 12 July 1936.

"drowned at midnight"—"British Actor and Son Drown in Malibu *(sic)* Lake," *The Baltimore Sun*, 1 November 1936.

The Shierry & Walling Funeral Parlor—John Buckler death certificate.

Chapter Twenty-Six Notes:

"The most romantic title ..." Herve Dumont, *Frank Borzage: The Life and Films of a Hollywood Romantic* with a Foreword by Martin Scorsese, translated by Jonathan Kapansky (McFarland & Company, NC, 2006), p. 245.

... bathing suits ... Matthew Bernstein, *Walter Wanger, Hollywood Independent* (University of California Press, 1994), p. 118.

Page 68: "Political censor boards ..." Letter to Walter Wanger from Joseph Breen, *History Is Made at Night*, MPAA/PCA File, Margaret Herrick Library, Academy of Motion Picture Arts and Sciences, Los Angeles CA.

Salaries—Karl Thiede, 23 July 2018.

In 1933, when Carrillo was 52 ... *The Fresno Bee The Republican*, 4 December 1933, p. 8.

"On Colin Clive in *History Is Made at Night* ... " Letter to author from DeWitt Bodeen, Woodland Hills, CA, 16 February 1978.

"It has fascination for all the femmes ... "—"Reviews of the New Films," *The Film Daily,* 8 March 1937.

Worldwide rental—Karl Thiede, *ibid.*

Canton of Fribourg—MPAA/PCA file, *ibid,* 4 March 1938.

Irish Free State—MPAA/PCA file, *ibid,* 13 October 1937.

sound of revolver—Quebec Censorship report, MPAA/PCA File, *ibid,* 31 May 1937.

"Clive dives down very deep ... "—Dan Callahan, The Chiseler website: http://Chiseler.org/post/23947765431/highly-strung-colin-clive.

Chapter Twenty-Seven Notes:

Budgeted at $618,807.06 ... Financial figures, shooting dates on production information for *The Woman I Love* come from the RKO Collection, UCLA Performing Arts Library.

... Hopkins had stolen focus ... Charles Higham, *Bette: The Life of Bette Davis* (Dell Publishing Co., 1981), p. 54.

Muni and Hopkins—Allan R. Ellenberger, *Miriam Hopkins: Life and Films of a Hollywood Rebel* (University Press of Kentucky, 2018), p. 132.

"A disturbing element during the shooting"—Jerome Lawrence, *Actor: The Life and Times of Paul Muni* (G.P. Putnam's, 1974).

Salaries—Karl Thiede, Los Angeles, CA.

"All Clive scenes had to be shot ..." James Curtis, *James Whale: A New World of Gods and Monsters* (Faber and Faber, Boston and London, 1998), p. 316.

"Miriam Hopkins and Colin Clive ..." Jimmie Fidler, *Baton Rouge State Times,* 11 February 1937.

Amelia Earhart—A photo of Ms. Earhart with Paul Muni taken on the set of *The Woman I Love* appears in Jerome Lawrence's book, *Actor: The Life and Times of Paul Muni, ibid,* p. 231.

Hopkins spoke admirably ... Louella Parsons, *Los Angeles Examiner,* 26 June 1937.

"Of course, Clive's good ..." Parsons, *ibid.*

Worldwide rental—Thiede, *ibid.*

"... after a couple of days of work, he had to leave because of illness"—20th Century-Fox Legal Department records. Cited in "Notes" on *Lancer Spy* at the Turner Classic Movies Internet site (www.tcm.com/tcmdb/title/80740/Lancer-Spy/notes.html).

A Spanish-style house, built in 1927 ... Zillow Internet site (www.zillow.com) estimates the home's current value as $3,966,284.

Iris ... spouse ... U.S. City Directories 1822-1995; Residence Year, 1938.

Chapter Twenty-Eight Notes:

Myrtle Ward—"Mother Hurls Baby, Leaps Off Bridge," *Los Angeles Times,* 2 May 1937, p. 1; "Bridge Victim Recovering," *Los Angeles Times,* 3 May 1937, p. A1. Also, see Hadley Mears, "A History of L.A.'s Suicide Hot Spots, from the Colorado Street Bride to the Hotel Cecil," *L.A. Weekly,* 10 April 2017.

"God sent his angels and saved me"—Steve Lauria, "When Angles Saved Her: Only Known Survivor of 'Suicide Bridge' Recalls the Fateful Day," *Los Angeles Times,* 26 November 1992.

1937 had been one of Hollywood's most tragic years—See the author's "1937: Hollywood's Year of Tragedy," *Cult Movies,* Issue # 11, 1994, pages 68-73.

... Jean Harlow died ... David Stenn, *Bombshell: The Life and Death of Jean Harlow* (Doubleday, 1993), pages 225-242.

"people teased him about it ..." Author's interview with Stella Zucco, Santa Monica, CA, 19 July 1991.

"We'd heard he'd gone ..." Zucco, *ibid.*

"James Whale told me ..." Author's interview with Mae Clarke, Woodland Hills CA, 11 May 1983.

Edwin Martin—"Journey's End', Cinemania," *HCN,* 28 June 1937.

The weather that day ... "The Weather," *Los Angeles Times,* p. A1.

Death—Colin Clive death certificate.

Obituaries—Among those consulted: "Colin Clive Dies at 37; Funeral Services Tues.," *Variety,* 26 June 1937, p. 5; "English Actor Dies on Coast," *Baton Rouge State Times,* 25 June 1936; "English Actor Colin Clive Dies in Hollywood," *San Francisco Chronicle,* 26 June 1937. Also reviewed were various Clive obituaries, un-sourced but obviously from Los Angeles newspapers, in the files of the University of Wisconsin Center for Film and Theatre Research.

Iris Lancaster was informant ... Colin Clive death certificate.

Wee Willie Winkie ... "'Wee' Debuts Over Mutual," *Variety,* 15 June 1937, p. 4; "'Winkie' Sure of $5,500 Carthay Opening Fri." *Variety,* 22 June 1937, p. 2.

Chapter Twenty-Nine Notes:

Established in 1930 ... "New Mortuary Home Will Open," *Los Angeles Examiner,* 18 October 1930.

"Next of Kin"—Thanks to Ms. Sameerah W.S. Muhammad, receptionist, at Angelus-Rosedale Mortuary and Cemetery and Crematory, Los Angeles, CA, who graciously made copies of the papers and documents regarding Colin Clive's cremation when I visited there 28 June 2001.

"Do you remember in the beginning ...?"—Author's telephone interview with Forrest J Ackerman, Los Angeles, CA, 1991.

The funeral for Colin Clive ... The sources describing Colin Clive's funeral include: "'Last Scene' Final Tribute Paid Colin Clive," *Los Angeles Examiner,* 30 June 1937; "Colin Clive's Services," *Variety,* 30 June 1937; "Services for Colin Clive," *Hollywood Citizen News,* 30 June 1937; "Colin Clive Funeral Held," *San Francisco Chronicle,* 29 June 1937.

... a fair day ... "The Weather," *Los Angeles Times,* p. A1.

The Great Garrick—Details of the shooting on that film on 29 June 1937 come from the "Daily Production and Progress Report" in *The Great Garrick* Production File, Warner Bros. Archives, Los Angeles, CA., material emailed to author, 3 August 2017. Thanks to Brett Service.

"Prince" Mike Romanoff ... Iris Lancaster—Hubbard Keavy, "Movie Fan's Corner," *Valley Morning Star,* Harlington, TX, 1 July 1937.

"Yesterday at lunch ..."—"Main Street, Ol' Scoops Daily," *Radio Daily,* 15 July 1937, p. 4.

"Russette"—Read Kendall, "Around and About in Hollywood," *Los Angeles Times,* 5 May 1938.

"Dennis O'Keefe ... "Harrison Carroll, "Hollywood," *The Morning Herald,* Uniontown, PA, 26 May 1938.

Chapter Thirty Notes:

"Dear Boris," always game ... *House of Frankenstein,* Assistant Director Daily Reports, Universal Collection, USC Performing Arts Library.

The Cat Creeps—*The Cat Creeps,* Universal Collection, USC Performing Arts Library.

Lt. Col's Colin Philip Greig ... death and probate date ... England & Wales, National Probate Calendar (index of Wills and Administrations), 1858-1966.

... the end of the Greig line—Noel Audrey Greig, Colin's younger sister and born in 1903, died in 1977. No death date has been found for her sister, Cicely Margaret Greig, who was born in 1901.

Iris Lancaster ... divorce, "Hitching Post: Unhitching," *Variety,* 21 August 1952, p. 10. This article referred to her as "Iris Clive, ex-Earl Carroll showgirl."

$250—"Alimony Cut to $250 a Month for Ex-Movie Actress Iris Dietel,"

"Do not grieve for me ..." James Curtis, *James Whale: A New World of Gods and Monsters* (Faber and Faber, Boston and London, 1998), p. 384.

$556,764.21—James Whale Estate, Statement of Assets, 19 August 1957.

... Las Encinas Sanitarium ... James Whale Will and Estate File. According to a creditor's claim, Whale was at Las Encinas Sanitarium January 19, 1957 to January 26, 1957; February 16, 1957 to March 2, 1957; and March 16 to March 23, 1957.

"Oh, we had such a time ..." Mae Clarke had a copy of the *Nightmare!* script in her files, having sued KTLA and Ottola Nesmith after the telecast. After Ms. Clarke's death, her friend Doug Norwine acquired the script and provided a copy for me.

807%—KRON-TV full-page advertisement, *Variety*, 16 October 1957, p. 30.

The Reverend Father John Glennie Greig ... England & Wales, National Probate Calendar (index of Wills and Administrations), 1858-1966.

Jeanne de Casalis Stephenson ... settled her ex-spouse's estate ... England & Wales, National Probate Calendar (index of Wills and Administrations), 1858-1966.

Jeanne de Casalis ... archive ... See the webpage or Heritage Auctions, Dallas, TX and check the archives for details of the items in the archive.

"At the time of purchase ..." Letter to author from Ronald A. Hast of the Abbott and Hast Colonial Mansion, Los Angeles, CA, 6 March 1980.

"There are no records of abandoned remains ..." Letter to author from C. Garnette, crematory operator, Los Angeles County Crematory, postmarked 8 November 2017.

Clive's cremation—The late Everett Grant Jarvis, in the 1996 edition of his book *Final Curtain: Deaths of Noted Movie and Television Personalities*, wrote: *Colin Clive—(Cremated in Los Angeles, CA)—Ashes unclaimed.* A story that the ashes were dropped by plane into the Pacific Ocean in 1978 by an anonymous admirer has also made the rounds, but is completely unsubstantiated. Also, a June 7, 2012 post on the Classic Horror Film Board from "kelgo1" wrote, "I have Colin Clive's ashes and urn. My great uncle was in the mortuary chemical supply business and he bought the urn and ashes for $100 bucks back in '77 when the funeral home went bankrupt ... The urn (engraved "Colin Clive" 1900-1937) and human remains are in my possession to this day." My personal message sent to "kelgo1" via the Board went unanswered and he posted no more information on this topic. The poster was presumably a crank.

Iris Lancaster died ... Death certificate for Paula Iris Markus, California Department of Public Health, postmarked 22 March 2017.

Iris Lancaster—In April of 1939, Iris had been the leading lady of the "B" Western *Ridin' the Trail*, starring Fred Scott. According to Les Adams, it was an Atlas production for Spectrum Pictures, both Atlas and Spectrum went bust before its release, and Arthur Ziehn—who Adams describes "one of Hollywood's great 'junk' dealers"—salvaged it "from a trash bin of undistributed films." It was released in 1940. Iris had un-credited bits in *South of Dixie* (Universal, 1944), *Till We Meet Again* (Paramount, 1944), and *Rainbow Island* (Paramount, 1944). As "Iris Clive," she tried a "comeback" in Universal's *Renegades of the Rio Grande* (as the maid to leading lady Jenifer Holt, 1945) and in three Monogram Westerns: *Lonesome Trail* (1945), *West of the Alamo* (1946), and *Song of the Sierras* (1946).

"I started looking ..." Email to author from Denise Fetterley, 21 August 2018.

Sources and Bibliography

Interviews and Correspondence:

Lew Ayres, personal letters to author, 6 September 1982 and 24 January 1984.

Charles Bennett, telephone interview, Beverly Hills, CA, 29 October 1992.

DeWitt Bodeen, interview Woodland Hills, CA, 8 December 1981.

Mae Clarke, interview, Woodland Hills, CA, 11 May 1983; personal letter to author, postmarked 2 March 1984.

Frances Drake, telephone interviews, Beverly Hills, CA, 7 June 1986 and 19 March 1988; interview, Beverly Hills CA, 13 July 1987.

Marilyn Harris, telephone interview, San Gabriel, CA, 9, 11, and 30 May, 1991; interviews, San Gabriel CA, 20 July 1997 and 26 July 1998.

Katharine Hepburn, personal letter to author, 5 April 1978.

Rose Hobart, personal letter to author, Woodland Hills, CA, 25 April 1985.

Valerie Hobson, telephone interview, Basinstoke, England, 19 April 1989.

Josephine Hutchinson, interview, New York City, 17 August 1978; telephone interview, 12 October 1994.

Zita Johann, telephone interviews, West Nyack, NY, 3 November 1979 and 16 May 1989; interview, West Nyack, NY 27 December 1979.

Carla Laemmle, telephone interview, Los Angeles, CA, 5 June 2001.

Elsa Lanchester, telephone interview, Hollywood, CA, 10 June 1979; interview, Hollywood CA, 11 December 1981.

David Lewis, personal letter to author, 24 January 1983.

David Manners, interview, Pacific Palisades, CA, 30 July 1976; personal letter to author, postmarked 29 July 1977.

Marian Marsh, interview, Palm Desert, CA, 14 May 1983; telephone interview, Pam Desert, CA, 15 December 1992.

Pauline Moore, telephone interview, Tucson, AZ, 26 September 1991.

Alan Napier, Interview, Pacific Palisades, CA, 15 May 1983.

Gil Perkins, Telephone interview, Los Angeles, CA, 25 August 1991.

Gloria Stuart, telephone interview, Brentwood, CA, 19 May 1986.

Stella Zucco, telephone interview, Santa Monica, CA, 22 May 1991; interview, Santa Monica, CA, 19 July 1991.

Archives:

Billy Rose Library for the Performing Arts, Lincoln Center, New York City.

British Film Institute, London.

Enoch Pratt Library, Baltimore.

Johns Hopkins University Library, Baltimore.

Margaret Herrick Library, Academy of Motion Picture Arts & Sciences, Los Angeles.

Sandhurst Royal Military College, Archives, London.

Stonyhurst Preparatory School Archives, London.

UCLA Performing Arts Library, RKO Collection, Los Angeles.

USC Performing Arts Library, Newspaper Files, Los Angeles.

USC Performing Arts Library, Universal Collection, Los Angeles.

Victoria and Albert Theatre Archive, London, England.

Warner Bros. Archive, USC, Los Angeles.

University of Wisconsin Performing Arts Library.

Books

Rick Atkins, *Let's Scare 'Em!* (McFarland, 1997).

Noel Barber, *Fires of Spring* (Geoffrey Bles, 1952).

Kendra Bean, *Vivien Leigh: An Intimate Portrait* (Running Press, Philadelphia/London, 2013).

Matthew Bernstein, Walter Wanger, *Hollywood Independent* (University of California Press, 1994).

Gene Brown, *Movie Time* (Macmillan, New York, 1995).

James T. Coughlin, *Forgotten Faces of Fantastic Films* (Midnight Marquee Press, 2015).

Ronald Culver, *Not Quite a Gentleman* (Kimber, 1979).

James Curtis, *James Whale: A World of Gods and Monsters* (Faber & Faber, 1998)

Jeanne de Casalis, *Things I Don't Remember: Short Stories and Impressions* (William Heinemann Ltd., Melbourne, London, Toronto, 1953).

Homer Dickens, *The Films of Katharine Hepburn* (Citadel Press, Secaucus New Jersey, 1973).

Herve Dumont, *Frank Borzage: The Life and Films of a Hollywood Romantic* with a Foreword by Martin Scorsese, translated by Jonathan Kapansky (McFarland & Company, NC, 2006).

Allan R. Ellenberger, *Miriam Hopkins: Life and Films of a Hollywood Rebel* (University Press of Kentucky, 2018).

Denis Gifford, *Karloff: The Man, The Monster, The Movies* (Curtis Books, New York, 1973).

Denis Gifford, *Movie Monsters* (E.P. Dutton & Co. Inc., New York, 1969).

David Harris, *Civil War and Democracy in Wes Africa: Conflict Resolutions, Elections and Justice in Sierra Leone and Liberia* (I.B. Taurus, 2012).

Charles Higham, *Kate: The Life of Katharine Hepburn (*Signet, 1976).

Joel Hirschhorn, *Rating the Movie Stars* (by the Editors of *Consumer Guide*) (Beekman House New York, 1983).

Stephen Jacobs, *Boris Karloff: More than A Monster* (Tomahawk Press, 2011).

Ivone Kirkpatrick, *The Inner Circle: Memoirs* (St. Martin's Press, 1959).

Cynthia Lindsay, *Dear Boris*, (Knopf, 1975).

Pat O'Brien, *The Wind at My Back* (Avon Books, New York, 1967).

Thomas Pakenham, *The Boer War* (Cardinal, 1991).

George Pearson, *Flashback: An Autobiography of a British Film Maker* (George Allen & Unwin LTD, London, 1957).

Ayn Rand, *Letters of Ayn Rand,* Michael S. Berliner, editor (NAL Reprint Edition, 1997).

Basil Rathbone, *In and Out of Character* (Doubleday, 1962; Second Limelight edition, 1991).

R.C. Sherriff, *No Leading Lady: An Autobiography* (Victor Gollancz LTD, London 1968).

David J. Skal, *The Monster Show*, (W. W. Norton & Company, New York and London, 1993).

Robert Speaight, *The Property Basket: Recollections of a Divided Life* (Collins & Harvill press, 1970).

Brian Taves, *Robert Florey, the French Expressionist* (BearManor Media, 2014).

Lawrence J. Quirk, *Fasten Your Seat Belts: The Passionate Life of Bette Davis* (Signet, 1990), p. 116.

J. P. Wearing, *The London Stage, 1910-1919* and *1920-1929* (The Scarecrow Press, Metuchen, N.J. and London, 1982).

Mason Wiley and Damien Bona, *Inside Oscar: The Unofficial History of the Academy Awards* (Ballantine Books, New York, 1987).

Scott Wilson, *Resting Places: The Burial Sites of More Than 14,000 Famous Persons, Volumes I and II* (Third Edition, McFarland and Co., Jefferson, NC, 2016).

Norman Zierold, *The Moguls* (Coward-McCann, Inc., New York, 1969).

Magazines

Castle of Frankenstein
Cult Movies
Famous Monsters of Filmland
Films in Review
Film Weekly
Midnight Marquee
Monsters from the Vault
Picture Play
Picture Show
Theatre Arts Monthly
The Dark Side
Sky and Telescope
The Stonyhurst Record
Theatre World
The Magazine Programme
The Picturegoer

Newspapers

Bradford Evening Star and the *Bradford Daily Record*, Pennsylvania
Brooklyn Standard Union
Decatur Daily Review, Illinois
Detroit Free Press
Hollywood Citizen News
Hollywood Daily Citizen
Hull Daily Mail
Indianapolis Star, Indiana
LA Weekly
London Gazette
London Times
Los Angeles Daily Illustrated News
Los Angeles Evening Express
Los Angeles Examiner
Los Angeles Record
Los Angeles Times
Miami Daily News-Record, Oklahoma
Mount Carmel Item, Pennsylvania
Nevada State Journal
New Orleans Times Picayune
New York Times
News-Palladium, Benton Harbor Michigan
Ogden Standard-Examiner, Utah
Pittsburgh Post-Gazette, Pennsylvania
Richmond Times Dispatch
San Antonio Express, Texas
Seattle Daily Times, Washington
Sunday Times, (Perth, Western Australia)
The Film Spectator
The Hollywood Reporter
Variety
Wilkes-Barre Times Leader, Pennsylvania

Online Documents

Ancestry.com
1881 England Census
1911 British Census
1930 United States Federal Census
1940 United States Federal Census
British Phone Books, 1880-1984
California Death Index, 1905-1939
England & Wales, Marriage Index, 1837-1915
England & Wales, Marriage Index, 1916-2005
England & Wales, National Probate Calendar (Index of Wills and Administration), 1858-1966
Genealogy Message Boards
Historical Newspapers, Birth, Marriage & Death Announcements, 1851-2003
India Births and Baptisms, 1786-1947
London, England, Electoral Registers, 1832-1965
New York Passenger Lists, 1820-1957
New York Passenger and Crew Lists, 1909, 1925-1957
U.K. Outward Passenger Lists, 1890-1960
U.S. Border Crossings from Canada to U.S., 1895-1956
U.S. City Directories, 1822-1995

Acknowledgements

First of all, I must thank all those who, over several decades of research, have generously provided me memories of Colin Clive and the London, New York, and Hollywood in which he lived:

Lew Ayres, Charles Bennett, DeWitt Bodeen, Mae Clarke, Frances Drake, Marilyn Harris, Katharine Hepburn, Rose Hobart, Valerie Hobson, Josephine Hutchinson, Elsa Lanchester, David Lewis, David Manners, Pauline Moore, Alan Napier, and Stella Zucco.

The memories of these people, all of whom are now deceased, comprise the true core of the book. It's especially fortunate to have had access to them in the case of a subject who's been dead for 81 years.

Also, up front and center, I must thank several gentlemen whose skill and generosity have played a major role. In alphabetical order:

Frank Dello Stritto, whose books include the acclaimed *I Saw What I Saw When I Saw It*, provided a wealth of material on Clive's ancestry, as well as everything from ship passenger lists to probate files. He also made important contributions and suggestions.

Scott Gallinghouse, currently making his mark as a film historian, provided literally hundreds of documents from various sources, including copies of the 1911 divorce papers of Clive's parents. He also located and sent essential documentation of Piercy Greig's incarceration at the Jersey Lunatic Asylum.

Neil Pettigrew, whose superb articles have recently appeared in *The Dark Side* magazine, made trips around London, locating and copying (among many other items) Colin Clive's 1928 divorce petition vs. Evelyn Taylor. I felt a bit guilty challenging him to locate a picture of Jeanne de Casalis in her infamous pajamas in *Potiphar's Wife*. Within days, however, he sent me a copy.

These men boldly ran with any request for information that I threw them, no matter how esoteric or eccentric. I'm tremendously grateful.

Many thanks to friend and writing colleague Patrick McCray, who generously invited me to join him on a trip to London in 2010. During a whirlwind week there, Patrick indulged my classic horror fascination, including a trip to Regent's Park to see the swans (a Regent's Park swan had inspired Elsa Lanchester's hiss in *Bride of Frankenstein*), and tracking down the Gloucester Place house where Colin Clive had lived in the early 1930s.

A special thanks, too, to Sally Stark, a friend and fellow Clive enthusiast for almost four decades. Sally provided several important leads in this project and, over the years, has faithfully kept the candle burning in Clive's memory.

Many thanks to:

Ned Comstock, all-star curator of the University of Southern California Performing Arts Library, outdid himself—again—in providing all variety of information on Colin Clive and his films.

Julie Graham, curator of the University of California Los Angeles Performing Arts Library, made important files available, notably the RKO Collection.

Kristine Krueger, National Film Information Service coordinator of the Margaret Herrick Library at the Academy of Motion Picture Arts & Sciences, made it possible to see the censorship documentation on several of Clive's films that faced Production Code hassles.

David Knight, curator of the archives at Stonyhurst College, England, provided valuable information on Clive's years there in preparatory school, as well as some wonderful photographs.

Dr. Anthony Morton, Curator of the Sandhurst Collection, Royal Military Academy Sandhurst, Camberley, Surrey, England, made available material related to Clive's time there.

G.D. Hamann and his "Filming Today Press" have produced a wonderful collection of books on vintage Hollywood personalities—actors, directors, scandals, you name it—containing transcripts of the newspaper interviews, articles, and reviews of the era. His book of assembled Colin Clive material was enormously helpful.

Karl Thiede has a remarkable archive on a very specific aspect of film history—costs and rentals. The facts and figures he graciously shared with me accurately put Clive's films in perspective as to which were hits and which were misses at the box office.

Thanks to: the late Forrest J Ackerman; Ron Adams and the staff at the Monster Bash Convention; John Antosiewicz; Lionel Anthony Atwill; Buddy Barnett; the Billy Rose Library for the Performing Arts at Lincoln Center, New York; the late Richard Bojarski; Ron Borst; The British Film Institute; Danny Brown (Asst. Property Manager, the Hollywood Tower); the late Robert Clarke; Jim and Marian Clatterbaugh; the Colin Clive Forever Blog; David Colton and the Classic Horror Film Board; Robert Connors; Dr. James T. Coughlin; Gioia de Blasio-Moore; the late Lillian Lugosi Donlevy; The Enoch Pratt Free Library, Baltimore; Denise Fetterley; the late Dwight D. Frye; Kerry Gammill; Martin Grams, Jr.; Dan Gunderman; Ronald A. Hast; Charles and Sherry Heard; Roger Hurlburt; Tom Jackson; The Johns Hopkins University Library, Baltimore; Sara Karloff; Bela Lugosi, Jr.; Kevin McLaughlin; Julie and Dick May; the late Linda Miller; Bryan Moore; the late Evelyn Moriarty; Bill Nelson; Doug and Kelley Norwine; Pensar IT Management, London; Gary Don Rhodes; Tracy Surrell; Gary and Susan Svehla; Constantine Timothy Vlahos (The Villa Sophia, Los Angeles); Tatiana Ward; Tom Weaver; Wisconsin Center for Film and Theater Research; Scott Wilson; Charlie Wittig; and Valerie Yaros.

Finally, all my thanks, and all my love to Barbara. "Still on our feet ... and more in love than ever."

GWM
September 2018

Author's Biography

Gregory William Mank is the author of the books *It's Alive! The Classic Cinema Saga of Frankenstein; The Hollywood Hissables; Karloff and Lugosi; Hollywood Cauldron; Women in Horror Films, 1930s; Women in Horror Films, 1940s; Hollywood's Maddest Doctors; Bela Lugosi and Boris Karloff: the Expanded Story of a Haunting Collaboration; The Very Witching Time of Night;* and *Laird Cregar: A Hollywood Tragedy.* He's co-author of *John Carradine: The Films* (with Tom Weaver); *Hollywood's Hellfire Club* (with Charles Heard and Bill Nelson); and *Dwight Frye's Last Laugh* (with James T. Coughlin). He's written the production histories for a dozen of the MagicImage Filmscript books and has written and narrated the audio commentaries for the DVD releases of *Abbott and Costello Meet Frankenstein, Dr. Jekyll and Mr. Hyde (1931), Cat People, The Curse of the Cat People, The Mask of Fu Manchu,*

Chandu the Magician, The Mayor of Hell, The Walking Dead, Island of Lost Souls, and *The Lodger.* Greg has written many magazine articles, contributed to various anthologies, and has appeared on various documentaries, as well as the TV shows *Entertainment Tonight, Rivals!* and *E! Mysteries and Scandals.* He won the Rondo Award for Best Book (*Bela Lugosi and Boris Karloff*), as well as the Rondo Writer of the Year award in 2010, and received a Rondo Hall of Fame Award in 2014. A graduate of Johns Hopkins University with a Masters degree in Liberal Arts, he's a retired teacher of 30 years and, as an actor in Baltimore Theater for 50 years, played such roles as Professor Harold Hill in *The Music Man,* "Il Stupendo" in *Lend Me a Tenor,* and (for 35 Christmas seasons) Barnaby, the villain of *Babes in Toyland.* He and his wife Barbara live in Delta, PA.

INDEX

"One Man Crazy ...!"

"One Man *Crazy* ...!"

207, 228, 274
The Road Back (film), 284
The Romantic Age (play), 38
The Romantic Young Lady (play), 97
The Sacred Flame (play), 203
The Show (radio program), 198
The Spirit of Notre Dame (film), 109, 111
The Sting (film), 103
The Story of Louis Pasteur (film), 277, 281
The Stronger Sex (film), 98, 99, 100, 135
The Swan (1930 London stage), 95, 178
The Three Stooges, 80, 297
The Tidings Brought to Mary (play), 42, 64
The Trail Beyond (film), 206
The Twilight Zone (TV series), 255
The Walking Dead (1936 film), 284, 367
The Way of an Eagle (play), 37
The Whip (play), 39
The Widow from Monte Carlo (film), 253, 254, 255
The Witch (play), 45
The Wizard of Oz (film), 156
The Wolf Man (film), 298
The Woman I Love (film), 277 – 283, 297, 337
The Woman in Room 13 (play), 30
Thesiger, Ernest, 51, 94, 213, 216, 217, 224, 233, 310, 329
This Is Your Life (TV series), 131
Thomson, Kenneth, 217
Thorndike, Sybil, 70
Thoroughly Modern Millie (film), 103
Thriller (TV series), 80
Tinee, Mae, 138
To Each His Own (film), 37
Tobin, Genevieve, 204, 228
Toland, Gregg, 240
Torres, Raquel, 163
Tovarich (play), 285
Towne, Gene, 268
Travaglini, Tony Jr., 286

Tree, Lady, 70
Tree, Sir Herbert Beerbohm, 29
Tsar Nicholas II, 294
Turner, Lana, 292
Twelvetrees, Helen, 119
Ulmer, Edgar G., 80, 182
"Uncle Robbie," 167
Up in Mabel's Room (play), 30
Valle, Rudy, 255
Van Sloan, Edward, 104, 109, 114, 115, 116, 117, 118, 123, 137, 248
Veidt, Conrad, 30
Victoria Regina (play), 258, 285
Von Sternberg, Josef, 218, 260
Von Stroheim, Erich, 30
Wallis, Hal, 196, 204
Walpole, Hugh, 51
Walton, Izaak, 262
Wanger, Walter, 265, 268
Warburton, John, 202
Ward, Jeanette Louise, 284
Ward, Myrtle, 284
Warner, Jack L., 190, 204
Waterloo Bridge (1931 film), 104, 105, 106, 109, 114, 119
Watkins, Don, 102
Waxman, Franz, 221, 232
Wayne, John, 206
Wee Willie Winkie (film), 289
Weaver, Tom, 186, 367
Wegener, Paul, 27
Weissmuller, Johnny, 265
Welles, Orson, 240
Whale, James, 11, 13, 19, 46, 50, 51, 52, 53, 54, 55, 57, 60, 62, 63, 69, 70, 71, 72, 74, 75, 78, 81, 84, 86, 87, 88, 89, 92, 93, 94, 95, 100, 102, 104, 105, 106, 107, 108, 109, 110, 111, 112, 113, 114, 117, 118, 119, 120, 121, 123, 124, 125, 126, 127, 129, 130, 131, 132, 133, 135, 137, 138, 142, 147, 149, 150, 151, 156, 166, 167, 168, 184, 185, 186, 193, 194, 195, 197, 207, 212, 213, 215, 216, 217, 218, 220,

223, 225, 226, 227, 228, 232, 233, 234, 255, 264, 266, 268, 274, 283, 284, 285, 292, 294, 296, 298, 300, 301, 306, 310
Whalen, Michael, 290
Whatmore, A.R., 37, 98
Wheeler, Bert, 119
White, Dora, 64, 66, 67, 70
White, Pearl, 26
Whitty, Dame Mae, 167
Wilcox, Herbert, 206
William, Warren, 178, 254
Wills, Brember, 69, 151
Wilson, Marie, 292
Wilson, Scott, 17, 305
Winchell, Walter, 259, 260
With Byrd at the South Pole (film), 95
Wolfe, Ian, 243, 247
Wong, Anna May, 95, 97
Wood, Peggy, 204
Wooll, Edward, 255
Woolsey, Robert, 119
Wuthering Heights (1939 film), 240
Wyatt, Jane, 185, 186, 194
Wynyard, Diana, 40, 183, 184, 185, 186, 194, 195
Yeaman, Elizabeth, 218
Young, Loretta, 206
Young Frankenstein (film), 125
Yurka, Blanche, 211
Zanuck, Darryl F., 206, 252
Zeitlin, Frank, 247
Zero (film), 48
Zucco, Frances, 285
Zucco, George, 52, 53, 54, 57, 60, 61, 62, 64, 69, 70, 78, 90, 258, 285, 290, 298
Zucco, Stella Francis, 54, 62, 64, 65, 66, 69, 285

If you enjoyed this book,
write for a free catalog of
Midnight Marquee Press titles
or visit our website at
http://www.midmar.com

Midnight Marquee Press, Inc.
9721 Britinay Lane
Baltimore, MD 21234
410-665-1198
mmarquee@aol.com